Supplement to THE RECORD OF CONNECTICUT MEN...DURING THE WAR OF THE REVOLUTION, 1775–1783

Volume I
ROLLS AND LISTS OF CONNECTICUT MEN IN THE REVOLUTION, 1775–1783

Connecticut Historical Society

Originally published as
Volume VIII
of the
Collections of the Connecticut Historical Society

CLEARFIELD

Originally published as
Collections of the Connecticut Historical Society, Vol. VIII:
Rolls and Lists of Connecticut Men in the Revolution, 1775–1783
Hartford, Connecticut, 1901

Reprinted for
Clearfield Company, Inc. by
Genealogical Publishing Co., Inc.
Baltimore, Maryland
1997

International Standard Book Number: 0-8063-4753-8
Set Number: 0-8063-4752-X

COLLECTIONS

OF THE

Connecticut Historical Society.

VOLUME VIII.

HARTFORD:
PUBLISHED BY THE SOCIETY.
1901.

ROLLS AND LISTS

OF

CONNECTICUT MEN

IN THE

REVOLUTION.

1775–1783.

HARTFORD:
CONNECTICUT HISTORICAL SOCIETY.
1901.

CONTENTS.

OFFICERS OF THE SOCIETY.

Elected May 21, 1901.

PRESIDENT, SAMUEL HART.

VICE-PRESIDENTS,
- JAMES J. GOODWIN, HARTFORD.
- JAMES TERRY, NEW HAVEN.
- RICHARD A. WHEELER, STONINGTON.
- MORRIS W. SEYMOUR, BRIDGEPORT.
- THEODORE S. GOLD, CORNWALL.
- FRANK FARNSWORTH STARR, MIDDLETOWN.
- ELLEN D. LARNED, THOMPSON.
- E. STEVENS HENRY, ROCKVILLE.

RECORDING SECRETARY, ALBERT C. BATES.
CORRESPONDING SECRETARY, W. DE LOSS LOVE.
TREASURER, JOHN E. MORRIS.
LIBRARIAN, ALBERT C. BATES.
AUDITOR, JOSEPH G. WOODWARD.

MEMBERSHIP COMMITTEE,
- SAMUEL HART, *ex officio.*
- JOSEPH G. WOODWARD.
- JULIUS GAY.
- JOHN E. MORRIS.
- HORACE E. MATHER.
- JANE T. SMITH.
- ALBERT C. BATES.
- JOSEPH L. BLANCHARD.

LIBRARY COMMITTEE,
- SAMUEL HART, *ex officio.*
- FRANCIS H. PARKER.
- WILLISTON WALKER.
- THOMAS S. WEAVER.

PUBLICATION COMMITTEE,
- SAMUEL HART, *ex officio.*
- ALBERT C. BATES.
- LEVERETT BELKNAP.
- GEORGE S. GODARD.

COMMITTEE ON MONTHLY PAPERS,
- P. H. WOODWARD.
- CHARLES B. WHITING.
- ARTHUR L. SHIPMAN.

INTRODUCTION.

The State of Connecticut issued in 1889 through the Adjutant-General's office the splendid volume edited by Prof. Henry P. Johnston, entitled "Record of Service of Connecticut Men in the War of the Revolution." Later investigations have brought to light new rolls and additional information not contained in that volume. It is these new rolls which are here printed to serve as a supplement to the volume issued by the State.

This volume of Rolls and Lists is published under the provisions of a recent special Act of the General Assembly making an annual appropriation of one thousand dollars to the Connecticut Historical Society; one of the purposes specifically named in this act being "to publish its rolls of soldiers in the revolutionary and colonial wars, not heretofore printed." Another provision is that the Society "shall deposit in the State Library three hundred copies of each catalogue, report, or other work published" under this act, to be disposed of by the State Librarian. This is the third publication issued under the provisions of this act, and the first important work so issued.

The late Judge Sherman W. Adams, while chairman of the Society's publication committee, undertook the task of preparing the manuscript copy for this volume for the printer. He placed the Society's unpublished rolls in his office-safe where they would be conveniently at hand for the work, examined and compared them with those already in print, and began the labor of copying. But poor health soon caused him to lay aside the work for many months, only to take it up a second time and be again forced by illness to drop it, this time permanently, and he sadly returned the manuscript to the Society's vault.

Meanwhile work was progressing, with considerable delays and occasional cessations, upon two other volumes of Collections, the fifth and seventh, which the Society already had in press; and between the issuing of these two another, the sixth volume, was published, the gift of our first Vice-President.

While the last of these three volumes was yet in press another effort was made to prepare the volume of Revolutionary War Rolls for the printer, the Corresponding Secretary and the Librarian of the Society undertaking the work as a special volunteer committee. But the task was greater than either had, perhaps, anticipated, and after a spasmodic effort and the preparation of about one hundred pages of copy the work again came to a standstill.

At the annual meeting last May the Standing Committee of the Society took the matter in hand and instructed the publication committee to take up and carry to completion the publication of the Revolutionary Rolls belonging to the Society, and such others remaining unpublished as could be found. From that time to the present the work has been constantly in progress, the labor falling naturally upon the chairman of the publication committee. He has been fortunate in having the assistance of Edmund C. Thomas of Trinity College, Hartford, in making the copy, and of Miss Alice M. Gay, also of Hartford, in writing the cards for the index. All of the proofs, however, have been read by him, and with a half-dozen exceptions the proof of every roll or list has been read with the original manuscript. The index cards also were all compared by him with the printed sheets before they were printed.

The fact of this volume being in the nature of a supplement to one already in print made its preparation more difficult in some ways than it would otherwise have been ; for it became necessary to examine each manuscript roll in order to determine whether it had been printed in the volume already issued by the State, or whether it should be copied for the Society's volume. A further complication was the frequent finding of rolls the names on which appeared to have been already printed though in a different arrangement. Often a part or all of the names appearing on a manuscript company roll would be found scattered through an alphabetically arranged regimental roll in the printed Record of Connecticut Men in the Revolution. In many such cases it was only after the most careful comparison that a decision as to printing the manuscript could be reached.

Every roll and list here printed is either entirely new, or contains sufficient that is new in the way of new names, additional service, or names of the towns from which the men came to justify its printing. In a work of this character it is difficult to avoid duplicating some of the matter already printed, but it is believed that there is very little of such duplication. It has been thought better to print, with a few exceptions, the whole of each roll or list, even at the risk of occasional duplication, than to attempt to extract and print new names from lists already partially in print. In a few cases a roll has been reprinted entire from another source than the State's publication, to show variations in spelling. The name of a town from which a man came has in many instances proved an important means of identification, and special attention has been paid to giving the towns wherever they appear on the rolls.

The arrangement of the material in this volume follows closely the arrangement adopted in the Record of the Service of Connecticut Men in the War of the Revolution, and a reference to that work accompanies many of the rolls here printed, showing where the roll would have appeared had it been printed in that volume. In many instances it is difficult to decide whether an organization served as State Troops or as Militia, and later investigation may change the present arrangement of many companies in this respect. It seems probable that some companies now credited to the Militia will prove to have served as State Troops.

This work does not profess to be more than a list of men who served as soldiers, with an account of their service and such further records as will aid in identifying them. Consequently much has been omitted in the printing of these rolls which has appeared irrelevant to the object in view. It has seemed outside the scope of the work to give the amount with which a soldier was charged for his gun, cartouch-box, or blanket, the number of months and days in service when dates of both his enlistment and discharge are given, the total amount disbursed by a captain for the wages and expenses of the men in his company, and numerous similar items. As the location of the manuscript of each roll is given, the curious can find such items as occur by reference to the originals.

In indexing all names have been spelled exactly as they appear in the text, with the following exceptions. Where an abbreviation appeared and there was no reasonable doubt as to the name for which the abbreviation stood, the name has been given in full in the index. The names of a few prominent officers have been indexed under one uniform and recognized spelling rather than to follow the various misspellings found in the text. All place names have been properly spelled in the index regardless of their spelling in the text.

The rolls here printed from the Society's archives have been presented to the Society at various times by sundry persons; many of them are from the collection of Trumbull papers received in 1845 from the executor of the estate of William T. Williams, a grandson of the elder Governor Trumbull. The Revolutionary War manuscripts in the State Library which have been examined for this work comprise thirty-seven folio volumes consisting of every description of document relating to the subject mounted upon or between the leaves of the volumes; also documents mounted in one large folio volume which were presented in 1877 by Charles Hebard of Lebanon, great-grandson of Hon. William Williams; also a package of documents purchased in 1893 from Samuel A. Drake of Boston. The manuscripts in the Comptroller's office include several small unbound or paper-covered books of accounts; the thick folio volume of Haskell's Receipts; and a large, square, thin volume referred to as "Copy in Comptroller's Office." This last mentioned volume was evidently made in recent years and consists of copies of rolls, probably made from original manuscripts. Originals of some of these are found in the State Library, many are already in print in the Record of Connecticut Men in the Revolution, though probably taken from another source, while the others are new material and the location of the originals from which they were copied is unknown. The volume of Haskell's Receipts is of much interest. It consists of records of accounts preferred by the State of Connecticut against the United States for payments made by the State for the wages and expenses of State Troops and Militia, each of which is certified as correct by "E. Haskell Com[r] Eastern States."

A complete roster of Col. David Waterbury Jr.'s regiment of Connecticut volunteers, 1776, was published in 1897. As the original rolls are in private hands and the pamphlet was issued under the United States copyright law, the material is not included in this volume.

Sufficient material is at hand to form another volume of the size of the present one. This material consists not of rolls but of returns forwarded from the different towns to the Colony and State authorities, giving the names of soldiers serving from each town, and of lists of soldiers prepared by their commanding officers, giving the town from which each soldier came. The Society hopes to publish this material soon and would welcome the knowledge of any other unpublished rolls or lists which might add to the interest of the volumes.

ALBERT C. BATES,
Chairman of the Publication Committee,
and Editor of this Volume.

THE SOCIETY'S LIBRARY, DECEMBER 26, 1901.

LEXINGTON ALARM LIST.

EAST WINDSOR.

[*See Record of Connecticut Men in the Revolution, page 9.*]

Name		Rank
Samuel King	11	Sarj
Ichabod Wadsworth	11	Sarj
John Hall	9	Sarj
Daniel Warner	11	Sarj
James McKenney Jr	2	Corp
John Craw Jr	8	Corp
Jacob Bottom	10	Corp
Isaac Mason	11	Corp
Stephen Warner	11	Drumr
Stephen Russell	11	Drumr
Oliver Chapman	11	fifer
Lemuel Pinney	11	fifer
Chauncey Foster	10	fifer

Name		Name	
John Aldich Jr	11	Aaron Damon	10
Samuel Andress	11	Charles Day	11
Christopher Allien	8	David Davis	11
Benjamin Allien	10	Joseph Durfy Jr	10
Eliphas Bartlet	8	Jedediah Durfy	11
Alexander Buckland	11	Adonijah Day Jr	6
Edmond Bragg	11	Hezekiah Elsworth	11
Stephen Burroughs	8	Daniel Elsworth 3rd	10
Abner Burroughs Jr	11	Jesse Fitch	2
Francis Belknap	9	Wareham Foster	11
Edmond Bartlet Jr	11	Josiah Frost Jr	10
Samuel Bartlet	3	Noah Frost	6
Stephen Bradley	11	Ephrim Frost	10
Zebulon Burroughs	10	Daniel Green	11
Josiah Bradley Jr	11	Seth Gibbs	10
Reuben Bradley	10	Levy Gibbs	10
Jonathan Brown	4	Oliver Gibbs	2
Stephen Bartlet	10	Nathan Hall	10
Mathew Campbell	11	Amos Huntley	3
Thomas Cook	9	Thomas Kennedy	10
George Charter	10	Andrew Kenedy	11
John Charter Jr	11	Elijah H. Kingsbery	3
Eli Carpenter	9	Joseph Kingsbery	10
Timothy Cook	11	Joseph Kneeland	9
Hoseah Chapman	2	Simon Kingsbery Jr	2
Zenus Cleavland	1	Jesse Ladd	11
Rufus Cleavland	6	Elijah Lee	7
Caleb Downer	6	Eliphalet Lord	8
Jonathan Damon Jr	11	David Lovet	8

Name		Name	
John Lovet	10	Ephrim Parker Jr	11
Samuel Lovet	11	Thomas Pember	11
James Lovet	10	Samuel Peak	11
Benjamin Lewis	11	John Pease	8
Wiliam McKenney	11	Edward Pain	[ ]
Andrew McKenney	11	Seth Parker	6
Peter Mills	7	Hezekiah Russell	11
Ezekiel McKenstry	10	Silas Read	9
Wiliam McCray Jr	11	Philip Read	3
Reuben McCray	11	Nathan Russell Jr	11
David McCray	11	Wm Shurtliff	1
James McKenney 3rd	11	Lothrup Shurtliff	10
Nathan McWavy	9	Wm Spear Jr	10
Thomas McKnight	11	Moses Smith Jr	11
Caleb More	7	John Stiles	10
Ephrim McWavy	3	Aaron Slade	11
Isaac Newton	11	Abner Slade	11
Daniel Newhall	11	John Shurtliff	5
John Newhall	11	Asael Shurtliff	10
Jacob Newhall	11	Graves Smith	8
Andrew Pember	11	Daniel Slade	1
John Porter	11	Jonathan Sexton	11
Joseph Pinney Jr	7	Moses Slafter	2
John Pinney	6	James Thompson	9
Samuel Pember	11	John Taylor	8
James Parsivel	6	John Taylor Jr	8
Jonathan Porter Jr	11	James Wallace	10
Daniel Porter	5	John Wallace	11
Joseph Parkhurst	10	Benjamin Woodward	9
Elezer Pinney	8	Abram Walace Jr	1
Daniel Pearson	11	Wiliam Wallace	11
Samuel Pearson Jr	9	Alexander Young	6
Ephrim Pearson Jr	2		

[ ]ue Coppy from [ ] Rooles Errors Excepted
[ ] those th[ ]ent in the Alarrum
[ ]

[*Connecticut Historical Society.*]

LEBANON.

[*See Record of Connecticut Men in the Revolution, page 15.*]

The following is the Names of those that inlisted under my Command in the time of the Alarm with the Money they Spent & the time when they left the Service. Marched from home Sat. 22 Apl 1775

Left Service		Name			
		Capt Daniel Tilden	Com		
		Lieut Thos Tirrel	Com		
		Ensign Thos Bill	Com		
		Jeddiah Phelps	Sargt		
May	1	John H. Buell	Sargt	12/	
Apl	26	Nathan Lee	Sargt	9/	
May	7	Peletiah Holebrook	Corpl	10/	
	10	Jos Howes	Corpl	20/	
	11	Simon House	Corpl		
	1	Ephram Bemiss		12/	8
	11	Adonijah White		15/	
	11	Ebenr Gillit Jur		12/	
	3	Andrew Dewey			
	8	Simon Jones			

Listed 7 M	Beriah Sprague	6/	8
23	Andrew Richardson		
1	Dan[ll] Badcock		
11	Eben[r] Bailey	12/	
	Jabez Foster inlisted 8 May		
Ap[l] 25	Jonah Gross	2/	
	Asahel Williams	13/	
May 8	Edmund Daman	6/	
1	James Barnaba	12/	8
Ap[l] 26	Rufus Rude Ju[r]		
May 15	Sam[ll] Beamont		
	Tho[s] Brooks		
7	Michael Bestow	6/	6
Ap[l] 26	Jonathan Bliss		
	Abner Doubleday	6/	
	Oliver Hyde	12/	
26	Adonijah Crocker		
7	Jerom Clark	15/	
May 1	Joseph Severoy		
7	Garshom Gillet	4/	
Ap[l] 26	Sam[ll] Davis		
May 1	Zebedee Goodwine		
	Asa Loomise provision found for him by Cap Tisdale to amt of 0 4 0	12/	
2	Jacob Loomise	8/	6
15	Asel Gay		
	Amos Miner Cap. C. says listed ye 8 May	7/	
1	Tho[s] Saveroy		
11	Lem[l] Clark	12/	
11	Benjamin Woodwarth		
Ap[l] 25	Jacob Gillet Returned with horses: sit out for boston 21 of April	6/	

[*Connecticut Historical Society.*]

D[r] Colony, To Wages & Billeting, of sundry Officers & Soldiers who marched, from Lebanon, to the Relief of y[e] Country in the late Alarm at Lexington & Concord &c under Dan[ll] Tilden as Capt 1775

N B the Soldiers 1d P Day too High

	Days in ye Service	Wages		
Dan[ll] Tilden Cap[n]	9	1	18	8
Tho[s] Tyrrel L[t]	19	2	14	3
Tho[s] Bill Ens[n]	9	0	19	4
Jed[h]: Phelps Serj[t]	3	0	5	1½
Jn[o] H. Buell Serj[t]	13	1	2	2½
Nath[n] Lee Serj[t]	5	0	8	6½
Pel[a] Holbrook Serj[t]	18	1	10	9
Jos. Howes Corp[o]	22	1	13	11
Simon House Corp[o]	21	1	12	4½
Sam[ll] Bemont Cor	24	1	17	0
Ep[m] Bemus	13	0	18	5
Adonij: White	23	1	12	7
Eb[r] Gillet Ju[r]	23	1	12	7
And: Dewey	11	0	15	7
Simon Jones	21	1	9	9
Beri: Sprague	15	1	1	3
And: Richardson	35	2	9	7

	Days in ye Service	Wages		
Dan[ll] Badcock	13	0	18	5
Eb[r] Bailey	22	1	11	2
Jabez Foster	16	1	2	8
Elisha Hutchin[n]	3	0	4	3
Jonah Gross	4	0	5	8
Asa[l] Williams	19	1	6	11
Edm[d] Daman	19	1	6	11
Ja[s] Barnabee	12	0	17	0
Rufus Rude Ju[r]	07	0	9	11
Sam[ll] Bemont	27	1	18	3
Tho[s] Brooks	27	1	18	3
Micha[l] Barstow	18	1	5	6
Jon[n] Bliss	7	0	9	11
Abner Doubleday	7	0	9	11
Oliv[r] Hyde	7	0	9	11
Zenas Howis	2	0	2	10
Adonij: Crocker	7	0	9	11
Jerom Clark Cap Wrights Lad	16	1	2	8
Jos. Savory	12	0	17	0
Ger. Gillet	16	1	2	8
Sam[ll] Davis	7	0	9	11
Zebedee Goodwin	12	0	17	0
Asa Loomis	12	0	17	0
Jacob Loomis	14	0	19	10
Asael Gay	27	1	18	6
Amos Miner	16	1	2	8
Tho[s] Savory	12	0	17	0
Lem[ll] Clark	22	1	11	2
Benj[n] Woodworth	22	1	11	2
Jacob Gillet returnd w[h] horses	5	0	7	1
Elijah House	2	0	2	10
John Sprague				
Sol[o] Parker Case	3	0	4	3
Jn[o] Doggett				

The following Persons set out on the March & did not go thro:

	Days gone	Wages		
Cap[t] Dan[ll] Dewey	3	0	12	11
Lieu[t] James Pinneo as a L[t] is so at home	3	0	8	7
Serj[t] Dan[ll] Dunham	3	0	5	0
Cler Sam[ll] West	3	0	4	9
Corp[o] Henry Bliss	3	0	4	9
Corp[o] Ab[m] Bliss	2	0	3	2
John Henry	3	0	4	3
John Joy	3	0	4	3
Azariah Brown	3	0	4	3
Dav[d] Treadway	3	0	4	3
Josiah Fitch	3	0	4	3
Tho[s] Clark	3	0	4	3
Reuben Woodworth	3	0	4	3
Benj[n] Gary sick on ye road & returned	11	0	15	7
Wm Swift 3[d]	5	0	7	1
Jos. Doubleday, & was sent Post to N London from Cambridge	9	0	12	9

The foregoing is a just & true Acc[o] & Roll of the 2[d] Comp[n] in Lebanon who marchd under the Command of Dan[ll] Tilden as Captain, in the late

Alarm occasioned by the Ministerial Troops, firing on the Inhabitans of Lexington &c in April 1775 & of their Expences Provisions &c in the most exact & perfect manner We have been able to come at it

Test

Aug[t] 30 1775

W[m] Williams
Vetch Williams
Elijah Hyde Jun[r]
Jeams Pinco Jun[r]
Pelatiah Marsh
} Select Men of Lebanon

[*Connecticut Historical Society.*]

D[r] Colony Connecticut, To Wages, Billiting, Horse Hire &c for sund: Officers & Soldiers, who marchd from Lebanon, to relief of y[e] Country &c in the late Lexington Alarm &c marched 22 April 1775 under Cap James Clark

N B ye Soldiers 1[d] P D . too high

	Days	Wages		
James Clark Cap	9	1	18	8
And[w] Waterman Lieu[t]	19	2	14	3
Dan Throop L[t]	19	2	14	3
Joel Chamberlin Ens	19	2	0	9
Jos. Abel Serj[t]	16	1	7	4
Malachi Thomas Ser	19	1	12	5½
Ich[a] Bosworth Serj[t]	16	1	7	4
Jos. Loomis Serj[t]	6	0	10	3
And[w] Fitch Cler	9	0	14	3
Josh[a] Chappel Ju[r] Cor[l]	16	1	5	4
Cha[s] Williams Cor[l]	19	1	10	1
Jehiel Williams Cor[l]	23	1	16	5
Elip[t] Hyde Cor[l]	18	1	8	6
Rog[r] Strong Fifer	23	1	16	5
Dav[d] Barber	15	1	1	3
Cary Prat	15	1	1	3
Abel Hackly	15	1	1	3
Asa Loomis in T.				
Oliver Hide in T.				
Sam[ll] Lothrop	15	1	1	3
James Law	15	1	1	3
Beri: Sprague in T.				
Zera Page	16	1	2	8
Abner Doubleday in T.				
Tim[o] Peepoon	15	1	1	3
Jn[o] Fowler	16	1	2	8
Jon[a] Blackman	15	1	1	3
Amos Miner in T.				
Ich[a] Fitch Ju[r]	16	1	2	8
And[w] Chapman	15	1	1	3
Benj[a] Keeney	16	1	2	8
And[w] Williams	16	1	2	8
Sam[ll] Wattles Ju[r]	16	1	2	8
Tho[s] Loomis	16	1	2	8
Billy Williams	16	1	2	8
Beri[h] Badcock	23	1	12	7
Squire Lee	26	1	16	10
Rich[d] Lyman	27	1	18	3
Sam[ll] Goodwin	20	1	8	4
Dan[ll] Rockwell	24	1	14	0

	Days	Wages		
Sol° Tracy	26	1	16	10
Jacob Baldwin	37	2	12	5
Vetch Williams Jr in ye Caps return	29	2	1	5
Benja Payn Jur	18	1	5	6
Jona Wills	18	1	5	6
Nathl Porter	18	1	5	6
Cap Wright, says is payd Jerom Clark marchd 22 Apl & listed 8 June } in T				
Benj: Seabury Jur	18	1	5	6
Stephen Payn	15	1	1	3
Nehh Payn	14	0	19	10
Stephen Payn Jr	5	0	7	1
Jona Webster Jur	15	1	1	3
Guida Webster	13	0	18	5
James Webster	15	1	1	3
Jno P. Bissell	18	1	5	6
Andw Clark	18	1	5	6
And Clark is not twice enterd see below				
Danll Wilcox	19	1	6	11
Theodore Metcalf	19	1	6	11
Jno Williams retur'd for Killingley	6	0	8	6
Thos Wattles Do	6	0	8	6
Dan Payn Do	6	0	8	6
Geo. Webster Do	6	0	8	6
Jos. Barstow Do	6	0	8	6
Davd Webster	4	0	5	8
Jude West	16	1	2	8
Andw Clark	18	1	5	6
A B	20	1	8	4
Jona Brewster	5	0	7	1
David Stoddard	6	0	8	6
Wm Torrey Jur	7	0	9	11

The foregoing is a just & true Acc° & Roll of the Company who marchd under the Command of Cap James Clark of Lebanon, in the late Alarm occasioned by the Ministerial Troops, firing on the Inhabitants of Lexington &c in April 1775 & of their Expence Provisions &c in ye most exact and perfect manner, We are able to get at it

Test

Wm Williams
Vetch Williams
Elijah Hyde Junr
Jeams Pinneo Jur
Pelatiah Marsh
} Select Men of Lebanon

30 Augt 1775

[*Connecticut Historical Society.*]

SIMSBURY.

[*See Record of Connecticut Men in the Revolution, page 21.*]

Wee the Subscribers Hearing of the Distressing Situasion our Breathceren are in at Boston by the mourders and Barberaties Committed on them By the King Troop: wee Do volontarely Enlist our Selves to Go to Boston to assist our Brothering and to Defend our Just Rights and Prevledges under the Command of Elisha Phelps & Job Case or any other man wee

Shall Chuse to be our Commander as witness our hand this 21[t] Day of pril 1775

Jacob Pettibone	Joshua Egeton
Loam Nearen	Jacob Davis Jur
Benj[a] Bodwell	Joseph Grimes Jur
Theo[s] Woodbridge	Joseph Humphry
William Andrews	John Case Jur
Tho[s] Phelps J[r]	Daniel Barber Jur
Martain Case	Elisha Phelps
Seth Higley	Job Case
Parmeno Adams	

[*Connecticut Historical Society.*]

CONTINENTAL REGIMENTS-1775.

FIRST REGIMENT—GEN. WOOSTER.

SIXTH COMPANY—CAPT. DOUGLAS.

[*See Record of Connecticut Men in the Revolution, page 41.*]

[Extract from Capt. William Douglas' account book, giving names of soldiers in his Company in 1775, and the time for which they received wages. The privates each received 52 shillings bounty money, and the majority of them are credited with mileage for 253 miles.]

	Time of service Months	Days
Lieut. Sam[l] Barker		
Lieut. Jared Robinson	7	14
Ens. Ebenezer Trusdell	7	14
Serj. Levi Munson	4	17
Serj. Benj[n] Bartholomew	7	7
Serj. Thomas Smith	6	
Serj. Asahel Harrison	5	24
Sam[l] August[s] Barker	7	9
Qr. Master Serj. Mark Mazuzen	6	12
Corpl. Benj[a] Henshaw Jr.	6	18
Corpl. Josiah Fowler Jr.	8	7
Corpl. Abijah Bradly	5	29
Corpl. John Aberhart	5	8
Samuel Whedon	7	3
Drummer John Bunnel	5	1
Fifer Asahel Strong	5	27
Timothy Andrus	7	
Philemon Augur	6	28
Levi Baldwin	7	7
Aaron Baldwin	4	20
Timothy Barker	7	5
Isaac Barns	7	9
Solomon Barns	7	7
Eliphalet Barns	5	28
Gideon Bartholomew	7	7

	Time of service Months	Days
Zealous Blaksley	6	9
Samuel Britain	7	9
Zebulon Bradly	7	6
Joseph Brown	7	
Samuel Brown	7	
Abraham Bunnel	7	
Matthew Butler	5	29
Titus Butler	6	23
Walter Butler	6	10
Ebenezer Byintun	5	1
Joseph Cheney	6	3
Ephraim Chidsey	4	10
Street Chidsey	6	3
Samuel Cook	5	9
Caleb Cook	4	18
Abraham Cook	5	2
Eliakim Culver	7	7
William Evertun	5	20
Zebulon Farrin	5	
Ebenezer Foot	5	20
Heli Foot	7	23
Elias Forbs	4	24
Caleb Frisbie	7	23
Titus Frisbie	5	7
Samuel Goodsell	5	
Henry Gilner	6	5
Isaac Grannis	7	9
Amos Green	4	24
John Guy	6	27
Wooster Harrison	7	
Jarius Harrison	7	2
David Hill	7	7
Sam[l] Hoadly	4	29
Jared Heminway	5	4
Moses Heminway	6	1
Enos Heminway	7	5
Mason Hobart	7	5
Joel Howd	5	1
Zebulon Jacobs	7	7
Artemas Johnson	7	
Joseph Jones	6	10
Samuel Ludonton	7	5
Eliphalet Ludinton	5	25
David Mallery	5	21
John Mallery	4	29
Zaccheus Maltbie	6	26
Joseph Moltroup	4	26
Elihu Moltroup	4	11
Eli Moltroup	7	2
John Negus	7	7
Benjamin Norton	7	7
Jacob Page	7	
Luther Page	7	25
John Palmer	6	12
Barnabas Palmer	7	5
Jacob Pardee	7	
Isaac Pardee	7	7
Ephraim Rogers	6	29

	Time of service Months	Days
Thomas Pierpoint	5	2
Levi Potter	7	6
Jacob Rogers	7	7
Rufus Rogers	7	5
Levi Rogers	5	20
Philemon Rogers	4	20
Chandler Robinson	8	16
Levi Rose	7	7
John Shepard	5	4
Caleb Smith	7	20
Robert Stewart	5	7
Solomon Talmage	7	7
Abner Tharp	7	
John Thomas	4	21
Benjamin Pratt	7	1

[*Comptroller's Office.*]

PROVISIONAL REGIMENT—GEN. WOOSTER.

[*See Record of Connecticut Men in the Revolution, page 44.*]

CAPT. WOODBRIDGE'S COMPANY.

A Pay Roll of Cap[t] Theodore Woodbridge's Company in Gen[l] Woosters Reg[t] in the Service of the United Colonies from Nov[r] 10th 1775 to Feb[y] 29th 1776 both Days included.—Copy

Officers & Soldiers Names Officers Non Commisoned		which the Man Inlisted last Campain Companies and Colonies in		Time of entry Company into this	No. of Days in the Service between the time of to 29 Feb[y] inlistment
Theodore Woodbridge Cap[t]				18 Nov	104
Uriah Church 1 Lieu[t]		Cap[t] Woodbridge	Connecticut	"	104
Daniel Barns 2 Lieu[t]		"	"	"	104
Trial Tanner Serj[t].		"	"	"	104
William Hart Serj[t]		"	"	"	104
James Doal Serj[t]		Cap[t] M[c]Cracken	New York	"	104
Abraham M[c]Killiss Serj[t]		Cap[t] Noble	Massachusetts	23 Nov	99
Silas Sperry Corp[l]		Cap[t] Stanton	N. Hampshire	18 Nov	104
John Henderson Corp[l]		Cap[t] M[c]Cracken	N. York	"	104
Ezekiel Cook Corp[l]		Col[n] Hinman	Connecticut	"	104
Asa Darga Corp[l]		"	"	"	104
John Datton	—	"	"	"	104
James Ledley	"	Cap[t] Noble	Massachu[s]	23 Nov	99
Thom[s] Kane	"		New York	18 Nov	104
Richard Hodnett	"		"	"	104
Joseph Kitchel	"	Cap[t] Noble	Massa[s]	23 Nov	99
David Kitchel	"	"	"	"	99
Samuel Brown	"		Cannada	18 Nov	104
Stephen Hadlock	"	Cap[t] Badcock	Massac[s]	1 Jan.	60
Isaac Moon	"		Cannada	18 Nov	104
Richard Northover	"		Connecticut	"	104
James Steward	"		"	"	104
Peter Ferris	"	Cap[t] Noble	Massachu[s]	23 Nov	99
Aaron Bond		Cap[t] Stanton	N. Hampshire	18 Nov	99
Jairus Bonny	"		Connecticut	"	104
Lemuel Baker	"	Capt Stanton	N. Hamp[s]	"	104
Daniel Benjamin	"		Connect[t]	"	104
James Call	"	Cap[t] Grant	N. Hamp[s]	"	104
James Call Jun[r]	"	"	"	"	104
John Call	"	"	"	"	104
Joseph Chandler	"		Connecticut	"	104
Eliphalet Everit	"		"	"	104
Edward Fox	"		Cannada	"	104
Nath[nl] Spears	"		Connecticut	"	104
Samuel Cook	"	Cap[t] Hanchet	Massachu[s]	1 Jan.	60
John Doal	"	Cap[t] M[c]Cracken	N. York	18 Nov.	104
William Galaspy	"	"	"	"	104

Officers & Soldiers Names Officers Non Commisoned		which the Man Inlisted last Campain Companies and Colonies in		Time of entry Company into this	No. of Days in the Service between the time of to 29 Feby inlistment
John Green	——	Capt McCracken	N. York	18 Nov.	104
Saml Hall	"		Connecticut	"	104
John Harrison	"		Cannada	"	104
Ebenezer Hastings	"	Capt Stanton	N. Hamp	"	104
Gilbert Hall	"		"	"	104
Ebenezer Leech	"		Connecticut	"	104
Abel Moses	"	"	"	"	104
Robert McCauley	"	Capt McCracken	N. York	"	104
Neil McNeil	"		Connecticut	"	104
William Pierce	"	Capt Hanchin	Massachu^{s}	1 Jan	60
William Patterson	"	Col. Warner	N. Hamp^{s}	18 Nov	104
Daniel Russ	"	"	"	"	104
Charles Robinson	"		Connecticut	"	104
Solomon Tuttle	"	Capt Stanton	N. Hamp^{s}	"	104
Samuel Wiry	"	Capt McCra^{n}	2^{d} Batt^{n} N. York	"	104
Caleb Waddams	"		Connecticut	"	104
John Welch	"	"	"	"	104
Charles Tilden	"	Capt Stanton	New Hamp^{s}	"	104
Thomas Watkins	"	"	"	"	104
Jacob Norton*	"		Connecticut	"	39
Thomas Tibbals Drum^{r}			"	"	104
Mathew St John		Capt Stanton	N. Hampshire	"	104
Giles Gaylord			Connecticut	"	104

[*Connecticut Historical Society.*]

* Discharged 26 December

THIRD REGIMENT—GEN. PUTNAM.

FIFTH COMPANY—CAPT. KNOWLTON.

[*See Record of Connecticut Men in the Revolution, page 55.*]

[From roll and individual accounts entered by Thomas Knowlton in his account book.]

Capt Thoms Knowlton
Lieut John Kyes
Lieut Daniel Allen Signs his name Daniel Allen Jr.
Ensign Squire Hill Signs his name Squier Hill
Serjt Daniel Eldridge
Serjt Obadiah Perry
Serjt Tymothy Dimmick
Serjt Amos Woodward Signs his name Amos Woodard
Clark Samll Moseley Served from May 6 to Dec. 10, 1775
Serjt Joseph Snow Signs his name Joseph Snow Jr
Drumr Nathl Hayward
Corpl David Allen
Corpl Daniel Squire Signs his name Daniel Squier
Corpl Christor Boing Signs his name Christopher Bowen
Corpl Jeddih Ammidown Signs his name Jedidiah Amidown
Fifer Benjn Russel Signs his name Benjamin Russell Jr
Fifer Isack Abbe Signs his name Isaac Abbe
Phillip Abbot
Jonathan Avery
William Allen Signs his name Wm Allin
George Anderson
Thoms Anderson
Steven Anderson Signs his name Stephen Anderson
Amos Bugbe
Joseph Berney Signs his name Joseph Barney Jr
Thoms Bragg
Abihel Bugbe
John Braughton
Aseph Burley
Thaddeus Brown
Jacob Burley
Jonathn Badger
Daniel Bozwarth
John Bowing Signs his name John Boen
Joseph Bowing Signs his name Joseph Boen
Lemuel Boles
Jonathan Chase Signs his name Jonathan Chaffe
Jerimiah Cinnel
Jonathan Crane
William Cheney Kild June ye 17th
Christr Chapman
Thoms Chapman
William Curtis
Benjn Dimmick

Thom^{s} Davison
Asa Davison
Amos Dowset Signs his name Amas Douset
Isack Dimmick Signs his name Isaac Dimmuck
Jonath^{n} Dowset
Timothy Eastman
Josiah Eaton
Daniel Fitts
Steven Foster Signs his name Stephen Foster
James Grant
Hamilton Grant
Sam^{ll} Hale
Robert Hale
Caleb Hande Signs his name Caleb Hendee
Benjn Henfield Signs his name Benja Hanfield
John Holmes Signs his name John Holmes ye 3^{d}
Silas Holt
Josiah Holt Discharged August ye 26
Charles Kimbal
Steven Knowlton Signs his name Stephen Knowlton
Edward Kyes
Fred^{k} Knowlton
Asahel Lyon Kild June ye 17
Abraham Laflin
Alexand^{r} Macknel
William Morce Written on another page William More
Adin Marcy
Daniel Owens
John Potter
Robert Patterson
Benjn Pitts
Zera Preston
Benjn Rus Kild June ye 17
Eprai^{m} Squire
Ruben Simmonds Signs his name Reuben Simmons
James Shepard
Daniel Smith
Richard Smith
Salvanus Snow Discharg^{d} Sep^{t} 11th 1775
Abijah Smith
Josiah Smith
Steven Scrborough Signs his name Stephen Scarbrough
Thom^{s} Southward Signs his name Thos Southworth
William Watrous
William Watkins
Aron Wales
Nathan Ward
Nathan Watkins
Sam^{ll} Walker
Elieazr Wales Signs his name Eben^{r} Wales
James Walker
Daniel Ward
John Woodward Signs his name John Woodard
Zachariah Kyes
Amariah Lyons
John Laflen
Robert Hosmer signs receipt for service in the company "in the Room of Abijah Smith" from Oct. 18 to Nov. 10.
William Williams

[*Connecticut Historical Society.*]

BILLS.

[*See Record of Connecticut Men in the Revolution, pages 37-90.*]

[Names of soldiers extracted from a volume of "Sick Bills", 1775, being itemized accounts of the expenses of individual soldiers during sickness.]

Name of soldier	His Company	His Regiment	Remarks
William Whiting	Capt. Sedgwick	Hinman	Of Hartford Died
Silvanus Snow		Putnam	
Benajah Geer		"	
Capt. Abraham Tyler		Huntington	In Rhode Island
Daniel Brown	Capt. Putnam	Putnam	Of Coventry
Benjamin Babcock	"	"	"
Benjamin Hoskins	Capt. Wm Gaylor Hubble	Charles Webb	
William Raymont	Capt. Doolittle		
Chauncey Smith		Wooster	
Thomas Pierpont		"	
Ebenezer Hall		"	
Serj. Cochram	Capt. Mott's guard		
Jude Bill	Maj. Elmore		
Daniel Bill	Capt. Watson		
Samuel Hough	Capt. Cook	Wooster	
John Pearce	"	"	
Phineas Lyman	"	"	
Gideon Bill	"	"	
Jarius Harrison	Capt. Douglas		
Jacob Page	"		
Eli Moulton	"		
Samuel Orsborn	Capt. Cook		
Amos Austin	"		
Ichabod Merriam	"		
Reuben Rowleson	Col. Ward		
Abraham Bunnell	Capt. Douglas		
Titus Butler	"		
Clement Tuttle	"		
Ezra Prindle	Capt. Peck		
Samuel Donaldson	"		
Nathaniel Taylor	Maj. Dimon		
David Annibal	"		
Levi Mallery	"		
Lyman Jennings	"		
David Sturgis			
Chauncey Dowens			
Isaac Squires			
Nehemiah Thorp			
Nath' Whitehead			
John Knapp			
David Dickson	Maj. Elmor		
John Comstock	"		
Asa Cole	"		

Name of soldier	His Company	His Regiment	Remarks
Billy Hatch	Capt. Watson		
Thaddeus Betts	Col. Waterbury		
Timothy Scott	"		
Henry Scofield	"		
Aaron Peck	"		
Joseph Beebe	Capt. Peck		
Reuben Beebe	"		
Thomas Wedge	Maj. Elmore		
Elias Chapman	"		
Joseph Jones	Capt. Watson		
John Trowbridge	"		
Joseph Thomson	"		
Nathaniel Marvin	"		
Jason Perkins	"		
Jared Benham	Capt. Cook		
Amos Austin	"		
James Olcott	Capt. William G. Hubble	Webb	Went on to Cambridge in Sept. 1775.
John Camp	"	"	Went on to Cambridge in Oct. 1775.
Eli Tuttle	"	"	
Thomas Merchant	Capt. Caleb Trowbridge	Wooster	Of Waterbury
Benj. Freeman	Capt. Mott	Parsons	
Zebulon Butten	"	"	
Roger Billings	"	"	
Peter Quecheats	"	"	
Jabez Avery	"	"	
Isaac Teacomwaus	"	"	
Jonathan Cartwright	Maj. Thomson	Wooster	Died
Aaron Camp	Capt. James Arnold	"	Returned from St Johns
John Higbee	Capt. Meigs	Spencer	
Nathaniel Miller	"	"	
Dan[l] Churchill	"	"	
Samuel Markham	"	"	
William Lucas	"	"	
Wickham Brooks	"	"	
Amos Roberts	"	"	
Frederick Winthrop	"	"	
Benj. Pearce	Maj. Meigs	"	Dislocated shoulder
David Mallery	Capt. Douglas	Wooster	
Joseph Hotchkiss	Capt. Caleb Trowbridge	"	
Charles Parmerle	Capt. James Arnold	"	
David Hyllyard	Maj. Prentis	Parsons	Wounded with a bayonet
——— Tyler	Col. Street Hall	Webb	
Jonah Hall	Capt. Porter	"	From Stillwater
David Pease	Maj. Clark	Huntington	Of Somers
John Willson	Col. Store	Putnam	
Benajah Geer		"	Wounded at the Battle of Bunker's Hill
Capt. Joseph Eliot		"	Of the army at Cambridge. In his last sickness

Name of soldier	His Company	His Regiment	Remarks
Reuben Judd	Capt. John Sedgwick	Hinman	
James FitzGerald		Parsons	
Nathaniel Watson	Capt. Shubael Griswold	Hinman	Died Dec. 1775.
Samuel Benham	Capt. Isaac Cook	Wooster	Northern army
Titus Negro	Capt. Hanchet	Spencer	
John Hatchway	"	"	
Thomas McKnight		Huntington	At Roxbury
Jacob Tocomuaus	Capt. Mott	Parsons	
Peter Cochecks or Quochecks	"	"	
Beriah Brunson	Col. Pitkin	Hinman	Wounded
Samuel Dealing	Capt. Chester	"	
Thomas Brooks	Capt. Parsons	"	
Sim. Wright	"	"	
Enos Skinner	Capt. Putnam (?)	"	
James Converse	Capt. Levi Wells	Spencer	
Ens. James Peck	Capt. Cook	Wooster	Of Wallingford
Lieut. John Hough	"	"	Not sick
Judah Leaming	Maj. Welch	Wooster	From Ticonderoga
Bethuel Norton		Spencer	Of Farmington
——— Benham	Maj. Welch	Wooster	From Lake Champlain
Joseph C. Hawley	Capt. Starr	Hinman	Of Harrington From Northern Army
David Smith	Maj. Welch	Wooster	From Ticonderoga
Capt. Noadiah Hooker		Spencer	
Jabez West	Capt. Solomon Willes	"	Of Tolland
Sam[l] Savage	Capt. James Arnold	Wooster	Of Middletown
Silas Gaylord	Capt. Arnold	"	
Nathaniel Averill	Capt. Eleazer Curtiss	Hinman	
William Crane	Capt. Hezekiah Parsons	"	
Charles Hall	Capt. Cook	Wooster	Of Wallingford
Lieut. Jonathan Parker	Capt. Willes	Spencer	
Lieut. Moses Hall	Maj. Eno	"	
Jesse Converse	"	"	
David Rice	"	"	
Caleb Orcutt	Capt. Solomon Willes	"	
Jabez West	"	"	
Nathan Carpenter	"	"	
Justus Thomson	"	"	
Nathan Jennings Jr.	"	"	
Daniel Johnson	"	"	
Jacob Green	Capt. Robinson	"	
Daniel Colburn Jr.	"	"	
Stephen Cross	"	"	
Gideon Noble Jr.	Capt. Shipman	"	
Aaron Cadwell	Capt. John Sedgwick	Hinman	Of Hartford
William Russell	Col. Whiting	Waterbury	
Silas Gaylord	Capt. James Arnold	Wooster	Died. Probably Of Wallingford
——— Fowler		"	Died Sep. 5, 1775. Of Guilford
Jacob Averill			At Stillwater
Silas Brewster			"

Name of soldier	His Company	His Regiment	Remarks
Phicol Moody			At Stillwater
Samson Obey			"
Thomas Averill			"
——— Smith			"
Solomon Martin		Hinman	"
——— Way		"	"
Peter Jermain or German			"
Charles Jermain or German			"
Rev. William Seward		Waterbury	"Chaplain
Nathan Hicock			"
Thomas Andrus			"
Ezekiel Trumbull	Maj. Welch	Hinman	"
Friend Dickinson	"	"	"
David Morris			"
Elishia Burret			"
Elihu Burret			"
Nathan Newell	Capt. Watson	Hinman	"
Jesse Foster	Capt. Doolittle	Waterbury	"
Salmond Taylor	"	"	"
Joseph Thorp	Capt. Buel	Hinman	"
Phineas Allen	Gen. Wooster		"
Abraham Chittenton	"		"
Jasphat Tuttle	Capt. Porter		"
Isaac Camp	"		"
Jonah Hall	"	Wooster	"
Ashbel Beecher	Gen. Wooster		"
Jonathan Beecher	Capt. Peck		"
Daniel Gates	Capt. Doolittle		" Died
Job Marshall	Capt. Griswold		"
Stephen Marsh	Gen. Wooster		"
Phineas Squire	Capt. Reed		"
Samuel Gilbert	"		"
Daniel Silliman	Maj. Demon		"
Isaac Silliman	Capt. Reed		"

The above men noted as at Stillwater belonged to Wooster's, Waterbury's and Hinman's regiments.

Name of soldier	His Company	His Regiment	Remarks
Ezra Ramsdale		Spencer	
Bethuel Fuller		"	
Lieut. Daniel Cone	Gen. Spencer	"	At Brookline
Corpl. Phineas Cone		"	
William Smith	Capt. Mott	Parsons	At Hartford
Charles Hall	Capt. Isaac Cook	Wooster	
Ephraim Chamberlain	"	"	
Dan Smith	"	"	
Levy Ives	"	"	
James Corbett Jr.	"	"	
Ens. James Peck	"	"	Of Wallingford
Thomas Brooks Jr.	Capt. Chester	Huntington	
Joseph Lamb	Capt. Hanchet	"	
Elizur Brooks	Col. Douglas	Huntington	
Jonathan Riley	"	"	
Joel Buck	Capt. Smith	Waterbury	
Silas Gaylord	Capt. James Arnold	Wooster	
Andrew Hull	"	"	
Nathaniel Bull	"	"	
Asa Blakesley	"	"	
William Perkins	"	"	
Archibald Rice	"	"	

Name of soldier	His Company	His Regiment	Remarks
Oliver Bradley	Capt. James Arnold	Wooster	
Stephen Brooks	Lieut-Col. Street-Hall	Webb	
Josiah Smith	"	"	
Ebenezer Thomson		Wooster	
Cyperan Merrell	Capt. Griswold	Hinman	Dislocated Knee
Noadiah Emmons	Capt. John Willes	Spencer	
Timothy Tiffany	Capt. John Watson	Hinman	
Ashbel Beach	"	"	
Gibbon Wentworth	"	"	Of Canaan
Elias Lee	"	"	
Amos Phelps	"	"	
Reuben Rowlison	"	"	
Hiland Hall	"	"	At Fort Edward
Samuel Borden	"	"	
Nathaniel Clark	"	"	
Billy Hatch	"	"	
Samuel Hotchkiss	"	"	
Ens. Jehiel Hull	"	"	
Nathan Newell	"	"	
Samuel Fellows	"	"	
Asa Andruss	"	"	
Benjamin Austin	Capt. Isaac Cook	Wooster	
Jared Benham	"	"	
Salmon Stanly	"	"	At Fort George
Serj. Joseph Shaylor	"	"	
Lieut. Morgan Noble		Hinman	
Reuben Clark	Capt. Hanchet	Spencer	
Ichabod Fitch Jr.	Capt. James Clarke	Putnam	
Nathan Linkhorn	Capt. Ripley	"	
Jabez Frisbee		Hinman	Discharged Aug. 75
Ashbel Porter	Capt. Starr	"	"
Dan[1] Cook	"	"	"
Nathaniel Catlin	Capt. James Arnold	Wooster	
Dr. Francis Percival		Spencer	
Corpl. Abner Cole	Capt. Scott	"	
Samuel Savage	Capt. Arnold	Wooster	
Amaziah Barber	Capt. Pettibone	Spencer	Lame
Abiel Willson	Capt. Humphries	"	Wounded
Othniel Gillet Jr.	Capt. Pettibone	"	
Lieut. James Thomson	Capt. Sedgwick	Hinman	
Hezekiah Clark	"	"	
Jeremiah Hurlburt	"	"	
Serg. Abner Willson	Capt. Starr	"	
Benjamin Barber	"	"	Of Torrington
Simeon Barber	"	"	"
Oliver Phelps	"	"	Of Harwinton
Enos Scott	"	"	"
Adj. Jonas Prentice		Wooster	
Thomas Catlin	Capt. Samuel Willmot	"	Not sick
Benjamin Smith	"	"	
Joshua Morse Jr.	Parsons	Parsons	
Eli Tuttle	Capt. Wm Gaylord Hubble	Webb	
David White	Capt. Nathaniel Buell	Hinman	
Judah Lewis	Capt. Nathaniel Tuttle	Webb	Of Woodbury
Daniel Brown	Capt. Putnam	Putnam	
Joshua Leach	Capt. Shubael Griswold	Hinman	
Caleb Leach	"	"	

Name of soldier	His Company	His Regiment	Remarks
James Benham	Capt. Shubael Griswold	Hinman	
Job Marshall	"	"	
Serg: Charles Wright	Capt. John Sedgwick	"	
David Wright	"	"	
Tryal Tanner	"	"	
Lemuel Gillet	"	"	
Ezekiel Perry	"	"	
Ebenezer Shepard	"	"	
Kirtland Grifling	Capt. Nathaniel Buell	"	
Nathaniel Douglass	"	"	
Caleb Chatfield	"	"	
Samuel Kelcey	"	"	Of Salisbury
Eber Everts	"	"	
Aaron Mills	"	"	
Daniel Burton	"	"	
Samuel Williams	"	"	Of Canaan
Josiah Whitney	"	"	"
John McLean	"	"	
Joseph Plumley	"	"	
Henry Hull	"	"	
Reuben Smith	"	"	
James Russ	"	"	
Jonathan Russ	"	"	
Gideon Dunning	Capt. Joseph Smith	Waterbury	
Levi Bostwick	"	"	
James Fairchild	"	"	
Charles McDaniel	"	"	
Serg. Timothy Munson	"	"	Of New Milford
William Hamlin	"	"	Died
Serg. Jonas Brush	Capt. Nehemiah Beardsley	"	
Joseph Bearse	"	"	
Job Scribner	"	"	
Titus Brockett	Capt. Isaac Cook	Wooster	
Daniel Gates	Capt. Doolittle	Waterbury	
Caleb Hurlburt	Capt. Griswold	Hinman	
Eber Beach	"	"	
Obed Crosbey	"	"	
Amariah Clumb	Capt. Watson	"	
Dick Gudeahn	Col. Ward	"	
David Moretrup	Capt. Willmot	"	
Benj. Gaylord	Capt. Griswold	"	
Elihu Thomson	Capt. Cook	"	
Thomas Marsh	Col. Wooster	"	
Lieut. Jesse Cook	Capt. Hubble	Webb	
Abraham Catlin	Maj. Welch	Wooster	
Samuel Wesson	"	"	
George Jones	"		
Amos Gilbert	"	"	
Moses Steel	Capt. Sedgwick	Hinman	Of Hartford
William Whiting	"	"	
Martin Woodruff	Capt. Hanchet	Spencer	
Lieut. Timothy Holcomb	Capt. Buell	Hinman	Died at Shaftsbury
Jacob Sayer		Parsons	
Jonathan Reynolds	Lieut-Col. Hobby	Waterbury	Wounded
Sam[l] Whitman	Capt. Noadiah Hooker	Spencer	
Sam[l] Coe	"	"	
Jonathan Reynolds	Maj. Hobby	Waterbury	Wounded

Name of soldier	His Company	His Regiment	Remarks
Wm. Manning	Capt. Mott	Huntington	
Serg. Timothy Munson	Capt. Starr	Hinman	
Jeremiah Smith	Capt. Sedgwick	"	
Jabez Avery	Capt. Edward Mott	Parsons	Of Preston
William Hamlin	Capt. Joseph Smith	Waterbury	
Augustus Lewis	Capt. Gale	Parsons	
Reuben Bates	"	"	
Sam[l] Bone		Spencer	
Josiah Arnold		Parsons	
George Dear Jr.	Capt. John Sedgwick	Hinman	Of Goshen
William Beech	"	"	
Heman Smith	Capt. Starr	"	
Samuel Kellogg	Capt. Sedgwick	"	A minor
Joseph Brooks	Capt. Starr	"	Of Goshen
Charles Miles	Capt. Sedgwick	"	"
Abel Butler Jr.	"	"	"
Samuel Hayden	"	"	"
William Matson	Capt. Willmot	"	Died
Salmon Stanley	Capt. Cook	Wooster	Of Wallingford
Amos Austin	Capt. Cook	Wooster	
Jesse Fairchild	Capt. Smith	Waterbury	Of Newtown
John Willson		Storrs	
Lieut. Trowbridge		Webb	
Duke Hamlinton		"	
——— Cook		"	
Daniel Winchel		"	
Roger Umsted		"	Died
——— Filow		"	
Daniel Smith		"	
Benjamin Bennet		"	
——— Olcott		"	
Serg. Taylor		"	
Serg. Phelps		"	
William Hamlin		Waterbury	
Serg. Josiah Fowler	Capt. Douglas	Wooster	
Lieut. Elizur Hubbard	Col. Douglass	Huntington	Of Glastenbury
Levi Deans		Parsons	
Richard Olmsted		Waterbury	
Nathan Carpenter		Spencer	
John Fairchild	Col. Samuel Whiting	Waterbury	
Serg. John Jones	Capt. James Arnold	Wooster	Of Durham
Thomas Cheesborough	Capt. Jewett	Waterbury	
John Willson	Col. Storrs	Putnam	Of Yorkshire Eng.
Ebenezer Pitcher Jr. or Ebenezer Pritchard Jr.	Col. Hinman	Hinman	Of Woodbury
Jabez Syzer	Col. John Douglas	Huntington	
Aaron Minor	Capt. Phineas Porter	Hinman	
Timothy Pond		Spencer	
Fifer James Wells	Capt. Mott	Parsons	
Gilbert Crittenden	Col. Ward	Wooster	
Angus McFee	Capt. Peck	"	
James Fairchild	Capt. Smith	"	
Jedediah French Wells	Capt. Reed	"	
Capt. John Watson		Hinman	Of Canaan, Wounded at St. Johns Sept. 18, 1775.

Name of soldier	His Company	His Regiment	Remarks
Henry Norton	Col. Andrew Ward	Wooster	Of Guilford
John Scovill Jr.	"	"	
Eber Hall	"	"	Of Guilford
Zebulon Benton	"	"	
Thomas Cheeseborough	Capt. Jewet	Huntington	
Pettet Scofield	Col. Waterbury	Waterbury	
Jacob Scofield	Capt. Hait	"	
David Selleck	Col. Waterbury	"	
Isaac Brown		"	
Andrew Bennet	Capt. Bardsley	"	
Nathaniel Scribner	Capt. Mead	"	
Nathaniel Little	Capt. Joseph Smith	Wooster	
John Clemons	Maj. David Welch	"	
Smith Clark	"	"	
David Smith	"	"	
Beriah Birge	"	"	
William Russel Jr.	Col. Whiting	Waterbury	
Isaac Miles	Capt. Sedgwick	Hinman	Of Goshen
David Mitchell	Col. Hinman	"	Of Woodbury
William Hamblin Jr.	Capt. Joseph Smith	Waterbury	Died Sept. 30, 1775 Of New Milford
Thomas Olmsted	Capt. Doolittle	"	Died Oct. 26, 1775
Samuel Stubbs	Capt. Ebenezer Mosely	Putnam	Of Windham
Amos Ormsby	Capt. John Watson	Hinman	
John Curtiss	"	"	Of Canaan
Nathan Jennings		Spencer	
Jeremiah Chase	Capt. Mead	Waterbury	
Lieut. Morgan Noble	Capt. Eleazer Curtiss	Hinman	
Charles Kilborn	Maj. Welch	Wooster	Of Litchfield
Solomon Goodwin	"	"	"
Josiah Remington		Spencer	With Col. Arnold in Canada.
Thomas Averill	Capt. Edward Mott	Parsons	
Torrey Scranton	Col. Andrew Ward	Wooster	
Corp. Prentice Hosmer	Capt. Sedgwick	Hinman	Of Hartford
Isaac Willcox	Maj. Joel Clark	Huntington	His last sickness
Caleb Orcutt	Capt. Wells	Spencer	Of Willington
Luther Page	Capt. William Douglas	Wooster	
Daniel Johnson	Capt. Solomon Wells	Spencer	
William Bearce	Capt. John Sedgwick	Hinman	Of Cornwall
Justus Thomson	Lieut. Jonathan Parker	Spencer	Of Willington
Amos Mix	Col. Street Hall	Webb	
Moses Warner	Capt. Ellsworth	Huntington	
Eli Pease	"	"	
Roswell Blotchet		"	
David Shaw	Capt. Parsons	"	
Ebenezer Prior	Capt. Ellsworth	"	
Chester Allyn	Capt. Hanchet	"	
Samuel Barlow	Capt. Zalmon Read	Waterbury	Died at Poughkeepsie
John Patterson	Capt. Dimon	Wooster	
Ichabod Canfield	"	"	
Timothy Stevens	Capt. Rowley	Huntington	
Obediah Fox	Col. Douglas	"	
Elijah Hollister	Capt. Chester	Spencer	
Robert Harvey Jr.	Capt. John Willis	Wyllys	Of East Haddam

Name of soldier	His Company	His Regiment	Remarks
Mason Hobart	Capt. Douglas	Wooster	
Ebenezer Judd	Capt. Porter	"	
Daniel Williams	Capt. Peck	"	
Artemas Johnson	Capt. Douglas	"	
Isaac Camp	Capt. Porter	"	Of Farmington
Edmund Clarke	Capt. John Ripley	Huntington	
Ens. David Hitchcock	Capt. Peck	Wooster	Of Wallingford
Solomon Martin	Col. Hinman	Hinman	Of Woodbury
Lemuel Herrick	Capt. Mott	Parsons	Of Preston
Elijah Crane	Capt. Beardsley	Waterbury	
Benjamin Mack		Parsons	
John Willson	Col. Storrs	Putnam	Of Windham
Moses Warner	Capt. Cook	Wooster	
Samuel Hall	"	"	
Peter Van Dyke	Capt. Eleazer Curtis	Hinman	
Phinehas Sherwood	"	"	
Daniel Seward	Capt. Peck	Wooster	
Joel Buck	Capt. Smith	Waterbury	
Benajah Gears	Col. Storrs	Putnam	Wounded in Bunker Hill fight.
Samuel Stubbs	Capt. Moseley	"	Of Windham
Nathaniel Watson	Capt. Griswold	Hinman	Died
Silvanus Snow	Capt. Knowlton	Putnam	Wounded in the battle at Bunker Hill
Samuel Barlow	Capt. Zalmon Read	Waterbury	Died
Eleazer Fenton Jr.	Maj. Enos	Spencer	
Ebenezer Drinkwater	Capt. Starr	Hinman	
Serg. John Stevens	"	"	
Oliver Bostwick	"	"	
Thomas Perry	Capt. Ichabod Doolittle	Waterbury	
Andrew Minor	Capt. Solomon Willes	Spencer	Died
Asa Brownson	Capt. Starr	Hinman	
Elnathan Filley	Maj. Enos	Spencer	
Richard Gay Jr.	Capt. Elihu Humphry	Huntington	
Charles Tuttle	Capt. Isaac Cook	Wooster	Of Wallingford
Joseph Ruggles	Capt. Joseph Smith	Waterbury	Of New Milford
Edward Barnerd Jr.		Spencer	Of Windsor. Died.
Japhat Tuttle	Capt. Phineas Porter	Wooster	
Paul Wellman	"	"	
Serg. Amos Dutton	"	"	
Peter Bradley	Capt. David Dimon	Waterbury	
John Slater	Col. Whiting	"	
Samuel Perritt	Capt. Peck	Wooster	
Henry Bull	"	"	
Jeremiah Bull	"	"	
Reubin Rowlinson	Col. Ward	"	Of Guilford
William Morce	"	"	"
David Lewis	Capt. Hooker	Wyllys	
Titus Fulford	Capt. Trowbridge	Wooster	Of Waterbury
Ens. Ebenezer Banks Jr.	Capt. Ichabod Doolittle	Waterbury	
Serg. William Fowler	Col. Ward	Wooster	Of Guilford
Joel Norton	"	"	"
James Needham Griffin	"	"	"
Richard Dick	"	"	"

Name of soldier	His Company	His Regiment	Remarks
Joseph Barney Sr.	Capt. Knowlton	Putnam	Of Ashford
Eli Stevens	Capt. Noble Benedict	Waterbury	
Daniel Eldredge	Capt. Knowlton	Putnam	Of Ashford
William Williams	"	"	"
Caleb Smith	Capt. William Douglas	Wooster	Of East Haven
John Hills	Col. Ward	"	Of Guilford
Angus McFee	Capt. Samuel Peck	"	
George Clark Smith	Capt. Starr	Hinman	
Lieut. Ezekiel Sanford	Capt. Zalmon Read	Waterbury	
Talmage Hall	Capt. Nehemiah Beardsley	"	
Samuel Baldwin	Capt. Porter	Wooster	
John Bunnel	Capt. William Douglas	"	Of Branford
Allyn Steel	Capt. John Sedgwick	Hinman	
Edward Dimock	Capt. Solomon Willes	Spencer	
John Charter Jr.	"	"	
Amasa Allen	"	"	
Samuel Wright	"	"	
Samuel Perkins	Capt. John Ripley	Huntington	
John Babcock			Of Lebanon
Ichabod Hawley	Capt. Hooker	Wyllys	
Eli Wood	Capt. Nathaniel Buel	Hinman	
Isaac Perry	Capt. Zalmon Reed	Waterbury	
Amariah Plumb		Hinman	Wounded and taken prisoner at St. Johns
Jedediah French	Capt. Read	Waterbury	
Joseph Thorp	Capt. Buell	Hinman	
Jehiel Comstock	Capt. Coit	Parsons	

[*Comptroller's Office.*]

CONTINENTAL REGIMENTS-1776

SEVENTEENTH REGIMENT—COL. HUNTINGTON

[*See Record of Connecticut Men in the Revolution, page 101.*]

CAPT. BISSELL'S COMPANY.

An Ammunition Return of Capt Ebenezer Fitch Bissells Company ye 17th Reg^{t} New York May ye 15th 1776

Mens names that have Got Guns and other Ammunition

Serj^{t} Cornelius Russell
Serj^{t} John Roundey
Serj^{t} Eleazer House
Serj^{t} Hezek^{h} Haydon
Corp^{l} Sam^{ll} Bordman
Corp^{l} Aaron Porter
Corp^{l} Sam^{ll} Hall
Corp^{l} Elijah Bordman
John Atwood
Willm Andruss
Ozias Atwell
Willm Arvin
Ephriem Alderman
Joshua Burgess
Shubell Cook
Willm Cradock
Elisha Case
Jedidiah Case
Ira Clark
John Chambers
Abner Fuller
Lemuel Fuller
Benjamin Fuller
Hezekiah Filley
Roger Filer
Reuben Flowers
Daniel Gilburt
Carmi Higley
Obed Higley
Erastus Humphrey
Joel Humphrey
John Humphrey
Jesse Halley
Jonath^{n} Holaday
Jareth Ingraham
Henry Edwards
Phinihas Kellogg
Henery Kirkam
Samuel Kirkam
Nath^{ll} Lamberton
Elijah Loomis
Sam^{ll} Landers
George Lewardy
Elijah Lusk
James Lawrance
Isaac Merrell
Increas Mather
Alpheus Munsell
Daniel Moses
John Miller
Daniel Munsell
Frances Merrey
Isaac Mix
Elisha Messenger
Loammi Nearing
John Newbury
Daniel Olmsted
James Powers
Lewis Standley
John Smith
Wm Shephard
Joseph Sedgwick
Alex^{r} Thomson
Roswell Warner
Abner Warner
John Wilson
John White
John Whiting
Daniel Waller
Rhoderick Clark
Augustus Miller
John Flether

[*Connecticut Historical Society.*]

NINETEENTH REGIMENT—COL. WEBB.

CAPT. HALE'S COMPANY.

[*See Record of Connecticut Men in the Revolution, page 104.*]

A Pay Abstract of Capt. Hale's Company Colo. Webb's Regiment for ye Month of April 1776. June 10th 1776

Mens Names	Sum of Wages £	s	d
Capt. Nathan Hale	8	0	0
Lieut. Alpheus Chapman	5	8	0
Lieut. John Elderkin	5	8	0
Ens. George Hurlbut	4	0	0
Serg^ts^ Thomas Updike Fosdick	2	8	0
Stephen Hempsted	2	8	0
Francis Sage	2	8	0
Peter Robertson	2	8	0
Corp^ls^ Christopher Beebe	2	4	0
Asa Spink	2	4	0
Thomas Kingsbury	2	4	0
Christopher Woodbridge	2	4	0
Drum^r^ Lemuel Maynard	2	4	0
Fif^r^ William Willson	2	4	0
Privates Pigot Colin Adams	2	0	0
Ebenezer Allen	2	0	0
Alvin Ames	2	0	0
William Bacon	2	0	0
Guy Beckwith	2	0	0
Thaddeus Beebe	2	0	0
Gideon Beebe	2	0	0
Ephraim Beebe	2	0	0
Paul Beebe	2	0	0
Joseph Bolles	2	0	0
John Brown	2	0	0
Charles Brown	2	0	0
Eliphalet Button	2	0	0
Stephen Califf	2	0	0
David Canada	2	0	0
Silas Chapman	2	0	0
John Chappel	2	0	0
Alpheus Chappel	2	0	0
Joseph Church	2	0	0
William Clark	2	0	0
Thomas Cook	2	0	0
	£87	12	0
Thomas Fargo	2	0	0
Timothy Fargo	2	0	0
Stephen Ginnings	2	0	0
Daniel Ginnings	2	0	0
Stephen Hall	2	0	0

Mens Names		Sum of Wages £	s	d
Privates	Enos Greenfield	2	0	0
	Isaac Hammon	2	0	0
	John Hand	2	0	0
	Josiah Hand	2	0	0
	Timothy Hedges	2	0	0
	Henry Hopping	2	0	0
	John Holmes	2	0	0
	Lebbeus Houghton	2	0	0
	Robert Johnson	2	0	0
	Luther Martin	2	0	0
	John Martin	2	0	0
	Samuel Maynard	2	0	0
	Jabez Maynard	2	0	0
	Elkanah Meech	2	0	0
	Matthew Melony	2	0	0
	John Moltrop	2	0	0
	Isaac Morgan	2	0	0
	Josiah Osborn	2	0	0
	William Parish	2	0	0
	James Phillips	2	0	0
	Daniel Plumbe	2	0	0
	William Putnam	2	0	0
	Arthur Robertson	2	0	0
	Pharaoh Sharper*	2	0	0
	Jeremiah Tallmadge	2	0	0
	Nathaniel Tuttle	2	0	0
	James Ward	2	0	0
	Davidson Williams	2	0	0
	Asher Wright	2	0	0
		£70	0	0

The Following Privates, being inlisted after the Month commenced, draw pay but for part of it.

Names	When Inlisted	Days Servce	Sum		
Samuel Ames	April 2d	29	1	18	8
Silas Holley	23d	8	0	10	8
Ezra Smith	20th	11	0	14	8
			3	4	0
			87	12	0
			70	0	0
		Total	160	16	0

A Return of Capt Hale's Company Colo Webb's Regiment giving the Stat[ ] of it morning and evening each Day. Beginning April 20th 1776.

[In addition to the names in the above pay abstract the following names appear.]

Diarca Elderkin
Henry Wardon
Thomas Merrit

* Evidently an error for Sharp, as the name is written Pharaoh Sharp in three other places in the same book.

An Account of the Arms, Amunition &c used by Capt Hale's Company [ ] Regiment in the Campain of 1776.

[In addition to the names in the above pay abstract and return the following names appear]

Reynold Hooper
Ezra Williams
Simon Neil

An Account of Arms, Amunition and Accutrements Capt Hale's Company Col° Webb's Regiment

[In addition to the names in the above pay abstract the following names appear.]

Isaac Brun June 29 1 Gun N226 bay^t & Strap
Eliphalet Robinson Mar. 4. 1 G. N. 45. 24r. 1 bay^t & Car.b.
Joseph Weeks Jun. 27 1 K. arms Compt:

Casualties in Capt. Hale's Company Col° Webb's Regiment.

1776

May 12 Ser^t Thomas Updike Fosdick sent recruiting to the East end of Long Island & New London Instructions written not by Col° Webb but by his order.

Jeremiah Tallmadge sent on command to the eastern part of Long Island after arms belonging to himself & some others of the Company Living near by him.

28 Samuel Maynard Joined the Company

June 4 John Martin Joined the Company.

8 Enos Greenfield returned from 12 Days command.

Serg^t Thomas Updike Fosdick returned from recruiting & joined the Company.

29 Jeremiah Tallmadge returned having been detained at home by Sickness.

[*Connecticut Historical Society.*]

SIZE ROLL OF CAPT. HALE'S COMPANY.

[The following roll being imperfect the headings given are assumed and may not be correct.]

[Names]	[Age Y	M	Height F	I]	[Place of Enlistment State	Town]	[Birthplace State	Town]	[Date of Enlistment]
[ ] Robertson					Ibid	New London	Ibid	New London	
[ ] Sharp	25	10	5	9¾	New York				March 1
Jeremiah Tallmadge	28	6	5	8¼	New York				March 1
James Ward	24	7	5	3½	Connecticut	New London	Rhode Island	Newport	Nov. 15
Davidson Williams	21	2	5	6½	Connecticut	New London	Connecticut	New London	March [ ]
Henry Worden					Ibid	Stonington			[ ]
Asher Wright	22		5	9½	Ibid	Coventry	Connecticut	Coventry	Dec. 26 J [ ]
John Chappel	55	7	5	7½	Ibid	New London			March 27 Apr [ ]
Silas Chapman	16	8	5	4	Ibid			New London	March 23
Joseph Church	17	10	5	6½	Ibid				30
Samuel Ames Jun[r]	21	6	5	9½	Ibid				April 2
Elkenah Meech	16	6	5	9¾	Ibid	Groton		Groton	1
Thomas Merrit									March 9
Nathaniel Tuttle			5	7¾	New York				1
*Robert Johnson			5	6	Connecticut	New London	Connecticut	New London	Nov. 15
Corp[l] Christopher Woodbridge	20	10	5	8	Ibid	Stonington		Stonington	15
Silas Halley									Apr. 23
Ezra Smith									20
Simon Neil									
Ezra Williams									
Joseph Weeks									

* This entry is crossed out in the original

[*Connecticut Historical Society.*]

CAPT. PERRIT'S COMPANY.

[*See Record of Connecticut Men in the Revolution, page 104.*]

[Capt. Peter Perrit, Lieut. Joseph Hull, "and the Non Commissioned Officers and Matrosses of his Company Shewing to this Assembly that they were taken Prisoners of War the 16th of Novem[r] 1776 while in Continental Service" were granted certain allowances by special act of the General Assembly.]

Pay Table Office June 12th 1784

John Lawrence Esq. Treas[r]

Sir

Please to secure to the following Persons the Payment of the Sums annexed to their Names being for Service in the Army before January 1st 1780 agreably to a Special Act of Assembly in fav[r] of Cap[t] Peter Perritt passed in May 1784. . . . . .

Eleazer Wales Com[tee]

Cap[t] Peter Perrit
Lieu[t] Joseph Hull
Serj[t] Jam[s] Yatman
" Jon[a] Stricland
" Thomas Hinkley
Corp[l] Sam[l] Peck
" Preserve Edgcomb
" Landon Smith
" Jn[o] Hambleton
Jonathan Beecher
Jer[a] Norton
Benjamin Doll
James Burn
Ephraim Jackson
Lewis Clark
Andrew Yeumons
William Jones
Jn[o] Davis
Charles Walles
Gideon White
William Lock
Joseph Harrope
Jn[o] Bartrum
Jeremiah Durkee
Benjamin Harris
Jn[o] Colter
Shubael Johnson
Nathan Andrus
Jn[o] Wood
Francies Danaty
Richard Read
Jn[o] Camron
Benj[a] Pease
Daniel Haridon
Thomas Lawson
Samuel Lowell
Nathan Horton
William Whipple
Jon[a] Barnett
Mahu Tupper
Charles Brown
Francies Garrow
Jabez Sperry
Asa Beach
William Sanders
Adam Voas
William Gorden
Isaac Waterhouse
Jn[o] Pease
Asa Johnson

[*State Library, Revolution 17.*]

COL. BURRALL'S REGIMENT.

[*See Record of Connecticut Men in the Revolution, page 110.*]

FIELD AND STAFF.

We the Subscribers being Col^{ll} Lieu^{t} Coll^{ll} Major Chaplain Adjutant Quarter Master Surgeon and Surgeons Mate Acknowledge to have Rec^{d} of Epap^{s} Bull Duputy Pay Master of the Connecticut Battallion Rais'd by Virtue of the Governors Proclamation of the 27th of Jany 1776 — the Sums Affixt to our Names being our first Months Pay for Entering into S^{d} Service as Witness our hands. Feby 24th 1776.

Co^{ll} Charles Burrall Fifty Dollars	£15.	0.	0
Lt Co^{ll} Natha^{l} Buell forty Dollars	12.	0.	0
Maj^{r} John Sedgwick thirty three Dollars & one third of a Dollar	10.	0.	0
Ammi R. Robbins Chaplin Twenty six Dollars & ⅔ .	8.	0.	0
Thos. Converse Auj^{t} Eighteen Dollars & ⅓ . . .	5.	10.	0
Zerah Beech Quarter Master Eighteen Dollars & ⅓ . .	5.	10.	0
Edward Sutton twenty five Dollars Surgeon	7.	10.	0
Isaac Swift thirteen dollars & ⅓ & 10/ for Blanket Surg^{n} Mate	4.	10.	0
	68.	0.	0

[*Connecticut Historical Society.*]

[The Regimental Commissary book adds the following names and information.]

Jno Bigelow, captain of a company of Matrosses which formed a part of the regiment and went with the other companies at least as far as Albany.

Adonijah Strong, lieutenant in Bigelow's company and regimental commissary.

Reuben Murry, lieutenant in Swift's company.

Solomon Story, lieutenant in Throop's company.

Captain Swift's company contained at least 83 men.

[*Comptroller's Office.*]

CAPT. DOWNS' COMPANY.

A Pay Role of Capt David Downs's Compy being the 1st Compy in Cololl Charles Burrell's Battallion. We the Subscribers whose Names are underwritten having Enter'd & Enlisted ourselves into the Connecticut Battallion Rais'd by virtue of ye Governors Proclamation dated the 27th of Jany 1776, under the Command of Cololl Charles Burrell, to Reinforce the Northern Army, Acks to have Recd of Epaps Bull duputy Paymaster to Sd Battallion the Sums Affixt to our Names who have Sign'd hereuntoo for our first Months pay Bounty pay for Blankets & Napsacks as Carryed out in the Collum of Amt Witness our hands March 7th 1776.

Names & Quality	Time Enlisted
David Downs Capt	Jany 19
Adonijah Griswold	23
David Doty Liut	23
Samuel Johnson	23
David Rusco Sergt	Feby 1
David Strong "	"
Anthony Hoskins Serj	"
Oliver Hatch "	14
David Goodrich Jun. Corpor	1
Obadiah Matthews "	3
Oliver Crocker "	1
Samll Southworth "	2
James Bruester	1
Abner Buck drumr	6
Nathll Tyler Fifer	1
Isaac Pardee	1
Benjamin Macintire	"
David Randall	4
Caleb Jewett Junr	1
Jonas Knapp	3
Elisha Ticknor	"
Nathl Calkins	1
Simon Whitcomb	13
Saml Wright	10
James Hambleton	8
Daniel Parsons	1
Isaac Persons	"
Joshua Hambleton	10
Jacob Maxum	1
Wm Williams	10
Samuel Gray	6
Jesse Goodrich	20
Asa Rice	3
Benjamin Youngs	3
Jehiel Smith	"
Joel Chafe	"
Elijah Jackson	6
Joseph Doty	3
John Jackson Junr	6
Josiah Stronge	"
Joseph Calkin	3
Asa Hoskins	2
Charles Gillet	7

Names & Quality	Time Enlisted
James Laughlane	26
Abner Goodrich	3
Enos Pettit	27
Isaac Chamberlin	3
Lawrance Knickerbacor	1
Reuben Willis	3
John Reen	20
Jethro Delano	6
Stephen Wilcox	12
Wm Hyde	4
Judah Bill	3
Charles Gillet Senr	1
David Manning Junr	"
Cyrus Fillmore	12
Edward Bumpus	29
Henry Ingram	6
Wm Goodrich Weller	1
Elijah Bennett	6
Simeon Runo	10
Edmon Hunt	4
John Churcher	8
Eleazer Norton	6
Ephram Toby	3
Michael McKee	4
Adonijah Pangbourn	5
Ezra Chapman	"
Edward Richmernd	10
Amasa Warner	"
Thos Slitwill	1
Elijah Hurlburt	8
Jonas Adams	"
James Clary	Marh 1
Rosel Roberts	Feb 5
Peter Armstrong	8
Isaac Lamb	10
John Fisk	1
John Hall	4
Samll Brown	12
Dan Smith	8
James Barker	29
Jeduthan Gray	5
Danll Stuard	4
Samll Goodrich	6

[*Connecticut Historical Society.*]

CAPT. STEVENS' COMPANY.

A Pay Role of Capt John Stevens's Company being the 2nd Company in Co^{ll} Charles Burrells Battallion. We the Subscribers whose Names are underwritten having Enter'd into & Enlisted ourselves into the Connecticut Battallion Rais'd by virtue of the Governors Proclamation dated the 27th of Jany 1776 under the Command of Co^{ll} Charles Burrell to Reinforce the Northern Army, Ackno^{g} to have Rec^{d} of Epap^{s} Bull duputy Paymaster to S^{d} Battallion the Sums Affixt to our Names, who have Sign'd hereunto for our first Months pay Bounty & pay for Blank^{ts} & Napsacks as Carryed out in the Colum of Am^{t} Witness our hands – March 1776 —

Names & Quality	Time Enlisted	Names & Quality	Time Enlisted
Jno Stevens Capt	Jany 19	John Hewit	27
Jesse Kimball Liu^{t}	23	Randol Hewit	"
Matthew Patterson	23	Willard Kingsbury	19
Bayze Wells Esn	23	Phinihas Heath	9
David Fellows	24	Sippo Negro	24
Rufus Paine Serj.	Feby 24	Daniel Janeways [?]	Jany 29
Cornelus Flower Seg^{t}	5	Medad Newel	Feby 9
Jeddidiah Smith Cor^{ll}	19	Jabez Lewes	Jany 24
Elisha Hosmer Corp	5	Jonathan Davis	Feby 9
Samuel Green Drum	Jany 24	Samuel Steel	5
Zachariah Porter Fifer	Feby 19	Eleazer Fisher	4
Samuel Simmons	"	Abraham Webster	5
David Baldwen	"	Isaiah Gridley	4
Joseph Allen Tanner	6	Eliphas Steel	5
Daniel Everest	21	Amos Shepard	4
Elisha Bradford	6	Titus Merrel	5
Hezakiah Barce	15	Ebnezear Sedgwick	5
Ruben Dean	"	Eldad Kellogg	5
Ephram Simons	19	John Ledgyrd	4
John Cowle	6	Simeon Dupe	4
Thomas Fleming	15	Julus Davis	4
John Waterhouse	"	Jack Negro	8
James Claray	6	Uriah Ab^{ms} Bailey	27
John Spaulding	Jany 24	Jacob Wheeler	"
Thos Gilbert	22	Josiah Eaglestone	"
Stephen Fellows	"	Wm Wealer	"
Olover Stevens	"	Amaziah Palmeter	"
Edward Bow	24	Walter Whaling	"
Obel Fellows	29	Zadock Hawley	"
Josiah Cleveland	24	Joseph Foot	March 5
Ananias Pauridge	"	Abner Spencer	Feby 27
Samuel Pierce	"	Paulis Abune	"
John Green	29	Jonas Cleveland	Ap^{l} 13
William Chamber	24	Phineas Stephens	Feby 5
Samuel Fitch	29	Simeon Heath	15
Zebulon Stevens	24	Sam^{ll} Fellow	March 2
David Preston	Feby 15	Seth Raymond	3
Benjn Stevens	19	John Evens	2
Jehial Burr	15	Enos Lyon	12
Elias Lee	19	John Harrington	"
Aaron Lawrence	Jany 24	Joseph Henderson	19
John Squier	29	John McGoon	22
Benjn Hewit	Feby 26	Eben^{r} Evert Foot	5
Epheram Hewit	27		

[*Connecticut Historical Society.*]

CAPT. AUSTIN'S COMPANY.

A Pay Role of Capt Aaron Austin's Compy being the 3rd Compy in Colo^ll Charles Burrells Battallion. We the Subscribers whose Names are Under-written having Enter'd & Enlisted ourselves into the Connecticut Battallion Rais'd by Virtue of the Governors Proclamation dated the 19th of Jany 1776, under the Command of Cololl Charles Burrell to Reinforce the Northern Army Ackg to have Recd of Epaps Bull, duputy Paymaster to Said Battallion the Sums Affixt to our Names who have Sign'd hereunto for our first Months pay Bounty & pay for Blankets & Napsacks as Carryed out in the Collum of Amt Witness our hands March 1776.

Names & Quality	Time Enlisted	
Capt Aaron Austin	Jany	19
Moses Shepard Liut		23
Asahel Hodge Lieut		23
William Steel Ensign		"
James Benham Ser	Feby	1
James Austin Sergt		1
John Alford "		1
Seth Spencer "		6
Abraham Catting Corl		"
Zamri Skinner "		"
Leveret Kellogg "		"
Normand Filer "		"
Elias Benham drumer		"
Matthias Hurlburt fifer		"
Aaron Fay		"
Eli Andrus		6
Job Marsh		8
Benjn Frizby		9
Martin Wilcox		7
Benjn Gaylord		1
Isaac Bradly		8
Nehemiah Merrells		6
Jno Hale		8
Wm Seymour		6
Reuben Warren		9
Danll Kelcy		8
Wm Taylor		10
Martin Kellogg		10
Jno Steel		8
Roderick Hopkins		6
George Hopkins		"
Noah Kellogg		6
Benjn Parsons		9
Hezekiah Olcott		6
John Stanclift		6
Samll Pike		6
Joseph Ives		6
Elias Merrells		10
Jonas Webb		1
Benajah Abro, Negro		10
Benjn Abro, Negro		"
Benjn Ball		1
Thomas Gardiner		8
James Pike		6
Danll Fisher		"
Jesse Ives		6
Usebius Austin		6
Jno Sweet		6
James Spencer		6
David Humphrey		20
George Frazier		12
Jno Marr		12
Josiah Russel		8
Abraham Coval		6
Abel Tyler		6
Ezra Spencer		6
Joseph Kellogg		6
Asa Griswold		10
Hamlin Jonson		8
Joshua Thomson		1
Benjn Barber		8
White Griswold		10
Jno Matthews		8
Eliphelet Alford		8
Jabez Frisby		8
Elijah Scott		1
Elijah Loomis		6
Joseph Hally		9
Enos Scott		1
Joel Castel		9
Amasa Scott		6
Seth Meacham		9
Moses Nash	Mach	25
John Nearing		20
Phinehas Shepard		25
David Goff		24
Ezra Edgcomb		26

[*Connecticut Historical Society.*]

CAPT. STODDARD'S COMPANY.

A Pay Role of Capt Luther Stoddard's Company being the 6th Company in Colo^ll Charles Burrells Battallion. We the Subscribers whose Names are underwritten having Enter'd into & Enlisted ourselves into the Connecticut Battallion Rais'd by virtue of the Governor's Proclamation dated the 27 day of Jany 1776, under the Command of Colo^ll Charles Burrell to Reinforce the Northern Army Acknowledge to have Rec^d of Epap^s Bull duputy Paymaster to Said Battallion the Sums affixt to our Names who have Sign'd hereunto for our first Months Pay Bounty & Pay for Blankets & Knapsacks as carryed out in the Collum of Am^t Witness our hands. Feby 1776—

Names & Quality	Time Enlisted		Names & Quality	Time Enlisted	
Luther Stoddard Capt	Jan^y	19	Elezar Fuller	Jan^y	29
Eleazer Claghorn 1 Liu^t		23	Joseph Culver	Feb	11
Thos Converse Lieu^t		23	Benjamin Everest		6
John Hollenbeak Ensign		23	Timothy Holabird Ju^r		7
William Paterson Serg^t	Feb^y	6	Nethaniel Root		9
Rufus Whitney Serg^t		2	Moses Bishop		8
Sam^ll Richmond		"	Jasper Grinnel		9
Asahel Kellogg Serg^t		7	Rial Bingham		7
Oliver Church Corpo^l		2	Ebenezar Burch		2
Michael Brooks		"	Aaron Curtice		7
Edmund Grandey Corp^l		8	Eleanah Cleavland		7
John McClean Drum^r		2	Joseph Cowles		7
Jacob McClean fifer	Jan^y	29	Samuel Wilcox		7
Charles Evarts Clerk	Feb^y	7	William Robartson		16
Samuel Kelsey		8	Robert Whitcomb		2
Ebur Evarts		7	Elisha Mix		8
Stephen Hawley		"	John Musson		22
Thomas Edwards		2	Seth Hills	Jan^y	30
John Rose		7	Nathan Carter	Feb^y	12
Isaac Bird		6	John Thomson Ju^r	Jan^y	29
Sylvenus Tousley		6	Ambrous Collins		"
James Bradley		6	Nathan Norton	Feb^y	2
Timothy Capen		2	Asher Smith	Jan^y	30
Joshua Hide		10	John Grigry	Feb^y	4
Samuel Williams		6	Lewis Hinman		2
Curtis Chappel		2	George Deer		3
Billy Blinn		7	James Rogers		21
Samuel Waterhouse		8	Dan^ll Cady		"
Fraderick Stevens		6	Jonathan Sweet		13
Isaac Hugg		8	Thos E. Munson		9
Jesse Bishop		"	Isaac Trowbridge		22
Elenezar Birck		2	Jonathan Richmond		12
William Hinsdale		7	Asaph Nichols		21
Jesse Grandey		7	Champion Ackly		11
Joshua Jewell Ju^r		2	Isaac Smith		2
Elisha Everest		6	Benjn Vaughn		7
Joseph Hawley		7	Noah Nichols		8
Russell Hunt ye 2^d		"	Jonathan Chipman		6
Billy Munger Ju^r		2	Dan^ll Wilcox	Jan^y	29
Abraham Barthrong		"	Jonathan Ensign	Feb^y	7
William Blinn		7	Robert Jones Ju^r		13
Elijah Marsh		17	Jno Prevett	March	3
Joel Tuttle		20	Niel McNiel	Ap^l	15
Timothy Woodford		7	Francis Freeland		"
Henry Hull		2	Elijah Collins	Feb^y	28
Daniel Fuller		6			

[*Connecticut Historical Society*]

CAPT. PARMELEE'S COMPANY.

A Pay Role of Cap[t] Oliver Parmelee's Comp[y] being the 7th Comp[y] in Colo[ll] Charles Burrell's Battallion — We the Subscribers whose Names are underwritten having Enter'd & Enlisted ourselves into the Connecticut Battallion Rais'd by Virtue of the Governors Proclamation dated the 27th of Jan[y] 1776, under the Command of Colo[ll] Charles Burrell, to Reinforce the Northern Army Acks to have Rec[d] of Epap[s] Bull duputy Paymaster to S[d] Battallion, the Sums Affixt to our Names who have Sign'd hereuntoo for our first Months Pay Bounty Pay for Blankets and Napsacks, as Carryed out in the Collum of Am[t] Witness our hands March 1776 —

Names & Quality	Time Enlisted		Names & Quality	Time Enlisted	
Oliver Parmelee Cap[t]	Jan[y]	19	Jonah Goram		8
Nathan Stoddard Lu[t] 1st		23	Gideon Nichols		"
Asahel Hurd Liut.		23	Sam[ll] Galpen		"
Reub[n] Calkin Ens		23	Elijah Northrup		26
Sam[ll] Peet Serj[t]	Feb[y]	8	John Hally		"
Stephen Spary "		"	Dan[ll] Taylor		8
James Smith "		"	Caleb Whealer		26
Michael Goodrich		4	Amos Clark		"
Dan[ll] Tucker Cor[ll]		8	James Hannah		28
Asahel Weller "		"	David Runnell		29
W[m] Torrence "		"	Abraham Hill		10
Charles Jennings"		4	Philip Shattuck		4
Eli Baldwin drum[r]		8	Hezekiah Churchell	Ma[h]	2
Justus Gregroy fifer	Mar[h]	1	Noah Turrell	Feb[y]	8
William Beamont	Feb[y]	16	Ezekal Slate		6
Benj[n] Peet		26	Asahel Bissel		10
Dan[ll] Tucker Ju[r]		8	Elisha Goodrich		6
Jeremiah Finch		26	Matthew Parker		18
Josiah Sweet		16	Elijah Brace		4
Stephen Smith		26	Nath[ll] Richards		10
Caleb Nichols		9	Elisha Calkins		4
Dan[ll] Dudly		26	Dan[ll] Elmer Ju[r]	Ma[h]	1
John Root		8	Elnathan Botsford	Feb[y]	4
Jn[o] Barns Ju[r]		26	Amos Weller		10
Reuben Smith		8	W[m] Page		"
Dan[ll] Warner		"	Thos Wainwright		"
Robert Warner		"	Heman Gibbs		4
Abijah Stoddard		"	John Doud		6
Jn[o] Baldwin		"	John Sawyer		5
Simeon Taylor	Feb[y]	8	Sam[ll] Hurlburt Ju[r]		10
Dan[ll] Brown		26	Dan[ll] Elmer Ju[r]	Ma[h]	1
Phinhas Hill		9	Isaac Fisher	Feb[y]	4
Rich[d] Dale	March	11	Jn[o] Clark	Ma[h]	1
Cyrenus Stodard	Feb[y]	9	Sam[ll] Holms		1
Josiah Churchell	Ma[h]	2	Joshua Culvar	Feb[y]	4
Thaddeus Stoddard	Feb[y]	8	Jonathan Norris	Ma[h]	1
Aner Adee		9	Aaron Culver	Feb[y]	4
Dan[ll] Stilson		"	Preston Halbisk [?]		26
Benj[n] Avery		"	W[m] Norton		"
Michael Robbin		15	Justice Hurd		"
John Fitz Gerald		26	John Hurd		"
Tho[s] Munn		8	Joshua Hurd		"
Josiah Hooker		26	Phinehas Clark		"
W[m] Lamphear		10			

[*Connecticut Historical Society.*]

CAPT. WATSON'S COMPANY.

A Pay Role of Capt Titus Watson's Comp^y being the 8th Comp^y in Col^ll Charles Burrell's Battallion — We the Subscribers whose Names are underwritten having Enter'd into & Enlisted ourselves into the Connecticut Battallion Rais'd by virtue of the Governor's Proclamation dated the 27th of Jany 1776 under the Command of Co^ll Charles Burrell to Reinforce the Northern Army, Ack^g to have Rec^d of Epap^s Bull deputy Paymaster to 8^d Battallion the Sums Affixt to our Names, who have Sign'd hereunto for our first Months pay Bounty & pay for Blankets & Napsacks as Carryid out in the Collum of Am^t Witness our hands — March 1776 —

Names & Quality	Time Enlisted	
Titus Watson Cap^tn	Jan^y	19
Andrew Moor 1st L^t		23
John Rily 2^d L^t		23
Charles Wright En^sn		23
Elkanah Phelps Serj^t	Feb^y	1
Jarad Abernethy "		"
Joseph Butler Serj^t		"
Josiah Whitney "		"
Thos Curtis Corporal		"
Adam Mott "		"
Stephen North "		6
David Wright "		1
Silas Seward fifer		"
Isaac Williams		6
Heman Watson		1
Joseph Preston		3
Benjamin Murooy		24
Thomas Wiar		1
Nathaniel Clark	Jan^y	29
Ambrose Beech	Feb^y	6
Jonathan Munger		1
Ichabod Tuttle		"
Sam^ll Kellogg		"
Nathaniel Field		"
Seth Hayden		"
Israel Beech		"
Jacob Williams		6
Gibbens Wentworth	Jan^y	29
Shuble Wentworth	Feb^y	26
Brotherton Seaward	Jan^y	29
Wait Deming	Feb^y	6
Stephen Goodwin Junr		1
Rufus Thrall		15
Bille Hatch	Jan^y	29
Samuel Gaylord	Feb^y	6
Isaac Butler	Jan^y	29
Elijah Pettibon		"
John Gillit	Feb^y	26
Serajah Comstock	Jan^y	29
Nicholas Holt		"
Wm Leech		"
Alexander Leech		"
Moses Turner	Feb^y	26
Sam^ll Bishop		1
Nathan Tubbs	Jan^y	29
Samuel Wolcott	Feb^y	16
Amos Phelps	Jan^y	29
Asahel Case	Feb^y	6
Sam^ll Mills Ju^r		"
Nathaniel Balcam		"
Eli Filley		"
Joseph Jones		1
Abram Knap		16
Caleb Aspenwall	Jan^y	29
Levi Hotchkiss	Feb^y	16
Joel Grant		1
Amasa Parker	Jan^y	29
Justus Squier	Feb^y	1
Charles Walter		"
Jonathan Wheaten		6
Seth Hill		"
Jonathan Deming		"
Hose Willocks Ju^r		1
Abel Butler		6
Seth North		6
William Gillit		1
Joel Hamblen	Jan^y	29
John Bristoll Jr	Feb^y	1
Samuel Barden		16
Robert Macksun		16
Joseph Phelps		1
Joseph Knap		"
Asa Hewit		"
John Walter		"
Thomas Johnson	Jan^y	29
Edward Fuller		"
Roger Orvis	Feb^y	6
Simeon Mills	March	5
Abjah North	Feb^y	6
Chester Bingham	Jan^y	29
John Clark		"
John Curtis		"
Reuben Wilkinson	Feb^y	6
Seth Stanard		"
Martin Allen		"
Darius Gibbs		"
Spencer Gibbs		"
Abel Norton		"
Joel Miller		"
Geo. Hudson		'

[*Connecticut Historical Society.*]

CAPT. THROOPE'S COMPANY.

A Pay Roll of the Company Commanded by Capt Benj^{a} Throope in the Connecticut Battalion, Destined to Serve in the Province of Quebec

Names	When entered the Service
Benj^{a} Throope Captain	
Solomon Story 1st Lieutenant	
Thomas Bill 2nd "	
Jacob Fox Ensign	
Jessa Brown Sergeant	Jan^{ry} 20
John Pember "	"
Frances Fulton "	"
John Avery "	"
Samuel Lothrop "	"
Sherman Gardner Corporal	Jan^{ry} 20
Ebenezer Leonard "	"
John Tiffany Junr "	"
Samuel Loomer Drummer	"
John Lydleman Junr Fiffer	"
Ammon Fortune Private	"
Samuel Davis	"
Elijah Palmer	"

[*State Library, Hebard Papers.*]

COL. ELMORE'S REGIMENT.

CAPT. WOODBRIDGE'S COMPANY.

[*See Record of Connecticut Men in the Revolution, page 113.*]

A Pay Roll of Capt Theodore Woodbridge' Company in Col Elmores in the Service of the United States of America — From the 16th Day of April 1776 — to the 31st Day of July both Days included

Officers Non Commission:d Officers & Privates Names		Time of Inlisting or Reingageing	in what Company last Campaign	Number of Days in Service
Theodore Woodbridge	Capt	april 16th 1776		107
Uriah Church	First Lieut	"	Capt Woodbridge	107
Samuel Elmore	2d Lieut	"		107
Trial Tanner	Ensign	"	Capt Woodbridge	107
James Doal	Serjt	"	"	107
William Hart	"	"	"	107
Isaac Pardee	"	May 11th	Capt Downs	82
Bàrnabas Payne	"	June 6th		56
John Henderson	Corpl	Apr 16th	Capt Woodbridge	107
Benjamin Gidding	"	June 6th		56
Daniel Driggs	"	"		56
Samuel Spencer	"	"		56
Titus Allyn	Private	"		56
Samuel Benjamin	"	"		56
Azariah Bill	"	"		56
Simeon Blyn	"	"		56
Bartholomew Barret	"	"		56
John Bell	"	"		56
Thomas Brechin	"	"		56
Noah Chappel	"	June 1st		61
Silas Crippen	"	June 6th		56
Jonathan Culver	"	"		56
John Cain	"	"	Capt Cooper	56
John Call	"	April 16th	Capt Woodbridge	107
Joseph Chandler	"	"	"	107
William Chidester	"	June 6th		56
Jonathan Chidester	"	"		56
John Doal	"	June 7th	Capt Woodbridge	55
Samuel Dickinson	"	June 6th		56
Benjamin Darling	"	"		56
Gershom Flagg	"	May 24th	Capt Root	69
David Gold	"	June 6th		56
John Goodrich	"	"		56
Samuel Hall	"	April 16th	Capt Woodbridge	107
Ebenezer Hastings	"	"	"	107
John Harrison	"	"	"	107
Erastus Hills	"	June 6th		56
John Hubbart	"	"		56
Seth Hamilton	"	"		56
Phinehas Kingsbery	"	June 1st		61

Officers Non Commission:d Officers & Privates Names		Time of Inlisting or Reingageing	In what Company last Campaign	Number of Days in Service
Ebenezer Leech	Private	April 16th	Capt Woodbridge	107
John Moody	"	May 16th	Capt Parmalee	77
Abner Manley	"	June 6th		56
Sampson Marble	"	"		56
John Manley	"	"		56
David Rood	"			
William Ruston	"	"		56
David Rice	"	"		56
Thomas Watkins	"	April 16th	Capt Woodbridge	107
Levi Waller	"	June 6th		56
Samuel Willcocks	"	"		56
Samuel Wire	"	May 24th	Capt Woodbridge	69
Austen Wells	"	June 6th		56
James Warren	"	"		56
Thomas Tibbals Drumr		April 16th	Capt Woodbridge	107
Joseph Gilbert Fifer		June 6th		56

Capt Theodore Woodbridg—his Account Current with United States.
Augt 19th 1776 To Majr General Schuylers Warrant on the Pay Master general—£429 = 11 .. 6 .. ⅔
To Jonathan Trumble Jur Esqr P. M. genll in N. York Department
Sr:
Be Pleased to pay unto Capt Theodore Woodbridge the Sum of four hundred twenty-nine pounds eleven Shillings Six pence two thirds of one penny N. York Curency for which payment this with his Receipt thereon Endowed Will be to you Sufficient Voucher
Given under my hand at head Quarters
Albany Augt 19–1776

[*Connecticut Historical Society.*]

CAPT. WOODBRIDGE'S COMPANY.

A Roll of Cap[t] Woodbridgs Company in Co[ll] Elmores Reg[t] for Overplus Bounty Inlisted upon Gen[ll] Worsters Order Given in Canada: Albany Aug[t] 24th 1776

Mens Names		Overplus Money for Bounty
James Doal	Serj[t]	£0 16/ 0d.
William Hart	"	16/
Isaac Pardee	"	16/
Barnebas Payne	"	16/
John Henderson	Corp[l]	16/
Benjamin Giddings	"	16/
Sam[ll] Spencer	"	16/
Daniel Driggs	"	16/
Thomas Tibbals	Drum[r]	16/
Joseph Gilbert	Fifer	16/
Titus Allen	Private	16/
Sam[ll] Benjamin	"	16/
Azariah Bill	"	16/
Simeon Blyn	"	16/
Bartholomew Barret	"	16/
John Bell	"	16/
Tho[s] Brechan	"	16/
Noah Chappel	"	16/
Silas Crippan	"	16/
Jonathan Colver	"	16/
John Cain	"	16/
John Call	"	16/
Joseph Chandler	"	16/
William Chidester	"	16/
Jonathan Chidester	"	16/
John Doal	"	16/
Samuel Dickenson	Private	16/
Benjamin Darling	"	16/
Gershom Flagg	"	16/
David Gold	"	16/
John Goodrich	"	16/
Sam[ll] Hall	"	16/
Ebenezer Hastings	"	16/
John Harrison	"	16/
Erastus Hills	"	16/
John Hubbert	"	16/
Seth Hambleton	"	16/
Phinehas Kingsbury	"	16/
Ebenezer Leech	"	16/
John Moody	"	16/
Abner Manley	"	16/
Sampson Marble	"	16/
John Manly	"	16/
William Ruston	"	16/
David Rice	"	16/
Thomas Watkins	"	16/
Levi Waller	"	16/
Sammuel Wilcox	"	16/
Sam[ll] Wire	"	16/
Austin Wells	"	16/
James Warren	"	16

[*Connecticut Historical Society.*]

CONNECTICUT LINE 1777-1781.

OFFICERS.

[*See Record of Connecticut Men in the Revolution, pages 145-230.*]

The Arrangement of the Connecticut Line
Arrangement of the Connecticut Line recd
P Brown 3d Octr 79

First Regiment

Rank		Names		Date of Commissions
Colonel		Josiah Starr		27th of May 1777
Lt Colo		David F. Sill		5th of March 1777
Major		Chrisr Darrow		15th April "
Captains	1	Eliphalet Holmes		1st January 1777
	2	John Shumway		" "
	3	Willm Richards		" "
	4	Ithamar Harvey		1st of January 1778
	5	Ebenezer Perkins		" "
	6	Ezra Selden		" "
Capt Lieut		Enoch Reed		1th June 1778
Lieut	1	Henry Hill		1st Januy 1777
	2	David Dorrance		" 1778
	3	Richard Douglass		" "
	4	John Tiffany		6th Febry "
	5	Willm Colfax		18th March "
	6	James Lord		1st June "
	7	Simeon Avery		" "
	8	Ezra Lee		" "
Ensigns	1	Darius Peck	to rank as 2d Lieut	6th Febry "
	2	Ichabod Spencer	"	29th May "
	3	Rufus B. Able	"	1st June "
	4	Thos Anderson	"	" "
Ensigns	5	Willm Tracy		30th July 1777
	6	Robert Allen		1st November "
	7	Reuben Saunderson		29th Decembr "
	8	Josiah Tiffany		1st Jany 1778
	9	Joseph Fellows		1st June "
Adjutant		Simeon Avery		
P. Master		James Lord		
Q. Master		Ezra Lee		
Surgeon		Albigence Walds		
Mate		Saml Brown		

Second Regiment

Rank		Names		Date of Commissions
Colonel		Zebulon Butler		13th March 1778
Lt Colonel		Isaac Sherman		1st Jany 1777
Major		Ames Walbridge		27th May "
Captain	1	Ichabod Hinckley		1st Jany "
	2	David Parsons		" "
	3	Stephen Betts		" "
	4	Erastus Wolcott		27th May "
	5	James Beebe		25th Decr "
	6	Henry TenEyck		13th May 1778
Capt Lieut.		Roger Alden		1st June "
Lieutenants	1	Benoni Shipman		27th May 1777
	2	Timothy Taylor		1st Septr "
	3	Moses Cleaveland		7th Decemr "
	4	Peter Robertson		25th Decemr "
	5	James Andrews		29th " "
	6	Solomon Fenton		1st May 1778
	7	Joseph Austin		1st June "
	8	John Mix		16th " "
Ensigns	1	Isaac Keeler	to rank as 2d Lieut	27th May 1777
	2	Jabez Parsons	"	1st Septr "
	3	Eli Barnum	"	7th Decemr "
	4	Saml Hicock		1st Septr "
	5	Israel Strong		7th Decemr "
	6	Josiah Buell		25th " "
	7	Willm Linn		29th "
P. Master		Ichabod Hinckley		
Adjutant		John Mix		
Qt Master		Jabez Parsons		
Surgeon		Noah Coleman		
Mate		Jonathan G. Graham		

Third Regiment

Rank		Names		Date of Commissions
Colonel		Samll Wyllys		1st of Jany 1777
Lt. Colonel		Thos Grosvenor		13th March 1778
Major		Wills Clift		15th Octor "
Captains	1	Daniel Allen		1st Jany 1777
	2	Henry Champion		" "
	3	Robert Warner		" "
	4	John Barnard		" "
	5	Wm Judd		" "
	6	Edward Eells		" "
Capt Lieut		Elias Stilwel		1st June 1778
Lieutenants	1	Jonathan Hart		1st Jany 1777
	2	Peleg Heath		" "
	3	Saml Richards		" "
	4	Obadiah Gore		" "
	5	Sylvanus Perry		" "
	6	Charles Miller		14th April 1778
	7	Silas Godale		25th " "
	8	Ralph Pomeroy		1st June 1778
Ensigns	1	Hezekiah Hubbard	to rank as 2 Lieut	1st Jany 1777
	2	Elijah Ransom	"	" "
	3	Saml Gibbs	"	" "
	4	Theophilus Woodbridge	"	" "
	5	Reuben Pride	"	11th Novr "
	6	Hezekiah Bailey	"	14th April 1778
	7	Prentis Hosmer	"	25th " "

Rank		Names		Date of Commissions
Ensigns	8	Alex^r McDowel		1st Jany 1777
	9	Willm Higgins		23^d July "
Adjutant		Jonathan Hart		
P. Master		Saml Richards		
Qt Master		Willm Higgins		
Surgeon		John R^d Watrous		
Mate		Hezekiah Clarke		
		Fourth Regiment		
Colonel		John Durkee		1st Jany 1777
Lt Colonel		John Sumner		27th May "
Major		Benjamin Throop		25th " 1778
Captains	1	John Harman		1st Jany 1777
	2	John McGreigur		" "
	3	Nath^{ll} Webb		" "
	4	Andrew Fitch		" "
	5	Robt Hallam		31st July "
	6	Seth Phelps		25th May 1778
Capt Lieut		Saml Clift		1st June "
Lieutenants	1	Daniel Wait		1st Janu^y 1777
	2	John Buel		24th July "
	3	John Durkee		31st " "
	4	Joseph Chapman		" "
	5	Simeon Belding		25th May 1778
	6	Pownal Deming		15th Nov^r "
	7	Charles Fanning		" "
	8	Edward Slaxt^r Coleman		" "
Ensigns	1	Willm Adams	to rank as 2^d Lieut	24th July 1777
	2	Ezra Smith	"	31st " "
	3	Ebenezer Wales	"	" "
	4	Andrew Griswold	"	15th Nov^r "
	5	Silas Holt	"	13th Jany 1778
	6	Lebbeus Loomis	"	1st March "
Ensigns	7	Diah Hartshorn		31st July 1777
	8	Elias Robinson		27th Decem^r "
	9	James Hyde		" "
Adjutant		Lebbeus Loomis		
Pay Master		Willm Adams		
Qt Master		Joseph Chapman		
Surgeon		David Adams		
Mate		Jonathan Knight		
		Fifth Regiment		
Colonel		Philip Burr Bradly		1st Jany 1777
Lt Col^o		Jonathan Johnson		15th April 1778
Major		Albert Chapman		5th March "
Captain	1	Abner Prior		1st Jany 1777
	2	Joseph Allen Wright		" "
	3	Josiah Lacy		" "
	4	Saml Hait		" "
	5	Willm Greene		17th March 1778
	6	John St John		25th May "
Capt Lieut		Thaddeus Weed		1st June "
Lieutenant	1	Elizah Chapman		1st Jany 1777
	2	James Morris		" "
	3	David Strong		" "
	4	Roger Wadsworth		" "
	5	Edward Palmer		" "

Rank		Names		Date of Commissions
	6	Hezekiah Rogers		12th July 1777
	7	Cornelius Higgins		17th March 1778
	8	Thaddeus Keeler		25th May "
Ensigns	1	Cornelius Russel	to rank as 2d Lt	15th Decemr 1777
	2	Nehemiah Gerham	"	" "
	3	Othniel Clark	"	1st Jany 1778
	4	Willm Henshaw	"	4th " "
	5	Daniel Bradly	"	13th " "
	6	Job Smith	"	9th May "
	7	Jasper Mead	"	1st June "
Ensigns	8	Saml Deforest		15th Decemr 1777
	9	David Beach		4th Jany 1778
Adjutant		Hezekiah Rogers		
P. Master		Willm Henshaw		
Qt Master		Jasper Mead		
Surgeon		Sempson		

Sixth Regiment

Rank		Names		Date of Commissions
Colonel		Return Jonan Meigs		12th May 1777
Lt Colonel		Ebenezer Gray		15th Octor 1778
Major		Eli Levenworth		18th Septr 1777
Captains	1	Jonas Prentice		1st Jany "
	2	Joseph Mansfield		" "
	3	Elijah Humphry		" "
	4	David Humphry		" "
	5	Elisha Ely		" "
	6	Eleazer Claghorn		19th April 1779
Capt Lieut		Stephen Potter		" "
Lieutenant	1	David Starr		1st Jany 1777
	2	Saml Still A Barker		" "
	3	Asa Lay		" "
	4	David Hull		" "
	5	Willm Smith		" "
	6	John Ball		15 Novr 1778
	7	Joseph Shaler		" "
	8	John Mansfield		19th April 1779
Ensigns	1	Charles Burret	to rank as 2d Lt	1st Jany 1777
	2	Levi Munson	"	" "
	3	John Trowbridge	"	" "
	4	Gideon Bailey	"	" "
	5	John Sherman	"	17th Octr 1777
	6	Giles Curtiss	"	15th Novr "
	7	Elias Mather	"	15th Novr 1778
	8	Thos Farmer		15th Feby 1777
Adjutant		Samuel S. A. Barker		
P. Master		John Sherman		
Qt Master		Elias Mather		
Mate		Theodore Wadsworth		

Seventh Regiment

Rank		Names		Date of Commissions
Colonel		Heman Swift		1st Jany 1777
Lt Colo		Hezekiah Holdridge		25th May 1778
Major		Theodore Woodbridge		10th Feby 1778
Captains	1	Titus Watson		1st Jany 1777
	2	Stephen Hall		" "
	3	Aaron Stephens		" "
	4	Ebenezer Hills		1st Septr "
	5	Thos Converse		3d Novr "

Rank		Names		Date of Commissions
	6	Ephraim Chamberlain		15th Novr 1778
Capt Lieut		Caleb Baldwin		1st June "
Lieutenant	1	John Holomback		1st Jany 1777
	2	Charles Miel		" "
	3	Saml Barnum		" "
	4	Tryal Tanner		1st Sept^{r} "
	5	James Chapman		25th Octo^{r} "
	6	Stephen Billings		3^{d} Nov^{r} "
	7	Phineas Grover		2^{d} Decem^{r} "
	8	James Barnes		15th Novr 1778
Ensigns	1	Augustine Taylor	to rank as 2^{d} L^{t}	1st Jany 1777
	2	Joseph Wilcox	"	1 Sept^{r} "
	3	Willm Starr	"	3^{d} Nov^{r} "
	4	Thos Starr	"	2^{d} Decem^{r} "
	5	Philemon Hall	"	10th March 1778
	6	Henry Dagget	"	24th April "
Ensigns	7	James Bennit		1st Septr 1777
	8	Talmadge Hall		25th Oct^{r} "
Adjutant		Trial Tanner		
P. Master		Augustine Taylor		
Qt Master		Henry Dagget		
Surgeon		Launcelot Jacques		
Mate		Timothy Mather		

Eighth Regiment

Rank		Names		Date of Commissions
Colonel		Giles Russel		5th March 1778
Lt Col^{o}		Joseph Hart		18th Septr 1777
Major		David Smith		13th March 1778
Captains	1	Saml Mattocks		1st Jany 1777
	2	Paul Brigham		" "
	3	Saml Comstock		" "
	4	Theop^{s} Manson		" "
	5	Nehemiah Rice		15th Nov^{r} "
	6	Saml Sanford		15th Dec^{r} "
Capt Lieut		Daniel Barns		1st June 1778
Lieutenants	1	Asahel Hodges		1st Jany 1777
	2	Selah Benton		" "
	3	Richard Sill		15th Decem^{r} "
	4	Ephraim Kimberly		14th Febr^{y} 1778
	5	David Judson		10th March "
	6	Nath^{ll} Jackson		20th " "
	7	Aaron Benjamin		7th May "
	8	Salmon Hubbel		19th May 1779
Ensigns	1	John Strong	to rank as 2^{d} L^{t}	10th March 1778
	2	Levi Hotchkiss	"	21st " "
	3	John Hubbard	"	" "
	4	Eli Curtiss	"	21st April "
Ensigns	5	Willm Beaumont		15th Decem^{r} 1777
	6	James Olmsted		24th " "
	7	Joshua Whitney		31st " "
Surgeon		David Holmes		
Mates		Jedediah Eansworth		
Adjutant		Asahel Hodges		
P. Master		Richard Sill		
Qt Master		Willm Beaumont		

Officers on the Supernumerary List—To be especially recommended.

1st Regiment

1st Lieut.	Avery
2d Lieut.	Hale
3d Lieut.	Fox
4th Lieut.	Tracy
5th Lieut.	Spencer

2d Regt

1.	Capt.	Manning
2.	Ensign . . .	Stewart

3d Regt

1.	Capt.	Abbey
2.	Lieut.	Sprague
3.	Lieut.	Durkee

4th Regt

1.	Capt.	Bacon
2.	Capt.	Bill
3.	Lieut.	Bishop
4.	Lieut.	Cleaveland

5th Regt

1.	Capt.	Childs

6th Regt

1.	Capt.	Barker
2.	Capt.	Kirtland
3.	Lieut.	Potter
4.	Lieut.	Robertson

7th Regt

1.	Capt.	Beardsly

8th Regt

1.	Capt.	Brown
2.	Lieut.	Mack

[*State Library, Hebard Papers.*]

PROMOTIONS.

List of promotions in the Conn. Line 1780 1781

David Dorrance	Capt.	July 1, 1780
Richard Douglass	Capt.	Aug. 21, 1780
Selah Benton	Capt.	Aug. 21, 1780
Joshua Whitney	Lieut.	Aug. 21, 1780
Richard Sill	Capt.	Apr. 22, 1781
Josiah Tiffany	Lieut.	Apr. 22, 1781
William Fowler	Ens.	Feb. 27, 1781
Aaron Keelor	Ens.	Apr. 22, 1781
Elijah Chapman	Capt.	June 20, 1780
James Morris	Capt.	Apr. 1, 1779
Thadeus Weed	Capt.	Aug. 27, 1780
David Strong	Capt.	May 2, 1781
William Henshaw	Lieut.	June 20, 1780
Samuel DeForest	Lieut.	Aug. 27, 1780
Timothy Allyn	Capt.	Feb. 10, 1781
Nathan H. Whiting	Lieut.	Feb. 10, 1781
Benjamin Dimmick	Lieut.	May 4, 1781
Asa Lay	Capt.	Aug. 28, 1780
Thomas Farmer	Lieut.	Sep. 8, 1780
Elias Robinson	Lieut.	Oct 26, 1780
William Higgins	Lieut.	Oct. 28, 1781
William Lord	Lieut.	Dec. 6, 1781

The Gentlemen above named were appointed to the respective Officies annexed to their several Names at the Time specified in the List, as appears from the Minutes & Journal of His Excellency the Governor & Council of Safety.

Test
Jedediah Strong Clerk

[*State Library, Revolution 25.*]

FIRST REGIMENT—COL. HUNTINGTON.

[*See Connecticut Men in the Revolution, page 145.*]

CAPT. REED'S COMPANY.

Pay Roll of Capt Reeds Company 1st Connecticut Reg^t of Foot Commanded By Col^o Josiah Starr, for November 1779.

Names	Rank	Remarks
Enoch Reed	Capt	
Ichabod Spencer	L^t	
John Davol	Srg^t	
John West		
Thomas Leeds	Corp^l	
David Fellows		
Henry Worden		
Thomas Frink	Drum	
James Satterlee	Fife	
James Alexander	Privat	
George Buttolph		
Abell Brown		
Danl Browning		
Saml Butler		
Augustus Clark		
Elihu Church		
Simeon Cadwell		
Nathan Cottrill		
Benoney Congdon		Sick Absent
Amos Dennison		
Nathl Fellows		
James Griffing		
Simon Hubbart		Sick Absent
Thomas Henry		
Hezk^h Ingraham		
Wm Little		
Valentine Lewis		
James Philips		
Oliver Rouse		
Saml Shelley		
Danl Smith		
Grant Wickwire		
Jo^s Westland		
Wait Worden		
Shubal Cook		
Carpenter Elliss		
Elisha Lord		Omitted in October
Reuben Phelps		"
George Foot		"

E. Reed Capt

[*Connecticut Historical Society.*]

SHORT TERM LEVIES, 1779.

Return of the Eight Months Men In the 1st Connecticut Regt in the year 1779

Names	Town	Commencement of Service	Expiration of Service
Eli Starr	N. Milford	Novr 1	Jany 15
Jno Pulman	Preston	Octr 1	15
Asa Woodroof	Hartford	1	15
Monmoth Simons	Horse Neck	1	15
Joseph Hinman	Canaan	20	15
Nathl Morriss	Waterbury	16	15
Elisha Lord	Salisbury	1	15
Reuben Phelps	Simsbury	1	15
George Foot	New Town	1	15
Seth Frink	Sharon	19	15
Jeremiah Fisher	Washington	19	15

[*State Library, Revolution 16.*]

SECOND REGIMENT—COL. BUTLER.

[*See Record of Connecticut Men in the Revolution, page 157.*]

RETURN, 1779.

Return of the Non Commissioned Officers and Soldiers engaged for the war Specifying the Towns they Belong to and by whom Hired, In the 2nd Connecticut Reg^{t} Commanded by Zebulon Butler Colonel

Nathaniel Booth	Stratford	Robert Chandler	Woodstock
Nathan Brown	Norwalk	Silas Phelps	Lyme
Joshua Geecocks	Fairfield		

Those in Major Walbridges Company

Daniel Sherwood	Stratford	William Quirk	Summers
Benjn Cady	Woodstock	Peter Stephens	Killingsworth
Amos Fuller	Fradricksburgh	William Taylor	Simsbury
John Fuller	Fairfield	Joshua Wheeler	Stafford
Nathl Johnson	Greenfield		

Those in Capt Betts Company

Aaron St John	Norwalk	Justin St John	Norwalk
Isaiah Betts	"	Thomas Black	New heaven
Aaron Reymond	"	Joseph Hait	Stanford
David Webb	Stanford	Uzual Knap	"
John Dickeson	"	Sam^{ll} Bush	"
John Kelley	Litchfield	Hezekiah Bracket	New heaven
Aasa Hase	Woodbury	Christopher Tully	"
Selah Scoffield	Stanford	Joseph Clinton	Norwalk
John McNally	"	Thadeous Scofield	"
Jacob Wardwell	"	John Downing	Fairfield

Return of Lieu^{t} Colonel Haits Company in the 2nd Connecticut Regiment of Foot Commanded by Zebulon Butler Esqr Col^{o} of the Non Commis^{d} Officers and Soldiers who are engaged for the war Decr 12th 79

Enoch Meriman	Wallingford	Sam^{ll} Gookins	Suffield
Richard Lord	Lyme	Sam^{ll} Henman	Stratford
George Hubard	Tolland	Nero Hawley	"
James Downs	Northstatford	Shelden Pater	Woodbury
Richard Austin	Suffield	Comma Simons	"
John Demmon	Waterbury	John Widger	Sea Brook
Daniel Evitt	N Stratford	Benjn Weed	Stanford
Ceasar Edwards	Stratford	Sam^{ll} Whitney	Stratford
James Fuller	Suffield		

Return of the Non Commision'd officers and Soldiers Inlisted for the war in Capt Parsons Company in the 2nd Connecticut Regiment of Foot Commanded by Zebulon Butler Esqr Col^{o} Decr 12th 79

William Basset	Woodbury	John Avery	Norwalk
Abiather Evens	Hartford	David Bullin	Enfield
Daniel Winchel	Farmington	John Baker	Fairfield

Moses Ellsworth	East Windsor	Stephen Meeker	Redding
Nathan Elwood	Fairfield	Jonath^n Parsons	Enfield
John Jemson	Enfield	Abraham Reymond	Norwalk
Patrick Hines	New London	Aaron Tharp	Fairfield

Those of Capt Aldens Company

Jaquess Harmon	Suffield	Joel Masher	Stratford
Thomas Wood	Stanford	Abraham Murry	Woodbury
John Downs	Stratford	Sam^{ll} Manning	Stratford
Abraham Hawley	"	Galloway Peter	Woodbury
Abijah Perrey	"	Simeon Rood	Woodbury
Nath^{ll} Beach	Fairfield	David Rymond	Fairfield
Richard Denrary	Stratford	Elijah Spear	Suffield
Phineas Granger	Suffield	Elihue Spear	"
Nathan Harslen	Stratford	Charles Stwart	Salem
David Hurd	"	Benjn Waklee	Stratford
Brestor Jude	Waterbury	James Shop	Woodbury
Peter Lewis	Stratford	Jana Turney	Stratford
Benoni Moss	Wallingsford		

Those in Capt Hinckleys Company

Jonathan Luce	Tolland	Thomas Wilson	Horse Neck
Amos Harris	"	Peter Johnson	New haven

Those belonging to Capt Wolcotts Company

Caleb Orcutt	Willington	John Churcher	Fairfield
John Mitchel	Fairfield	Stephen Ludlow	Sea Brook
Gideon Nobels	Willington	William Reymond	Fairfield
Moses Allen	Fairfield	Tiras Turkens	Canterbury
John Ammit	New haven	Prince Negro	Norwinch

Those in Capt Ten Eycks Company

Ruben Beach	Stratford	Lewis Hurd	Stratford
Nathan Bradley	Fairfield	Abraham Couch	Greenfield
Jonah Cushman	Stafford	Joseph Porter	Fairfield
William Daskomb	Stratford	Daniel Potter	"
Joseph Harrap	Fairfield	Elias Shaw	Woodstock
James Hide	"	Jesse St John	Norwalk

J Hait Lt Col^o Com^{dt}

[*State Library, Hebard Papers.*]

SHORT TERM LEVIES, 1779.

Return of the Eight Months men that belong'd to the 2[d] Connecticut Regiment Commanded by [ ] 1779
[The expiration of the service of each man is Jany 15]

Names	Town	Commencement of Service
Thomas Kettle	Providence R. I.	July 14
Daniel Hoskins	Norfolk	Aug. 20
John Mills	Groton	"
Benajah Tracey	Preston	July 14
Daniel Thomas	Lebanon	"
Stephen Post	Salisbury	"
Asa Prissnear	Hartford	18
Increase Waymend		23
Moses Walsore	Harwington	Aug. 23
Solomon Chitingdon	Killingsworth	July 28
Gideon Roberts	Waterbury	Aug. 18
Allen Lain	Middletown	1
Moses Bradley	N Haven	July 29
Lenard Bishop	Guilford	27
Benj[n] Waters	Symsbury	Aug. 20
Nathan Wordwell	Somers	4
Jonathan Amedown	Willington	July 5
John Poole	Ashford	29
David Allen		Aug. 8
Joshua Hartshorn	Cornwall	July 20
Sam[l] Davis	Litchfield	7
Sam[l] Lambart	Harwington	15
Oliver Gibbs	Cornwall	15
Benajah Smith	Norwich	Aug. 1
Elnathan Beach	Cornwall	July 26
Elijah Buck	Somers	Aug. 2
Allen Clinton	Norwalk	18
Daniel Chapin	Somers	25
John Douning	Fairfield	18
Alpheus Pease	Somers	July 26
Ruben Stephens	Stamford	Aug. 18
Elijah Sexton	Somers	24
Joseph Scofield	Cornwall	July 26
Joshua Wedge	Norwich	Aug. 1
Moses Bradley	N Haven	July 27
Caleb Atwater	"	25
Edward Griswold	Killingsworth	28
Solomon Evit	Guilford	27
Nath[l] Root	Canaan	Aug. 14
Jeremiah Page	N. London	3
John Beckwith	"	3
Thom[s] McKnight	E. Windsor	3
Charles Elsworth	"	July 18
Nath[l] Tharp	Fairfield	Oct. 1
Edward Thomson	Symsbury	Aug. 20
Amas Reed	Mansfield	July 31
[ ] Hill	Tolland	Aug. 9
[ ] Atwater		July 20
[ ] Moory	Killingsley	Aug. 3
[ ]	Woodbury	Oct. 1
[ ]	Ashford	Aug. 3
[ ]	Norwalk	10

Names	Towns	Commencement of Service
John Wheeler	Norwalk	10
Daniel Smith	"	Oct. 12
James Sellick	"	Aug. 14
John Curch	Symsbury	" 20
Increase Brainard	Haddam	July 27
Richard Goff	N. London	Aug. 1
Sam[l] Parlms (?)	Lyme	1
Ashbel Waller	Cornwall	1
Hait Scofield	Stamford	13
Timothy Scofield	Cornwall	13
Evins Chancy	Killingsworth	13
W[m] McFall	N. London	13
Calvin Fuller	Somers	3
Pierce Boney	Cornwall	July 25
James Thresher	Stafford	Aug. 3
Richard Bogs	Hebron	3
Benajah Brown		June 25
John Ausborn	N. Fairfield	Aug. 11
Moses Coay (?)	Tolland	1
Derias Carlton	"	1
Tho[s] Foster	Guilford	July 27
Abra[m] Grimes	Cornwall	Aug. 1
Sam[l] Hubbard	Louden Mass.	25
[ ]	Guilford	9
Elijah Johnson	Tolland	July 20
John Lade	"	Aug. 1
Jesse Tinker	Haddam	July 27
Jared Tozen (?)	Symsbury	20
Eli White	Cornwall	26
Beriah Wright	Symsbury	Aug. 28
Stephen Wedge	Norwich	July 26
[ ] White	Tolland	Sep. 29
[ ] Selleck	Danbury	1
[ ]th[l] Ames	Stonington	Aug. 1
Ruben Harrington	Stafford	14
Jeduthan Dimack	Mansfield	1
Joseph Newcomb	Lebanon	1
John Taylor		1
James Wood	Scituate R. I.	1

[*State Library, Revolution 16.*]

THIRD REGIMENT—COL. WYLLYS.

[*See Record of Connecticut Men in the Revolution, page 168.*]

[The Connecticut Historical Society contains a collection of some two hundred interesting documents relating to this regiment, which, however, do not come within the scope of this volume. They are chiefly returns of the men serving in various companies at certain periods, and lists of clothing furnished to individual soldiers. The men signed receipts for each article of clothing, so that the autograph of almost every man in the regiment appears.]

CAPT. DANIEL ALLIN'S COMPANY.

Names	Residence	Names	Residence
Serg. Isaac Barrows	Killingly	James Dodge	Colchester
" Amasa Brown	Colchester	Willm Baker	"
" Ezra Beckwith	Windsor	Nicholas Ackley	"
" David Gibbs	"	Ezekiel Daniels	"
Corp. Saml Allen	Ashford	Champlin Haris	"
" John Fox	Colchester	Lucius Hulbert	Suffield
" Wm Osborn	Hartford	Mark Filley	E. Windsor
" Ebenez^{r} Cheeney	Ashford	Thomas Parsons	Windsor
Abijah Smith	"	Benjn Bawdell	Simsbury
William Waters	"	Benjn Hayse	"
Joshua Isham	Colchester	Jacob Holiday	"
Titus Prescott	Ashford	John Lain	Ashford
Peletiah Pomroy	Suffield	Joshua Knolton	"
Saml Chapman	E. Hadam	Chester Rogers	"
John Farrow	Simsbury	Lemuel Barrows	Killingly
Robert Hall	Ashford	David Coy	Volintown
Peter Smith	"	John Roberts	Colchester
John Smith	Mansfield	Wm Burnham	"
John Finigan	Danbury	Nathan Roberts	"
Silas Pease	Suffield	Aaron Chamberlin	"
Israel Osborn	E. Windsor	Joshua Isham	"
John Warren	Bolton	Wm Isham	"
Daniel Wheeler	Suffield	Nehemiah Daniels	"
Amos Couch	Farmington	Elezer Russell	Ashford
Obadiah Brown	Ashford	Perley Hering	Kilingsley
Henry Lyon	"	Elezer Smith	Ashford
Caleb Conant	Mansfield	John Wakins	"
Nathan Scovil	Colchester	Stephen Eaton	"
Hezekiah Marks	Hebron	Jedediah Smith	"
Lewis Ackley	Colchester	James Jones	Colchester
Ebenez^{r} Isham	"	Jonathan Isham	"
Elihu Mather	Windsor	John Hambleton	N. Fairfield

[*Connecticut Historical Society.*]

CAPT. HENRY CHAMPION'S COMPANY.

Henry Champion	Colchester	Henry Evans	E. Hartford
Charles Miller	Hartford	Josiah Evans	E. Hartf^{d}
Theo^{s} Woodbridge	Simsbury	Comfort Foster	Windham
Amasa Brown	Colchester	Abner French	"
Homer Phelps	Hebron	Richard Ferman	Infield
Abner Chapman	Colchester	Aaron Fargo	Windsor
Abner Mark	Hebron	James Gray	Hartford
Daniel Wheeler	Suffield	Saml Glass	Canterbury
Henry Brown	New Haven	Asahel Goodrich	Weathersf^{d}
Joseph Copp	N. London	Champlin Harrison	Colchester
Joseph Rouse	Preston	Thos Hill	Pomfret
Ezra Ames	"	Jonath Hill	"
Stephen Brumon	Farmington	James Keeney	E. Hartf^{d}
Francis Baxter	Windsor	Silas Pease	Suffield
Jonath Brister	Milford	Comfort Ranney	Middletown
Eben^{r} Brown	Waterbury	John strong	Chatham
John Brown	Coventry	Joseph Starkweather	Killingly
Zeph^{h} Bates	E. Windsor	Micah Towsley	Suffield
Benj^{a} Bullen	Union	Alex^{r} Tompson	E. Windsor
Edwd Coburn	Windham	Aaron Ward	Middlet^{n}
Wm Chafee	Infield	Elias Wares	Glastenbury
Wm Cook	Middletown	John Wright	Union
Ez^{l} Daniels	Colchester	James Walker	"
Neh^{h} Daniels	"	John Warren	Bolton

[*Connecticut Historical Society.*]

Return of Non Effectives in Capt Henry Champion's Company.

Alex^{r} McDowell	Glastenbury	Job Bennet	
Eli Bigelow	Colchester	Eph^{m} Seeley	
David Elgar	E. Hartford	George Delaby	Union
Wm Earl	Pomphret	Levi Loveland	Glastenbury
Eliakim Johnson	Wallingford	Levi Otis	N. Haven

[*Connecticut Historical Society.*]

CAPT. CHAMPION'S COMPANY.

A Return of the Non Commission'd officers and Soldiers inlisted in Capt Henry Champion's Company in the Regiment Commanded by Col^{o} Samuel Wyllys, with the places of their abode, the town for which inlisted & the names of the persons who have hired any of them.

Names	Term of Inlistment	Place of abode	Casualties
Alex^{r} McDowell	Dur^{g} war	Glastenbury	Promoted to an Ens^{n}
John Parker	3 Years	Stratford	Deserted
[ ]^{m} Tompson	Dur^{g} war	Bolton	
Israel Johnson	"	Colchester	
Daniel Whiting	"	"	
Elisha Brown	3 Years	"	Dead
Patrick Murfey	Dur^{g} war	Mass.	Deserted
Samuel Coe	3 Years	Farmington	
Levi Frisby	Dur^{g} war	Sinsbury	Dead
Thomas Collat	"	Farmington	
Jared Teuky (?)	"	New Haven	
Levi Fox	"	East Haddam	

Names	Term of Inlistment	Place of abode	Casualties
John Chariey	3 Years	Killinglee	Dead
Josiah Barrows	"	"	Dead
Henry Cone	"	East Haddam	
David Clark	"	Simsbury	Dead
Joseph Andras	"	Chatham	
Eliphalet Lord	"	Windsor	
Wm Matthews	"	N. Y. State	
Zeb^n Woodruff	"	Farmington	Captivated by the Enemy
Micah Towsley	Dur^g war	Suffield	
[ ]siah Lindsey	3 Years	Farmington	Dead
[ ]hn Johnson	"	"	
Obadiah Andras	"	"	
Stephen Brunson	"	"	
Ladwick Hodgkiss	"	"	
John Conner	Dur^g war	"	
Daniel Powel	"	Hartford	Inlisted in 4th Georgia Batt^n
James A. Johnson	"	"	Deserted
Nath^{ll} Merrills	"	"	
Wm Higgins	3 Years	Lyme	Promoted to Q M
Ezra Ames	Dur^g war	Norwich	
Elijah Mann	"	Mass.	
Abijah Gardiner	"	Rhode Island	
[ ]ick Thomas	3 Years	Hartford	
Aaron Ward	Dur^g war	Middletown	
Daniel Judd	3 Years	Colchester	
Gardiner Gilbert	"	Hebron	Discharged
Abijah Pratt	"	Colchester	
John Higgins	Dur^g war	Chatham	Dead
Gideon Cole	3 Years	Wethersfield	
Luke Wadsworth	Dur^g war	Farmington	
Thomas Dick	3 Years	Norwich	Deserted
Ephraim Judd	"	Colchester	
Asher Carty	Dur^g war	"	
Abner Chapman	3 Years	"	
Alex^r Porter	"	Hebron	
James Couch	Dur^g war	Farmington	Dead
Jonathan Bill	3 Years	Colchester	
Hosea Gridley	Dur^g war	Farmington	
Edward Eli	3 Years	Weathersfield	
David Enos	"	Farmington	
Elisha Heart	"	"	
Tim^o Heart	"	"	
Seth (?) Knowles	"	Chatham	
[ ] Davis	"	Simsbury	Deserted (?)
Elisha Harwington	"	"	
Zeckry Prince	Dur^g war	"	
Thos Phelps	3 Years	"	Deserted
Saml Lomis	Dur^g war	Colchester	
Eli Bigelow	"	"	
Daniel Wright	3 Years	Glastenbury	
Eben^r Welch	"	New Hamp.	
Reuben Hart	"	Farmington	
Charles Wampey	"	"	Dead

West Point Feby 17th 1778

Henry Champion Capt

[*State Library, Hebard papers.*]

CAPT. CHAMPION'S COMPANY.

Capt Champion's Return of Officers & men during the war, as P Division Orders of December 7th 1779

Names	Towns	Names	Towns
Henry Champion Ct	Colchester	Nehh Daniels	Colchester
Charles Miller Lt	Hartford	Henry Evans	East Hartford
Theos Woodbridge Lt	Simsbury	Jonah Evans	"
Abner Mack Corpl	Hebron	Aaron Fargo	Windsor
Danl Wheeler "	Suffield	James Gray	Hartford
Joseph Copp Drumr	New London	Silas Pease	Suffield
Joseph Rouse Fifer	Preston	John Strong	Chatham
Ezra Ames	"	Micah Towstey	Suffield
Jonathan Brester	Milford	Elias Wares	Glastenbury
Ebenr Brown	Waterbury	Aaron Ward	Middletown
Wm Cook	Middletown	John Warren	Glasenbury
Ezl Daniels	Colchester	Henry Brown Corpl	New Haven

Second River 12th Decr 1779

H. Champion Capt

[*State Library, Hebard papers.*]

CAPT. EELLS' COMPANY.

A Return of Non Commissioned Officers and Soldiers in Capt Edward Eells Co in the Regt Commanded By Colo Samuel Wyllys with the Place of their abode the term for which Inlisted & the Names of the Persons who have hired any of them

Names	Term	Place of abode
Benjn Bowers	3 Years	Chatham
Peter Graves	"	Colchester
Wm Combs	D war	
David Canida	3 Years	Glastenbury
Benjamin Bowers	"	Chatham
Ebenr Billings	"	Stonington
Gideon Chapman	"	Colchester
Charles Brown	"	Stonington
Wm Tryon	D war	Weathersfield
James Morgain	3 Years	Colchester
Aaron Carter	D war	"
James Dewey	"	Middletown
Robart Douglass	3 Years	Colchester
Nathan Dodge	"	"
Stephen Dart	D war	"
David Elger	"	Hartford
Joseph Egleston	"	Windsor
Jacob Freeman	3 Years	Colchester
Abrm Freeman	"	"
Joseph McHood	D war	Lyme
Dick Loomis	"	Weathersfield
Nathnl Miller	3 Years	"
Dick Molatto	"	"
Asahel Newton	"	Colchester
Jack Bulkley	D war	"
Jno Nickalds	3 years	Middletown

Names	Term	Place of abode	
Syfax Negro	D war	Glastenbury	
Newport Negro	"	"	
Thos Pilgrim	3 Years	Colchester	
Jno Robison	D war	Middletown	
Stephen Ranney	3 Years	"	
Comfort Ranney	"	"	
Ezry Tryon	D war	Glastenbury	
Thos Watrous	"	Hartford	
Elias Wires	"	Glastenbury	
Thos Durfey	"	L. I. Prisnor	Inlisted 4 years Regt
Dunkin Read	"	Deserter	"
Oliver Ocain	"	Weathersfield	Deserted
Darby Connel	"	L. I. Prisnor	"
Mical McNe[ ]	[ ]	"	"

[*State Library, Hebard papers.*]

CAPT. ROBERT WARNER'S COMPANY.

Robert Warner	Middletown	John Harris	Middletown
Hezekiah Hubbard	"	Charles Loveland	"
Daniel Whitney	Colchester	Joseph Lung	"
Levi Goodrich	Chatham	Willm Mathews	Farmington
Abner Hubbard	Middletown	Daniel Morgan	Middletown
Lemuel Potter	Farmington	Charles O. Martin	Chatham
Daniel Parks	Chatham	John Oakley	
Bethuel Goodrich	"	John Parks	Chatham
Jacob Wood Junr	"	Jesper Pratt	Saybrook
Huet Alvord	"	Samuel Pierce	Union
Abel Abels	"	Thomas Rohds	New Haven
David Butler	Middletown	Elijah Royce	Wallingford
Thomas Brown	Chatham	Samuel Simmons	Middletown
Ephraim Bowers	"	John Stilwell	New Haven
Wolcott Burham	Farmington	Josiah Steal	Farmington
Samuel Comstock	"	Jonathan Stocking	Chatham
Lamberton Clark	Middletown	Solomon Townsand	New Haven
Cornelius Dunham	Farmington	Jered Trickey	"
John Foster	Middletown	Jonathan Verrey	Chatham
David Foster	"	Jacob Wood	"
Joseph Graham	Chatham	John Wright	" [N. Y.
John Graham	"	Frances Wright	West Chester
Jonathan Goff	Middletown	David West	Chatham
Samuel Goff	Chatham	William Wickham	"
David Hull	Middletown	Benj^a Welton	Farmington

[*Connecticut Historical Society.*]

CAPT. ROBERT WARNER'S COMPANY.

Return of Non effectives who have Serv^{d} in the 4 C^{o} third Connecticut Reg^{t} Since January 1st 1777

	Rank	When Ingag^{d} in Service	Town from which Inlisted	Tirm of Service	Unmarried	Casualties
Elihue Mott	Private	May 26th 77	Chatham	3 Years	1	Died July 26th 77
Paul Topping	"	Apr^{l} 30th 77	Middletown	"	1	died June 26th 77
John Barkley	"	June 6th 77	Weathersfield	D. Warr	1	" Decem^{r} 25 78
John McMullin . . .		Jany 1st 77	Middletown	3 Years	1	disarted Apr^{l} 21st 79
John Towers	"	Feby 22^{d} 77	Windsor	"	1	" Novm^{r} 3^{d} 78
Richard Clark	"	Apr^{l} 25th 77	Middletown	D. War	1	" August 8 79
John Grogan	"	June 3^{d} 77	Weathersfield	"	1	" Sepr 22^{d} 77
Nicholas Charles . . .	"	Jany 1st 77	Hebron	3 Years	1	Died Feby 2^{d} 77
Charles Wallis	"	March 11th 77		D. War	1	Disarted Apr^{l} 2^{d} 77
Charles Brune	"	" 11th 77		"	1	" August 12th 77
John Douaal	"	June 3^{d} 77	Weathersfield	"	1	" " 3^{d} 77
John Hughs	"	" 6th 77		"	1	" July 9th 77
Livenus Holt	"	Feby 28th 77	Harwinton	"	1	died Decem^{r} 9th 78 [Married
Samuel Smith	"	May 28th 77	Middletown	D. War.		Inlisted in 4th George Bat Sepr 1st 1777

R. Warner Capt^{t}

[*Connecticut Historical Society.*]

FOURTH REGIMENT—COL. DURKEE.

[*See Record of Connecticut Men in the Revolution, page 182.*]

SHORT TERM LEVIES, 1777.

A Return of the N° of Eight M^s^ Men that were in Col° Durkees Reg^t^ 1777

Privates Names		Names of Cap^ts^
Nath^n^ Draper		Capt Bills
John Gary		"
Wm Burroughs		"
Elijah Smith		"
Thos Cheney		"
Jon° Orms	Died 4th Decr 1777	
Nath^n^ Stowell	Inlist^d^ for 3 years 30 Aug^t^	
Gideon Waters	Dischg^d^ 27 Aug^t^	Capt Harmons
Ezekiel King	Died 19 Sep^t^	
Daniel Palley	Died 1 Jany 1778	
Zenas Kent		
David Ens		
Caleb Austin		
Medad Pomeroy		
Jo^s^ King		
Gideon Waters		
Saml Weaver		
Abram Skinner		
Ovorus Yeomans		
Jon^a^ Russell		
Eleaz^r^ Skinner		
Saml Pratt		
Joshua Sumner		
Jon^a^ Reed		Capt Webb
Benj^a^ Fuller		"
Eliph^t^ Colburn		"
Jon^a^ Webb		"
Wm Oliv		"
Eph^m^ Durphee	Died 27 Decr 1777	
George Michal	" 26 Oct. "	
Richard Harvey	Enlisted During War 15 May	Capt Lee
Ithamer Smith	" " " "	"
John Hill		Capt Fitch
Martin Stiles		"
Edward Burns		"
Aaron Hulet		McGreguiers
Jacob Wilson		"
Lem^l^ Parkhurst		"
Duthan Parkhurst		"
Ja^s^ Hawkins		"
John Almey		"
W^m^ C		"

Privates Names		Names of Cap^ts
Jacob Kinney		Bacons
Jacob Averil		"
Jesse Fosset		"
Stephen Baker		"
Nahum Cady		"
Saml Wright		"
Jonathan Cady		"
Phin^s Stephens		"
Benj^a Fosset		"
Ebenez^r Besster		"
John Ames	Enlist^d 29 Dec^r	
Jo^s Morey	Died 4 Sep^t	
Andr^w Hibberd	Enlist^d 27 "	
Moses Tracy	Enlist^d 27 "	
Saml Coburn	Enlist^d 27 "	
Hannibal Bassul		Capt Hallam
Zach^s Waldo	these 10 paid 27 Oct 1778	
Roger Carey	"	
Jarod Lilly	"	
David Harvey	"	
Jesse Kimbal	"	
Elijah Lilley	"	
Eliphas Cleveland	"	
Levy Kyesby	"	
Elijah Manning	"	
Joel Manning	"	

[*Copy in Comptroller's Office.*]

SHORT TERM LEVIES, 1779.

Return of the Eight M^s Men that belonged to the 4th Conn^t Reg^t comm^d by John Durkee Col: 1779

Names		Commencement of Service	Expiration of Service
Oliver Ladd	Coventry	Sept 20	Jany 15
David Noiles	Lyme	" 13	" 15
Jesse Foster		Augt 13	" 15
Tim^o Tucker	R Island	" 16	" 15
Jon^a Putney	Killingly	" 16	" 15
Henry Brown	"	" 16	" 15
Isaac Sweet	Voluntown	July 27	" 15
Jesse Childs	Killingly	Augt 16	" 15
Lem^l Falkner	Milford	" 2	" 15
Obed Gridley	Farmington	July 29	" 15
Willard Evans		Augt 13	" 15
Asher Williams	Norwich	Oct 4	" 15
William Parker	Killingly	" 4	" 15
John Adams	Coventry	" 1	" 15
John Howard	Deserted		
Abel Baker	R Island	Augt 16	" 15
John Morris		June 21	
Danl Palmer	Stonington	Augt 16	" 15
Thos Condin	Woodstock	" 16	" 15
Amos Mansfield	N. Haven	July 23	" 15
Sol^o Wilton	Farmington	" 28	" 15
Wm Cramer	Saybrook	Augt 16	" 15

Names		Commencement of Service	Expiration of Service
Isaac Rood	Killingly	Sep^t 15	Jany 15
Steph^n Emerson		Augt 10	" 15
Nehem^h Hulet	Killingly	Sep^t 21	" 15
Asa Alger	"	Augt 16	" 15
Danl Bixbey	"	" 16	" 15
Moses Bixby	"	" 16	" 15
John Banford	Farming^tn	" 2	" 15
Saml Bishop	Bolton	" 21	" 15
Lem^l Foster	R Island	" 16	" 15
Ambrose Cleavland	"	" 16	" 15
David Hosmer	Killingly	" 16	" 15
Basok Heath	"	" 16	" 15
Lewis Leach	R. Island	" 16	" 15
Eph^m Page	Branford	July 20	" 15
Silas Taft	Killingly	Augt 16	" 15
Saml Price	Danbury	Oct 22	" 15
Danl Wright	Farmington	July 29	" 15
Geo: Harris		Oct 1	" 15
Thos Fox	Simsbury	July 15	" 15
Moses Robinson	Killingly	" 15	" 15
Oliver Brown	Stonington	Augt 16	" 15
Alpheus Bowers		" 16	" 15
Abial Chafe	Ashford	" 13	" 15
Saml Chafe	Killingly	" 16	" 15
James Chafe	Woodstock	" 16	" 15
Hiram Chappel	Lebanon	" 16	" 15
Steph^n Downing	Canterbury	" 16	" 15
Henry Franklin	Woodstock	" 16	" 15
Thos Galford	Farmington	July 29	" 15
Wm Harrington	Mansfield	Augt 16	" 15
James Knapp	N. Fairfield	" 14	" 15
Aaron Rologg		July 31	" 15
Nath^n Martin	Mansfield	Augt 16	" 15
Steph^n Martin	Hebron	" 16	" 15
Richd Robinson	Windham	" 16	" 15
Henry Smith	Hf^d	July 29	" 15
Micha Taylor	Killingly	Augt 16	" 15
David Walding	Windham	" 16	" 15

[*Copy in Comptroller's Office.*]

SHORT TERM LEVIES.

Return of the Eight Months Men that belonged to the 4th Connecticut Regiment commanded by John Durkee Col^o 1779.

Names		Commenc^t of Service	Expiration of Service
Benjamin Lines	N. Haven	June 28	Jany. 15
Thomas Simons	Plainfield	Augt 16	" 15
Stephen Wilbur	"	" 16	" 15
William Fullour	Windham	" 16	" 15
John Adams	Colchester	" 16	" 15
John Casye		" 16	" 15
Benjn Williams	Voluntown	" 16	" 15
Elijah Herrick	Coventry	" 16	" 15

Names		Commenc^t of Service	Expiration of Service
Oliver Webster	New Haven	Augt 16	Jany. 15
Cyrus Powers	Killingly	" 16	" 15
Joseph Munn	Farmington	" 21	[ ]
Cotton Evens	Woodstock	" 28	" 15
Thomas Shephard	Middletown	" 24	" 15
Elijah Cady	Killingly	" 26	" 15
William Allen	Norwich	" 26	" 15
Benjamin Strong	Woodbury	Novr 26	" 15
Edward Washbon	"	" 26	" 15
Ahial Answorth	Woodstock	Augt 16	" 15
William Merritt	Hebron	" 16	" 15
Eli Perce	Ashford	" 16	" 15
Elias Tracy	Preston	" 16	" 15
Freeman Burnham		" 16	" 15
Benjn Perry	Preston	" 16	" 15
Thomas Eldridge	Rhod Island	" 16	" 15
Joshua R———l	Ashford	" 16	" 15
Uriah Carpenter	"	" 16	" 15
Robert Sumner		Augt 16	" 15
Samuel Perry		July 29	" 15
Eleazer Whipple	Farmington	" 28	" 15
Elijah Carpenter	Woodstock	Augt 13	" 15
Nathaniel Nash	Norwalk	July 20	" 15
David Growse	Killingly	Sep^t 14	" 15
Stephen Johnson	Haddam	Augt 1	" 15
Thomas Gardner	Milford	" 16	" 15
Henry Bennitt	Voluntown	Augt 13	" 15
Manassah Cady	Killingly	" 16	" 15
Jeremiah Durkee	Windham	" 16	" 15
Jed. Gilbert	Pomfret	" 16	" 15
Rufus Gossord	Simsbury	Sep^t 18	" 15
Levi Gossord	Simsbury	" 18	" 15
Israel Farnam		Augt 16	" 15
John Joyce	Woodstock	" 16	" 15
Wm Leatch	Winchester	" 1	" 15
Levi Meeks	Waterbury	" 3	" 15
Wm Palmister	Coventry	" 16	" 15
Simeom Robertson	Windham	" 16	" 15
David Weltch	Plainfield	" 7	" 15
Nathl Beecher	Farmington	July 29	" 15
Charles Childs	Woodstock	" 16	" 15
Seth Gary		" 16	" 15
Wm Johnson	"	" 16	" 15
James Russell	"	" 16	" 15
Moses Robinson	"	" 16	" 15
Henry Morris	"	" 16	" 15
Ja^s Leygoit	"	" 16	" 15
Edward Foster	Middletown	" 29	" 15
Moses Beegbe	Woodstock	Sep^t 14	" 15

[*State Library, Revolution 16.*]

FIFTH REGIMENT—COL. BRADLEY.

[*See Record of Connecticut Men in the Revolution, page 193.*]

SHORT TERM LEVIES, 1779.

Return of the Eight Months Men In the 5th Connecticut Regiment Commanded by P. B. Bradley Col[o] In the Year 1779.

The expiration of the service of each was Jan. 15, [1780].

Ebenez[r] Huntington	Woodbury	Aug.	31
Jn[o] Porter	"		31
Stephen Childs	Killington		16
Nath[l] Bacon	Litchfield	Sep.	24
Phineas Holcomb	"		24
Elijah Hays	"		24
Zenas Hays	"		24
Zebina Smith	Sharon	July	26
Will[m] Trowbridge	N. Milford		26
Bela Hill	Winchester		26
Ezra Pratt	Symsbury		26
Nath[l] Griffin	"		20
Absalom Griffin	"	Sep.	27
Dan[l] Ensign	Hartland	July	20
Amos Holcomb	Simsbury	Sep.	12
Dosa Holcomb	"		12
Phin[s] Holcomb	"		12
Hamlin Johnson	Harrington		12
Joseph Bradley	"		12
Isaac Broker	Symsbury		12
Abijah Scofeld	"	Ju[ ]	20
James Chappel	Tolland		20
Isaac Eno	Symsbury	Nov.	27
Orange Barns or Burns	Litchfield	May	15
Return Byer	"	Aug.	15
Joab Gillet	Simsbury	Sep.	30
Jn[o] Winchel	Torrington		24
Cyrenus Knapp	Simsbury		30
Abijah Clemmonds	Litchfield	Nov.	24
John Garratt	Symsbury	July	27
John McMann 1st	"	Aug.	3
Jn[o] McMann 2[d]	"		3
Nathan Odle	Fairfield		23
Will[m] Phelps	Symsbury		15
Simeon Holladay	"		15
Ezekiel Hays	"		15
Lemuel Messenger	"		15
Jacob Finch	Danbury		17
Thaddeus Wheelock	Ridgfield		13
Grove Lommis	Windsor		28
Zacheus Holcomb	Simsbury	Sep.	24
Bradford Kellogg	Goshen	July	26

[*State Library, Revolution 16; also Copy in Comptroller's Office.*]

RETURN.

A Return of the Non Commissioned Officers & Privates in the 5th Connec^{t} Reg^{t} who are engaged during the War, The Town to which they belong & by whom hired.

1st Company

Names	Towns	Names	Towns
Martin Denslow Serg^{t} Maj^{r}	Windsor	Jason Crawford	Woodstock
Edward Fields Drum Maj	Fairfield	John Gould	Goshen
Ambrose Filer Fife Maj		Gideon Hurlbut	Fairfield
Louden Bailey Serg^{t}	Haddam	Asbel Mason	Litchfield
Jaazmah Howe Corp^{l}	Goshen	Joseph Norton	Goshen
Stephen Wheeler Serg^{t}	New Milford	Giles Olcutt	Litchfield
Calvin Jenkins Drum	Norwalk	[ ]	"
Putnam Catlin Fife	Litchfield	Osburn Parsons	Norwalk
Cash Africa	"	John Rockwell	
James Columbus	"	Henry Smith	Litchfield
Reuben Craw	"	John Seely	"
		Josiah Whitney	Ridgefield
		James Wright	Litchfield
		Ephraim Wheeler	

2nd Company

Thomas Wilson	Hartford

3^{d} Company

Jonath^{n} Ambler		Enos Pettit	
Elias Balcom	New Hartford	Azor Patchen	
Jacob Bateman	Horseneck	Jon^{a} Russ	Sharon
Ben Boston	Meriden	Edward Runnels	
John Burgoyn		Jon^{a} Tobias	Sharon
Benjn Bennet		John Taylor	Horseneck
Daniel Davison	Stonington	John Taylor	New Hartford
Daniel Fenn		George Tankerd	
Henry Keeler	Norwalk	Samuel Witherill	Stamford
Edwd McClanning		Coker Wiggins	"
Abijah Olmsted	Norwalk		

4th Company

Amos Lawrence Serg^{t}	Windsor	Joseph Whippell Corp^{l}	Hartford
Danl Bissell Serg^{t}	"	George Anger	Middletown
Willm Anderson Corp^{l}	Hartford	John Brangin	"

4th Company

Amos Lawrence Serg^{t}	Windsor	Zebulon Hoskins	Windsor
Danl Bissell Serg^{t}	"	Obed^{h} Lamberton	"
Willm Anderson Corp^{l}	Hartford	Ephraim Loatwell	"
Joseph Whippell "	"	Phillip Negro .	Simsbury
George Anger	Middletown	Plymouth Negro	Windsor
John Brangin	"	Alvan Owen	"
Jeremiah Barrit [?]	Hartford	Daniel Porter	"
John Beecher [?]	Windsor	Jacob Pason	"
Cornelius Cahale	"	Grove Rockwell	Middletown
Ozias Cone	Middletown	Sherman Rawland	Windsor
David Daniels	Windsor	Eben^{r} Woolworth	"
William Graves	Middletown	Christopher Welch	Middletown
Jesse Gilbert	"	Robert Weston	Windsor

5th Company

Names	Towns	Names	Towns
Jared Knap Sergt	Litchfield	Simon Crosby	Litchfield
Mark Mildren "	Farmington	John Farnum	"
Enos Barns "	Litchfield	Wm Jackson	Norwalk
Richd Cornell Drum	Middletown	John Mason	Litchfield
Eber Stocking Corpl	Chatham	Denis Parkiton	Stamford
Paul Price "	Litchfield	Saml Stannard	Litchfield
Jude C. Brown	Windsor	Moses Scott	Norwalk
Ezra Bates	Stamford	Jona Dykeman	Danbury
Ambrose Barns	Litchfield	Joseph Thompson	Malbury

6th Company

Names	Towns	Names	Towns
Isaac Odell Sergt	Fairfield	Isaiah Jones	Stamford
Stephen Hall "	Stratford	Isban Jennings	Fairfield
Elijah Patchen Corpl	Fairfield	Josiah French	Stratford
Willm Cummins "	"	John Ludeman	Danbury
Wakeman Hull "	"	David Morehouse	Fairfield
Hezh Meaker Drum	"	Ebenr Meaker	"
Charles Burrit	Stratford	Joseph Moger	"
Danll Burr	Fairfield	Woolcot Patchen	"
Pink Clark	Stratford	John Parker	Stratford
John Chaps	"	Nehh Sherwood	Redding
Ephraim Chorse	"	Baruck Taylor	Fairfield
David Cogins	Fairfield	Aron Wailey	"
Peter Fegro		Joseph Wallace	"
William Gould	Fairfield		

7th Company

Names	Towns	Names	Towns
Samuel Mead Fife	Norwalk	Thomas Keeler	Ridgefield
John Ashley	Haddam	Baruck Nickerson	"
Eliph^t Allen	Fairfield	Wiram Pond	Colchester
Joseph Boynton	Cape Ann	Enoch Sperry	Litchfield
Enos Barns	Litchfield	Sylvanus Scofield	Stamford
Timothy Gibbs	"	Benjn Tarbox	Lyme
[ ]	[ ]	Micajah Weeks	Redding
Jeremh Keeler	Ridgefield	Jabez Williams	"

8th Company

Names	Towns	Names	Towns
Henry Bacon Sergt	Pomfret	William Jones	Colchester
Elias Bigsby "	Reading	Elijah Phelps	Middletown
Nathan Coley Corpl	"	Clark Roberts	Windsor
Samuel Woodcock "	Litchfield	James Stanton	Ridgefield
EdmundFowlerDrum	Fairffeld	Enoch Sperry	New Haven
Truman FrenchFifer	NorthStratford	Gregory Thomas	Norwalk
John Cordrick	[ ]	Thadeus Waugh	Litchfield
David Clark	Windsor	Nathan Winton	Fairfield
Abel Culver	Litchfield	Nathan White	[ ]
Isaac Grant	"		

9th Company

Names	Towns	Names	Towns
John Ryon Sergt		Jacob Lewis	
Samuel Waugh "	Litchfield	Gamaliel Parker	
James Knapp Corpl	Sharon	Thomas Reed	
Nathll Tylar Drum	"	Nathll Richards	
[ ] Davis Fife	Middletown	William Stuart	Sharon
[ ]	[ ]	William Smith	
[ ]	[ ]	[ ]	["]
Daniel Elmore	Somers	Daniel Tobias	"
Eleazar Gilson	"	Dennis Torrey	
William Jackways		Ezekiel Whitney	Sharon
John Jackson		Isaac Welden	
Noah Kelsy	Sharon	Zelophehad Williamson	

J. Wright Capt Comd.

[*State Library, Hebard Papers.*]

SIXTH REGIMENT—COL. DOUGLAS.

[*See Record of Connecticut Men in the Revolution, page 205.*]

CAPT. STEPHEN POTTER'S COMPANY.

Return of the Non Commisiond officers and Privates Ingaged for the war in Capt S. Potters Company In the 6th Conn^{t} Reg^{t} Commanded by R J Meigs Col^{o}

Mens Names	Rank	towns they Belong to
Saml Brown	Serj^{t}	Branford
James Gold Smith	"	Milford
Phinehas Squires	"	Durham
Saml Hadley	Corp^{l}	Branford
John Eberhard	"	"
Joel Potter	Drum	"
George Cook	Fife	N haven
Chandler Benton	Privat	Guilford
Ezekiel Butler	"	Branford
David Roggers	"	"
Saml Chapman	"	Fairfield
Elihu Cook	"	Wallingford
Benjamin Foord	"	"
Jonathan Foord	"	"
Pratt Jones	"	"
Charles London	"	"
Zenos Mix	"	"
John Parker	"	"
Amasa Tharp	"	"
Amos Tharp	"	"
Skylor Goddard	"	Durham
David Hull	"	Darbey
Joel M. Daniel	"	"
John Hancock	"	N haven
Anthony M. Daniel	"	"
Bennajor Woolcut	"	"
Amos Warnor	"	"
John Lerrow	"	Licthfield
Charles Purkines	"	Stanford
Isaac Robberts	"	Middletown
David Hungerford	"	"
Joseph Hawkings	"	Branford
Roswell Whedon	"	"
David Hodge	"	Milford

Camp December 10th /80

[*Connecticut Historical Society.*]

MAJ. LEAVENWORTH'S COMPANY.

Muster Roll of Major Eli Leavenworth Comp^{y} 6th Conn^{t} Reg^{t} in the Service of the United States of America Commanded by Col^{o} Retwin J. Meigs for Octr 1779

Commissioned
- Major Eli Leavenworth Sep^{t} 18/77
- Lieu^{t} Asa Lay Jany 1st/77 Prisoner of War
- Lieu^{t} Giles Curtiss Novr 15/77

Appoint^{d}		Time	Remarks
	Sergeants		
Feby 6/77	Eliakim Strong	3 y^{s}	
" 17	And^{w} Andrews	3 y^{s}	
	Jair^{s} Harrison		On Com^{d} Middletown
	Corporals		
Jan 31/77	Hugh^{n} Hinman	3 y^{s}	On Duty
	Luther Page		
Ap^{r} 10/77	Benjn Crampton	3 y^{s}	"
	Drum		
Ja^{n} 31/77	Reuben Brown	3 y^{s}	
	Fife		
Mar^{h} 4	Saml Brown	3 y^{s}	
Inlisted	Privates		
	Cesar Bagdon		On Duty
	Saml Barker		
Feby 17	Joel Bishop	3 y^{s}	"
	Paul Beebe		
	Ja^{s} Cooper		On Com^{d} N River
	Thos Cook		sick in Camp
	Wm Carr		sick Fishkill July 16
	Sharper Camp		On Duty
" 6th	Amos Davis	3 y^{s}	
	Ja^{s} Dinah		"
	Reuben Frisbie		"
May 20	Jno Francis	3 y^{s}	On Com^{d} Robinsons farm
	Jno Garrett		On Duty
	Dav^{d} Hitchcock		"
Decr 8/76	Jno Hatchet	3 y^{s}	
	And^{w} Jack		
	Wm Johnson		"
May 13/77	Jno Johnson	3 y^{s}	sick Wallingford May 11/78
Mar^{h} 3	Nath^{n} Kelsey	3 y^{s}	
	Jack Little		
Feby 3^{d}	Phin^{s} Meigs	3 y^{s}	On Duty
	Jno Meeker		sick in Camp
	Warren Murray		
	Meade Merrils		On Duty
	Phillip Niger		sick at Branford Apr 11/79
	Abr^{m} Norton		
	Nathan Palmer		on Com^{d} wth Genl Parsons
Feby 17/77	Wm Parker	3 y^{s}	
	Benjn Potter		
	Jno Peck		
Ap^{l} 13	M^{s} Robinson	3 y^{s}	sick at Fishkill Octr 12
Feby 6	Saml Seward	3 y^{s}	Brigade Waggoner
" 17	Seth Strong	3 y^{s}	
	Jord^{n} Smith		On Com^{d} N^{o} River

Inlisted	Privates	Time	Remarks
May 7	Selah Stedman	3 y^s	
	Abia^r Squire		On Duty
	London Sawyer		On Duty
	Thos Sanford		"
	Tory Scranton		
	Enos Tuttle		"
	Jacob Towner		"
May 14	Saml Teale	3 y^s	
	Jno Voigson		
	Rufus Wheedon		
	Step^n Wade		
Decr 10/76	Saml Wood	3 y^s	On Duty
	Thos Wheeler		
May 27/77	Limbo Stannard	3 y^s	Dischargd Octr 11 [ ]

Novr 3 1779 Musterd then Major Leavenworth's Comp^y as specified in the above Roll

Jacob Jno Lansing [?]

[*Connecticut Historical Society.*]

Return of the Eight Months Men In the 6 Connecticut Reg^t In the Year 1779

Name	Town	Commencement of Service	Expiration of Service
Jno Linsley	Branford	July 20	Jany 15

[*State Library, Revolution 16.*]

SEVENTH REGIMENT—COL. SWIFT.

[*See Record of Connecticut Men in the Revolution, page 217.*]

CAPT. HILLS' COMPANY.

The following is the balance due to the State of Connecticut from Each Man as anexed to their Respective Names for States Cloathing Received of Capt Wm Redfield States Cloather by Capt Ebenr Hills and delivered to them by Sd Hills at diferant times before Novr 1778 taken from accounts Receipts &c. with Remarks

John Cole	2	2	0	dead June 10 1778
Grig Trumbul	2	8	0	discharged
Christopher Coflin	0	14	6	disarted Feby 17 1778
Edward Booth	0	12	0	" December 1779
David Wells	2	0	0	Exchanged for John Cobb
James Taylor	1	16	0	deserted June 27 1778
Thomas Brooks	1	9	0	
Elijah Parker	0	8	6	deserted
John Colson	0	14	6	deserted May 2 1778
Chiliab Palmer	0	7	0	
James Lanford	0	8	6	
Mingo Treet	0	5	6	discharged
Joel Botchford	0	19	0	
Prince Simbo	0	6	0	
Ichabod Wilkinson	0	19	0	discharged
David Dean	0	11	6	"
Elijah Parker	0	8	6	deserted Jany 8 1779
William Barnit	1	9	1	" August 2 1778
Edward Goodyear	0	7	0	
Robart Nicols	0	7	0	
Daniel Averil	0	8	6	discharged
Jacob Galusha	1	16	6	"
Gad Taylor	0	18	0	
Thomas Brooks	0	9	6	
Ebenezer Keelor	0	7	0	
total	22	12	1	

The above named Soldiers ware Serving in the 8th Compy 7th Connect Regt at the time of Receiveing the above sd Cloathing

Ebenr Hills Capt In sd Regt

Kent Apl 2d 1782

[*Connecticut Historical Society.*]

RECRUITS.

Return of Men recruited for the United States of America

[The list here given appears to be of recruits for the seventh regiment of Connecticut Line, formation of 1777—1781, Heman Swift, Colonel, where the names are found in the printed *Record of Connecticut Men in the Revolution.* The names are here reprinted because of the added information of "where inlisted"; the dates of inlistment and term agree with the printed *Record* and are here omitted.]

Mens Names	Where inlisted
John Bingham	Windham
Nathan Morgan	Stonington
Jabez Rouse	Windham
Asa Hebard	"
James Kingsley	Norwich
Nathan Morgan	Windham
Andrew Warner	"
Aaron Bailey	Norwich
Elijah Backus	Windham
Walter Chace	"
Mason Abbee	"
Zebulon Ames	Preston
Elias Kingham	Windham
Levi Bingham	"
Elisha Baldwin	Preston
John Bill	Coventry
Samuel Burdain	"
Gershom Dunham	Windham
Ezekiel Dunham	"
Stephen Dunwell	Preston
Robert Davison	"
Ezekiel Daniels	Glastonbury
John Dugard	Preston
Caleb Fitch	Windham
Uriah Heberd	"
Timothy Hebard	"
Eben^{r} Heberd	"
Jed^{h} Hebard	"
Samuel Hallows	"
Richard Howard	"
Lemuel Herrick	Preston
Lebeus Herrick	Stonington
Joseph Jinnings	Windham
Cyrus Killam	Groton
Elijah Linkon	Windham
Nathan Loveland	Glastonbury
Amos Loveland	"
Benjn Lamb	Windham
Seth Larrabee	"
John Leathercoat	"
Andrew McClarry	Preston
Joseph Mezen	Windham
Jonah Palmer	"
Jabez Pottage	"
Eleazer Robertson	"
Joseph Reed	Windham
Jabez Rockwell	Stonington
Joseph Robbins	Windham
Adariah Simons	"
John Spears	Preston
Elisha Stoddard	Groton
Theodore Taylor	Glastenbury
John Taylor	"
Benone De Wolf	"
Ephraim Jerry	Windham
Amos Woodward	"
David Young	"
Charles Ripley	"
Gideon Seartes	Glastenbury
David Yerrington	Preston
William Placey	Windham
Charles Riley	Glastenbury
Gershom Treat	"
Moses Scott	"
Seth Eddy	Chatham
Joseph Gladding	Seabrook
Selah Griswould	"
Reuben Taylor	Glastenbury
Azariah Taylor	"
Aaron De Wolf	"
Jacob Meach	Groton
Ezekiah Rood	"
Salmon Treat	Preston
Luther Jones	"
Samuel Stubbs	Windham
John Jonson	Preston
Eleazer Westcoat	Cituate
Jabez Shoals	Groton
Edwd John Witt	Plainfield

[*State Library.*]

Return of the Eight Months Men in the 7 Connecticut Reg^{t} in 1779

Name	Town	Commencement of Service	Expiration of Service
Joseph Lindsley	Cornwall	July 26	Jany 15

[*State Library, Revolution 16.*]

EIGHTH REGIMENT—COL. SHERMAN.

[See Record of Connecticut Men in the Revolution, page 229.]

RETURN, 1779.

Return of the Commission'd & Staff Officers Non Commission'd officers and Privates in the Eighth Connecticut Regiment Inlisted for during the war

Names	Rank	Town they belong too
1st Capt Compy		
Paul Brigham	Capt	Coventry
Richard Sill	Lieut & P.M.	Lyme
Nathll Thompson	Serjt	Coventry
Jonah Mallery	Corpl	Waterbury
Saml Granger	Private	Sufield
Benjn Frizbee	"	Torringsford
Eliphilet Philips	"	New britton
Amos Temple	"	Stratford
Japhura Primas	"	"
Cash Palingtine	"	Lebanon
6th Capt Compy		
Asahel Hodge	Capt	Harrington
Egbon Hubbell	Serjt	Fairfield
Burr Gilbert	Corpl	"
John Gilbert	Privates	Stratford
David Pendleton	"	"
Seth Buckley	"	Fairfield
Jno McKinsey	"	"
Simeon Persons	"	Farmington
Levi Persons	"	"
James Fostor	"	
Joseph Frudom	"	Waterbury
Patrick Linch	"	
Jno Frame	"	Windom
Wm Woodruff	"	Farmington
Eli Denslow	"	Milford
4th Capt Compy		
Samuel Sanford	Capt	Milford
John Strong	Lieut	Woodbury
William Beamont	Ens & Qr Master	Lebanon or Woodbury
Heber Smith	Serjt	Stratford
Abiel Linley	"	Woodbury
Anthony Stoddard	Corporal	"
Julan Easton	Fifer	"
Amor Eadee	Private	"
Peter Bristoll	"	Milford
Jehial Bradley	"	Woodbury
Titus Minor	"	"
Jethro Toney	"	"

Names	Rank	Town they belong too
Daniel Tucker	Private	Woodbury
Abiel Wakeley	"	"
Nathan Walker	"	"
James Cebree Jr	"	Milford
Abner Lee	"	Woodbury
Robert Freeman	"	Stratford
John Fontine	"	Waterbury
Pomp London	"	Woodbury
Elisha Walker	"	"
Simeon Taylor	"	"
James Hooker	"	"
Isaac Pollard	"	"
Lt Colo Comdt Company		
Selah Benton	Lieut	Stratford
John Hobart	"	Branford
Daniel Provost	Private	Stanford
Abraham Holley	"	"
David Bates	"	"
Jeremiah Blackman	"	Stratford
Elisha Pulford	"	"
Eli Stodard	"	Woodbury
Benjn Wheeler	"	"
London Goodluck	"	Stratford
4th Capt Compy		
Nehemiah Rice	Capt	Waterbury
Joshua Whitney	Ensign	Canaan
Ozias Elwell	Private	Waterbury
Abel Lewes	"	Wallingford
Ethiel Scott	"	Harwinton
Levi Hitchcock	"	Wallinford
Prince Hotchkiss	"	"
Majors Compy		
David Smith	Major	Waterbury
David Judson	Lieut & B. Qr M.	Woodbury
John Gillet	Serjt	Milford
Elihu Sanford	"	New Haven
Jonathan Davis	Corporal	Waterbury
Joseph Cutler	"	"
William Russel	Drumer	Stratford
Elijah Picksley	"	Waterbury
Ozem Cook	Private	"
Reuben Culver	"	"
Samuel Eells	"	Milford
Joseph Martin	"	"
Jonathan Preston	"	Waterbury
Strong Sanford	"	New Haven
Silas Glasgow	"	Stratford
John Jones Wakeley	"	"
5th Capt Compy		
Daniel Barns	Capt	Farmington
James Olmsted	Ensign	Hartford
Abraham Clark	Serjt	"
David Dixon	"	Woodbury
Thomas Wells	Corporal	Hartford
Thomas Spencer	"	"
Amos Clark	"	Woodbury
John Ducitt	Fifer	Windsor

Names	Rank	Town they belong too
Rich[d] Case	Private	Hartford
Asa Seymour	"	"
Daniel Stevens	"	Woodbury
Amos Sanders	"	Stratford
David Reynolds	"	Woodbury
Stephen Ranney	"	"
Philamon Stedman	"	Hartford
Grove Kellogg	"	"
Hezekiah Goodwin	"	"
James Libberty	"	Woodbury
Abram Yellis	"	Waterbury
Job Uffott	"	Woodbury
Charles Hollister	"	Hartford
Aaron Olds	"	Woodbury
Reuben Hadlock	"	Hartford
Asher Hecock	"	Farmington
Samuel Lee	"	Woodbury
Enoch Thomas	"	"
Jared Dixon	"	"
Hezekiah Keeler	"	"
Timothy Andruss	"	Hartford
Aquilla Sturgis	"	Woodbury
2[d] Cap[t] Comp[y]		
Sam[ll] Comstock	Cap[t]	Norwalk
Ephraim Kimberly	Lieu[t]	Newton
Salmon Hubbel	"	Norwalk
Elijah Taylor	Serj[t]	"
Abel Baldwin	"	Newtown
Aaron Keeler	"	Norwalk
Matthew Marwin	Corporal	"
Moses Gilbert	"	"
William Brown	"	Stanford
Uriah Mead	Fifer	Norwalk
Stephen Hait	Drum[r]	"
John Bouton	Private	"
Isaac Baldwin	"	Newtown
David Bouton	"	Norwalk
Jack Botsford	"	Newtown
Alben Cole	"	Norwalk
Sam[l] Fairweather	"	Newtown
Peter Fairchild	"	"
Elijah Foot	"	"
Robert Freman	"	Waterbury
Sam[l] Green	"	Norwalk
Nathan Hubbel	"	Newtown
Timothy Hanford	"	Norwalk
Samuel Nichols	"	"
Abijah Prindle	"	Newtown
Zalmon Prindle	"	"
William Spurr	"	Boston
Isaac Smith	"	Norwalk
Josiah Taylor	"	"
Enoch Kellogg	"	"
Azur Patchen	"	"
Seth Hubbell	"	"
John Williams	"	"
Theophilus Mead	"	"
Josiah Green	"	"

Staff

Names	Rank	Town they belong too
Thomas Skinner .	. Surgeon	. Colchester
Jedediah Eansworth	. Mate	. Canterbury
Samuel Hait . . .	. Q^{r} Master Serj^{t} . . .	. Stanford

N: B: The Light Infantry are not Included in this Return

Isaac Sherman Lieu^{t} Col Com^{t}

[*State Library, Hebard Papers.*]

CAPT. MONSON'S COMPANY.

Return of Capt Monsons Comp^{y} Lt Inf^{y} Who are during the War 8th Reg^{t}.

Capt T. Monsons Return of Officers & Men during the War as pr Division Orders of Decemb^{r} 7th 79.

Names	Town	Names	Town
Theop^{s} Monson Capt	New Haven	Isiah Moss	Wallingford
Aaron Benjamin L^{t}	Stratford	Linus Moss	Waterbury
Salmon Hubbel "	Wilton	Alex^{r} Mills	Woodbury
Ebenez^{r} Shelly Serj^{t}	Stratford	Jesse Mathews	Waterbury
John Fulford "	Waterbury	John McRowe	Stratford
John Fletcher Corp^{l}	Danbury	Nathl Pardee	Norwalk
Moses Churchel Drum^{r}	Woodbury	David Parsons	Wilton
Alex^{r} Fairchild Fifer	Stratford	Justice Reynalds	Woodbury
Willm Burnes Priv^{t}	Coventry	Stephen Thompson	Waterbury
Willm Bundy	Woodbury	Henman Wooster	Woodbury
George Fields	"	Asa Thaires	Waterbury
Sam^{ll} Jackson	"	Daniel McRowe	Stratford
Uriah Keeler	Wilton	Peter Fairchild	New Town
Eli King	Suffield	Sam^{ll} Fairwether	"
Thomas Lewis	Stanford		

2^{d} River Decemb^{r} 12th 1779
T. Monson Capt

[*State Library, Hebard Papers.*]

SHORT TERM LEVIES, 1779.

Return of the Eight M^{s} Men in the 8th Conn^{t} Reg^{t} Comn^{d} by Isaac Sherman Co^{l} for the year 1779

Names		Commencem^{t} of Service	Expiration of Service
Edwd Ensworth	Groton	Augt 11	Jany 15
Tim^{o} Anderson	Windham	" 24	" "
Johnson Cleveland		" 16	" "
Jo^{s} Gray	Lebanon	" 16	" "
Rufus Gibbs	Windham	" 24	" "
Jesse Long	Coventry	" 16	" "
Jonth Stawson		" 11	" "
Augustus Stawston	E Windsor	" 24	" "
Elisha Tucker	Coventry	" 16	" "
Jesse Whitman	Killingly	" 16	" "
Chas Warner		" 16	" "
Nath^{n} Blackman	Winchester	Sept 24	" "
Christ^{r} Swan	Colchester	" 10	" "
Adonij^{h} Crane	Windsor	Nov 1	" "
Hez^{h} Lewis	Killingly	Augt 16	" "
Saml Norton	Farmington	July 29	" "

Names		Commencem^{t} of Service	Expiration of Service
Jno Paine	Windham	Augt 16	died Oct^{o}
Isaih Plank	Killingly	" 16	Jany 15
Jo^{s} Woodford	Kensington	July 29	" "
Asa Torrey	Lebanon	Augt 16	" "
Jno Sweet	Millington	" 16	" "
Uriah Finney	Lebanon	" 16	" "
Ja^{s} Ball	Coventry	" 16	" "
Geo. Bissell	"	" 16	" "
Ja^{s} Field	Saybrook	" 12	" "
Eben^{r} Merritt	Fairfield	Oct 1	" "
Lem^{l} White	Coventry	" 1	" "
Israel Wood	Stamford	Sep^{t} 19	Oct 14
Eric McPharson	"	" 19	Jany 15
Jno Larkin	"	" 19	" "
Jo^{s} Boyd	Killingly	Augt 16	" "
Selah Cook	Waterbury	" 22	" "
Asa Davidson	Ashford	" 16	" "
Amos Green	Killingly	" 16	" "
Henry Green	"	Sep^{t} 5	" "
Jno Lovejoy	Plainfield	" 5	" "
Saml Mobbs	"	Augt 21	" "
Benjn Sweet	Killingly	" 16	" "
Saml Wait	Plainfield	" "	" "
Hez^{h} Bonnet	Farmington	Nov 1	" "
Thos Love	Killingly	Augt 16	" "
Jno Crammer	Woodbury	Sep^{t} 1	" "
Lyman Mott	"	Augt 16	" "
David Walker	"	Sep^{t} 1	" "
Gulielmas Hodg	"	" 1	" "
Deliverance Eastman	"	Nov 1	" "
Chauncy Adkins	Farmington	Augt 16	" "
Jno Barns	"	" 4	" "
Saml Ingraham	Farmington	July 27	" "
Joel Lane	Voluntown	Augt 7	" "
Saml Manson	"	July 27	" "
Rayner Page	"	Augt 2	" "
Amaziah Raymond	Pomphet	Augt 16	" "
Elias Harp or Tharp	Farmington	" 16	" "
Reuben Hill	Woodbury	Oct 10	" "
Ira Mandwill	"	Sep^{t} 22	" "
Benj Porter	"	" 22	" "
Roswill Burnham	Windham	Augt 16	" "
Saml Barns	Farmington	" 17	" "
Ezekiel Curtis	"	" 17	" "
Selah Deming	"	" 17	" "
Israel Fitts	Windham	Augt 15	" "
Beriah Foote	Harrington	July 2	" "
Robt Huntington	Ashf^{d}	Augt 16	" "
Ja^{s} Harden	"	" 16	" "
Eben^{r} Littlefield	Windham	" 16	" "
Elijah Lilley	"	" 16	" "
Jerem^{h} Neal	Farmington	July 17	" "
Moses Parsons	"	Augt 13	" "
Ja^{s} Powers	"	July 30	" "
Jno Tossell	Woodbury	Sep^{t} 10	" "
Ichabod Talmage	Farmg^{n}	July 17	" "

[*Copy in Comptroller's Office.*]

NINTH REGIMENT—COL. WEBB.

SHORT TERM LEVIES, 1779.

[*See Record of Connecticut Men in the Revolution, page 245.*]

Abstract of Pay for the Six Months Recruits in the 9th Connect Regt from the Commencement to the Expiration of their Service. [With rolls for 1779.]

Names	Towns	Commencement of Service	Expiration of Service
Colonels Compy			
Joseph Atwood	Wethersfield	18 July	4 Dec
Joseph Andrus	"	7 Aug	"
James Antony	"	18 July	"
Levy Bulkley	"	"	"
John Deming	"	"	14
David Deming	"	"	4
Abel Edgerton	Norwich	23	14
Hezekiah Hartshorn	"	"	"
Nehemiah H [		] Aug	"
Robert Francis	Wethersfield	18 "	9
Abraham Guthrie	Fairfield	26	4
Samuel Kent	Suffield	28 July	"
Asa Lewis	Woodbury	23	16
Ezekiel Main	Reading	26 Aug	"
Huit Olvord	Hebron	23 July	4
Joseph Root	Woodbury	"	"
Francis Weaver	Middletown	7	14
3d Company			
Elisha Allyn	Windsor	20 Sep	4 Dec.
Bartholemew Arthur	Groton	24 Aug	"
Stephen Burnham	Hartford	13	17
Charles Clark	Wethersfield	18	4
Samuel Castle	Chatham	28 July	"
Rufus Gillet	Suffield	"	13
William Grey	Chatham	1 Oct.	14
Nathaniel Hale	Wethersfield	18 Aug	"
Isaac Johnston	Chatham	23 July	"
Daniel Lee	"	"	1 Oct.
Daniel Lyman	Labanon	"	12 Dec.
Giddeon Phillips	Litchfield	24 Aug	9
Samuel Robbins	Wethersfield	18	20 Sep.
Tom Tommas	Lebanon	23 July	12 Dec.
Nathaniel Tibbles	Washington	24 Aug.	4
Josiah Tryon	Wethersfield	18	"
Jedediah Woodworth	Lebanon	23 July	2
John Porter	"	"	14
Richard Robbins	Wethersfield	"	12
Jonah Stricklin	Middletown	16 Aug.	9
Daniel Taylor	Hartford	23 July	16
David Stillman	Wethersfield	1 Oct.	9
Bigelow Waters	Hebron	23 July	14
David Ward	Durham	16 Aug	9

Names	Towns	Commencement of Service	Expiration of Service
Majors Comp[y]			
Elijah Bemus	Hebron	23 July	13 Dec.
John Carrier	"	"	14
Benjamin Denilo	Suffield	"	4
Nathan Eluzzad [?]	Durham [?]	[	]
John Hurlburt	Wethersfield	17 July	4
Eliphelot Hill	"	16 Aug.	14
Russell Hill	Glastenbury	"	"
Daniel Holmes	Wethersfield	23 July	9
George King	New Haven	18 Aug.	14
Hazia Landon	Litchfield	26	16
Henry Moriner	Middletown	18 July	14
James Shaw	Saybrook	18 Aug	9
Dudley Tracey	Norwich	25 July	14
James Tiley	Say Brook	18 Aug.	"
[			]
David Wetherty	Wethersfield	18 July	4
John Welch	Chatham	28	14
4th Company			
James Brown	Coventry	23 July	16 Dec.
Nathaniel Baldwin	Wethersfield	"	14
John Bailey	Haddam	28	12
Joseph Briggs	Suffield	"	4
Joseph Brooks	Danbury	18 Aug.	14
Silas Crane	Durham	16	16
Joseph Flower	Wethersfield	18	9
Simeon Goodrich	"	"	"
Theodore Harrison	"	15 July	"
Barnabus Hall	Wallingford	16 Aug.	16
Adney Gillet	Hartford	"	4
Jacob Miller	Durham	"	9
Josiah Prior	Middletown	17 July	"
L[t] Infantry Comp[y]			
David Baxter	Glastenbury	23 July	14 Dec.
John Bliss	Lebanon	"	4
Asa Blush	Colchester	"	17
Elisha Card	Vollentown	"	14
Stephen Commens	Coventry	25	9
James Downer	Lebanon	23	4
John Follen	Glastenbury	"	"
Philer Goodrich	Wethersfield	"	14
Daniel Lane	Moodus	17	"
Justin Lumbard	Suffield	28	14
James Pratt	Wethersfield	9 Aug.	4
John Smith	Suffield	8 July	14
Elisha Smith	Middletown	18	4
1st Company			
Abel Baldwin	Waterbury	16 Aug.	14 Dec.
Amos Cook	Chatham	17 July	4
Joseph Churchell	"	18 Aug.	16
Uriah Finney	Lebanon	23 July	9
Edward Fenn	Wallingford	16 Aug.	16
Elnathan Gary	Lebanon	28 July	9
Asahel Hall	Wallingford	16 Aug.	4
Jesse Lyman	Lebanon	23 July	9
John Gipson	Wethersfield	18 Aug.	14
Aron Overton	Norwich	23 July	20
Zenus Pieno	Lebanon	"	4

Names	Towns	Commencement of Service	Expiration of Service
Nathaniel Robarts	Chatham	17	14
John Rice	Wallingford	18 Aug.	"
Amasa Stocking	Chatham	17 July	4
Abel Spicer	Lebanon	23	14
Ephraim Spalding	Ashford	16 Aug.	9
Silas Tracey	Washington	23	4
James Wilson	Middletown	17 July	"
Aaron West	Chatham	"	"
Samuel Woolcut	Wallingford	16 Aug.	16
David Welch	Plainfield	"	17
Jonathan Whipple	"	23 Aug.	14
Lt Colonels Compy			
Samuel Ames	Waterbury	23 July	14 Dec.
Daniel Avery	Cornwall	"	"
Joseph Austin	Middletown	17	9
John Codner	"	"	4
John Downes	Groton	30 Aug.	14
Jonathn Hutchinson	Coventry	23 July	9
Samuel Jones	Hebron	"	4
John Kirtland	Suffield	28	14
Allen Lane	Middletown	17	"
Joseph Lewis	Stratford	28	"
Jesse Morgan	Chatham	1 Sep	"
Isaac Owen	Hebron	23 July	4
5th Company			
Sylvanus Avery	Lime	26 Aug.	14 Dec.
William Almy	Volentown	23 July	14
Ebenezar Clark	Labanon	"	9
Phinehas Dean	Chatham	26 Aug.	4
Jacob Fenton	Lebanon	17 July	9
Squire Goff	Colchester	23	14
Japhet Hanmon	"	28	20 Nov
Saml Kingsbury	Plainfield	16 Aug.	16 Dec.
Isaac Lacey	Fairfield	17 July	9
George Little	Killingley	16 Aug.	14
Thomas Marvell	Coventry	23 July	"
Amos Ranney	Chatham	17	4
Jonah Thomas	Lebanon	23 Aug.	"
Daniel Stoddard	Litchfield	26	14
Isaac Utter	New Milford	18	4
Stephen Williams	Fairfield	"	"
Ambrous Woodward	Lebanon	17 July	14
Fredrick Woodward	"	9	"
2nd Compy			
Jonathan Francis	Wallingford	15 Aug.	14 Dec.
Fredrick Fuller	Wethersfield	18	4
Jason Gay	Fairfield	"	14
Clark Hide	Stratford	15	19
Charles Johnson	Wallingford	18	20 Nov.
Benjamin Porter	Hartford	20	4 Dec.
Elias Purple	E Haddam	4 Oct	"
Elisha Perkins	Cheshire	18 July	9
Paul Griffis	Killingsley	15 Aug.	14
Peregrine Garner	Norwich	31	4
Jonathan West	Lebanon	23 July	4 Oct

I do hereby certify that the above Pay abstract is just & true according to the best of my Knowledge. Jno P. Wyllys

Majr Comdt 9th Connect Regt

[*State Library, Revolution 16.*]

COL. HAZEN'S REGIMENT.

DESERTERS, 1779.

[*See Record of Connecticut Men in the Revolution, page 260.*]

A Return of sundry Deserters from Col. Moses Hazen's Regiment inlisted in the State of Connecticut, and returned to the Board of War, as a Part of that State's Quota, and not included in the Return delivered by Capt. Munson to the Assembly of that State.

Names &c		Town	Names &c		Town
John Cornelius	Priv.	New Haven	Aaron Tuttle	Priv.	Ridgfield
Edward Gilbertson	"	"	Michael Welch	"	New Milford
Christopher Gale	"	Canaan	William Baker	"	Salisbury
Benjamin Hindman	"	Woodbury	James Daurough		Stamford
John M[c]Coy	"	New Haven			

Moses Hazen Col.

[*State Library, Revolution 16.*]

THREE MONTHS' REGIMENT—COL. WYLLYS.

OFFICERS.

[On June 30, 1780, the Council of Safety in consequence of Gen. Washington's representations voted to raise 1000 men to serve for three months in the "Connecticut Line."]

The United States D^r To the State of Connecticut, for Disbursements for the Pay &c of three Regiments under the Command of Col. Hezekiah Wyllys, for three Months, raised in consequence of a requisition from General Washington in June 1780.

Companies	Regiments	Companies	Regiments
Field & Staff	Hez^h Wyllys's	Capt D. Godfrey	Saml Canfield's
Capt Smith	"	Capt J. Carter	"
Capt D. Stewart	"	Capt E. Couch	"
Capt B. Norris	"	Capt A. Sloper	"
Capt J. Green	"	Capt A. Mills	"
Maj^r J. Clark	"	Col. B. Richards	Richards
Lt S. Smith	"	Maj^r D. Cone	"
Capt D. Johnson	"	Capt E. Palmer	"
Capt Mathew Grant	"	Capt A. Hotchkiss	"
Field & Staff	Saml Canfields	Capt D. Collins	"
Capt J. Pennoyer	"	Capt S. Ely	"
Capt Joseph Smith	"	Col. B. Richards	"
Capt H. Hait	"	Capt J. Brian	"

[*Comptroller's Office, Haskell's Receipts.*]

BOUNTY ROLLS.

Account of Bounties paid to recruits raised for 3 mo. to join the Continental Army in the year 1780 by Col. Jonathan Dimon Viz^t

Siras Hawley
Bille Lacey
T. Porter
S. Gregory
J. Meeker
D. Brown
D. Raymond
A. Wheeler
S. Ranny
D. Jennings 3d
T. Rynes
Samuel French
S. Scovil
Silas Dayton
G. Welles
N. Morehouse
John Lockwood 3d
J. Adams
Elias Sturges
J. Squire
C. Godfrey
S. Daten
Peter Winton
J. E. Olcott
A. Pillias
E. Sherwood
Elijah Raymond
Joseph Platt
J. Crowfeet
Jonas Platt
E. French
A. Cable
Waker Bates
D. Drew

[*State Library, Revolution 17.*]

Bounty Roll of the 3 mo. Men who joined the Continental Army from the 9th Reg. of Militia in the year 1780

Isaac Smith
Reuben Mead
John Morrel
Jonathan Read
Levi Sherwood
John Reymond
Jacob Richards
Samuel Waring Jr
Samuel Penoyer
Benjamin Reymond
Samuel Reynolds
Joseph Patchen
Isaac Hubbell
Gol[ ]kwood
[ ]eed
John Butler
Abraham Raymond
Isaac Reymond
Abraham Seymour
Stephen Reed
Daniel Mills
Eliakim Smith Jr
William Raymond
Ira Scott
Moses Gates
Samuel Hait
Gideon Weed
Gold Ferris
William Patchen
Joseph Gregory
Dodatey Hendrick
Matthew Betts
Jesse Taylor
Reuben Mead Jr
Jedediah Nash
Jonathan Platt

[*State Library, Revolution 17.*]

Account of Bounties paid to recruits raised for 3 mo. to join the Continental Army in the year 1780 by Col° Increase Mosely

Elijah Hinman
Andrew Graham
John Thomas &c
Justus Hinman &c
Benja Hitchcock Jr &c
John Graham
Wait Hinman
Dan Chatfield
Danl Squier
David Rumsey
Thomas Knapen
Gershom Holmes
Joseph Hamlin
Agur Beach
Reuben Miner
Noah Bunnell
Thaddeus Lacey
John Skeel
S. Ingraham

[*State Library, Revolution 17.*]

State of Connecticut To Nehemiah Beardsley Paymaster to the Men raised in the 16th Regiment for three months in the year 1780 Bounties to the Men & for Guns Blankets &c Dr July 1780

Matthew Olmstead
Thaddeus Whitlock
Ebenezer Moody
Daniel Rockwell
Eanos Rockwell
Uriah Raymond
Amos Griffin
Robert Wilson
Jeremiah Andrews
Thomas Neal
Elijah Hait
Sedeman Harrard
Dan Towner
Nathaniel Fuller
John Potter
David Hall
Job Jones
Jonathan Griffin
Elnathan Beers
Joseph Boughton
Eliphalet Peck
Amos Hoyt
James Platt
John Benedict
Samuel Hoit
John Barnum
Samuel Brown
Ezra Barnum
Oliver Clark
Joseph Thomas
Hezekiah Wetherbee
Asa Powers
Benjamin Rockwell
Peleg Finch
Oliver Burton
James Lincoln
Simeon Baldwin
Joseph Rockwell

Abner Judd
Jehiel Smith
John Fairchild
Abiel Prindle
Bennet Perry
Joseph Barnum
Enoch Fairchild
Jacob Keeler
Thomas Hodges
Moses Gray
Jabez Wakeman
Samuel Crane
Elizer Taylor
Silas Dunning
David Beers
Jonathan Benedict
Thomas Kellogg

[*State Library, Revolution 17.*]

COL. FLOWER'S ARTIFICERS.

[*See Record of Connecticut Men in the Revolution, page 295.*]

A Return of the Names of the Officers & men in the Military Department at Springfield under the Direction of Col. Ezekiel Cheevers D Commissary General Military Stores and who are Lawfull Inhabitants of the State of Connecticut together with the time of their Engagements in the Department also the towns and Counties to which they Severally Belong.

Names	Time of Engagement	Towns
John Collins D Commissary Military Stores	Jan. 1, 1777	Wethersfield
Amasa Loomis Clerk Military Stores	Feb. 28, 1777	Bolton
William Barton Caplain of Armory	Aug. 20, 1777	Farmington
John Conant Asst Harness Maker	Apr. 20, 1779	Mansfield
Jacob Sergants Armorer	May 13, 1779	"
Rufus Payne "	Mar. 28, "	East Windsor
William Barton "	Apr. 1, "	Farmington
Ashbel Fox "	May 6, "	East Hartford
Michael Jenson "	"	Colchester
Samuel Weaver "	Aug. 15, "	"
Hiram Roberts "	Oct. 6, "	Farmington
Joseph Barton "	Jan. 1, 1779	"
Amasa Polley "	Sep. 1, "	Suffield
Henery Pooley "	Dec. 16, "	Farmington
Joseph Daley "	Dec. 1, 1778	"
Ephraim Luce Harness Maker	Apr. 13, "	Sumers
David Davis "	May 5, 1779	Mansfield
Ephraim Richardson "	June 8, 1779	Coventry
Lemuel Southworth "	" 16, "	Mansfield
Abijah North Blacksmith	Oct. 20, "	Farmington

These may Certifie that the officers & men contained on this Roll is Engaged in the Service of the United States of America for three years or During the War, & that they have not been absent from their Respective Duties unless by proper authority

Attest Ezek[l] Cheever D C G M S

[*State Library, Revolution 15.*]

SOLDIERS DISCHARGED AND DESERTED.

The United States Dr to the State of Connecticut for supplies to the families of Officers & Soldiers of the Connecticut Line who were discharged from or deserted the service before the first day of January 1780 & were not included in the settlement for depreciation on their pay: Vizt

Names of the Persons supplied	By what Town supplied
Daniel Allen Capt	Ashford
Jonathan Allen	New Haven
John Adams	Farmington
William Andruss Artif.	East Windsor
Thomas Abbe Capt	Enfield
Thomas Avery Lt	Groton
John Anthony	Wallingford
Saml Barker Capt	Brandford
Abner Bacon "	Canterbury
William Bacon Artily	Middletown
Eli Biggelow	Colchester
Beriah Bill Capt	Norwich
Robin Blanchard	Colchester
Nathl Bishop Lieut.	Norwich
Silas Baldwin	Derby
Caleb Baldwin Lt	Killingsworth
Henry Baldwin	Say Brook
Jona Brown Capt	Farmington
Charles Brown	Stonington
Oliver Brown	"
James Barns Lt	New Fairfield
David Barns	Wallingford
Increase Brainard	Haddam
Stephen Buckland Capt	Hartford
Asa Burnham	Litchfield
Joseph Burnham I. C.	Lyme
Asa Burnham	Preston
Humphrey Ball	Lebanon
Jona Blackman	"
Elijah Blackman Capt	Middletown
Ebenezer Blake	"
Edward Benton Serjt	Guilford
Gideon Bailey Lt	Haddam
Robert Bailey	"
Jona Beeman	East Windsor
Friend Beeman	Washington
Boanerges Beebe	New London
Edward Brind	Haddam
John Burk	Milford

Names of the Persons supplied	By what Town supplied
Phinehas Beardsley Capt	New Fairfield
David Bewel	New Milford
Josiah Burrows	Stratford
Benjn Burnap	Windham
Abisha Bingham	"
Danl Culver	New London
Timothy Cleaveland Lt	Canterbury
Darius Cady	Stonington
Reuben Carter	Canterbury
James Carter	Lebanon
Marcus Cole Lieut	Chatham
John Cole	Farmington
Nathan Clapp	Coventry
John Chapman	Say Brook
David Clark serjt	New Haven
Asahel Clark Ensn	Woodstock
Elijah Churchill	East Windsor
Ames Curtiss	Farmington
Phinehas Camp	Woodbury
John Conlee	Glastenbury
Walter Chase	Haddam
Ebenezer Church	Woodbury
Joseph Cone	Middletown
Noah Coleman Doct.	Lebanon
Josha Chappel	New London
Comfort Chappel	"
Curtiss Chappel	Salisbury
Jona Corwin	Norwich
Selah Corwin	"
John Comstock	Say Brook
Wm Lock Collins	Stratford
Robert Davinson	Greenwich
Stephen Downing	Canterbury
Christopher Downing	Norwich
Thomas Duffe	Fairfield
Josha Disborough	"
Titus Dutton	Waterbury
Saml Dealing	Glastenbury
Stephen Davis	Waterbury
Israel Dayton Artifr	New Haven

Names of the Persons supplied	By what Town supplied
Moses Dowd	Guilford
David Deming Lieut	Hartford
Daniel Die	Kent
Daniel Dodge	Lyme
Nathan Dodge	Colchester
James Dewy	Middletown
Joseph Dickerman	New Haven
William Drinkwater	New Milford
Benjn Durkee Lieut	Windham
Jeremiah Durkee	"
Zebulon Dudley	Say Brook
Miles Dunbar	Waterbury
Solomon Douglas	New London
Everet Eams	Danbury
Saml Evans Junr	Hartford
Isaac Evans	Preston
Ezra Edgcomb	New Hartford
Vine Elderkin Cap^{tn}	Windham
Jack Freeman	Colchester
Samson Freeman	Glastenbury
Providence Freeman	New London
John Fox	Colchester
Jacob Fox Lieu^{t}	Norwich
Nehemiah Fowler	Fairfield
Caleb Fowler Corp^{l}	Guilford
Saml French	Fairfield
John Fenton	Willington
Reuben Farnum	Windham
Francis Fillets	Woodbury
John Garret	New Hartford
Elihu Geer	Chatham
Richard Giddens	"
D. Tubbs Gardner	Norwich
Wm Green Capt	Hartford
Robert Green	Voluntown
Nathl Gates Lieu^{t}	Canterbury
Joseph Graham	Chatham
Ephraim Goodrich	Wethersfield
Simeon Graves	Waterbury
Azariah Grant	East Windsor
Saml Gross	Lebanon
Phinehas Granger	Suffield
Saml Gorham	Stratford
Wm Hall	Ashford
Saml Hall Corp^{l}	Killingsworth
Nathl Hall	Waterbury
Wm Hall Artif^{r}	New London
Elihu Hubbard	Chatham
Wm Harrison	Lyme
Aaron Hale Lieut	Chatham
Cornelius Higgins "	Haddam
Levi Hotchkiss "	Derby
Ithamar Harvey Capt	East Haddam
Simeon Hagar serj^{t}	Enfield
Titus Hayes	Hartford
Joseph Hannabal	Groton
Joseph Hannabal	Stonington

Names of the Persons supplied	By what Towns supplied
Joseph C. Hawley	New Milford
Rufus Hyde	Lyme
John Hudson	Stonington
James Hull	Waterbury
Stephen Hull	Woodbury
Champlin Harris, alias Harrison	Colchester
Frederick Harden Artif^{r}	New Haven
Richd Hunt	"
Thos Hiscox	Stonington
Hawk's Son	"
Wm Heacock	Waterbury
David Heacock	Woodbury
John Hastings	Wallingford
James Stoughton	Union
Daniel Hendry	New London
Lemuel Hitchcock L^{t}	Willinton
Wm Hambden	Woodstock
Joseph Jones	Brandford
Thomas Jones	Wallingford
Henry Jones	New London
Elnathan Jennings	Chatham
Robert Johnston	Sharon
Danl Judd Serj^{t}	Colchester
Nathan P. Jackson L^{t}	Fairfield
John Jordan	Washington
M. Jacobs	Norwich
Usell Knapp	Stanford
Thomas Kinning	New Fairfield
Thos Kirtland Capt	Say Brook
John Kirrit	Symsbury
Wm Lane	New London
Levi Lee	"
Elisha Lee Capt	Lyme
Moses Loomis	East Windsor
Saml Lockwood Capt	Greenwich
Levi Loveland	Glastenbury
Samuel Lucas	Hartford
Allen Leet	Killingsworth
John Lines	New Haven
Ebenezer Lewis	Wallingford
Saml Lewis serj^{t}	Waterbury
Willet Larrabee	Salisbury
Sylvester Minor	New London
James Minor	"
Andrew Minor	Tolland
Wm Mackhall	New London
Cyprian Merrills	Farmington
Thomas Mercy	Ashford
Enoch Miller	Chatham
W^{m} McCorne	"
George Mitchel	Norwich
Stephen Meeker	Redding
Noah Murray serj^{t}	Kent
McDowal Ens.	Glastenbury
John McDonald	Groton

Names of the Persons supplied	By what Town supplied
Saml Mattocks Capt	Hartford
Orlando Mack Lieut	Hebron
James McKensey	Stonington
Jedediah Mackinborough	Hebron
John Main jun^{r}	Kent
Danl Munger	Litchfield
Alexander McCoy	Lyme
Comfort Marks	Middletown
Wm Munson Cap^{tn}	New Haven
Joseph Moulthrop	"
Lewis Martin	"
John Moss	"
Wm Manning Captn	Woodstock
Urane Nickerson	Greenwich
Briston Negro	Say Brook
Cuff Negro	Colchester
Colonel Oswald	Farmington
Timothy Oharra	New London
Wm Ollin	Norwich
Israel Patten Lieut	New Haven
David Pelton	Groton
Levi Price	Cornwall
Rufus Price L^{t}	Tolland
Thomas Picket	Danbury
Danl Perkins jun^{r}	Enfield
Peter Peas Serj^{t}	Glastenbury
Jacob Pomp	Groton
Zebulon Peck	Goshen
Silas Peck jun^{r}	Lyme
Darius Peck	Norwich
Benj^{a} Pomeroy Doct	Hebron
Lazarus Puffer	"
Sylvanus Perry	Killingley
Eben^{r} Perry Serj^{t}	Windham
Jonas Prentice Captn	New Haven
Jeremiah Parmelee Captn	New Haven
Eliab Parker	Waterbury
Alpheus Polley	Lebanon
Andrew Patterson	Tolland
Jon^{a} Pardee	Waterbury
Danl Pendleton Artif^{r}	"
John Robinson	Middletown
Jared Robinson Lieut	New Haven
Saml Robinson Q M	"
Simeon Robinson jun^{r}	Windham
Abial Roberts	Waterbury
Jeremiah Roswell	Danbury
Laban Riggs	Derby
Saml Raymond	Redding
Amos Rowe	Farmington
Simeon Rouse	Preston
Reuben Reed	Norwich
John Roach	Lyme
Nathan Root L^{t}	Willington

Names of the Persons supplied	By what Town supplied
David Rice	Willington
Peter Stevens j^{r}	Canterbury
Roswel Stevens	Farmington
Elias Seymour	New Hartford
John Shipman	Say Brook
Saml Shipman Serj^{t}	"
Jaspar Stannard	"
Geo. Smith Ens.	Hartford
Job Smith Ens.	Ridgefield
Saml Smith Artif.	Waterbury
James Smith	Windham
Wm Shaw	Canterbury
Benjn Shaw	"
Timothy Stark	Colchester
Stephen Stark	"
Stephen Stark	Hebron
James Simmons	Stonington
Robert Swift	Groton
Benajah Strong	Lebanon
Daniel Seward	Milford
Wm Seward	"
Saml S. Squier	Farmington
David Spencer L^{t}	East Haddam
Obadiah Spencer	Hartford
James Sally	East Haddam
Wm Smithers	Glastenbury
Aaron Suntsimons	Groton
John Spears	"
States Spears	"
Josep Sharp	Milford
Wm Shortman	Groton
John Shelley	Litchfield
Josiah Stone	"
David Stone	Wallingford
Jonah Sizer	Middletown
Ezekiel Sandford	Waterbury
Wm Sherman	New Haven
Chauncey Sperry	"
Nathl Sturdevant	Norfolk
John Sydleman	Norwich
Saml Spicer	"
Asa Starkweather	"
Elisha Stowel	Pomfret
Obadiah Sears	Preston
Constant Searl	Stonington
Nathl Suncheman	"
Prince Summit	Voluntown
James Sprague	Union
Stephen Scovill	Waterbury
Absalom Thomas	New London
James Thomas	New Haven
John Taylor	New Hartford
David Tomlinson Ens.	Derby
John Treat	Glastenbury
Ezekiel Tuttle	Waterbury
Timothy Tuttle	"

Names of the Persons supplied	By what Town supplied
Hezekiah Tuttle	Waterbury
Hezekiah Tracy Lieut	Norwich
Isaiah Wright	Hebron
Ezekiel Wright	Norwich
Joseph Weeks	New London
Henry Whiting P Mr	Derby
Uriah Wise	Cornwall
Thomas Wooster Capt	New Haven
Richard Watrous	Derby
Jona Webb	Norwich
Stephen Welton junr	Waterbury
Joshua Webster	Glastenbury

Names of the Persons supplied	By what Town supplied
Thomas Wiard	Goshen
Hammon Way	Hartford
Wm Walter Art:	New Haven
Wm Ward	Lebanon
Martin Wade	Lyme
Wm Whitely	New Milford
Josha Wedge	Norwich
Walter Warden	Stonington
Oliver Woodward	Windsor
Joseph West	Windham
Benjn Western Ens.	Weathersfield
Albigence Waldo	Windham
Michael Welch	Washington
Gael Landor	New Haven

[*Comptroller's Office, Haskell's Receipts.*]

CONNECTICUT LINE, 1781-1783.

FIRST REGIMENT—COL. DURKEE.

[*See Record of Connecticut Men in the Revolution, page 315.*]

SHORT LEVIES, 1781.

The United States D[r] To the State of Connecticut, For the Pay of sundry Persons who joined the 1st Regiment, as short Levies in the Year 1781. Viz[t]

Names	when entered the Service 1781	when Discharged
Seth Garnsey	July 28	Dec. 14
Daniel Pierce	Aug. 30	" 30
Amos Westland	July 10	" 19
Benjamin Cushman	Aug. 31	" 26
Zebulon Hawkins	June 27	" 31
Benjamin Wood	" 27	" 25
Caleb Edson	Aug. 8	" 15
James Morgan	June 1	" 29
Josiah Terry	July 2	" 29
Seth Geary	Sept. 3	" 28
Nathan Fairchild	" 10	" 25
John B. Emmes	" 14	" 25
Araunah Kilborne	" 1	" 25
Elijah Griswold	Aug. 24	" 31
John Wilcoxon	July 1	" 19
Jabez Bottom	" 30	" 14
Thomas Peck	Aug. 27	" 25
Nath[l] Sabins	" 18	" 25
Derby Donavin	July 10	" 31
John Green	" 7	" 25
Cudgoe Shepard	" 1	" 25
Joseph Pratt	Aug. 10	" 13
William Fuller	" 27	" 25
Josiah Rogers Dodge	" 27	" 14
Daniel Perkins	" 18	" 25

Names	when entered the Service 1781	when Discharged
Ichabod Blackman	July 13	Dec. 25
John Spencer	Sept. 14	" 31
Ephraim Babcock	July 1	" 28
Philip Perkins	Aug. 18	" 19
Solomon Brooks	" 21	" 30
Stephen Simmons	July 3	" 12
William Austin	" 1	" 31
Bernard Bagley	" 12	" 25
Thomas Evans	Sept. 11	" 29
Robert Hammond	" 5	" 25
Aaron Baxter	" 1	Nov. 28
Stephen Commins	July 10	Dec. 25
Timothy Green	Aug. 18	" 25
Thomas Marble	" 22	" 30
Roswell Beach	July 1	" 25
Nehemiah Blackman	Sept. 7	" 28
Jack Gregory	Aug. 23	" 31
Samuel Brewster	" 15	" 27
John Cumbo	July 19	" 30
Aaron Kellogg	Aug. 14	" 31

[*Comptroller's Office, Haskell's Receipts*]

SHORT LEVIES, 1782.

Pay Roll of the eight Months Men who served in the 1st Connecticut Regiment in the Year 1782

Names	Time of Inlistment	Time of Discharge
John Ayer	Apr. 8	Dec. 25
Isaac Snow	22	9
John Whitcomb	28	29
Samuel Cole	28	9
Mark Hamblin	May 1	9
Henry Waldo	Apr. 22	28
Willm Knapp	22	Feb. 1783
David Hull 2d	May 3	"
James Heart	Nov. 1	Dec. 17
Chas Rice	"	5
Fred Smith	"	20
Ebenr Doolittle	"	31
Elijah Northrop	"	9
Joseph West	"	13
Zacchs Doud	"	5
Bemmir (?) Morgan	Apr. 15	Jan. 1
David alias Daniel Pease	"	"
Amos Holden	7	
Jonn Fosket	May 1	Jan. 1
Jack Gregory	Apr. 24	"
Emanus Lilley	May 4	Nov. 15
John Green	June 10	Jan. 1
Jonah Webb	Nov. 1	"
Caleb Barrows	"	"
Willm Coltrain	"	"

Names	Time of Inlistment	Time of Discharge
Eben' Cobuck	Nov. 1	Jan. 1
Rob' Follett	"	"
Elip' Burnham	"	"
Jacob Norton	"	Nov. 22
Wolcott Burnham	May 14	Dec. 9
Ira Cannon	8	Nov. 16
Ezra Tupper	June 7	Sept. 23
James Hopkins	12	Dec. 8
Levi Parker	22	"
David Carpenter	1	Nov. 5
Daniel Bird	Nov. 1	Dec. 16
Step[n] Moucher	"	6
Will[m] Davis	"	"
Asael Hull	"	Nov. 5
Amasa Ingham	"	Dec. 31
Asa Burr	"	6
Daniel Pick	"	Nov. 5
John Butler	May 4	17
Shubal Snow	30	Jan. 1
Hezekiah Davison	"	"
John Blocker	"	Aug. 19
Jesse Peck	13	Jan. 1
Tho[s] Fox	6	Dec. 9
James Kennedy	Nov. 1	Jan. 1
Moses Allyn	"	Dec. 5
Elisha Marshall	"	6
Will[m] Reed	"	"
Jed[h] Cox or Coc	"	29
Isaac Boxford	"	"
Sam[l] Andrews	"	28
Jon[n] Egglestone	"	Nov. 29
Arnold Worden	Apr. 15	Jan. 1
Elias Tracey	22	"
Phin[s] Hulett	1	"
Joseph Morgan	26	Nov. 17
Bethuel Norton	1	16
Ezra Bates	26	Jan. 1
Joshua Martin	July 16	
Sam[l] Martin	"	
Tho[s] Rindge	"	
Lemuel Barber	Nov. 1	Dec. 5
Sam[l] Cook	"	"
Abel Barnes	"	"
Jachish Holcomb	"	"
Fred. Avery	Apr. 14	Jan. 1
Benj[n] Ward	May 18	"
Solom[n] Howard	1	"
John Conolly	June 21	"
Noah Spencer	Nov. 1	"
John Robinson	"	"
Will[m] White	"	"
Israel Frisby	"	"
Abrah[m] Tomkins	"	"
Sam[l] Collins	"	"
Edmund Griswold	"	"
Thomas Watson	"	"
Elijah Howard	May 1	Dec. 5

Names	Time of Inlistment	Time of Discharge
James Morse	Apr. 8	Dec. 8
John Martin	May 16	6
David Pratt	June 10	9
Gad Page	May 6	29
Sylvanus Pease	May 19	9
John Ford	Apr. 1	"
Edw[d] Holmes	Nov. 1	7
Josiah Rockwood	"	16
Amos Rich	"	28
Solomon Cone	"	18
Prince Crosby	"	31
Peter Maranday	"	9
Elisha Carrell	"	5
Shipman Clark	"	"
Joseph Cromb	Apr. 1	Nov. 24
Joseph Howe	16	Dec. 20
Gilbert Hatch	26	Jan. 1
Amos Starkweather	"	Dec. 9
Elisha Dyer	May 1	Jan. 1
Joel Mack	27	"

[*State Library, Revolution 25.*]

SECOND REGIMENT—COL. SWIFT.

[See Record of Connecticut Men in the Revolution, page 322.]

CAPT. CALEB BALDWIN'S COMPANY.

Return of Capt Baldwins Comp^y Specifying the time they have to serve.

Names	Term y	Term m	Names	Term y	Term m
Serj Hall	War		Eleazer Baldwin	1	6
Serj Meigs	War		Eli Hull	1	6
Serj Turner	1	7	John Warrin	War	
Corp^l Call	War		Cornelius Chittenden	1	7
Corp^l Mix	War		Joel Gaylord	War	
Corp^l Sillick	War		Nathan Teall	1	8
J. Airey D^r	1	1	Amasa Warner	War	
J. Coon Fifer	War		Robart Watkins	1	6
Benjamin Knapp	1	5	Call Fruman	War	
Hilderick Barritt	War		John Wright	1	9
Samuel Lynds	1	7	Cuff Smith	1	7
David Cole	War		Joel Willcon	1	8
Jonah Carter	1	6	Whala Springger	1	7
Reuben Stevens	War		Samuel Rucket (?)	1	6
John Griswold	1	8	Ezeriah Canfield	War	
Joel Spencer	1	6	Solomon Chittenden	1	7
Robart Hull	1	5			

[The remainder of the roll is missing.]

[Connecticut Historical Society.]

SHORT LEVIES, 1781.

The United States D^r To the State of Connecticut for the Pay of sundry Persons who joined the second Regiment as short Levies in the Year 1781.

Names	when entered the Service	when Discharged
Reuben Morey	July 31	Dec. 12
Samuel Stanliff	" 31	" 31
Ashbel Olmstead	Aug. 21	" 24
Samuel Nye	" 7	" 13
Samuel Dimmock	" 7	" 20
John Dimmock	" 7	" 30
Lothrop Burgiss	" 16	" 7
Joshua Simmons	" 7	" 13
Taman Kimball	" 16	" 20

Names	when entered the Service	when Discharged
Samuel Tibbals	July 11	Dec. 31
Richard Skinner	" 12	" 24
Increase Brainard	" 12	" 12
George Healy	Aug. 27	" 12
Abel DeForrest	" 27	" 12
Thomas Newcomb	" 5	" 30
William Harris Fox	" 6	" 30
Timothy Linsey	July 31	" 12
Ephraim Hull	Aug. 21	" 12
Anthony Sizer	" 21	Nov. 21
Uriah Finney	" 16	Dec. 12
Nathan Gregory	" 29	" 31
Timothy Rundalls	July 27	" 24
Joseph Mead	" 27	" 24
Josiah Apley	" 31	" 31
Samuel Church	" 9	" 13
Nathan Hinman	Aug. 27	" 12
John McClentock	" 7	" 31
Jonathan Talbott	July 9	" 13
Silas Leonard	Aug. 3	Jan. 4
Noah Munroe	" 21	Dec. 31
James Lincoln	" 21	" 31
John Benidict	" 27	" 12
Matthew Barnum	" 27	" 30
Elihu Judd	" 29	" 12
Phineas Taylor	" 29	" 12
Benjamin Peck	" 27	" 31
William Coltrain	" 16	" 14
Jannah Sutliff	July 11	" 12
Elias Johnson	Aug. 24	" 27
Grove Loomiss	" 21	" 24
Isaac Mead	July 27	" 13
Timothy Herrington	Aug. 16	" 13
Abner Moses	July 13	Nov. 13
Idem	April 25	June 11
William Tisdale	July 12	Dec. 30
Phineas Gorham	Aug. 2	" 24
Caleb Bailey	July 11	" 21
Andrew Chidester	Aug. 27	" 12
Danl (for Matthew) Hubbard	July 11	" 31
James Fuller	Aug. 16	" 20
Jeremiah Tharp	" 29	" 31
Phineas Smith	" 27	" 31

[*Comptroller's Office, Haskell's Receipts.*]

DESERTIONS, 1781, 1782.

List of deserters from the 2d Connecticut Regt Commanded by Colonel Swift from the 1st of Jany 1781 to the 31st July 1782

Names	Time Deserted 1781	Names	Time Deserted 1781
Ephraim Cohorse	Jan. 28	Ebenezr Drinkwater	July 19
Benjn Tarbox (late Q Mr Serj)	Feb. 1	Moses Dutton	"
Jonah Jones	Mar. 16	David Andrus	Aug 9
John Smith	Feb. 22	Jesse Smith	"
Abraham Gillet	Apr. 10	Hiram Wm Howard	Sep. 4
Cocher Wiggins	Apr. 1	Stephen Jones	Oct. 31
John Taylor (of N. Hartford)	Jan. 1	Christopher Blake	Oct. 11
John Condrick	Apr. 8	Samuel Lummis	Nov. 13
Charles Goodwin	May 2		1782
Abraham Quakenbush	May 4	Peter Surdan	Feb. 11
Thomas Reed	Jan. 1	Aaron Culver	Mar. 5
Isaac Fisher	May 20	William Jackson	Apr. 10
Noah Fulford	May 30	Isaac Squires	"
John Springer	June 26	Daniel Davidson	"
Samuel Whitney	July 1	Samuel Sturdivant	June 3
Henry Stevens	"	Joseph Ross	June 21
Prince Cato	June 20	Thomas Allen	"
Elipht Nickerson	Aug. 1	Jeremiah Wheaton	July 17
Elisha Bradford (late Corporal)	July 14	Elipht Allen	July 21
John Dennison	Aug. 5	James Tobias	"
		George States	July 22
		John Ashley	"

H. Swift Col.

[*State Library, Revolution 25.*]

THIRD REGIMENT—COL. WEBB.

[*See Record of Connecticut Men in the Revolution, page 331.*]

FIRST COMPANY—CAPT. BULKLEY.

Roll and Muster of the First Company in the 3rd Conn. Regiment Commanded by Colonel Samuel B. Webb.

Ranks	Names	Term of Inlistment	Casualties	Alterations since last Muster
Captain	Edward Bulkley	1st Jan 1777		
Lieut	Daniel Bradley	20 July 1780	In Connecticut	On Recruiting Service
Serg^t Major	Jonathan White	D. W.		Transfered to the Roll of Field & Staff 25th Ap^l 82
Q M. Serg^t	Simon Griffin	D. W.		
Serg^t	Elijah Bordman	D. W.		
"	Darius Orcutt	1 Year & 6	21st Feb. 1782 at Nyack D. Ferry	
"	Moses Griswold	D. W.		
"	Daniel Sizer	D. W.		
Corporal	Hezekiah Nott	D. W.		
"	Thomas Stanley	D. W.		
"	Gideon Goff	D. W.		
Drum Major	David Pratt	D. W.		" " "
Fife Major	John Kirkum	D. W.		" " "
Drummer	Moses Hatch	D. W.		" " "
"	David Lindsey	D. W.		" " "
Fifer	Asa Squire	D. W.		
"	William Armstrong	D. W.		
	Daniel Bushnell	D. W.		
	Abraham Belding	D. W.		
	Jonathan Bullock	1 Year & 8 Months		
	Simeon Barnes			Discharged 13 Ap^l 82
	Jeremiah Bennet	1 Year & 8 Months	12th Ap^l 82 on the lines	
	John Ballard	1 & 11		
	Ward Colton	1 & 8	22 Feb. 82 on the lines	
	Moses Coy	1 & 9		
	Robert Chandler	1 & 8		
	Daniel Dunham	1 & 10		
	Joseph Douglass	1 & 9	12th Ap^l 82 on the lines	

Ranks	Names	Term of Inlistment	Casualties	Alterations since last Muster
	Alphred Dresser	1 & 8	7th Feb '82 Pomphret in Conn. by Col. Grosvenor's order	
	Jack Freeman			
	Brince Freeman			
	Cato Freeman			
	Stephen Fox			
	Samuel Herrington			
	Arunah Hackley			
	Samuel Lyon			
	Daniel Mosley			
	David Peck			
	Nathaniel Price			
	Joseph Preston			
	Joseph Pease			
	Samuel Roberts			
	Reuben Roberson			
	Abel Stowel			
	Samuel Stowel			
	Nathaniel Stowel			
	John Smith			
	Joseph Treat			
	Hezekiah Wheeler			
	Peter Whitney			
	Joseph Willson			

I certify the above Roll to be the true State of said Company the 25th Day of April 1782

Edward Bulkley Cap't.

[*Edward Bulkeley, New Haven.*]

EIGHTH COMPANY—CAPT. ROGERS.

[*See Record of Connecticut Men in the Revolution, page 336.*]

Size Roll of Captain Rogers's Company 3d Connecticut Regiment

Mens Names	Age	Size Feet	Inches	Born	Residence	Complection	Eyes	Hair	Inlistments When	Term	What Town
Serjt Richard Lord	31	5	7	Lyme	Lyme	Dark	Dark	Brown	March 77	D War	Willington
William Basset	39	5	10½	N. Haven	Water Town	Light	Light	D Brown	Feb. 1777	D War	Watertown
Abiather Evans[1]	40	5	9	Hartford	Hartford	Dark	Dark	Dark	Feb. 1777	"	Hartford
Peter Stalker[2]	27	5	11	Fairfield	Fairfield	Dark	Dark	Dark	Aug. 1777	"	Fairfield
Reuben Beach	24	5	11	"	Stratford	Light	Light	Brown	Mar. 1, 1777	"	Stratford
Henry Hull											
Thomas Wells	23	5	7½	Hartford	Hartford	Fair	Grey	Light	Apr. 15, 1777	D War	Hartford
Corp Jesse St John	22	5	9½	Norwalk	Norwalk	Dark	Dark	Black	Mar. 15, '78	D War	Norwalk
James Crane	22	5	9	Saybrook	Goshen	Light	Light	Dark	Dec. 26, 1780	3 years	Goshen
Amasy Grenold[3]	27	5	5	Saybrook	Salsbury	Light	Grey	Brown	Apr. 1777	D War	Salsbury
Nicholas Howell[4]	46	5	4½	Sandy Cruse	N. Haven	Dark	Black	Black	Jan. 1777	D War	N. Haven
Reuben Carter	31	5	11½	Canterbury	Canterbury	Dark	Black	Black	Mar. 11, '77	D War	Canterbury
Drummer John Avery	17	5	5	Norwalk	Norwalk	Light	Light	Dark	Mar. 1779	D War	Norwalk
William Kane[5]	16	5	2	Fradericks-burg, N. Y.	N. Milford	Light	Grey	Brown	Feb. 1, 1781	3 years	N. Milford
Fif Frederick Whipple[6]	17	5	4½	Norwich	Norwich	Dark	Dark	Black	Feb. 1781	D War	Norwich
Isaac Higgans[7]	17	5	7	Stratford	Stratford	Light	Light	Brown	July 5, 1781	3 years	Fairfield
Private Anor Adee	22	5	11	Woodbury	Woodbury	Dark	Grey	D Brown	May 12, 1777	D War	Woodbury
Reuben Adams	16	5	5	Voluntown	Voluntown	Light	Light	Brown	Dec. 20, 1780	3 years	Voluntown

Ephraim Bates[8]	30	5	7½	Colchester	Litchfield	Light	Light	Light	May 1, 1781	3 years	Litchfield
Ephraim Burgess	41	5	4	Harwich, Mass.	Enfield	Light	Light	Brown	Feb. 1, 1781	3 years	Enfield
William Burrus	21	5	9	Killingly	Killingly	Light	Light	Dark	Jan. 1, 1781	3 years	Killingly
Osias Butts	17	5	5	Canterbury	Canterbury	Light	Light	L B	Mar. 15, '82	1 year	Canterbury
Comfort Chapman[9]	21	6		Norwich	Norwich	Light	Light	Dark	Feb. 1, '81	3 years	Norwich
Eliphalet Carpenter	17	5	8	Woodstock	Woodstock	Light	Light	L Brown	Jan. 9, 1781	3 years	Woodstock
David Clark	24	5	5½	Union	Wethington Mass.	Light	Dark	Dark	Feb. 1777	D War	
Ephraim Coy	21	5	10	Preston	Norfolk	Light	Light	Light	April 1777	3 years	N. Haven
John Dingly	36	5	5	Windham	Windham	Dark	Light	Brown	Nov. 1781	D War	Windham
James Duggan	36	5	3½	Ireland	Canterbury	Dark	Dark	Dark	Jan. 1, 1781	3 years	Canterbury
Moses Elsworth	34	5	7½	E. Windsor	E. Windsor	Light	Light	L Brown	April 1777	D War	E. Windsor
Jonathan Edwards[10]	22	5	9½	Rochester, Mass.	Rochester Mass.	Light	Dark	L Brown	Jan. 1777	D War	
Samuel Eells[11]	25	5	10	Milford	Milford	Light	Light	L Brown	April 1777	D War	Milford
Aron Eaton	19	5	7	No. 1, N. H.	Kent	Light	Light	L Brown	Apr. 8, 1782	1 year	Danbury
Thomas Frink				Conn.							
Amos Holden	20			Glastenbury	Glastenbury	Dark	Grey	Light	June 15, 1782	3 years	Bolton
Samuel Hull	16	5	6	Milford	N. Milford	Dark		Black	Feb. 1, 1781	3 years	N. Milford
Philip Hill[12]	39	5	4½	Lebanon	Lebanon	Light	Light	D Brown	Jan. 1, '81	3 years	Lebanon
David Hammond	17	5	4½	Woodstock	Woodstock	Light	Light	L Brown	Mar. 15, 81	3 years	Woodstock
Jacob Haladay	24	5	7½	Simsbury	Simsbury	Light	Dark	L Brown	Dec. 18, '80	3 years	Simsbury
David Hodge[13]	27	5	4½	Milford	Milford	Dark	Dark	D Brown	Apr. 1, 77	D War	Milford
Joel Hait	25	5	8	Stamford	Stamford	Light	Light	L Brown	Feb. '77	D War	Stanford
Samuel Jenkins	17	5	3	Norwalk	Norwalk	Dark	Light	D Brown	June 1780	D War	Norwalk
Justin St John	34	5	5	N. Haven	Norwalk	Light	Dark	Black	Mar. 1777	D War	Norwalk
Chandler Judd											
Jedediah Kimball[14]	32	5	5	Norwich	Norwich	Dark	Dark	Dark	Mar. 15, '81	3 years	Norwich
Uriah Kecler	23	5	10	Norwalk	Norwalk	Light	Grey	Light	Apr. 19, '77	D War	Norwalk
Abner Lord	20	5	3	Lime	Lime	Light	Light	Brown		D War	
James Liberty	31	5	4	N. Y. City	Woodbury	Black	Black	Black	April '77	D War	Woodbury
Weight Lewis[15]	21	5	6	N. Town	N. Town	Dark	Dark	Dark	May 1, '79	D War	N. Town
Joel Mosher	21	5	6	Stratford	Stratford	Light	Light	L Brown	April '77	D War	Stratford
David Mattesson[16]	22	6		N. London	Norwich	Light	Light	D Brown	Feb. 1, '81	3 years	Norwich
Abraham Murrey	44	5	10	Providence, R. I.	Danbury	Dark	Dark	Dark	April '77	D War	Stratford

Occupation.—[1]C & Joiner [2]Weaver [3]Joiner [4]Taylor [5]Hatter [6]Joiner [7]Weaver [8]C Warner [9]Carpenter [10]Cocker (?) [11]Cooper [12]Weaver [13]Weaver [4]Cooper [15]Shoe Mak[r] [16]C Winder

Mens Names	Age	Size Feet	Inches	Born	Residence	Complection	Eyes	Hair	Inlistments When	Term	What Town
Private Stephen Meigs	18	5	8	Guilford	Guilford	Light	Light	Brown	May 1780	D War	Guilford
Peter Mix	25	5	5	Ginea	Durham	Black	Black	Black	May 5, '77	D War	Branford
Cato Negro	18	5	9	E. Windsor	E. Windsor	Black	Black	Black	July 5, '81	3 years	E Windsor
Aron Parks	16	5	3½	Preston	Ashford	Light	Light	L B	Nov. 26, '80	D War	Ashford
Joseph Phinney[1]	30	5	9	Lebanon	Lebanon	Light	Light	Dark	Jan. 1 '81	3 years	Lebanon
Thomas Palmer	22	5	10	Hartford	Rockehill	Dark	Dark	Dark	Apr. 10, '82	3 years	N. Milford
Ebenezer Platt	18	5	5	Danbury	Danbury	Light	Light	Red	Apr. 10, '82	1 year	Danbury
James Raymond	17	5	10½	Canterbury	Canterbury	Dark	Dark	Dark	Mar. 15, '82	1 year	Canterbury
Ethiel Scott	22	5	5	Waterbury	Harwinton	Light	Grey	Light	Apr. 19, '79	D War	
William Short	20	5	6½	Killingly	Killingly	Light	Light	L B	Mar. 6 '81	3 years	Killingly
Sariel Squires	19	5	7½	Ashford	E. Windsor	Dark	Dark	D B	Apr. 20, '82	Dec. 31, '82	E. Windsor
Darius Trusdell	30	5	11	Pomfret	Woodstock	Dark	Dark	Dark	Jan. 11, '81	3 years	Woodstock
Enos Tuttle[2]	24	5	7	Norwalk	Norwalk	Dark	Black	Black	Aug. 15 '78	D War	Norwalk
Stephen Thompson	22	5	8	N. Haven	Waterbury	Dark	Black	Black	Mar. 1777	D War	Waterbury
Amos Temple	21	5	6	Stratford	Stratford	Copper	Black	Black	June 1777	D War	Stratford
Eli Tuller	42	5	4½	Simsbury	Simsbury	Dark	Dark	Dark	Jan. 21, '81	3 years	Simsbury
Johnson Tiff	17	5	11½	Simsbury	Simsbury	Dark	Dark	L B	Jan. 11, '81	3 years	Simsbury
John F. Tone	24	5	4½	Germany	Volunton	Light	Light	L B	Jan. 5, '81	3 years	Voluntown
Jethro Toney	23	5	7	Woodbury	Woodbury	Copper	Dark	Black	April '77	D W	Woodbury
William Waterbury[3]	25	5	7½	Stamford	Stamford	Red	Grey	Brown	Apr. 11 '77	D War	Stanford
Nathan Walker	16	5	8	Woodbury	Woodbury	Light	Blue	L Brown	Sep. 1777	D War	Woodbury
Cato Wilborn	21	5	2½	Ginea	Durham	Black	Black	Black	May 1777	D War	Durham

Occupation.—[1]Weaver [2]Weaver [3]Shoe Maker

Size Roll of the 8th Company 3d Connecticut Regiment for the year 1782

[*State Library*, *Hebard Papers.*]

Other monthly muster rolls in the same volume show that the regiment was commanded by Col. Samuel B. Webb; that the Captain was Hezekiah Rogers; and that the following persons were at sundry times Lieutenants: John Hobart, William Lynn, John Mix, Nathan H. Whiting, Benjamin Dimmick.

SHORT LEVIES, 1781.

The United States D[r] To the State of Connecticut, for the Pay of sundry Persons who joined the third Regiment as short Levies, in the year 1781 — Viz —

Names	when entered the Service	when Discharged
Noah U. Norton	July 5	Oct. 16
John Dailey	" 23	Dec. 14
Lemuel Gillet	" 20	" 13
Abiel Hinsdale	" 20	" 24
Timothy Catlin	" 15	Sept. 9
Josiah Gaylord	" 16	Dec. 13
Jesse Seymour	" 11	Oct. 3
Joseph Rogers	" 15	Nov. 29
Jonathan Wright	" 30	Dec. 31
Eleazer Payne	" 28	" 13
Elias Bascomb	" 28	" 31
Joseph Allen Jun[r]	Sept. 7	" 23
Isaac Snow	" 7	" 24
Russell Pratt	" 7	" 16
Robert Follet	Aug. 29	" 16
Moses Wright	July 29	Jan. 1
Nathan Hovey	Aug. 23	Dec. 1
Jonathan Babcock	July 27	" 25
Jonathan Pasco	" 30	" 8
William Leach	Aug. 1	" 13
Christopher Willoughbey	Sept. 8	Nov. 12
Ebenezer Rockwell	Aug. 5	" 12
Simeon (for Elijah) Hunt	July 27	Dec. 8
Bliss Willoughbey	" 26	" 13
Joseph Bacon	" 27	" 24
John Ives	Sept. 8	" 12
George Burrows	" 8	Oct. 3
Noah Barber Jun[r]	July 29	Dec. 2
Hervy Whiting	" 15	" 24
William Mattison	Aug. 26	" 30
Jonathan Bemont	" 8	" 25
Charles Warner	July 27	" 13
Benjamin Loomiss	Aug. 11	Nov. 25
Daniel Eaton	" 8	Dec. 24
John Marsh	" 27	" 24
Michael Freeman	" 26	" 24
Caleb Burrows	" 20	" 26
Joseph Allen	" 7	" 31
Samuel Kimball	July 15	" 16
William Porter	" 27	" 24
Ephraim Kingsbury	" 27	Nov. 28
James Carpenter	" 27	Dec. 21
Josiah Fassett	Sept. 5	" 24
Reuben Grant	July 24	" 26
Helmont Kellogg	" 15	" 24
Tracey Cleveland	Sept. 5	" 13
Stephen Long	July 27	" 30
Abner Richmond	" 27	" 13
Archelaus Deane	Oct. 10	" 13
Samuel Strong	July 24	" 30
Hezekiah Grant	" 24	" 24
Ashley Rathburn	Aug. 26	" 14
Harba Childs	July 27	" 29

[*Comptroller's Office, Haskell's Receipts.*]

SHORT LEVIES, 1782.

Return of Levies who served in the 3d Connect Regmt part of the Year 1782

Names	Commenct of Pay	Expiration
Jacob Haskell	May 1	Dec. 29
Samuel Bliss	6	"
Samuel Parks	Apr. 20	"
John Bliss	May 1	"
Moses Barnard	Apr. 17	"
Bereiah Bliss	27	"
Daniel Lyman	"	"
John Haskell	June 5	"
Andrew Hazen	May 16	"
Joshua Olmsted	June 17	9
Noah Norton	July 1	"
David Hubble	"	"
George Foott	Apr. 27	20
Nehemiah Seeley	30	9
Amos Gustin	June 10	10
Daniel Knight	May 1	26
Benoni Robbins	"	22
Janna Willcox	"	28
Elisha Catlin	23	28
Ebenez Durffee	Apr. 29	5
Elijah Durffee	May 13	9
Noah Kesley	Apr. 19	24
Jacob Fenton	29	9
James Bliss	May 15	5
Hezh Terrell	Apr. 24	31
Nehemiah Barnes	June 29	31
Edward Duncan	May 11	"
Charles Lewis	"	"
Aaron Wayley	June 3	"
Zacheus Gillett	May 9	10
Benoni Gillett	"	"
Nathan Fenton	June 6	9
Sorel Squire	"	31
Nathaniel Conant	20	6
Levi Hall	May 4	31
Simeon Stimpson	Feb. 3	Nov. 8
Daniel Jackson	May 15	Dec. 9
Miles Bennett	"	"
Jonathan Beamont	July 17	6
Nathan Potter	Apr. 29	Oct. 7
Royal Manton	July 1	Nov. 7
Adonijah Chapman	Apr. 15	Oct. 2
Wm Cooke	June 1	"
Jonathan Curtiss	Apr. 9	June 12
Reubin Clark	1	Aug. 11
Ebenr Chapman	May 24	Oct. 2
David Gardner	Apr. 13	"
David Hawley	May 11	Dec. 15

[*State Library, Revolution* 25]

FOURTH REGIMENT—COL. BUTLER.

[*See Record of Connecticut Men in the Revolution, page 337.*]

RETURN, 1781.

Return of the Non Commiss^{d} Officers & Men in the 4th Conn^{t} Reg^{t}

Names	Rank	Date of Inlistments	Term they Engag'd for	Town for which they Serve
Edw. Miller	Serg M^{r}	Ap^{l} 19 '77	War	Middletown
Oliver Munn	Fife	Mar^{h} 7 '79	"	"
Geo. Doolittle	Serg^{t}	May 1 '78	"	"
Jabez Atkins	Private		"	"
Willm Bacon	"		"	"
Saml Frothingham	"		"	"
Jon^{n} Tayler	"	Jany 1 '77	"	"
Joseph Willis	"		"	"
Aaron Rawles	"		"	"
John Codner	"	July 2^{d} '81	6 Months	"
Lem^{l} Wilcox	"		War	"
Mich^{l} Maloney	"	July 14 '81	6 Months	"
Jon^{n} Hubbard	"	Ap^{l} 1st '77	War	"
Nat^{l} W Benton	"	June 1 '80	"	"
Jacob Gilson	"	Jany 17 '77	"	"
Isaac Roberts	"	Mar^{h} 16 '80	"	[ ]
Peter Freeman	"		"	[ ]
Cuff Liberty	"	Mar^{h} 1 '78	[ ]	"
Phil^{n} Freeman	"		[ ]	"
Cuff Freeman	"		[ ]	"
Zach^{s} Stow	"	Mar^{h} 12 '78	[ ]	"
Saml Lucas	Serg^{t}	Jany 31 '77	[ ]	Durham
Gid^{n} Chittendon	"	Octr 9 '77	[ ]	"
Phin^{s} Squires	"	May 5 '77	"	"
Nat^{l} Brown	F Maj^{r}	Decr 13 '77	"	"
[ ]ry[ ]ssetter*	Serg^{t}	Jany 1 '77	[ ]	"
John [ ]shop †	Corp^{l}	Decr 25 '77	"	"
Miles Cook	Drum	Ap^{l} 1 '80	"	"
Silas Stanbrough	fife	Jany 31 '81	3 Years	"
Lem^{l} Stanbrough	Drum	Feby 2^{d} '81	3 Years	"
Schuyler Goddard	Priv^{e}	Feby 1 '78	War	"
John Meeker	"	Feby 27 '77	"	"
Willm Johnson	"	May 24 '77	"	"
Asher Squire	"	May 5 '77	"	"
Dudley Squire	"	June 15 '81	1 Year	"
Willm Carr	"	Ap^{l} 1 '77	War	"
Warren Murray	Corp.	Feby 10 '77	"	"
Robt Carr	Priv^{e}	Jany 31 '81	3 Years	"
Nat^{l} Clark	"	Feby 9 '81	3 Y^{s}	"
Jon^{n} Loveland	"	Mar^{h} 15 '81	3 Y^{s}	"

---

* Bryant Rossetter † John Bishop

Names	Rank	Date of Inlistments	Term they Engag'd for	Town for which they Serve
Eben^{r} Carr	Priv^{e}	Jany 31 '81	3 Years	Durham
Clement Carr	"	"	"	"
Sharp Camp	"	Decr 1 '77	War	"
Cato Wilbrow	"	Mar^{h} '77	"	"
Ahim^{s} Punderson	Serg^{t}	Decr 13 '76	"	N. Haven
David Alcock	"	Jany 1 '77	"	"
Edwd Baker	"	Novr 24 '76	"	"
Geo. Cook	fife	Feby 1 '77	"	"
[ ]ld*	fife	Decr 13 '76	"	"
[ ]d	Corp^{l}	Mar^{h} 1 '77	"	"
[ ] Howell†	"	Dec^{r} '76	"	"
[ ]	Private	Ap^{l} '77	"	"
[ ]	"	Nov^{r} '76	"	"
[ ]ael Dodge	"	Ap^{l} '77	"	"
Amos Frost	[ ]	[ ] '77	"	"
John O Briant	[ ]	[ ] '77	"	"
Abel Stockwell	[ ]	[ ] '78	"	"
Asahel Salmon	[ ]	[ ] '77	"	"
Moses Potter	"	[ ] '77	"	"
Ambrose Smith	"	[ ]	"	"
Amos Tinker	"	[ ]	"	"
Jared Blakslee	"	[ ]	"	"
Martin Clark	"	Fe[ ]	"	"
Ja^{s} Sales	"	Jany 27 '77	"	"
Benajah Bracket	"	Aug[ ] '79	"	"
Medad Potter	"		"	"
Abr^{m} Cooper	"		"	"
Hez^{h} Bracket	"		"	"
Steph^{n} Shattuck	Serg^{t}		"	"
Amos Mallery	"		"	"
Robt Marsh	Private		"	"
Ward Peck	"		"	"
Elijah Wolcut	"		"	"
Tim^{y} Mansfield	"	Jany 10 '77	"	"
Dav^{d} Bradley	"		"	"
Willm Cook	"		"	"
Robt Climet	"		"	"
Abr^{m} Sugden	"	Feby 8 '77	"	"
Eph^{m} Thomas	"		"	"
Jesse Smith	Serg^{t}	Jany 4 '77	"	"
Daniel Moss	Private	Jany 1 '77	"	"
Saml Thomas	"	Decr 14 '76	"	"
Augus^{ts} Peck	"	Decr 14 '77	"	"
Thomas Sanford	"	May 20 '77	"	"
Anthony M Daniel	"	July 6 '78	"	"
Benajah Wolcut	"	Jany 20 '78	"	"
Amos Warner	"	July 6 '80	"	"
Caleb Blakslee	Drum^{r}	Augt 10 '79	"	"
Simeon Bishop	Private		"	"
Elnathan Tolles	"		"	"
Dav^{d} Eagleston	"		"	"
Jno Nales	"	May 2 '78	"	"
Bristol Baker	"	May '77	"	"
And^{w} Tack	"	May '77	"	"
Jack Little	"		"	"
Lewis Martin	"		"	"

* Charles Mansfield † Nicholas Howell

Names	Rank	Date of Inlistments	Term they Engag'd for	Town for which they Serve
Sharp Rogers	Private	Feb^{y} '77	War	N. Haven
Jess^{s} (?) Sill *	"		"	"
Ezekiel Toppand	"	Decr 13 '76	"	"
Hector Williams	"		"	"
Jabez Lord	"	May 1 '78	"	"
Abr^{m} Johnson	"	Decr 14 '76	"	"
John Wilson	"	Feby 1 '77	"	"
R^{d} L[ ]nsberry †	"		"	"
Jer. Wooding	"	May 10 '77	"	"
Ja^{s} Goldsmith	Serg^{t}	Feby 10 '77	"	Milford
Willm Ovitt	"		"	"
John Belding	Private		"	"
Elijah Bryan	"		"	"
Tim^{y} Johnson	"		"	"
Phinehas Johnson	"		"	"
John Peck	"		"	"
Dav^{d} Hodge	"	Ap^{l} 12 '77	"	"
Ichabod Walden	"	Jany 27 '81	"	"
Benjn Pritchard	"	Ap^{l} 1 '77	"	"
John Stewart	"	Jany 1 '77	"	"
Jared Hitchcock	Corp^{l}	Ap^{l} 25 '77	"	"
Abel Hitchcock	"	May '77	"	"
Isaac Northrup	"	Ap^{l} 25 '77	"	"
Joseph Goldsmith	Private		"	"
Titus Hine	"		"	"
Benjn Burns	"		"	"
Willm Goldsmith	"	Ap^{l} 15 '77	"	"
Job Cesar	"	Mar^{h} '77	"	"
[ ]be	"		"	"
[ ]rus	"	Nov^{r} '76	"	"
[ ]hapman	"	May '77	"	"
[ ] Gibbs ‡	"	May '77	"	"
[ ]ll^{m} So[ ]s §	"	Mar^{h} '77	"	"
[ ]ongo Z[ ]	"	Ma^{h} '77	"	"
Juba Freeman	"	May '77	"	"
Jasper Jones	"	Novr 24 '76	"	Stratford
Gershom Bardsly	"	[ ] 30 '77	"	"
David Hawley	"	[ ] '81	6 Months	"
Benjn Treadwell	"	[ ] '81	3 Years	"
Isaac Hawley	"	[ ] '81	6 Months	"
Joseph Wakely	"		War	"
Sam Gregory	"	July [ ] '81	6 Months	"
Nat^{l} Clark	"	July 5, '81	6 Months	"
Hen^{y} Baley	"		War	"
Hez^{h} Mitchel	"	July 28 '81	6 Months	"
Saml Chapman	"	Mar^{h}. 19 '79	War	Fairfield
Asa Sherwood	fife		"	"
Joseph Elwood	Priv^{e}	Jany 1 '81	3 Years	"
Isaac Higgins	"	July 5 '81	3 Y^{s}	"
David Jones	"		War	"
Ned Freedom	"	May '78	"	"
Step^{n} Hall	Serg^{t}	Jany 10 '81	3 Years	"
Enos Tuttle	Priv^{e}		War	Norwalk
John Parrot	"	July 21 '78	"	"
John Rogers	"	Ap^{l} '78	"	"
Sol^{o} Soutice	"		"	"

* Jeff^{y} (?) Sill † Richard Lounsberry ‡ Peter Gebbs § Willm Sowers

Names	Rank	Date of Inlistments	Term they Engag'd for	Town for which they Serve
Jon^{n} Newman	Priv^{e}	Jany 1 '81	3 Y^{s}	Ridgefield
Harry Williams	"	Feb^{y} '81	War	"
Benjn Bennit	Serg^{t}	Novr 25 '76	"	"
Jacob Patchen	Private	Mar^{h} 1 '81	3 Y^{s}	Reading
Josiah Hendrick	"	Jany 1 '81	3 Y^{s}	"
Danl Couch	"	Jany 1 '81	3 Y^{s}	"
Ja^{s} Dixon	"		War	"
Wm Dewen	"	Augt 24 '81	6 Months	"
Ezra Ketcham	"		War	Danbury
Jeremiah Rosel	"	May 1 '78	"	"
Edwd Goddard	Corp^{l}	May 5 '79	"	"
Brigs Ingersol	Private	June 25 '81	6 Months	New Milford
Nat^{l} Porter	"		War	"
Thad^{s} Jacklin	"	July '81	6 Months	"
Willm Cain	Fife	Feby 1 '81	3 Y^{s}	"
Jno Davenport	Corp^{l}		War	"
Jno Murray	Private	July 13 '81	6 Months	"
Salmon Bostick	"		War	"
Damon R Converse	"	July 13 '81	6 Months	"
Hanford Newell	"	July 5 '81	6 Months	"
Benjn Ruggles	"	July 5 '81	6 Months	"
Jared Hotchkiss	"	July 3 '81	6 Months	"
Saml Nichols	"	July 2 '81	6 Months	"
Sol^{o} Warner	"	July 3 '81	6 Months	"
Joseph Tomlinson	"	March 20 '77	War	Derby
John Hatchet	"	Jany 20 '77	"	"
Eli Hull	"	Mar^{h} 10 '80	"	"
Willm Smith	"		"	"
Prince Freeman	"	Feby 1 '81	War	"
Edwd Warren	"		6 Months	"
Ja^{s} Canada	"		"	"
Joseph White	"		"	"
Danl Brown	Serg^{t}	Novr 25 '76	"	"
Eben^{r} Durand	Private	Jany 1 '78	"	"
Eben^{r} Botchford	"	July 7 '81	6 Months	"
Reub^{n} Chapman	"	Feby 19 '81	3 Y^{s}	"
Reub^{n} Blake	"	Feby 20 '78	War	"
Thos Phillips	"	Decr 27 '76	"	"
Shub^{l} Johnson	"	Feb^{y} '77	"	"
Ezra Foot	"		"	"
David Hull	"	Mar^{h} 20 '78	"	"
Jon^{n} Brown	"	Novr 24 '76	"	"
Richd Pitts	"	Decr 27 '80	3 Y^{s}	"
Saml Bristol	"	July 17 '81	6 Months	Woodbury
John Herrick	Corp^{l}	Novr 24 '76	War	"
Zach^{h} How	Private	July '81	6 Months	"
Joseph Brooks	"	Augt 13 '81	6 Months	"
Amos Davis	"	Jany 1 '81	3 Years	"
Justus Taylor	"	June 20 '81	3 Y^{s}	Washington
Wm Lament	"	June 15 '81	3 Y^{s}	"
Eleazer Curtiss	"	June 11 '81	6 Months	"
John Davidson	"	May 1 '78	War	"
Ezekiel Newton	"	June 22 '81	6 Months	"
John Jordan	"	Augt 17 '81	6 Months	"
Isaac Davidson	Serg^{t}		War	"
John McLean	"	May 19 '77	"	Salisbury
Jacob McLean	"	Feby 15 '78	"	"

Names	Rank	Date of Inlistments	Term they Engag'd for	Town for which they Serve
[ ]iam[l] Tarry	Serg[t]	May 21 '77	War	Salisbury
[ ][s] Bradley *	"	May '77	"	"
[ ] Hull †	"	March 1 '78	"	"
[ ]enton	Private		"	"
[ ] Cool ‡	"		"	"
[ ] Griswold	"		"	"
[ ] Griswold	"		"	"
[ ] Whitney	"		"	"
[ ]sa Owen §	"	May 8 '78	"	"
Champ[n] Ackley	Corp[l]		"	"
W[m] Tupper	Q M [ ]	May 28 '77	"	"
Daniel Hull	Corp		"	"
Martin Tubbs	"	Feb[y] 15 '77	"	"
Phinehas Strong	"	May 14 '77	"	"
Jon[n] Hull	"	Feb [ ] '78	"	"
Simeon Meigs	Priv[e]	May 5 '77	"	"
W[m] Yates	"	May 7 '77	"	"
Amasa Grinnol	Corp[l]	May '77	"	"
Artemas Blodget	Priv[e]	May '77	"	"
Curtiss Chappel	"		"	"
Himan Cool	"	Feb[y] '77	"	"
Nat[l] Emorson	"	May '77	"	"
W[m] Eldredge	"	June '78	"	"
H[y] Fitzgerald	"	May '77	"	"
Benj[n] Graves	"	May '77	"	"
Will[m] White	"	May 10 '77	"	"
Bille Munger	"	Ap[l] '78	"	"
John Lerow	"	Mar[h] 16 '77	"	Litchfield
Isaac Cluff	"	Dec[r] 5 '76	"	"
Sam[l] Rossetter	"		"	"
John Bricks	"	May '78	"	"
Joseph Colyer	"		"	"
Phinehas Parker	"	July 1 '78	6 Months	Watertown
Alex[r] Judd	"		War	"
Medad Merrills	"	June 5 '78	"	Waterbury
Elkanah Smith	"	July 10 '81	6 Months	"
Barn[s] Clark	"		War	"
Jonah Webb	"	July 4 '81	6 Months	Cheshire
David Barns	"	Jan[y] 1 '77	War	"
Joel Barns	"	Feb[y] 27 '81	3 Years	"
Sam[l] Stone	"	Feb[y] 1 '81	War	"
Reuben Moss	Corp[l]	Ap[l] 3 '77	War	"
Benj[n] Bristol	"	Feb[y] 20 '77	War	"
Amos Mix	Priv[e]		War	"
Edmond Fields	Serg[t]	Mar[h] 1 '78	War	Wallingford
Joseph Clark	"	Feb[y] 1 '77	"	"
Dan[l] Bradley	"		"	"
Isaac Parker	"	Ap[l] '77	"	"
Sam[l] Collins	"	May 5 '77	"	"
Abr[m] Parker	Corp[l]		"	"
Edm[d] Merriam	"	May 20 '77	"	"
Eph[m] Merriam	fife	May 5 '77	"	"
Jotham Rice	Priv[e]	Feb[y] 9 '77	"	"
Tim[o] Parker	"	Ap[l] 14 '77	"	"
Will[m] Prout	"	Mar[h] 2 '78	"	"
John Parker	"	Feb[y] 9 '77	"	"

* Zenas Bradley † Henry Hull ‡ Isaac Cool § Asa Owen

Names	Rank	Date of Inlistments	Term they Engag'd for	Town for which they Serve
Joel Cook	Corp^{l}	May 10 '77	War	Wallingford
Johnson Cook	Priv^{e}	Jany 20 '77	"	"
Warren Cook	"		"	"
Jotham Hall	"		"	"
Thad^{s} Todd	"	Ap^{l} '77	"	"
Moses Hale	"	Mar^{h} 2 '78	"	"
Orange Munson	Drum	Feby 10 '78	"	"
Chas Merriman	D Maj^{r}	Jany 23 '77	"	"
Nash Yale	Priv^{e}	Ap^{l} 1 '77	"	"
Lemuel Cook	"	June 30 '81	6 Months	"
Pratt Jones	"	Feby 10 '78	War	"
Chas London	"	Feby 15 '78	"	"
Elihu Cook	"	Mar^{h} 7 '77	"	"
Amasa Thorp	"	June 21 '77	"	"
Amos Thorp	"	June 21 '77	"	"
Zenas Mix	"	June 1 '77	"	"
Benjn Ford	"	Jany 5 '78	"	"
Jon^{n} Ford	"	Jany 12 '78	"	"
David Atkins	"		"	"
Jno Verguson	"	Ap^{l} 25 '77	"	"
Elisha Bishop	"		"	"
Ja^{s} Coban	"	Ap^{l} 3 '77	"	"
Isaac Hawley	"	Augt 6 '81	6 Months	"
Levi Robinson	"		War	"
Jesse Vose	Corp^{l}	Mar^{h} 1 '78	"	"
Lent Munson	Drum	Mar^{h} '78	"	"
Dick Freedom	Private	Mar^{h} '78	"	"
Saml Brown	Serg^{t}	Feby 2 '77	"	Branford
Luther Page	"	Ap^{l} 21 '77	"	"
Jairus Harrison	"	Ap^{l} 21 '77	"	"
Rufus Whedon	"	May 9 '77	"	"
Saml Wardell	fife	Jany 16 '78	"	"
[ ]l Potter *	Drum	Ap^{l} 1 '77	"	"
[ ]iel Smith †	Private		"	"
[ ] Potter	"		"	"
[ ] Butler	"	May '77	"	"
[ ] Palmer	"	May '77	"	"
[ ]on^{n} Finch ‡	"	Ap^{l} 1 '77	"	"
Ezekiel Butler	"	Feby 10 '78	"	"
Jordan Smith	"	Ap^{l} 26 '77	"	"
David Rogers	"	Feby 10 '78	"	"
Joseph Hawkins	"	June 7 '78	"	"
Roswell Whedon	"	Decr 14 '76	"	"
Hermon Rose	Corp^{l}	Feby 12 '77	"	"
Hen^{y} Johnson	Private	Ap^{l} '77	"	"
Saml Barker	Serg^{t}	Jany 1 '81	3 Years	"
John Eberhard	"	Jany 7 '77	War	"
Saml Hoadley	Corp^{l}	Feby 2 '77	"	"
Ja^{s} Cooper	Priv^{e}	Ap^{l} 3 '77	"	"
John Garrett	"	Mar^{h} 8 '77	"	"
Reuben Frisbie	"	Feby 18 '77	"	"
Willm Cooper	fife	Decr 1 '77	"	"
Ziba Robinson	Private		6 Months	"
Cesar Bagdon	"	Ap^{l} '77	War	"
James Dinah	"	May '77	"	"
Prince George	"	Feb^{y} '77	"	"

* Joel Potter † Jehiel Smith ‡ Jonathan Finch

Names	Rank	Date of Inlistments	Term they Engag'd for	Town for which they Serve
Peter Lion	Private	June '77	War	Branford
Pomp Liberty	"	Marh '77	"	"
Peter Mix	"	Marh '77	"	"
Joseph Otis	"	Marh '77	"	"
Dick Violet	"	Marh '77	"	"
Heman Rogers	Corpl	Apl 25 '77	"	"
David Dowd	Private	Feby 1 '78	"	Guilford
Timy Scranton	"	Apl 12 '77	"	"
Timy Stevens	"		"	"
Benjn Watrous	"		"	"
Joel Johnson	"	Feby 13 '81	3 Years	"
Timy Shelley	"	July 5 '81	6 Months	"
Abr Norton	"	Apl 6 '77	War	"
Thos Wheeler	Corpl	Apl 10 '77	"	"
John Lewis	Private	July '81	6 Months	"
Jehiel Munger	"	July 5 '81	6 Months	"
Presto Kelsey	"	July 5 '81	6 Months	"
Chandr Benton	"	Marh 7 '77	War	"
Isaiah Atkins	Corpl		"	"
Hy McLean	Private		"	"
Benjn Welton	"	May '77	"	"
Eber Hall	"	Apl 2 '81	6 Months	"
Jehiel Dowd	"	Feby 1 '80	War	"
Stephn Meigs	"	May 1 '80	"	"
Bartt Rawlinson	"	Marh 9 '81	3 Years	"
Reubn Rawlinson	"	Marh 5 '81	3 Ys	"
Ira Atkins	"	Apl 3 '81	3 Ys	"
Reuben Everts	"	Feby 1 '81	3 Ys	"
Gilbert Graves	"	Feby 1 '81	3 Ys	"
Jehiel Wilcox	"	Feby 1 '81	3 Ys	"
Danl Newton	"	July '81	6 Months	"
Zachs Dowd	"	July 5 '81	6 Months	"
Davd Thompson	Sergt	Jany 25 '77	War	"
Torry Scranton	"	May '77	"	"
Thos Cook	Private		"	Killingsworth
Willm Wellman	"		"	"
Jesse Graham	Drum		"	Say Brook
Joseph Whittlesey	Prive	Decr 13 '80	3 Years	"
Giles Clark	"	July 2 '81	6 Months	"
Jas Grant	"	Feby 1 '81	3 Years	"
Gidn Buckingham	"	Feby 1 '81	3 Ys	"
Saml. Comstock	"	Marh 1 '81	3 Ys	"
Robt Newell	"	Jany 1 '81	3 Ys	"
Oliver White	"	Apr. 21 '77	War	"
Cyrus Graham	"	Feby 1 '77	"	"
Simon Hough	"	July 1 '81	1 Year	"
Richd Stokes	"	July 6 '81	6 Months	"
Thos Freeman	"		War	"
Const Chapman	Sergt	Jany 1 '81	3 Years	"
John Lay	Private	Jany 15 '81	3 Ys	Lyme
Rufus Holdridge	Drum	Marh 1 '81	3 Years	Groton
Cato Robinson	Private	Apl '77	War	"
John Nugen	"	Jany 10 '77	"	Stonington
Saml Hill	"	Jany 29 '81	6 Months	Lebanon
Benjn Bissel	"	June 29 '81	6 Months	"
Nathan Law	"	Jany 1 '81	1 Year	"
Benjn Bissel	"	July 4 '81	6 Months	"

Names	Rank	Date of Inlistments	Term they Engag'd for	Town for which they Serve
[ ]erry Reed	Private	Jany 16 '81	3 Years	Lebanon
[ ]nj^{n} Bennit	"	June 4 '81	6 Months	"
[ ] Wadsworth	"	June 29 '81	6 Months	"
[ ] Moulton	"	June 12 '81	1 Year	"
[ ] Hill	"	Feby 8 '81	3 Years	"
[ ]d Davidson	"	Feby 8 '81	3 Years	"
[ ]ep^{n} Buckingham	"	July 25 '81	6 Months	"
Ezekiel Lyman	"	July 26 '81	6 Months	"
Danl Puffer	"	July 26 '81	6 Months	"
Prince Williams	"	June 26 '81	6 Months	"
Ja^{s} Sharp	"	June 30 '81	6 Months	"
Joseph Abby	"	Jany 4 '81	3 Years	Windham
Daniel Neff	"	July 3 '81	6 Months	"
Abner Lilley	"	Decr 15 '80	3 Years	"
Asa Cleaveland	"	June 25 '81	6 Months	"
Danl Woodward	"	Novr 24 '80	3 Years	"
Phillip H Stish	"	June 1 '78	War	"
Juba Dyer	"	Feb^{y} '81	3 Years	"
Prince Johnson	"	Decr 1 '80	3 Years	"
John Dingley	"		War	"
Elisha Back	"	Mar^{h} 3 '81	3 Years	"
Salathiel Neff	"	June 3 '81	6 Months	"
James Dean	"	Mar^{h} 20 '81	2 Years	"
Jesse Gilbert	"		War	"
Chester Lilley	"	July 1 '81	6 Months	"
Elias Upton	"	July 1 '81	6 Months	"
Lothrop Frink	"	Novr 24 '80	3 Years	"
Enos Robins	"	June 26 '81	1 Year	"
Nat^{l} Abby	"	Jany 15 '81	3 Years	"
Chas Ripley	"	Decr 25 '80	3 Y^{s}	"
Eleaz^{r} Robinson	"	Novr 25 '80	3 Y^{s}	"
Jedediah Hibbard	"	Decr 4 '80	3 Y^{s}	"
Oliver Parish	"	July 1 '81	6 Months	"
Zacheus Hovey	"	July 3 '81	6 Months	"
James L Flint	Serg^{t}	May 1 '78	War	"
Sol^{o} Bixbee	Private	May 1 '81	3 Years	Stafford
Elijah Norton	"	July 1 '81	6 Months	Hebron
Henry Booth	Serg^{t}	Mar^{h} 1 '81	3 Y^{s}	Coventry
And^{w} Peters	Priv^{e}	Feby 8 '81	3 Y^{s}	"
Jon^{n} Ball	"	Feby 7 '81	3 Y^{s}	"
Jesse Peck	"	July 10 '81	6 months	Canterbury
Sol^{o} Goff	"	Feby 20 '81	3 Y^{s}	E^{t} Haddam
Ansel Patterson	"	Jany 2 '81	3 Y^{s}	"
John Lee	"	Ap^{l} 6 '81	3 Y^{s}	Ashford
Allen Prior	Serg^{t}	Jany 1 '81	War	Windsor
Tim^{o} Hoskins	Private	Decr 21 '81	3 Y^{s}	"
Calvin Wilson	"	Feby 20 '81	3 Y^{s}	"
Elihu Mather	Serg^{t}	Jany 1 '81	War	"
Jno Rowley	Private	Jany 1 '81	3 Y^{s}	"
Sampson Cuff	"	Jany 1 '81	3 Y^{s}	"
John Hosmer	"	Jany 1 '77	War	Hartford
Uri Hungerford	fife	Mar^{h} '81	War	Farmington
Roswell Cook	Drum	Jany 22 '81	"	"
Ichabod Bailey	Priv^{e}	Novr 10 '76	"	"
Josiah Cole	"	Decr 7 '76	"	"
Jno Horlehoy	"		"	Simsbury
Ja^{s} Eldiidge	"	Jany 2 '81	3 Y^{s}	"

Names	Rank	Date of Inlistments	Term they Engag'd for	Town for which they Serve
Dan[l] White	Priv[e]	July 1 '81	6 Months	Southington
Jam[s] Powers	"	July 6 '81	6 Months	"
Nathan Beacher	"	Feb[y] 1 '81	6 Months	"
Dav. Andrews	Fife	Jan[y] 1 '81	War	"
Ja[s] Powers	Private		"	"
Zeb[n] Dudley	"	Dec[r] 20 '80	3 Years	"
Elijah Bailey	"	July 1 '81	6 Months	"
Joseph Beacher	"	July 7 '81	6 Months	"
John Wellman	"	June 30 '81	6 Months	"
Isaac Hill	"	July 6 '81	6 Months	Ripton
Will[m] Bailey	"		War	Haddam
Jacob Rowell	"	July 1 '81	6 Months	Springfield
Jack Arrabas	"	Nov[r] '77	War	Fishkill
W[m] Smith	"		"	Wyoming
Leonard Cole	"		"	"
Matt[w] Grace	"		"	Fredericksburgh

S. Major	Q. M. Seg[t]	D. Major	Fife Maj[r]	Sergeants	Music	R & file	Total
1	1	1	1	40	20	389	453

Eben[r] Gray L[t] [ ]
& Com 4th C[ ]

[*Connecticut Historical Society.*]

SHORT TERM LEVIES, 1781.

Return of Men Engaged for 6 Months 4 Conn^{t} Reg^{t} Commanded by Col^{o} Zebulon Butler for 1781.

All ranking as privates

Names	Comment^{t} of Service	Time of Discharge	
Benjn Bissell	June 29	Jan. 1 '82	
Eleazer Curtiss	July 11	Dec. 8 '81	
Jared Hotchkiss	July 3	" 12	
Samuel Hills	June 29	" 26	
Zacheus Hovey	July 3	Jan. 1 '82	
Saml Nichols	July 2		Sick Virginia
Elijah Norton	July 1	Nov. 1 '81	
Oliver Parrish	July 1	Dec. 24	
Sol^{o} Warner	July 3	" 26	
Daniel Newton	July 2	" 13	
Thad^{s} Jacklin	July 12	" 13	
Salathiel Neff	July 3	" 20	
Michael Maloney	July 14	" 26	
John Codnor	July 2	" 31	
Nathan Beacher	July 1	" 30	
Preston Kelsey	July 5	" 2	
Jehiel Munger	July 5	" 24	
Jonah Webb	July 4	" 22	
Benj^{a} Bennet	July 4	" 30	
Heman Woodworth	June 29	Nov. 26	
Benj^{a} Bissell	July 4	Dec. 18	
Saml Bristol	July 17	Dec. 12	
Wolcut Blakley	July 17	Jan. 1 '82	
Giles Clark	July 2	Dec. 24 '81	
James Powers Jr.	July 16	Dec. 11	
Joseph Beecher	July 7	Dec. 31	
Jesse Peck	July 10	Dec. 8	
Asa Cleaveland	June 30	Dec. 16	
Brigs Ingorson	June 25	" 14	
Ezekiel Lyman Jr.	June 26	" 23	
Daniel Puffer	June 26	" 27	
Prince Williams	June 26	Jan. 1 '82	
Benjn Ruggles	July 5	Dec. 23, '81	
Hanford Nichols	July 5	Dec. 31	
Tim^{o} Shelly	July 5	Dec. 12	
John Maney or Murray	July 13	Dec. 25	
Damon R Converse	July 13		
Daniel Neff	July 2	Dec. 25	
Phinehas Parker	July 1	" 12	
Daniel Wright	July 1	" 12	
John Wellman	June 30	" 12	
Elijah Bailey	July 1	" 24	
John Lewis	June 30	" 24	
Zach^{s} Dowd	July 3	Jan. 1 '82	
Chester Lilly	July 3	Dec. 24 '81	
Elias Upton	July 1	" 24	
Eben^{r} Botchford	July 7	Nov. 27	
Lemuel Cook	June 30	Jan. 1 '82	
Saml Gregory	July 10	"	
Ezekiel Newton	June 22	"	
Zachariah How	June 22	Nov. 16 '81	

Names	Comment of Service	Time of Discharge
Joseph Brooks	Aug. 13	Jan. 1 '82
Isaac Hill	July 6	"
David Hawley	July 3	Nov. 24 '81
Isaac Hawley	July 5	Nov. 10
John Jordan	Aug. 17	Jan. 1 '82
Wm Dervan	Aug. 24	"
Zechariah Mitchel	July 28	"
Stepn Buckingham	July 25	Dec. 31 '81
Jacob Rowel	July 1	Dec. 1
James Thorp	June 30	Dec. 29
Richard Stokes	July 5	" 12
Nehemiah Clark	July 5	" 22
Elkanah Smith	July 10	Jan. 1 '82
Ziba Robinson	July 10	"
Isaac Hawley	Aug. 16	"

Jno Sherman P M 4th Connt Regt

[*State Library, Revolution 25; Comptroller's Office, Haskell's Receipts.*]

SHORT TERM LEVIES, 1782.

Short Levies 4 Connt Regt (filed "1782")

Samuel Androus
Moses Allyn
Daniel Burr
Abel Barns
Lemuel Barber
Caleb Burrows
Jeddiah Coe
Elisha Cone
Solomon Cone
James Cook
Solomon Cole
Job Cole
William Coltrain
Job Cole
Robert Follet
Israel Frisby
William Davis
Ebenezer Doolittle
Zephaniah Dowd
Edmund Griswold
Joel Gurnsey
James Hart
Increase Holcomb
Abner Hall
Asahel Hall
Chandler Judd
Elisha Marshall
Peter Morando
Stephen Moshier
Jacob Norton
Elijah Northrup
Daniel Peet
Charles Rice
Isaac Rexford
John Robinson
William Reed
Joseph Rockwell
Amos Rich
Jared Smith
Noah Spencer
Jonah Webb
Thomas Watson
William White
Joseph Wert

[*State Library, Revolution 25.*]

DESERTERS, 1781, 1782.

A Return of the Deserters from the 3d & 4th Connecticut Regimts since the Return for Settlmt of their Pay for the Service of 1780

Names	Regt	Time when	Towns they belong to
Samuel B Hotchkiss	3d	1 Feb. '81	Wallingford
Stephen Herrington	"	2 Mar. 81	Norwich
Daniel Pelton	"	16 Apr. 82	Chatham
Nehemiah Daniels	"	4 May 81	Colchester
Robert Freeman	"	20 June 81	Hartford
Elias Crow	"	5 July 81	"
Benjamin Kenny	"	19 July 81	"
Samuel Goff	"	1 Jan. 82	Chatham
Hezekiah Phelps	"	30 Mar. 82	Symsbury
Jehiel Gibbs	"	30 Mar. 82	Somers
William Flowers	"	10 Apr. 82	Hartford
Henry Watton	"	11 Apr. 82	Danbury
Gilbert Whitney	"	11 Apr. 82	Symsbury
Josiah Evans	"	11 Apr. 82	Hartford
John Hamilton	"	20 Apr. 82	New Fairfield
Jacob Hurd	4th	1 Jan. 81	Plainfield
John Grant	"	14 Feb. 81	Europe
Lot Chace	"	14 Feb. 81	Plainfield
Recompense Woodworth	"	1 Jan. 81	Lebanon
Serg. Elijah Spafford	"	15 July 81	Windham
Lemuel Chester	"	19 July 81	Norwich
Roswell Crocker	"	20 July 81	"
John Barker	"	1 Sep. 81	Pomfret
Isaac Bassett	"	26 Nov. 81	Canterbury
John Winship	"	1 Dec. 81	Norwich
Philimon Tiffany	"	1 Feb. 81	Lyme
Samuel Thompson	"	21 Feb. 82	Canterbury
John Casey Dm	"	30 Mar. 82	Providence
William Racke	"	2 Apr. 82	Bolton
Andrew Gay	"	11 Apr. 82	Stonington
Enos Mix	"	21 June 82	Wallingford
Austin Brown	"	25 July 82	Hebron

The above is a true Extract from the Regimental Book
Thos Grosvenor Lieut Col Com.

Camp Aug. 15, 1782

[*State Library, Revolution 25.*]

FIFTH REGIMENT—LT.-COL. SHERMAN

[*See Record of Connecticut Men in the Revolution, page 343.*]

SHORT TERM LEVIES, 1781.

Pay roll of the Short levies that serv'd in the 5th Connecticut Regiment (commanded by Lt Colo Comdt Isaac Sherman) in the year 1781.

Names	Commencement of pay	Time in Service Mo	Days
Bishop Crammer	June 7	5	24
William Johns or Jones	20	6	
Elisha Frost	July 16	5	
Thomas Turner	5	5	15
Simeon C. Stoddard	Aug. 3	4	8
Benjamin Chapman	16	3	15
William Gregory	24	3	6
Thomas Wakely	1	3	18
Alexr Baxter	July 14	5	11
John Fenton	1	5	12
Daniel Root	14	5	18
Stephen Simons	14	5	5
Adino Chapman	13	5	16
Amasa Hutchinson	14	5	
Jonah Cook	5	2	1
Jared Cone Jr.	12	4	26
Peletiah Alford	22	4	21
Levi Scovill	5	5	7
Ashbel Upson	5	5	24
Benjamin Hall	5	5	19
Gideon Barnes	Oct. 26	1	20
Samuel Dart	July 7	5	5
Daniel Williams	5	5	19
Elijah Porter	15	4	29
Benjamin Gaylord	3	5	10
Asahel Hodge	10	5	6
Ephraim Smith	5	5	13
Benjamin Loomis	1	5	24
John Tucker	1	5	29
David Hummiston	1	5	29
Enoch Sherman	Aug. 5	4	13
Ephm Moorhouse	28	3	21
Caleb Terrill	Sep. 8	3	4
Appleton Hollister	June 1	6	14
Consider Hanks	28	6	2
Benjn Stacy Evans	July 3	5	27
Simeon Booth	1	5	6
Benoni Stiles	1	5	16
Joseph Emerson	10	5	15
Thaddeus Osburn	1	5	29
Allen Carpenter	22	4	28

Names	Commencement of pay	Time in Service Mo	Days
James Dunham	July 2	5	26
Phillip Kibbee	1	5	25
Philip Manning	1	5	25
Caleb Thomas	22	5	9
Ebenezer Avery	1	5	12
Daniel Fowler	1	3	14
John Skinner	1	6	
Abiel Grant	1	5	24
Alpheus Russel	14	3	9
Frederick Kibbee	14	5	3
Daniel Edwards	26	4	22
Henry Waldo or Waldon	1	5	28
Nathan Hovey	4	4	26
Daniel Woodward	June 28	5	11
Elijah Fantom	July 1	6	
Jonathan Hill	12	5	20
James Johnston	7	5	14
Pliny Green	6	5	26
John Clark	5	4	19
Elijah Hurd	Aug. 16	2	17
Caleb Rowell	16	4	17
David Hubbell	22	3	8

Manoah Crowell	entered service	Aug. 26,	discharged	Dec. 18
John White	"	July 2,	"	" 31
Samuel Calkins	"	Aug. 7	"	Oct. 19
John Miller	"	" 7	"	Nov. 30
Asahel Osborn	"	July 30	"	Dec. 30

N. B. Jared Cone & James Johnston Rec[d] a months pay hard money in Virginia

Benj[a] Throop Maj[r] Comd[t] of y[e] 5th Conn[t] Reg[t]

[*State Library, Revolution 25; Comptroller's Office, Haskell's Receipts.*]

LIGHT INFANTRY, 1781

[*See Record of Connecticut men in the Revolution, page 351.*]

Pay abstract of the Infantry who Marched to the Southard under the Command of the Marq[s] De la Fayette and were Omitted in the Abstract for February 1781.

Names	Rank	Fro	To	
John P. Wyllys	Major	Feb. 1	Mar. 1	
Infantry C[o]				
Roger Welles	Capt.	Feb. 1	Mar. 1	
William Lynn	Lieut.	"	"	
Jacob Kingsbury	Ens.	"	"	
Lewis Hurd	Serj.	"	"	
Silas Phelps	"	"	"	
Reubin Beach	"	"	"	
James Wasson	"	"	"	
Stephen Meeker	"	"	"	
John Downs	Priv.	"	"	
David Lounsbury	Corp	"	"	
Stephen Butler	"	"	"	
David Bullen	"	"	"	
Benjamin Dix	"	"	"	
Joseph Clinton	"	"	"	
Daniel Winchell	Fifer	"	"	
John Dixon	Drum.	"	"	
John Allyn	Priv.	"	"	
Noah Barnum	"	"	"	
Ichabod Goodrich	"	"	"	
Benjamin Kirkum	"	"	"	
Jonathan Miller	"	"	"	
Bryon Montigou	"	"	"	
Nathaniel Beach	"	"	"	
Vaniah Fox	"	"	"	
Samuel Gookins	"	"	"	
Seth Gregory	"	"	"	
James Hide	"	"	"	
Jedediah Kimball	"	Jan. 15	Apr. 1	
Sheldon Potter	"	Feb. 1	Mar. 1	
Samuel Whitney	"	"	"	
Jeremiah Cunnell	"	Jan. 1	Apr. 1	
Jacob Achor	"	Feb. 1	Mar. 1	
Hondrick Baile	"	Jan. 1	Apr. 1	
John Barnum	"	Feb. 1	Mar. 1	
Edward Burghes	"	"	"	
Reubin Cadwell	"	"	"	
William Chadwick	"	"	"	
Jeremiah Chamberlain	"	"	"	Deserted
Allyn Corning	"	"	"	

Names	Rank	From	To	
Allyn Evens	Priv.	Feb. 1	Mar. 1	
Remb. Filley	"	"	"	
David Hurd	"	Jan. 1	Apr. 1	
Joseph Johnson	"	Feb. 1	Mar. 1	
David Robbarts	"	"	"	
Isaiah Smith	"	"	"	
Justin St John	"	"	"	
Ezra Tryon	"	"	"	
Samuel Vallet	"	"	"	
Benjamin Wakeley	"	"	"	
Joshua Wheeler	"	"	"	
Joseph Hand	"	"	"	Deserted
Seth Stannard	"	"	"	
Samuel Manning	"	"	"	
Samuel Pulford	"	"	"	
David Williams	"	"	"	
Joel Mashier	"	"	"	
Samuel Hinman	"	"	"	
Ebenr Huntington	Lt Co			
Stephen Betts	Cap.			
Nathan H. Whiting	Lieut.			

. . . .

Hopkins Co continued

Names	Rank	From	To	
Stephen Gavett	Priv.	Jan. 16	Mar. 1	
Ephraim Harrey	"	Jan. 1	Apr. 1	
John Pearle	"	Feb. 15	"	
James Anderson	"	Mar. 1	"	
Thomas Brewer	"	Feb. 27	"	
Garner Cleveland	"	Jan. 1	"	
Ichabod Downing	"	Mar. 1	"	
Daniel Davis	"	"	"	Deserted
David Spencer	"	Jan. 1	"	
Jacob Strong	"	Feb. 1	"	
Edmund Shelly	"	Feb. 13	"	
Joseph Smith	"	Jan. 1	"	

Capt. Walkers Co

Names	Rank	From	To	
Samuel Barden	Priv.	Jan. 1	Apr. 1	
John Clarke	"	"	"	
Benjamin Durfee	"	"	"	
John Fagin	"	" 22	"	
Mason Green	"	Feb. 14	"	Deserted
Joel Hamlin	"	Jan. 1	"	Deserted
Jabez Morten	"	" 11	"	
Lemuel Stanclift	"	Feb. 26	"	
Jonathan Simons	"	Mch. 1	"	
William Scheeswick	"	Feb. 4	"	
Seth Dodge	"	Jan. 1	"	
Reubin Dodge	"	"	"	
Joshua Fuller	"	Feb. 1	"	
Heman Hatch	"	Jan. 1	"	
Henry Ponds	"	Feb. 7	"	
Chester Upham	"	Jan. 1	"	
Jacob Weight 1st	"	"	"	
Jacob Weight 2d	"	"	"	
Hubbard Burrous	"	Mar. 25	"	

Allyn's C°

Names	Rank	From	To	
[ ]	Priv.	Jan. 4	Apr. 1	
[ ]	"	Feb. 1	"	
[ ] Beebee	"	Jan. 29	"	
[ ] Chaffee	"	Feb. 6	"	
[ ] Eggleston	"	Jan. 29	Mar. 6	
Benedict Eggleston	"	Jan. 1	Apr. 1	
Simeon Fox	"	Jan. 3	Mar. 25	
Bassett Fox	"	Jan. 15	"	
Jabez Edgcomb	"	Mar. 1	Apr. 1	
David Gardner	"	"	"	
Jacob Gillet	"	Jan. 17	"	
Cudjo Holmes	"	Jan. 1	"	
John G. Holcomb	"	Jan. 1	Mar. 6	
[ ] Horton	"	Jan. 29	Apr. 1	
[ ] Kingsley	"	Jan. 16	Mar. 25	
Eliel London	"	Jan. 17	Apr. 1	
Elias Meason	"	Jan. 1	Mar. 25	
Nathan Mallery	"	Jan. 19	Apr. 1	
John Mills	"	Mar. 1	"	
James Neason	"	Jan. 1	Mar. 25	
Robin Neason	"	Jan. 8	Apr. 1	
Isaac Nellson	"	Jan. 1	Mar. 25	
Daniel Perkins	"	"	Mar. 6	
Isaiah Pratt	"	Mar. 5	Apr. 1	
Adonijah Rose	"	Jan. 1	Mar. 25	
John Robertson	"	Mar. 1	Apr. 1	
[ ] Sharp	"	"	"	
Ebenezer Shaw	"	Jan. 1	"	
David Taylor	"	"	Mar. 6	

Cap Betts C°

Names	Rank	From	To	
Anthony D^eFlorus	D^m	Jan. 12	Apr. 1	
Jonathan Brown	Priv.	Jan. 1	"	
Parley Cay	"	Jan. 19	"	
Joseph Davis	"	Jan. 1	Mar. 28	
David Dix	"	"	" 26	
Edward Freeman	"	Mar. 17	Apr. 1	
Benjamin Greenslit	"	Feb. 3	Mar. 23	
John Gates	"	Jan. 1	Mar. 28	
Abel Guthcrie	"	"	Apr. 1	
Jason Gay	"	Feb. 1	"	
Robert Holdridge	"	Jan. 1	Mar. 23	
David Jackson	"	Feb. 28	Mar. 26	
Theophilus Luther	"	Jan. 1	Apr. 1	Deserted
Joseph Lawson	"	Jan. 19	"	
William Moore	"	Jan. 1	"	
Jesse Olmsted	"	Jan. 8	"	
Jacob Pettingall	"	Feb. 6	Mar. 6	
Asaph Pettengall	"	Feb. 6	Mar. 23	
Samuel Peters	"	Jan. 1	Apr. 1	
Abel Stimson	"	Jan. 29	"	
Daniel S^tJohn	"	Jan. 1	"	
David Thompson	"	Jan. 19	"	
James Thompson	"	"	"	
Chester Waterman	"	Jan. 1	Mar. 23	
Thomas Warden	"	Jan. 15	Apr. 1	
Phinehas Granger	"	Jan. 1	"	

Cap Rileys Comp.

Names	Rank	From	To	
Richard Dammorg	Priv.	Jan. 1	Mar. 24	Prisoner
Jonathan Luce	"	"	Apr. 1	
Ozias Barker	"	Feb. 6	Mar. 24	
Benjn Cady	"	Jan. 1	Apr. 1	
John Kimball	"	Feb. 1	"	
Marshall Keyes	"	Jan. 1	"	
Jared Kimball	"	Feb. 1	"	
Jabez Kirtland	"	Jan. 27	"	
Phinchas Knight	"	Feb. 3	"	
Joshua Reynolds	"	"	Mar. 24	
James Miner	"	Feb. 23	"	
John Munsill	"	Feb. 1	"	
Levi Munsill	"	Feb. 6	"	
Joel Hide	"	Feb. 5	"	
Ichabod Wording	"	Jan. 1	Apr. 1	
Joseph Cockeel(?)	"	"	Mar. 26	
[ ]	"	"	[ ]	
[ ] Latham	"	Jan. 17	Apr. 1	
George Seeley	"	Feb. 3	"	
David Chester	"	Jan. 8	"	
Abijah Downing	"	Mar. 1	"	
Eliezer Hatch	"	Feb. 1	"	
Sylvenus Gage	"	"	"	
Ichabod West	"	"	"	
Jacob Robbins	"	"	"	Deserted
Noah Merrills	"	Jan. 15	"	
Nathan Tubbs	"	Jan. 1	"	
John Wheeler	"	Mar. 1	"	
Joseph Cheney	"			

Cap. Williams C°

Names	Rank	From	To
Joel Clarke	Fifer	Jan. 1	Apr. 1
Jedediah Adams	Priv.	"	"
Christopher Avery	"	Feb. 2	"
Hezekiah Catlen	"	Jan. 29	"
Nathaniel Gates	"	Jan. 1	"
Silas Glass	"	"	"
Pileman Kirkum	"	"	"
Eliakim Seward	"	"	"
Charles Walters	"	"	"
Joseph Burrous	"	Feb. 3	"
Samuel Fargo	"	Jan. 1	"
Jim Holt	"	Mar. 2	"
Elijah Fayer	"	Mar. 1	"
Selah Hart	"	Mar. 5	"
Peter Holt	"	Jan. 1	Mar. 1
Abijah Smith	"	"	Apr. 1

Cap Parson's C°

Names	Rank	From	To
James Crane	Priv.	Jan. 1	Apr. 1
Frederick Whipple	"	Feb. 1	Mar. 2
Reubin Addams	"	Jan. 1	Apr. 1
Eph^m Burghes	"	Feb. 1	Mar. 6
William Burrous	"	Jan. 1	Apr. 1
Elias Carpenter	"	Jan. 9	Mar. 26
Eliphalet Carpenter	"	Jan. 1	"

Names	Rank	From	To	
Comfort Chapman	Priv.	Feb. 1	Mar. 3	Deserted
Joseph Phinney	"	"	Mar. 29	
Jacob Halladay	"	Jan. 1	Mar. 6	
Phillip Hills	"	Feb. 1	Mar. 29	
Andrew Hausey	"	Mar. 1	Mar. 30	
David Matterson	"	Feb. 1	Mar. 3	
Aaron Parks	"	Jan. 1	Apr. 1	
William Short	"	Mar. 6	"	
Reubin Smith	"	Feb. 1	"	
Johnson Tiff	"	Jan. 11	"	
David Hammond	"	Mar. 13	"	
Darius Trusdale	"	Jan. 11	Mar. 26	
Eli Tullar	"	Jan. 15	Apr. 1	
John F. Jone	"	Mar. 1	Mar. 30	
Thomas Poghcegh	"	Feb. 4	Mar 22	Deserted
Arcules Ames	"	Mar. 1	Apr. 1	

[*State Library, Revolution* 25.]

VARIOUS REGIMENTS.

LEVIES, 1782.

Return of Certificates Rec[d] from Sundry Pay Masters for payment of Levies in 1782.

A List of Certificates lodged in this Office by L[t] John Sherman Agent for the 2 Connecticut Regiment which Cert[s] are signd by Jn[o] Peirce Esq drawn in favour of the following persons who were short Levies in s[d] Reg[t] in 1782

Jonah Steckland
Abijah Batterson
Gilbert McGeer
David Brooks
Roswell Clark
Edward Gibbs
Nathaniel Parker
Jeremiah Rumsey
John Booth
Simeon Saxon
Oziel Richmond
William Norton
Asahel Sawyer
Richard Bishop
Charles Squires
Isaac Olcutt
Daniel Cowen
John Cowen
Samuel Patchers
Samuel Shipman
Niles Gideon
Abijah Elswood
Elijah Rood
Abraham Couch
Otis Ensign
John Ives
Solomon Johnson
Chipman Clark
Abisha Bard
Abisha Forbes
Daniel Bliss

A List of Certificates lodged in this Office by Lieu[t] Nathan Beers Agent for the 3[d] Connecticut Reg[t] which Cert[s] are Signd by John Pierce Esq[r] drawn in favour of the following Persons who were Short Levies in said Reg[t] in 1782

Jacob Haskell
Samuel Bliss
Samuel Parks
John Bliss
Moses Barnard
Beriah Bliss
Daniel Lyman
John Haskell
Adrew Hazen
Joshua Olmsted
Noah Norton
David Hubble
George Foot
Nehemiah Seeley
Amos Gustin
Daniel Knight
Benoni Robbins
Janna Wilcox
Elisha Catlin
Ebenezer Dufee
Elijah Duffee
Noah Kesley
Jacob Fenton
James Bliss
Hezekiah Torrell
Nehemiah Barnes
Edward Duncan
Charles Lewis
Aaron Wayley
Zacheus Gillett
Benoni Gillett
Nathan Fenton
Sarel Squires
Nathaniel Conant

Levi Hall
Simeon Stimson
Daniel Jackson
Jonathan Beamont
Miles Bennet
William Mitchel
Charles Minor
Amos Clark
David Hubbard
Solomon Ranny
Benjamin Webster
Neal McNeal
Gideon Russell
Jesse Thomas
Elijah Andrus
Elijah Kilby
James Packerr (?)
George Michel
Daniel Root
Samuel Peck
Jesse Terry
Thomas Marble
Stacy Evens
John Vaughn

A list of Certificates lodged in this Office by L[t] John Sherman Agent for the 4 Conn[t] Regiment which Certificates are signd by John Pierce Esq drawn in favour of the following persons who were short Levies in 4th Reg[t] in 1782

Moses Allen
Jedediah Coe
Elisha Marshall
Elisha Cone
William Reed
Peter Meranda
William Davis
Isaac Rexford
Daniel Peck
Stephen Mosher
Israel Frisby
Jacob Norton
John Robinson
Jonah Webb
Robert Follet
William Coltrain
Caleb Barrows
Solomon Cone
James Hart
Edmond Griswold
Daniel Bird
Amos Rich
Abner Hall
Asahel Hall or Hull
Charles Rice
Jared Smith
James Cook
Solomon Cole
Samuel Andrus
Abel Barnes
Noah Spencer
Lemuel Barber
Thomas Watson
Joseph Rockwell
Job Cole
Ebenezer Doolittle
Joseph West
Elijah Northrop
Zephaniah Dowd
Joel Gurnsey
Chandler Judd
William White
Increase Holcomb
Job Cole
James Burrill
Joseph Buratt
Abijah Beach
Eliphas Burnham
Elijah Beard
Ebenezer Chubbuck
Gideon Dunham
Samuel Elwell
Jonathan Eagliston
Ebenezer Elwell
Abisha Forbes
Philo Gibb
Elisha Hickum
Abraham Tomkins
William Turner
Jonathan Sheperd
Pely Simons
Samuel Nichols
Gurdon Molton
John McCarty
Stephen Luddenton
Abner Lilley
Nathan Law
Amaziah Ingraham

John Perries Certificates lodged in Pay Table Office by Jn° Sherman Agent for payment of Levies in 5th Conn. Regiment.

John Dawning
William Mitchell
Charles Miner
Amos Clark
David Hubbard
Solomon Ranney
Benjamin Webster
Neal McNeal
Gideon Russell
Jesse Thomas
Elijah Andrus
Elijah Kibbee
James Patchin
George Mitchel
Daniel Root
Samuel Peck
Jesse Toney
Thomas Marble
Stacey Evens
John Vaughn
Amos Westland
Roswell Lamphere
Ashbel Webster
John Clark

[*Comptroller's Office.*]

CONNECTICUT LINE, 1783.

THIRD REGIMENT—COL. WEBB.

[*See Record of Connecticut Men in the Revolution, page 367.*]

EIGHTH COMPANY—CAPT. ROGERS.

[In the volume of ***Hebard Papers*** the monthly returns of this company for a year previous to February 1783 can be seen.]
Roll and Muster of the 8th Company 3d Connecticut Regiment Commanded by Col° [S] B Webb for the Month of February 1783

Ranks	Names	Term of Inlistment	Time since last Muster, or Inlistment	Casualties
Captain	Hezekiah Rogers		December 5 1782	
Lieut	John Hobart		January 1 1783	[?]
"	William Lynn			
Ensn	Aron Keeler		January 26 1783	Forloughd Febry 26 83
Sergeant	Richard Lord	D W	December 5 1782	" by his Excellency Jany 3 83
"	William Bassett	"	January 26 1783	
"	Abiather Evens	"	December 5 1782	Sick Hartford Feby 1 83
"	Peter Stalker	"	January 26 1783	
"	Reuben Beach	"	"	Furloughd March 7 83
"	Henery Hull	"	April 2 1782	Sick Connet April 2 82
"	Thomas Wells	"	January 26 1783	

Ranks	Names	Term of Inlistment	Time since last Muster, or Inlistment	Casualties
Corporal	Jesse St John	D W	January 26 1783	
"	James Crane	9 M 12 D	October 13 1782	
"	Amasa Grenold	D W	January 26 1783	
"	Nicholas Howell	"	"	
"	Reubin Carter	"	"	
Drummer	John Avery	"	"	
"	William Kane	11 M 6 D	"	
Fifer	Frederick Whipple	D W	December 5 1782	Furlough^{d} by his Excellency Jan 3 83
"	Isaac Higgins	16 M 6 D	January 26 1783	
Privats	Aner Adee	D W	"	
"	Frank Buck	"	"	
"	John Dingly	"	December 5 1782	
"	Moses Elsworth	"	August 10 1782	Sick N Winsor June 30 82
"	Samuel Ells	"	January 26 1783	
"	Thomas Frink	"	"	
"	Jonathan Edwards	"	"	
"	Joel Hait	"	December 5 1782	
"	David Hodge	"	January 26 1783	
"	Samuel Jinkens	"	"	
"	Uriah Keeler	"	"	
"	Abner Lord	"	"	
"	James Liberty	"	"	
"	Wait Lewis	"	September 11 1782	
"	Stephen Meigs	"	January 26 1783	
"	Joel Mosher	"	"	
"	Peter Mix	"	December 5 1783	Connet with Capt Walker Jany 83
"	Abraham Murry	"	June 14 1782	
"	Aaron Parks	"	January 26 1783	Sick Ashford Febry 24 83
"	Justin St John	"	"	
"	Ethiel Scott	"	December 5 1782	
"	Enos Tuttle	"	January 26 1783	Furlough^{d} March 3 83
"	Amos Temple	"	"	Furlough^{d} March 3 83
"	Stephen Thomson	"	"	

Privats	Jethro Toney	D W	January	26 1783	
"	Nathan Walker	"		"	
"	William Waterbury	"		"	
"	Cato Wilborow	"		"	
"	Reubin Adams	9 M 11 D		"	
"	Esaias Butts	10 M 7 D		"	
"	Ephraim Bates	10 M 23 D	June	14 1782	Sick Connet Octr 2 82
"	William Burrus	9 M 23 D	January	26 1783	
"	Ephraim Burgess	10 M 23 D		"	
"	Eliphelet Carpenter	9 M 26 D		"	
"	John F. Tone	10 M 8 D		"	
"	Amos Holden	27 M		"	
"	Philip Hill	11 M 23 D		"	
"	David Hammond	12 M 6 D		"	
"	Samuel Hull	10 M 23 D	December	5 1782	
'	Jacob Haladay	9 M 9 D	January	26 1783	
"	Chandler Judd	1 M			Burring Line
"	Jedediah Kimball	12 M 9 D	January	26 1783	
"	David Matterson	10 M 23 D		"	
"	Cato Negro	15 M 28 D		"	
"	Thomas Palmer	25 M 23 D		"	
"	Joseph Pheney	10 M 23 D		"	
"	Ebenezer Platt	1 M 13 D		"	
"	James Raymond	1 M 7 D		"	
"	Aron Eaton	1 M 11 D		"	
"	William Short	12 M 6 D		"	
"	Johnson Tiff	10 M 4 D		"	
"	Darius Truesdil	10 M 4 D	December	5 1782	Sick Connet Decemr 8 82
"	Eli Tuller	10 M 4 D		"	Furloughd by his Excellency Jany 3 83
"	James Duggan	9 M 23	January	26 1783	
"	Brestor Negro			"	

I certify the above Roll to be the true State of said Company this 13th Day of March 1783
John Hobart Lieut

[*State Library, Hebard papers.*]

STATE TROOPS, 1775.

[*See Record of Connecticut Men in the Revolution, page 380.*]

LIEUT. LAY'S COMPANY.

[This company was ordered raised by the Council of Safety, Sept. 14, 1775.]

Lieut Lee Lays Pay Roll for Soldiers at Lyme Jan[y] 1776.
Soldiers at Lyme 1775, settled 1776
Entered into Service 20th Oct[r]

	Days
Lieut. Lee Lay	65
Sergt Benj[a] Higgins	65
Fifer Sam[l] Fosdick	41
Lem[l] Rogers	65
Paul Cooley	65
Phineas Huntley	65
Abner Smith	64
Martin Lee	65
Elisha Way	65
Silvanus Clark	57
Elisha Merrow	57
W[m] Mather	41
Ezra Lee	41
Elias Mather	41
Alex[r] Hyde	41
Geo. R. Lewis	41

[*State Library, Revolution 6.*]

STATE TROOPS, 1776.

[*See Record of Connecticut Men in the Revolution, pages 381-386.*]

SICK BILLS.

[Names of soldiers extracted from a volume of "Sick Bills," 1776, being itemized accounts of the expenses of individual soldiers during sickness.]

Levies in Jan'y 1776 for 2 Months

Name	Company	Regiment	Remarks
Abiel Crandle	Capt. Solomon Willes	Douglas	
Lieut. Lazarus Ives	Capt. Richards	Wadsworth	
Jonathan Tuttle Jr.	Capt. Peas	Douglas	
Isaac Newell Jr.	Capt. Noadiah Hooker	Wadsworth	Of Farmington
Zoeth Eldridge	Capt. Peas	Douglas	Of Willington
Jedediah Olcott	Capt. Prior	Wolcott	
Roswell Goodrich	Capt. Jonathan Hale	"	
Zechariah Kelsey	Capt. Prior	"	
Lieut. Samuel Pierce	"	"	
Jabez Chapman Jr.	Capt. John Willey	Wadsworth	
Elijah Whiton	Capt. Solomon Willes	Douglas	
Richard Spelman	Capt. Couch	Wadsworth	Of Durham
Samuel Lucas			Not ill
David Smith	Capt. Shepard	Wadsworth	
Giles Curtiss	Capt. Isaac Cook	Ward	
Chauncey Rowlee	Capt. Benjamin Richards	Wadsworth	
David Bunce	Capt. Prior	Wolcott	
James Whiton	Capt. Benjamin Clark	Douglas	
George Kimberly	Capt. Noah Fowler	Ward	
Dr. Robert Usher		Wadsworth	Not ill
Ens. Michael Brunson		"	
Corp^l Ebenezer Kilby	Capt. Hezekiah Welles	Wolcott	
John Thomas	Capt. Willey	Wadsworth	
Elijah Porter	Capt. Jonathan Welles	"	
Richard Risley	"	"	
Theodore Keeney	"	"	
Corpl. Joseph Porter	"	"	Died
Aaron Clark	"	"	Died

[*Comptroller's Office.*]

FIRST REGIMENT—COL. WADSWORTH.

[*See Record of Connecticut Men in the Revolution, page 386.*]

OFFICERS.

Coll James Wadsworth First Reg at Cambridge Winter of 1776— Roll of Capt Joseph Blagues Company & the Commis Officers of the Reg^{t}.

The officers of the first Reg^{t} of Militia under the Command of Coll James Wadsworth Jan 1776

1
Capt John Willey
Lt John Skinner
Lt Ithamar Harvey
Ens Roger Phelps

2nd Comp
Capt John Couch
Lt Simeon Parsons
Lt Joseph Newton
Ens Samuel Camp

3
Capt Eliph^{t} Bulkley
Lt Solomon Tarbox
Lt John Treadway
Ens Eliph^{t} Chamberlain

4
Capt Joseph Blague
Lt Joseph Churchill
Lt Jacob Wetmore
Ens Timothy Clark

5
Capt Jeremiah Mason
Lt Andrew Waterman
Lt Joel Chamberlain
Ens Elias Bliss

6
Capt Jared Shepard
Lt Edwd Ells
Lt David Smith 2^{d}
Ens Jabez Brooks

7
Capt Jesse Morse
Lt Thos Shepard
Lt Asa Beebe
Ens Miles Hull

8
Capt Benj Richards
Lt Lazarus Ives
Lt Moses Foot
Ens Michael Brunson

[*Copy in Comptroller's Office, location of original unknown.*]

CAPT. BLAGUE'S COMPANY.

Roll of Capt Joseph Blagues Company, at Cambridge in Winter & Spring of 1776

The Commissiond officers are given in No 4
Time of Enlisting Jany 25 '76
Time of Marching Feb. 8
Discharged April 6
Days in Service from 73 down to 69

Serj^{s} Samuel Tuels (?)
Nicholas Ames
John Johnson
Benj Cornell
Corp^{s} Gershom Hinkley
Jos Pelton
Amos Clark
Andrew Norton

Drummer Daniel Hamlin
Fifer Daniel Starr
Privates Atkins, Joel
Atkins, Isaac
Burton, Samuel
Brown, Thomas
Boardman, Timothy
Bunn, Paul

Privates Boardman, Nathan	Privates Lane, John
Clark, Daniel	Miller, Giles
Cook, Gideon	Pelton, Jonathan
Cook, Joshua	Parks, Daniel
Clark, Stephen	Penfield, Jesse
Cone, Joseph	Penfield, Simeon
Cone, Hubb Daniel	Prior, Jesse
Crittendon, Gideon	Plumb, Jesse
Cande, Theophilus	Rogers, Timothy
Cotton, Elisha	Reed, Jonathan
Doolittle, Thomas	Redfield, Samuel
Dana, Charles	Robbins, John
Duncan, James	Stocking, Eber
Davis, John	Strickland, Stephen
Doud, Richard	Jan 26 Discharged April 6
Gray, William	Stocking, Marshall
Goodwin, John	Stiles, Beriah
Griffith, Joseph	Story, John
Gilbert, Allen	Shepard, John
Gilbert, Williams	Sage, Michael
Hubbert, Gideon	Stone, Joseph
Hurd, Thomas	Ufford, Eliakim
Hale, Benjamin	Wilcox, Comfort
Hall, Timothy	White, William
Harris, Joseph	Wetmore, Josiah
Hulett, Joseph	Willcox, John
Johnson, Isaac	Wood, Joel

[*Copy in Comptroller's Office, location of original unknown.*]

COL. SWIFT'S BATTALION.

[*See Record of Connecticut Men in the Revolution, page 391.*]

STRATFORD SOLDIERS.

[Arms delivered to Stratford soldiers under the command of Capt. Elijah Beach, in Col. Swifts regiment bound for the Northern Department, July 1776.]

to What Soldier delivered	to What Soldier delivered
James Downs	Joseph Burton Jr
Samuel Edwards	William Burton
Willm Winwright	Thomas Weathers
Pheleg Sunderlin	Nathanel Booth
John Crawford	Gideon Peet

[*State Library, Revolution 6.*]

CAPT. LACEY'S COMPANY.

A List of the Minute Men Return'd to Col. Hinman by Capt. David Leavenworth Feby 5th 1776.

James Reynolds
James B. Reynolds
Samuel Hurd
Daniel Hurd
Ebenezer Lacey
Ebenezer Thomas Jr
George Newton Jr
Adam Hurd
Thaddeus Lacey
Abraham Post
Simeon Hurd
John Mallery Jr
Timothy Castle
Isaac Thomas
Asahel Booth
James Morehouse
Azariah Eastman
Samuel Blakeley
Aaron Olds
Benjamin Eastman
William Torrance
John Thomas
Samuel Torrence Jr
Jedidiah Elderkin
Noah Woodward Jr
Edward Collens
Thomas Torrence
Joseph Torrence
Eldad Baker
Lovewel Hurd
Hezekiah Reynolds
Ezra Lacey
Simeon Hurd Jr
Steph Hurd
Henry Wakeley
Curtis Hurd
Thomas Canfield
John Austin Norton
David Rumsey
Seth Mitchel
Noah Frisbie Jr
Phinehas Baker
William Castle
Isaac Blakeley
Eliphaz Worner
Noah Frisbie
Israel Miner
Asahel Frisbie
Abner Hurd
William Norton

Thadeus Lacey Capt of Sd Company

[Indorsed] List of Roxbury Minute Company

[*State Library, Revolution 6.*]

FIRST BATTALION—COL. SILLIMAN.

[*See Record of Connecticut Men in the Revolution, page 393.*]

STRATFORD SOLDIERS.

[Arms delivered to Stratford soldiers under the command of Capt. George Benjamin, in Col. Gold Sellick Silliman Regiment bound for New York, July 1776.]

To what Soldier delivered

Curtis Judson
Barnibas Cuningham
John Megraugh
John Downing
Elihu Mawwee

To what Soldier delivered

William Grant
Abner Elger
David Barlow Jr
Pink Clarke

[*State Library, Revolution 6.*]

SECOND BATTALION—COL. GAY.

[See Record of Connecticut Men in the Revolution, page 395.]

SEVENTH COMPANY—CAPT. WELLES.

Apprisement of the Soldiers guns under Com^{d} of Capt Saml Welles

Soldiers Names	Soldiers Names
Capt Saml Welles	Joseph Bidwell
Abraham Tallcott	Jonth Gains
George Tallcott	Leu^{t} Thos Hollister
Richd Smith	Serj^{t} Aaron Hubbard
Jesse Churchel	Elijah Hubbard
Josiah Lumis	Josiah Brooks
Josiah Stevens	Saml Daniels
Serj^{t} Benjn Stevens	Joseph Churchel
Benjn Howard	Eliz^{r} Hubbard
Frances Nichalson	Ebez^{r} Benton
Barnabas Fuller	Saml Hills Junr
Thomas Brooks	Wm Densmore
Ashbil Webster	Timothy Stevens
Steven Couch	Aaron Hollister
Peter Stevens	Josiah Hollister
David Hubbard	Timothy Wood
John Morley	John How
Jonth Loveland	Elemuel Tubbs
David Nigh fifer	Hez^{h} Wickham
Edward Potter	Nathan Nichalson
Elijah Covel	Thos Morley
Jonth Covel	Elez^{r} Goodale

Glastenbury 13th 1776
Samuel Welles Cap

[State Library, Revolution 6.]

SEVENTH COMPANY—CAPT. WELLES.

An account of 12 Blankets hired or impress^{d} by the Select Men of Glastenbury & delivered to Soldiers of Capt Saml Wells's Comp^{y} Col^{o} Gay's Reg^{t} 1776.

to whom delivered	their Casulties
Benjn Howard	Lost with him when he died supposed buried in it
Richd Smith	Lost in Retreat from Turtle Bay Sep. 15, 1776
Joseph Brooks	" " "
Benjn Hale	Buried with him
Stephen Couch	Lost in Retreat above mentioned
Jesse Churchill	No account of & to be paid for
Elihu Smith	Lost in sd Retreat
Josiah Hollister	" "
Jonth Gains	" "
Josiah Loomis	Shot to pieces
Lem^{l} Tubbs	No account of & to be paid for
Thos Morley	Lost in sd Retreat

[State Library, Revolution 6.]

LOST GUNS.

An account of the Guns that were Lost in the Reg^{t} late Col Gays while in the Continental Service under the Comand of Genl Washington A D 1776

Capt Stanlys Comp^{y}

Mens Names & what Companies they belonged to	What Place Guns lost at
Ambrus Sloper	on Long Island
Danl Darens	"
Eli Pardy	"
John Park	"
Thos Powers	"
John Thorp	on York Island in Retreat
John Andrus	" "
John Doty	" "
Amos Hawley	" "
Saml Lee	" "
Asahel Newel	" "
Josiah Smith	" "
Lemuel Wyard	" "
Ira Judson	" "
Samuel Hitchcock	in North River crossing River
Josiah Mix	in Baggage Waggon
Nathl Shepherd	"
Gideon Porter	in Amunition Cart
Mark Newel	in Baggage Waggon

Capt Jellits Comp^{y}

David Phelps	in Baggage Waggon
Jonathan Eccleston	"
Oliver Case	"
Zenas Hayse	"
Simeon Holliday	"
Ehud Fuller	"
Obed Lamberton	in Trenches

Capt Rogers Comp^{y}

Simeon Barns	in B Waggon
Danl Harris	"
James Willson	in Y. Island
John White	B Waggon
Benj^{a} Carrier	"
William Fellows	on L. Island
Nehemiah Smith	B. Wagon
George White	"
John Whitnay	L Island
Saml Franklin	"
Simeon Rude	B. Waggon
David Douglas	N. York in Retreat
Daniel Coo[ ]	Y. Island "
Thos Hamlin	" "
Peter Pratt	" "
Sluman Ables	B. Waggon
David Simons	"
Daniel Potter	"
William Jaquies	"
Asa Smith	"
David Franklin	"

Capt Goodwins Company

Mens Names & what Companies they belonged to	What Place Guns lost at
Lieut. Scovil	Y. Island in Retreat
Scarg^t Lockwood	B. Waggon
Joseph Gaylord	"
Joseph Gillet	"
Solomon Morse	Staten when on Guard
Levi Norton	B. Wagon
Bradford Kellogg	In Retreat York Island
Ebenez^r Scovil	" "
Joel Gaylord	B. Wagon
Ananias Porrage	"

Capt Bradleys Company

James Peat	Died on Long Island
Lieut. Blakesley	at White Plains when sick
Eli Easmon	Stolen on N. York
Saml Stannard	in Retreat N. York
Josiah Hatch	Stolen at Hackensack
James Corby	B. Waggon
[ ] Norton	"
David Rumsy	Armourers Shop L. Island
Isaac Blakesly	B. Waggon
John Preston	Y. Island

Capt Woolcotts Company

Ebenz^r Foot	Crossing N. River
Gideon Drake	"
William Jones	B. Waggon
Alexander Korton	"
Roz^{ll} Pryor	"
John Stely	"
Abner Slade	"
John Thompson	"

Capt Wells's Company

Ens. Reuben Phelps	B. Wagon
Thomas Brook	"
Josiah Brook	"
Jonathan Covel	"
Elias Chapin	"
Saml Danolds	"
John Hungerford	"
Saml Kibby	"
Jonathan Loveland	"
Josiah Loomis	"
Fransis Nickinson	"
John Phelps	"
Lemuel Tubbs	"

Capt Wilsons Company

Aron Bristol	York Island Retreat
Abel Bristol	" "
Benajah Heydon	B Wagon
Saml Hinsdale	"
Rufus Johnson	"

[*State Library, Revolution 6.*]

COAST GUARD.

CAPT. SALTONSTALL'S COMPANY.

A Return of Those Intitl[d] to a Bounty in the Company of Matross[s] Commanded by Nath[l] Saltonstall

Names	Time of Inlistment	Whose Company Came out of
Nath[l] Saltonstall Cap	July 1776	
Nath[l] Coit Jr Capt Lieut.	July 11	
Daniel Starr 1 Lieut	11	
Daniel Dee 2 Lieut	23	Capt. Kirtland's
Tho[s] Jones 1 Serj.	12	
Moses Fergo 2 Serj.	14	
John Chapman 3 Serj.	14	
Nath[l] Hempsted Jr 1 Corp.	12	
John Woodward 2 Corp.	14	
Jon[a] Miner 3 Corp.	26	Capt Kirtland's
Manuel Boix 1 Gunner	14	
George Rogers Drummer	12	
Gurdon F. Saltonstall Fifer	10	
John Howard Gunner	12	
Jeremiah Culver "	12	
Joseph Sharp "	12	
Thomas Mossett "	12	
John Buell "	26	Capt. Kirtland's
John Walker "	27	
Jonathan Miner "	12	
Abner Beebe Matross	12	
Samuel Mason "	12	
Nath[l] Tharp	12	
Ebenezer Colfax	12	
James Holt	13	
Nathan Spicer	14	
Jonathan Comstock	14	
Thomas Hopkins	14	
Ethiel Plant	23	Capt. Kirtland's
Robert Latimer	23	
Gideon Chapman	23	
Isaac Oliver	23	
John Bolles 4th	23	
John Clerk	26	Capt. Shapley's
Peter Stannard	26	Capt. Kirtland's
Titus Teal	26	"
William Stevens	26	"
William Bartholemew	26	"
Asa Baker Jr	27	
Palsey Baker	27	Capt. Shapley's
John Baker	27	"
Jeremy Bayley	26	Capt. Kirtland's
Thomas Quinley	27	Capt. Shapley's

Names	Time of Inlistment	Whose Company Came out of
Benjn Jones	26	Capt Kirtland's
Asa Denison	26	"
John Tredaway	27	Capt. Mather's
Joshua Griffing	27	"
Jeremiah Blake	27	"
Josiah Church	27	"
Augustus Lewis	26	Capt. Kirtland
Nathl Emerson	26	" [for Duty
John Hues	14	Discharged 29 being unfit
Aaron Jones	Aug. 10	Capt. Kirtland

[Indorsed] Capt Nathl Saltonstals Pay Roll of Matross Company at New London.

[*State Library, Revolution 6.*]

ENS. UFFOOT'S COMPANY.

A Pay Roll for the First Months pay of Ensign Samuel Uffoots Guard in Stratford

Ensign
Serj^nt
Nathan McCune
Josiah Hawley
John Uffoot
Benjamin Uffoot
Joseph Beers
John McCune
William Osborn
Joseph Prunwugh
Stephen Frost
Andrew Paylon
Ephraim McCune
Joseph Burritt
Charles Burrough
Samuel Patterson

[*State Library, Revolution 6.*]

THIRD BATTALION—COL. ENOS.

[*See Record of Connecticut Men in the Revolution, page 424.*]

CAPT. BLACKMAN'S COMPANY.

An acc^t of Prest Guns &c in Capt Elijah Blackmans C^o with the names of possesors &c Jany 23 1777

Possesors of Guns &c

Wm Colton
Benah Cone
Thos Norton
Allin Lane
Chris^r Whitehead
Josh^a Monroe
Sim^o Ranny
David Clark
Comfort Ranny
Nathl Ranny J^r
Danl Robberds
Ja^s Johnson
Saml Griffin

Possesors of Guns &c

Benj^a Babbit
Bennit Eglestone
Jo^s Bacon J^r
Wm Stow
John Gill
Allin Ward
Lamberton Clark J^r
Comfort Marks
Ebenez^r Robberds Fifer
Ebenez^r Bacon
Steph^n Robberds
Ashbel Cornwell

[*Copy in Comptroller's Office.*]

COLS. ELY'S AND ENOS' REGIMENTS.

[See Record of Connecticut Men in the Revolution, page 614.]

BOUNTIES.

The United States D^r To the State of Connecticut, for Bounty paid to the Subalterns in Col. Ely & Enos's Regiments in 1777, for extra Services. Viz.

Officers Names	Reg^{ts}	Officers Names	Reg^{ts}
Lt John Chick	Col. Enos	Lt A. Baldwin	Enos's
Lt Wm Morris	Ely's	Lt Danl Leffingwell	"
Lt Asa Bacon	"	Ens^n Joshua Gates	"
Lt E. Taylor	"	Lt Charles Goodwin	Enos's
Lt Joseph Hale	"	Ens^n John Francis	"
Ens^n Dav^d Scranton	"	Lt Josiah Cleaveland	Ely's
Lt Ezra Benedict	Enos's	Lt Nathl Bingham	"
Lt Noah Judson	"	Ens^n John Wiley	"
Lt Stephen Dodge	"	Ens^n L. Gaylord	Enos's
Ens^n Wm Torrance	"	Ens^n Job Smith	"
Lt Ich^a Bozworth	Ely's	Lt Jno Prudden	"
Lt John Shipman	"	Lt N. West	Ely's
Ens^n Jno Shipman 2^d	"	Lt B. Trowbridge	Enos's
Lt Saml Hozard	"	Lt R. Chapman	Ely's
Lt L. Grosvenor	"		

[Comptroller's Office, Haskell's Receipts.]

CAPT. PETTIBONE'S COMPANY.

An Account of the Arms Accoutrements &c that are going in Servis in Capt Abel Pettibones Comp^a with the prises thereto July 18th 1777.

Capt. Abel Pettibone
Ens. John Chick
Sr. Jededi^a Olcott
Asahel Andrus Jr
Obed Higley
Elihu Case 2^d
Joseph Presson
Eber Higley
Asa Hays
George Northway
Roswel Case
Jacob Davis 3^d
William Andrews Jr
Noah Humphry
Israel Tullar
Richard Lilley Jr
Eli Alderman
Daniel Olmsted Jr
Joel Barber Jr
Jonathan Alderman Jr
Judah Case
Amos Slarter
Jeremiah Willcox
Carmi Holcomb
Matthew Grifen Jr
Salmon Burr
Seth Grifen
Phineas Comstock
Eber Moor
Joseph Holcomb Jr
Serg^t Nath^{ll} Holcomb
James Slarter
Jonathan Andrus
Daniel Roe

[State Library, Revolution 11.]

CAPT. ROBINSON'S COMPANY.

A Role of a Company in the State of Rhode Island in October A. D. 1777 Commanded by Abner Robinson Capt.

Capt Abner Robinson
Lieut Samuel Campbell
Lieut Joseph Coye
Ensign Abijah Fuller
Serj[t] James Robinson
Serj[t] Nathan Robinson
Serj[t] Daniel Fobes
Serg[t] Joseph Burnam
Serg[t] Josiah Collins
Corpl Samuel Cook
Corpl Asa Royce
Corpl Elijah Simons
Corpl Daniel Denison
Fifer Uriah Kingsley
Jared Allen
Jonathan Avery
Isaac Abbe
Joseph Ashley
Samuel Ashley
Benjamin Burnit
Ethan Barrows
Daniel Badcock
Jonathan Burnit
Elias Blanchard
John Beamis
Thomas Crosby
Joseph Cary
Oliver Cary
Abner Church
Edmon Conent
William Cummins
James Clark
Thomas Coye
William Clark
William Durkee
Solomon Durkee
William D. Foster
James Fletcher
Moses Fith
John Flint
Amaziah Fisk
Ambros Grow
Abiel Holt
Jonathan Hovey
Richard Ingorsoll
William Loomis
Jonathan Loomis
Eleazer M[c]Call
Benjamin Molton
Elijah Miller
Stephen Ormsby
John Ormsby
Vaniah Palmer
Jacob Preston
Eber Robinson
Reuben Robinson
Uriah Roundy
William Rindge
Solomon Robins
Amaziah Storrs
Abner Webb
Frederick J. Whiting
Joseph Waldo
Samuel Whiting
William Young

[*State Library, Hebard Papers.*]

STATE TROOPS, 1777.

COL. McCLELLAN'S REGIMENT.

SIMSBURY SOLDIERS

[This regiment was raised for one month's service by a resolve of the General Assembly passed in August, and by further vote of the Council of Safety, September 23.]

Simsbury Septr; 8th 1777

We the Subscribers Soldiers belonging to a Regt; to be Commanded by Samll McClellan Col; have Each of us Recd of Capt Jona Humphry one Fire lock with Bayonet which Each of us am Accountable for witness Our hands —

Salem Burr
Nathaniel Butler
Stephen Rowely
Stephen Goodrich
Eli Hoskins
John Latimer
Daniel Rowel
Timothy Woodbridg
Francsis Salter
James Larrenc
Israel Case
Theodore Hilleyer
Elihu Case
Thomas wildor
David Phelps Jur
Joel Slater
Aaron Webster
Ashbel Webster
Theodore Cadwell
Asa Gillet
Aaron Brown
Asa Hubbard
Samuel Holton

Chattwil Parsons
Jonathan Bidwell Junr
Pelatiah Cadwell
Timothy Case
Charles Humphry
Solomon Humphy
Abel Case
Kaswell Halel (?)
Jedidiah Holcomb
Thomas Colton
Martin Humphy
James McNall
Daniel Graham J
William Willcocks
Francis Garrett Jr
Hosea Case Jr
George Hills
Dan Case
Asher Humphry
John Nearing
David Thomas
Charles Willcocks
David Messenger

Elijah Holcomb
Charls Dewolf
Elisha Pering
Dan Dibol
Peter Holcomb
Thomas Whiton
George Cornish
Benoni Humphry
Levi Godard
Ebenezer Holcomb
Thomas Allyn

arms rcd. of Capt woodbridge receipted by Capt. Humphry to him for Lieut. Johnson men viz

Salah Jackson
Samuel Wood
Joseph Johnson
David Sears
Isaac Johnson
Abraham Griffeth

Simeon Hollady not receipted } have got receipts for the
Seth Holcomb " } same Return[d].

[*Connecticut Historical Society.*]

Simsbury 8th Oct[r] 1777.

We the Subscribers soldiers in a Reg[t]; to be Commanded by Samuel M[c]Clellan Esq Co[l] have rec[d]; of Cap[t] Jon[a] Humphry the Several Sums Annexed to Our Respective Names, as part of our Pay or Bounty Rec[d] p[r] us.

Israel Case
Joel Slater
James McNall
Daniel Rowel
John Latimer
Eli Hoskins
Elisha Pering
William Roberts
Asher Humphry
Daniel Graham
Jehiel Wells (?)
Simeon Halladay
David Messenger
William Roberts
Elisha Pering
Simeon Holaday
George Hills
Timothy Woobrig
James M[c]Nall
Thomas Whiton
Charles D[e] Wolf
Isreail Case
Joel Slater
Israel Case
Timothy Woodbridge
Eli Hoskins
Daniel Rowel
John Latimer
Danel Grahom Jr
James Mc Nall
Seba Moses
John Nearing
Giles Humphry
Ithamer Colton
Francis Garritt Jr
Willam Roberts
Jehiel Wild (?)
Jedidiah Holcom
Timothy Woodbridge
Joel Slater
Phineas Holcomb
Daniel Dibble
Thomas Wilder
David Thomas
Israel Case
James Larrenc
Roswell Noble
Timothy Woodbridge
Timothy Woodbridge
Jehel Willcocks
Ithamer Colton
Jedidiah Holcomb
Daniel Rowel
John Latimer
George Cornish
Francis Garrit
Giles Humphry
Asher Humphry
Seth Holcomb
Micah Case
Charls Dolph
Simeon Halladay
Dan Dibbel
George Hills

Dan Case
George Cornish
Benoni Humphry
Timothy Case
Daniel Grimes
Phinehas Holcomb
Michiel Case
Charls Dewolf
Abraham Griffen
John Latimer
Daniel Rowel
Isaac Johnson
Ithamar Colton
Jehiall Willcoks
James Lawrence
George Cornish
Joseph Johnson
Samuel Wood
Benoni Humphry
L^{t}. John Johnson
Elisha Pering
Benoni Humphry
Eli Hoskins
Israel Case
Thomas Whiton
Theodore Hillyer
Jedediah Holcomb
John Nearing
Samul Colton
Asher Humphry
Jed Holcomb
John Latimer
Daniel Rowel
David Sears
Thomas Allyn
Salem Burr
Chattwil Parsons
Theodore Cadwell
Pelatiah Cadwell
Francis Garrit
Elihu Case
Salah Jackson
Isaac Johnson
David Sears
David Thomas
Eli Hoskins
Stephen Rowely
Daniel Rowel
Timothy Case
Hosea Case
Abel Case
Timothy Woodbridge
Charles Willcocks
James McNaal
Dan^{ll}; Graham
John Lattimore
David Messenger
Phineas Holcomb
Joel Slater
Charles Humphry
James Larrance
Thomas Wilder
Israel Case
Samuel Colton
Aaron Webster
Aaron Brown
Seba Moses
Dan Case
George Hills
William Roberts
Joel Cornish for
George Cornish
William Roberts
Benj^{a} Holcomb
Benj^{a} Holcomb
for money r^{d}. by En^{s} Hum
Martin Humphy

Simsbury Oct^{r}: 8th 1777

Rec^{d} of Capt Jon^{a} Humphy Eighteen pounds Eight Shillings L mony as a Bounty or advance pay to Raise a Company of men in a Reg^{t} to be Commanded by Sam^{ll} McClellan Esqr Col which I am to acc^{t} for £18 8 0

p^{r} me Benj^{a} Holcomb Leut

Simsbury Octr 8th 1777

Rec^{d} of Capt Jon^{a} Humphy Thirty pounds L money as a Bounty or advance pay for the Raising of a Company of men in a Reg^{t} to be Commanded by Sam^{ll} McClellan Esqr Co^{l} which I am to Acc^{t} for £30

p^{r} me Martin Humphy Ensn

[*Connecticut Historical Society.*]

We the subscribers have Rec^{d} of Capt Jon^{a} Humphry the full of Our Wages that was Due to us from the Town of Simsbury for service in an Expedition to providance in October Last in a Reg^{t} Rais^{d} by the state of

Connec[t] Commanded by Sam[ll] M[c]Clellen Esq[r] Co[l] & in S[d] Humphrys Company rec[d] p[r] us Simsbury March 24th 1778.

Timothy Case
Peter Holcomb Jr
Levi Gosard
Dan Case
Benoni Humphry
Joel Slater
Asher Humphry
James Hills for George
Francis Garrit for Son
Hosea Case Jur
Charles Willcocks
Thomas Wilder
Abel Case
Aaron Willcoks
David Thomas
Giles Humphry
Timothy Woodbridge
William Willcocks
James McNall
David Phelps
Seba Moses
Ebenezer Holcomb
George Cornish
Elijah Holcomb
John Nearing
Israel Case
Roswell Noble
Charles Humphry
James Larrance
Daniel Graham
Elihu Case
David Adams Jr
for William Roberts
Samuel Miller for
Jehial Willcocks
two pound aight

[*Connecticut Historical Society.*]

MILITIA REGIMENTS, 1776.

FIRST REGIMENT (?) — COL. WOLCOTT.

[*See Record of Connecticut Men in the Revolution, page 449.*]

CAPT. HYDE'S COMPANY.

[This company was inlisted as an independent company. See records of the Council of Safety August 16, 1776.]

A Travel Role of Capt Walter Hydes Company in Col^{o} Erastus Woolcot's Reg^{mt} of Militia from Lebanon To New York

Mens Names	Distance Traveled	Mens Names	Distance Traveled
Capt Walter Hyde	miles 150	Stephen Payne	150
Lieu^{t} Samuel Fuller	150	Silas Nye	150
Lieu^{t} John Vaughn	150	Dan Terrey	150
Doct^{r} Andrew Metcalf	150	Whighting Backus	150
Sarj^{t} Thomas Bingham	150	Samuel Woodard	150
Sarj^{t} Joseph Abel	150	Jeriah Wright	150
Sarj^{t} Robert Cambell	150	Solomon Wright	150
Serj^{t} Eliphalet Barker	150	Joseph Bissel	150
Serj^{t} Joseph Leech	150	Elijah Phelps	150
Corp^{rl} Joseph Throop	150	Joseph Phelps	150
Corp^{l} Elisha Doubleday	150	Daniel Smalley	150
Corp^{l} Jabez Foster	150	Abraham Merifield	150
Corp^{l} Benjn Throop	150	Daniel Rockwell	150
Drum^{r} Daniel Hyde	150	Moses Hyde	150
Fif^{r} Jacob Clark	150	Thomas Slooman	150
Samuel Hyde	150	Nehemiah Payne	150
Ezekiel Fitch	150	John Mackswell	150
Elisha Seabury	150	Dan Metcalf	150
James Baley	150	Ebeneazer Metcalf	150
Samuel Baley	150	Thomas Groas	150
Cumfort Bruster	150	Elijah Palmer	150
Bezelial Badger	150		
Dan Clark	150		Miles 6750
Jonathan Blackman	150		

Camp Near Kings Bridge Sep^{tr} 21st, 1776

Joseph Leech Clark

John Vaughan Lieut

[*Connecticut Historical Society.*]

THIRD REGIMENT—COL. JOHN ELY.

[*See Record of Connecticut Men in the Revolution, page 450.*]

CAPT. HOLMS' COMPANY.

Capt Thomas Holms Roll to North Castle New York 1776 under Colo Ely

	£	s	d			£	s	d
Capt Holms	5	1	4		Jeremiah Wheler	1	5	4
Lt Billings	3	3	5		John Wheler Geer	1	5	4
Doct Babcock	3	8	5		Amos Morgan	1	5	4
Serg Coats	1	10	5		John Utley	1	5	4
Corp Miner	1	7	10	2	Jedediah Randall	0	13	4
Corp Wheler	1	7	10	2	Joseph Wheler	1	5	4
Joshua Wilcox	1	5	4		Joshua Grant	1	5	4
Amos Miner	1	5	4		Stephen Main	1	5	4
David Miner	1	5	4		Amos Wheler	1	5	4
Isaac Williams	1	5	4		John Ayers	1	5	4
Isaac Williams 2nd	1	5	4		Amos Solomon	1	5	4
Nat Williams	1	5	4		Benedick Arons	1	5	4
Jonathan Morgan	0	13	4					
						39	1	8
					Sauce money	1	9	3
						40	10	11
					Benedicks	1	6	5
						39	4	6

whole Sause money while under Coll Ely is /15^{d} per mon
Except 2 men /3^{d}
December the 14th A D 1776

Recd of Sanford Billing Four pounds Nine Shilling & Four pence L Money Being part of Capt Thomas Holms Decasd wages Due while under Collonel Ely at North Castle

Sam. Holms administoratr

[A receipt for wages and sauce money signed by the men of the company is with this roll.]

[*Connecticut Historical Society.*]

FOURTH REGIMENT—COL. WHITING.

[*See Record of Connecticut Men in the Revolution, page 449.*]

CAPT. WHEELER'S COMPANY.

Cap[t] Nath[l] Wheelers Pay Roll for the C[o] under his command Belonging to the 4th Reg[t] of Militia of the State of Conn[t] under command of Col[o] Ichb[d] Lewis in a Campaign at New York

Mens Names		Entered into Service 1776		Discharg[d] and left the Service allowing 4 Days to get Home.		Mo.	Dys.
Cap[t] Nath[l] Wheeler		Aug[t]	10	Sep[t]	23	1	13
Jo[s] Curtis	Serg[t]	"	10	"	15	1	5
Stiles Judson	"	"	10	"	20	1	10
David Thompson	"	"	10	"	10	1	—
John Whiting	"	"	10	"	12	1	2
Josiah Peck	Corp[l]	"	10	"	10	1	—
W[m] Brooks		"	10	"	15	1	5
Curtis Beardsley		"	10	Aug[t]	28	0	18
Joel Judson		"	24	Sep[t]	18	0	24
Silas Judson	Drum[r]	"	10	"	10	1	—
Andrew Curtis		"	10	"	13	1	3
Nath[n] Birdsey		"	10	"	10	1	—
Elnath[n] Wilcockson		"	10	"	5	0	25
Judson Peck		"	10	"	0	1	—
Lewis Curtis		"	10	"	10	1	—
Abel Booth		"	10	"	20	1	10
Ja[s] Kirtland		"	10	"	23	1	13
Abr[m] Curtis		"	10	"	9	1	—
Steph[n] Lewis		"	10	"	9	1	—
Ja[s] Shearman		"	10	"	18	1	18
Thad[s] Curtis		"	10	"	8	0	28
Jo[s] Frost		"	10	"	15	1	5
Abel Judson		"	10	"	17	1	7
Abel Walker		"	10	"	12	1	2
Sam[l] Wheeler		"	10	"	10	1	—
Job Peck		"	10	"	10	1	—
Agur Curtis		"	10	"	15	1	5
Isaac Curtis		"	10	"	8	0	28
Nehem[h] Thompson		"	10	"	29	1	19
Abel Fairchild		"	10	"	17	1	7
Ebenez[r] Birdsey		"	10	"	29	1	19
Ebenez[r] Curtis		"	10	"	8	0	28
John Bardslee		"	10	"	19	1	9
Ja[s] Peck		"	10	"	20	1	10
Ja[s] Judson		"	10	"	20	1	10
Steph[n] Curtis		"	10	"	20	1	10
Elias Wells		"	10	"	10	1	6
Ja[s] Wells		"	10	"	19	1	9
Johon Beers		"	10	"	20	1	10

Mens Names	Entered into Service 1776	Discharg[d] and left the Service allowing 4 Days to get Home.	Mo.	Dys.
Rob[t] Curtis	Aug[t] 10	Sep[t] 15	1	5
Phine[s] Beers	" 10	" 29	1	19
Sam[l] Curtis	" 10	" 20	1	10
Silas Curtis	" 10	" 12	1	2
Abel Booth J[r]	" 10	" 20	1	10

[*Copy in Comptroller's Office.*]

FOURTEENTH COMPANY—CAPT. GODFREY.

A Ration Abstract for Cap[t] Dan[l] Godfrey[s] C[o] in Col. Sam[l] Whiting[s] Reg[t] of Militia which enter[d] upon Guard in Greens Farms. By order pursuant to Gen[l] Stillmans Order in Dec[r] 1776 —

Names	Time of Marching	Time of Discharge
Dan[l] Godfrey Cap[t]	Dec[r] 5	Dec[r] 17
Jo[s] Bennett Ens[n]	" 5	"
Jonah Squire Serg[t]	" 5	"
David Morehouse	" 5	"
Joel Gilbert Corp[l]	" 5	"
Joshua Disbrow "	" 5	"
Bradley Dean Fifer	" 5	"
Jesse Morehouse	" 5	"
John Andrews J[r]	" 5	"
Isaac Disbrow	" 5	"
Gideon Couch	" 5	"
Tho[s] Nash Couch	" 5	"
Dan[l] Bradley Jun[r]	" 5	"
Tho[s] Burnett J[r]	" 5	"
John Disbrow	" 5	"
Benj[n] Allen	" 5	"
Amos Gray	" 5	"
David Raymond	" 5	"
Isaac Elwood	" 5	"
John Crasman	" 5	"
Esra Thorp	" 5	"
Jaied Duncan	" 5	"
Henry Winkley	" 5	"
Steph[n] Dickman	" 5	"
Christ[r] Godfrey	" 5	"
Jon[a] Beers	" 5	"
Nath[n] Ogden	" 5	"
W[m] Batterson	" 5	"
Ichab[d] Canfield	" 5	"
Elias Bennett	" 5	"
Sturges Burr	" 5	"
Benj[n] Sol[o] Couch	" 5	"
W[m] Bennett	" 5	"
Justus Disbrow	" 5	"
Riab Beers	" 5	"
Straton Briant	" 5	"
Justus Smith	" 5	"

[*Copy in Comptroller's Office.*]

SIXTH REGIMENT—COL. CHESTER.

[*See Record of Connecticut Men in the Revolution, page 449.*]

CAPT. WELLS' COMPANY.

An abstract of Capt Chester Wells Company in Col Chesters Reg^{t} from the time of Enlistment untill march^{d} July 1776

Names	When Inlisted	When marched
Capt. Chester Wells	June 20	July 10
Lt. Edwd Bulkley	20	10
Lt. Eben^{r} Wright	20	18
Ens. Jon^{a} Stoddard	20	10
Serj. John Fraims	20	10
" Chas Curtiss	20	10
" Oliver Treat	20	10
" Jos. Andrews	20	10
Fife Jo. May	20	10
Drum Sim Dickinson	20	10
Corp. Fred. Robbins	20	10
" Lem^{l} Woodhoop	20	10
" Robt Warner	20	10
" Elijah Bordman	20	10
Priv. Eli Tryon	20	10
Ashbil Riley	20	10
Jos. Adams	24	10
Saml Andrews	24	10
Eben Bigelow	24	10
Henry Brown	24	10
Abr^{a} Blin	26	10
Thos Blackwell	24	10
Moses Belden	21	10
Fra^{s} Bulkley	24	10
Jon^{a} Brooks	Aug. 5	Aug. 17
Leo^{d} Bordman	June 24	July 10
O Burnham	24	10
Jared Brace	24	10
Thos Clark	Aug. 5	Aug. 17
Joseph Crain	June 24	July 10
James Curtiss	24	10
Joshua Cone	24	10
Jos. Combs	24	10
Jos. Curtiss	24	10
William Curtiss	24	10
Roger Clapp	24	10
Chas Churchill	July 8	Aug. 7
Joel Caatch	Aug. 5	17
Richd Demming	June 24	July 10
Eph^{m} Demming	24	10
Simeon Demming	24	10
Saml Dix	24	10
Benj^{a} Dix	24	10

Names	When Inlisted	When marched
Jesse Dix	Aug. 5	Aug. 17
Edmond Dorr	28	10
Waitstill Dickinson	25	10
Josiah Dickinson	5	17
Ozias Dickinson	5	17
William Dilling	5	17
Abel Fullar	June 28	July 10
John Fraines	24	10
John Furbs	24	10
Isaac Goodrich	24	10
Joh^{a} Goodrich	22	10
John Goodrich	24	10
Hosea Goodrich	Aug. 5	Aug. 17
Simon Griffin	July 1	July 9
Moses Griswold	June 24	10
Silas Hurlburt	24	10
James Hatch	24	10
Eben^{r} Kilbeŷ	July 1	9
David King	June 26	10
Stephen Kellogg	24	10
Mitchell Kingman	Aug. 5	Aug. 17
Levi Loveland	July 1	July 9
Luman Lary	4	24
Saml Lawson	Aug. 5	Aug. 17
Sol^{o} Lattimer	5	17
Hosea Millar	June 24	July 10
James Murpy	24	10
John Minor	July 1	15
Richd Montague	June 24	10
Zeb^{n} Myggott	July 4	12
Hez^{a} Nott	June 21	10
Wm Rood	Aug. 5	Aug. 17
Jos. Rood	June 24	July 10
John Russell	26	10
Saml Rockwell	24	10
Oswell Rockwell	24	10
Enoch Stoddard	24	10
Saml Stoddard	Aug. 5	Aug. 17
John Stoddard	5	17
Zach^{a} Seymour	5	17
Zach^{a} Seymour Jr	July 12	July 20
James Smith	June 24	10
Chas Treat	24	10
John Woodhouse	24	10
Elisha Wolcott	24	10
William Wolcott	24	10
Elizur Wolcott	24	10
Eben^{r} Wells	24	10
Elisha Wells	24	10
Sion Wentworth	24	10
Elisha Webster	Aug. 5	Aug. 17
Danl Warner	June 24	July 10
Jos. Wheeler	24	10
Joshua Wells	Aug. 5	Aug. 17
Joseph Wright	June 24	July 10
Saml Woodhouse	24	10

[*State Library, Revolution 32.*]

A Pay Roll of Capt Chester Wells Co in Colo Chesters Regt from their arrival in New York to the 1st Day of Octbr Including 6 days to Travel 120 Ml

Names & Rank	Time when arrid in N York 1776	Time when Dead, Desertd or Discharged	Ms & Days in Service Ms	Dys
Capt Chester Wells	July 10		2	27
Edwd Bulkley Lieut	" 10		2	27
Ebenezr Wright "	" 18		2	19
Jona Stoddard Ensign	" 10	Sept 3	2	22
John Francis Sergt	" 10	" "	2	27
Chas Curtis "	" 10	Augt 3	1	20
Jas Andrus "	" 10		2	27
Olivr Treat "	" 10	Augt 19	1	16
Leml Woodhouse Corpl promotd Augt 24	" 10		2	27
Fredk Robbins promotd Aug 20	" 10		2	27
Robt Warner Corpl	" 10		2	27
Elijah Boardman "	" 10		2	27
Joseph May Fifer	" 10		2	27
Simeon Dickison Drumr	" 10	Sept 3d	2	27
Joseph Adams Private	" 10		2	27
Saml Andrus	" 10		2	27
Alvin Bigelow	" 10		2	27
Henry Brown	" 10		2	27
Abrm Blin	" 10		2	27
Thos Wilson Buknel	" 10		2	27
Moses Belding	" 10		2	27
Francis Bulkley	" 10		2	27
Jona Brooks	Augt 15		1	22
Lincord Boardman	July 10		2	27
Orrin Burnham	" 10		2	27
Jered Bunce	" 10		2	27
Thos Clark	Augt 15		1	22
Jos Crane	July 10		2	27
James Curtis	" 10		2	27
Joshua Cone	" 10		2	27
Jas Combs	" 10		2	27
Jos Curtis	" 10		2	27
Wm Curtis	" 10		2	27
Chas Churchel	" 20		2	17
Roger Clap	" 10		2	27
Joel Conch	Augt 15		1	22
Richd Deming	July 10		2	27
Ephm Deming	" 10		2	27
Simeon Deming	" 10		2	27
Samuel Dix	" 10		2	27
Benja Dix	" 10		2	27
Jesse Dix	Augt 15		1	22
Edmond Dorr	July 10		2	27
Waitstill Dickerson	" 10		2	27
Osias Dickerson	Aug 15		1	22
Josiah Dickerson	" 15		1	22
Wm Dilkins	" 15		1	22
Jos Whealor	July 10		2	27
Joshua Wells	Aug 15		1	22
Abel Fuller	July 10		2	27
John Francis	" 10		2	27
John Farles	" 10		2	27

Names & Rank	Time when arrid in N York	Time when Dead, Desertd or Discharged	Ms & Days in Service Ms Dys
	1776		
Isaac Goodrich	July 10		2 27
John Goodrich	" 10		2 27
Hozea Goodrich	Augt 15		1 22
Simeon Griffin	July 10		2 27
Moses Griswold	" 10		2 27
Silas Hurlburt	" 10		2 27
Jas Hatch	" 10		2 27
Ebenezr Kilby	" 10		2 27
David King	" 10		2 27
Stephn Kellogg	" 10		2 27
Mitchell Kingman	Augt 15		1 22
Levi Loveland	July 10		2 27
Lumon Long	" 20		2 17
Saml Lawson	Augt 15		1 22
Solo Lattimer	" 15		1 22
Hosea Miller	July 10		2 27
Jas Murfy	" 10		2 27
John Miner	" 10		2 27
Richd Montigue	" 10		2 27
Zebelon Maggott	" 10		2 27
Hezch Nott	" 10		2 27
Wm Roads	Augt 15		1 22
Jos Roads	July 10		2 27
John Russell	" 10		2 27
Saml Rockwell	" 10		2 27
Oswell Rockwell	" 10		2 27
Enoch Stoddard	" 10		2 27
Saml Stoddard	Augt 15		1 22
John Stoddard	" 15		1 22
Zacheriah Seymour	" 15		1 22
Zachrh Seymour Jr	July 20		2 17
Jas Smith	" 10		2 27
Eli Tryon Corpl 20th Sept	" 10		2 27
Chas Treat	" 10		2 27
John Woodhouse	" 10		2 27
Saml Woodhouse	" 10		2 27
Elisha Woolcott	" 10		2 27
Wm Woolcott	" 10		2 27
Elizur Woolcott	" 10		2 27
Ebenezr Wells	" 10		2 27
Zion Wintworth	" 10		2 27
Elisha Wells	" 10		2 27
Elisha Webster	Augt 15		1 22
Danl Warner	July 10		2 27
Jos Wright	" 10		2 27
Ashbell Riley promotd to Drumr Sept 4	" 10		2 27

[*Copy in Comptroller's Office.*]

SIXTH COMPANY—LIEUT. ANDRUSS.

A Pay Roll of the Sixth Company in the Sixth Regiment of Malitia Commanded by Lieut Stephen Andruss, for service Done in New York in August & September Last with wages and Milage and sauce money when Entered & when Discharged.

Mens Name and Quality.	When Entered at York	When Dis-charged.	Wages				Travil Money		Sauce Money.	Total of each man's money.		
	August	September	L.	s.	d.	f.	s.	d.	d.	L.	s.	d.
Lieut Stephen Andruss	20th	11th	3	18	1		19	8	1/10	6	9	7
Sarjt Melitiah Nye	"	24th	3	8	10	1	19	8	2/11	4	11	5
" Jared Hollister	"	24th	3	8	10	1	18	8	2/11	4	11	5
" Joseph Churchel	"	11th	2	8	1	2	19	8	1/10	3	9	7
" Isaac Tallcot	"	6th	1	18	4		19	8	1/5	2	19	5
Corpl John Wire	"	24th	3	3	2		19	8	2/11	4	5	9
" Nehimiah Hollister	"	11th	2	2	10	3	19	8	1/10	3	4	4¾
" Ruben Risley	"	11th	2	2	10	3	19	8	1/10	3	4	4¾
" Henry Huxford	"	11th	2	2	10	3	19	8	1/10	3	4	4¾
Drumr David Fox	"	11th	2	2	10	3	19	8	1/10	3	4	4¾
Fifer David Hollister	"	11th	2	2	10	3	19	8	2/11	3	4	4¾
Charles Andruss	"	24th	2	17	4		19	8	1/10	3	13	11
John Andruss	"	11th	2	0	0		19	8	2/11	3	1	6
David Andruss	"	24th	2	17	4		19	8	2/11	3	19	11
Benjiman Andruss	"	24th	2	17	4		19	8	2/11	3	19	11
Levi Brooks	"	24th	2	17	4		19	8	2/11	3	19	11
Samuel Covill	"	24th	2	17	4		19	8	2/11	3	19	11
Philip Covill	"	24th	2	17	4		19	8	1/10	3	19	11
Elisha Couch	"	11th	2	0	0		19	8	2/11	3	1	6
Ebenezer Fox	"	24th	2	17	4		19	8	1/10	3	19	11
Israel Fox	"	11th	2	0	0		19	8	1/10	3	1	6
Isaac Fox	"	11th	2	0	0		19	8	2/11	3	1	6
Stephen Fox	"	24th	2	17	4		19	8	2/11	3	19	11
Joseph Goodale	"	24th	2	17	4		19	8	2/11	3	19	11
Timothy Goslee	"	24th	2	17	4		19	8	2/3	3	19	11
Aron Gosse	"	16th	2	6	8		19	8	2/3	3	8	7
David Hubburd	"	16th	2	6	8		19	8	2/3	3	8	7
Joseph Hubburd	"	11th	2	0	0		19	8	1/10	3	1	6
Israel House	"	24th	2	17	6		19	8	2/11	3	19	11
Elisha How	"	11th	2	0	9		19	8	1/10	3	11	0
William Holdrath	"	16th	2	6	8		19	8	2/3	3	8	7
William House	"	11th	2	0	0		19	8	1/10	3	1	6
Lazarus House	"	24th	2	17	4		19	8	2/11	3	19	11
Appleton Holmes	"	24th	2	17	4		19	8	2/11	3	19	11
Elisha Hills	"	24th	2	17	4		19	8	2/11	3	19	11
Ichabod Hollister	"	24th	2	17	4		19	8	2/11	3	19	11
George Hollister	"	24th	2	17	4		19	8	2/11	3	19	11
Israel Hills	"	6th	1	13	4		19	8	1/5	2	14	5
Frary Hale	"	24th	2	17	4		19	8	2/11	3	19	11
Isaac Hale	"	24th	2	17	4		19	8	2/11	3	19	11
Daniel House	"	11th	2	0	0		19	8	1/10	3	1	6
Joseph Hills	"	24th	2	17	4		19	8	2/11	3	19	11
Abner House	"	24th	2	17	4		19	8	2/11	3	19	11
Isaac Keeney	"	24th	2	17	4		19	8	2/11	3	19	5
Elizur Lovland	"	6th	2	17	4		19	8	1/5	2	14	5
Pelitiah Lovland	"	24th	1	13	4		19	8	2/11	3	19	11
Levi Loveland	"	24th	2	17	4		19	8	2/11	3	19	11
Samuel Risley	"	24th	2	17	4		19	8	2/11	3	19	11
Ruben Sparks	"	11th	2	0	0		19	8	1/10	3	1	6

Mens Names and Quality.	When Entered at York	When Discharged.	Wages				Travil Money		Sauce Money.	Total of Each man's money.		
	August	September	L.	s.	d.	f.	s.	d.	d.	L.	s.	d.
Samuel Smith	20th	16th	2	6	8		19	8	2/3	3	8	7
Ezekiel Skinner	"	24th	2	0	0		19	8	2/11	3	19	11
Lemuel Stratton	"	11th	2	17	4		19	8	2/11	3	1	6
Jonathan Treet	"	11th	2	0	0		19	8	1/10	3	1	6
Isaac Tubbs	"	24th	2	17	4		19	8	2/11	3	19	11
John Welles	"	11th	2	0	0		19	8	1/1	3	1	6
Peleg Welden	"	24th	2	17	4		19	8	2/10	3	19	11
Nehimiah Wire	"	16th	2	6	8		19	8	2/6	3	8	7
Joseph Wares	"	24th	2	17	4		19	8	2/11	3	19	11
John Wickham	"	11th	2	0	0		19	8	1/10	3	1	6

Lieu^t Stephen Andruss Roll to pay of his Men With. 1777. Feb. 25th

[*Dwight A. Andrews, Hartford.*]

TWELFTH REGIMENT—COL. HOSFORD.

[*See Record of Connecticut Men in the Revolution, page 450.*]

OFFICERS.

A Return of the Officers & Men that Serv^{d} Under Col^{o} Obadiah Hosford at West Chester
Septr 1776 Viz

		No. of Men			No. of Men
Capt. David Tarbox per	Roll	28	Capt. Ephraim Carpenter	Roll	35
Capt. David Miller	"	35	Capt. James Pineo	"	35
Capt. Andrew Waterman	"	[30]	Capt. John Wells	"	36
Capt. Eb^{r}. Hutchinson	"	41			
Capt. Danl Dewey	"	33			304
Capt. Joshua Phelps	"	30			

[*State Library, Revolution 6.*]

CAPT. TARBOX'S COMPANY.

A List of Capt David Tarbox C^{o} in Reg^{t} who march^{d} by order to East Chester Sept last (filed Hosfords Reg^{t})

David Tarbox	Capt	Diah Stark
Sol^{o} Tarbox	Lieu^{t}.	Danl Waters
Elisha Beach	Ens^{n}	Hez^{h} Cutting
Caleb Root	Serg^{t}	Jon^{a} Dunham
Christ^{r} Crouch	"	John Birg
Jo^{s} Waters	"	John Taylor
Jo^{s} Pepoon	"	Joshua Bigelow
Benjn Pepoon	Corp^{l}	Lawrence Powers
Jared Allen	"	Wm Darby
Levy Washborn	"	Zenas Tarbox
John Kellogg	" Desert^{d} Oct 18	Hazel Crandel
Joel Jones	Drum^{r}	Alex^{r} Phelps
Saml Jones	Fifer	Nathl Pease
David Skinner		Zebedee Cutting

Jere^{h} Mason Maj^{r}

[*Copy in Comptroller's Office.*]

CAPT. MILLER'S COMPANY.

A List of Capt David Millers C^{o} Lt Col. Obediah Hosfords Reg^{t} that march^{d} in Septr 1776 to East Chester to join Genl Washington's Army.

Names		Names
David Miller	Capt	John Huxford
Sol^{n} Phelps	Lieut	Epafrus Loveland
Wm Burt	Ens^{n}	Elisha Watrous
Jonah Root	Serg^{t}	Benjn Chamberlain
Eleaz^{r} Carter	"	Asa Loomis
Saml Finley	"	Ja^{s} Mackarel
David Blush	"	Abr^{m} Skinner 3^{d}
Israel Foot J^{r}	"	David Strong
Thos Carrier J^{r}	Corp^{l}	Jon^{a} Willis
Ebenez^{r} Coleman	"	Thos Hills
Benjn Darbee	Fifer	David Kellogg
Libbius Hills	Drum^{r}	Reuben Curtis
Adonij^{h} Strong		Benajah Jones
Chas Edy		Danl Loveland
Jeded^{h} Edgerton		Jacob Ingraham
Silvenus Norket		Asa Fuller
John Dewey		Hezekiah Kneland

Jerem^{h} Mason Maj^{r}

Gideon Waters Desert^{d}. Oct 24

[*Copy in Comptroller's Office.*]

CAPT. WATERMAN'S COMPANY.

A List of Capt Andrew Waterman Company in Lef^{t} Colo Obediah Hosford Regm^{t}

Andrew Waterman	Capt	Bela Devenport
Elihu Thomas	Left	Mark Fowler
Jacob Mackaul	Ensn	Amos Fowler
Joseph Lomis	Sargt	Daniel Ingraham
Simon Abel	Sargt	Benjamin Kinne
Dijah Fowler	Sargt	James Lothrop
Isaiah Loomis	Sargt	Dan Lee
Aaron Thorp	Corp	Thomas L Hyde
Otis Bigelow	Corp	Simeon Puffer
Jesse Brown	Corp	Sam^{ll} Robbinson
William Hyde	Drum^{r}	John Whitman
Olliver Strong	fifer	Sam^{ll} Wattles Jr
John Bartlet		Vetch Williams Jr
William Bentley		Joseph W Bissel
Caleb Chappel		Joseph Bartlet Jr
Benjamin Dike		

Jeremiah Mason Maj^{r}

[*State Library, Revolution 6.*]

CAPT. HUTCHINSON'S COMPANY.

Capt Eleaz^{r} Hutchinsons C^{o} Militia under Comman^{d} Col. Hosford^{s} Reg^{t} State Conn^{t}

Names		
Eleaz^{r} Hutchinson	Capt	
Paul Brigham	Lieut	
Thos Terril	Ensign	
John Henry	Serg^{t}	
Danl White	Serg^{t}	
Aaron Swetland	"	
Eliph^{t} Hendy	"	
Adonij^{h} White	Corp^{l}	
Jabez Loomis	"	
Jo^{s} Kingsbury	"	
Eph Beemas	"	
Eleaz^{r} Hutchinson	Drum^{r}	
Saml Jones	Fifer	
Wm Blackman		
Jon^{a} Badcock		
Wm Bowles		Desert^{d} Sep^{t} 28 return^{d} Novr 8
Adam Bingham		
Reuben Bill		
Levi Buell		
Danl Badcock		" " " "
Josiah Burnap		" " " "
David Brown		
Asariah Bell		" " " "
Tim^{o} Cowles		" " " "
Alex^{r} House		
Ja^{s} House		
Ja^{s} Hawkins		
Isahel Jones		
Benjn Jones		
Abiath^{r} Lyman		" " " "
Eleaz^{r} Lomiss		
Saml Perkins		
Jacob Fox		
Benjn Sprague		
Ebenez^{r} Sweetland		" " " "
Elisha Sprague		" " " "
Jo^{s} Savary		
Jon^{a} Savary		
David Townsen		" " " "
Jon^{a} Townsen		
Thos Tomson		" " " "

[*Copy in Comptroller's Office.*]

CAPT. DEWEY'S COMPANY.

A List of Capt Danl Deweys C^{o} in Lt Col^{o} O. Hosfords Reg^{t} that marched to East Chester Sep^{t} 1776 to join Genl Washington's Army

Danl Dewey	Capt	Elisha Hutchinson	Serg^{t}
And^{w} Huntington	L^{t}	Annis Fitch	"
Wm Mordock	Ens^{n}	Eleaz^{r} Manning	"
Chas Swift	Serg^{t}	Tim^{o} Allen	"

Jo^{s} Robinson Corp^{l}
Thos Laws "
Ezek^{l} Loomis "
Gersh^{m} Clark Drum^{r}
Andr^{w} Hide Fifer
Nath^{n} Lee
Peletiah Holbrook
David Potter
Ja^{s} Tickour
Rodolph^{s} Wacker
John Arnold
Saml Beemon
Richd Lyman
Beriah Sprague
Jon^{a} Bliss
Jon^{a} Edgerton
Gurdian geer
David Metcalf
Isaih Loomis
Asa Tiffeny
Adonijah Crocker
Benjn Tilden
Gideon Clark
Isaih Tiffeny
Asell Clark

Jer^{h} Mason Maj^{r}

[*Copy in Comptroller's Office.*]

CAPT. PHELPS' COMPANY.

A List of Capt Joshua Phelps C^{o} in Lieut Col^{o} Obadiah Hosfords Reg^{t} that March^{d} by order to Eastchester in Sep^{t} 1776 to join Genl Washington's Army

Joshua Phelps Capt
Saml Tyler Lieut
Roger Phelps Ens^{n}
Asa White Serg^{t}
John Gilbert "
Steph^{n} Barber "
Aaron Phelps "
David Strong Corp^{l}
Roswell Phelps "
David Carver "
Abel Bissel "
David Barber Drum^{r}
Beniah Phelps Fifer
Asa Boles
Amos Phelps J^{r}
Andrew Man
Eph^{m} Phelps
Saml Phelps
Inereas Porter
Joshua Phelps J^{r}
Joel Porter
Ja^{s} Pratt
Jon^{a} Tarbox
Obed^{h} White
Phinehas Strong
Silvester Garner
Tim^{o} Phelps J^{r}
John Gillet
Danl Phelps
Obediah Phelps

Jere^{h} Mason Maj^{r}

[*Copy in Comptroller's Office.*]

CAPT. CARPENTER'S COMPANY.

A List of Capt Eph^{m} Carpenters C^{o} in Col^{o} Hosfords Reg^{t} who march^{d} by order to East Chester Sep^{t} 1776

Eph^{m} Carpenter Capt
Danl Clark Lieut
Israel Williams Ens^{n}
Oliv^{r} Bill Serg^{t}
Malicha Thomas "
Joshua Carpenter "
Johiel Williams "
Chas Williams "
Amos Porter Corp^{l}
Jacob Clark "
Tabin Bosworth "
John Williams "
Roswell Clark Drum^{r}
Edwd Luther
Israel Bliss
Ja^{s} Gay
Danl Wilcox
Eliph^{t} Abel
Jon^{a} T Bissell
Abiel Bajcom
Hosea Birge
Amos Clark
Jon^{a} Cole
Joel Chamberlin

Rufus Lamb
Roswell Richardson
Noah Roberds
John Torry
Tim° Waters
Ja[s] Webster
W[m] Webster
Eph[m] Wilcox
Jared Clark
Eleazer Bill
Andrew Clark

[*Copy in Comptroller's Office.*]

CAPT. PINEO'S COMPANY.

A List of Capt James Pineo Company in Left Colo Hosford Regiment that Marched by order To East chester To Join General Washintons Army

James Pineo Capt
Elias Bliss Left
Daniel Dunham Ensn
James Woodworth Sarg[t]
Samuel West Sarg[t]
Henry Bliss Serg[t]
Joseph Hatch Corpl
Eldad Hunt Corpl
Benoni Loomis Cor
Rufus Collins Drummer
Jabez Persons fifer
Eliot Porter
Joseph Solland
Josiah Thomas
Sam[ll] Allen
John Joy
Jesse Wright
David Boles
Ephrm Hills
Edward Hawkins
John Holbrook
Elisha Warner
William White
Eleazer Collins
Zelotis Collins
Joshua Woodworth
Elijah Chappel
Sam[ll] Boston
Bethewell Newcomb
Jonath[n] Bissell
Fadrick White
Josiah Dewey
David Treadway
Joseph Demon
Samuel Guile

Jeremiah Mason Maj[r]

[*State Library, Revolution 6.*]

CAPT. WELLS' COMPANY.

A List of the 8th Company in the 12th Regiment of Melisha in the State of Conecticut that March[d] to West Chester in Sep[r] in 1776

Capt John H Wells
Lieutenant William Tallcott
Ensign Simeon Dunham
Daniel Bushnell
David Post
Sarg[t] Alexsander White
Gad Tallcott
Daniel Chapman Deserted
Corp[l] Eliphalet Youngs
Jehial Wilcox
Elihu Wells
Dru[r] Samuel Peters
Fifer Ashel Gilbert Deserted
Jonothan Hutchinson
Daniel Root
Joseph Hutchinson
Jeremiah Brown
Zachariah Perren
Isireal Hutchinson
Joshua Root
David Norton
Eli Phelps
Ezekiel Write
Joseph Peters Deserted
Ellis Luther
Isarel Skiner
Abel Write Deserted
Joseph Martin
Samuel Ingham
Zadock Man Deserted
Josiah Mack
John Post
Adenijah Skiner
Elisha Phelps
John Perren
Ezekiel Root

Test John H Wells Cap[t]
Jeremiah Mason Maj[r]

[*State Library, Revolution 6.*]

SEVENTEENTH REGIMENT—COL. SHELDON.

[See Record of Connecticut Men in the Revolution, page 449.]

DESERTERS.

List of Deserters from 17 Milit[a] Reg[t] on Service at N. York Aug[t] 1776 each of whom had 20/ advanc[d] before their March for which they are now Debtors to the State

Moses Bartholomew	of Cap[t] Barns C[o]
Jn[o] Malsby	" "
Abner Hancock	" "
Bela Graves	" "
Sam[l] Renner	" "
Jn[o] Griswold	" "
Isaac Bartholomew	" "
Benj[n] Doolittle	of Cap[t] Osborns C[o]
Steph[n] Plant	" "
Benj[n] Bissel	" "
Josiah Stone	" "
Jonas Leach	of Cap[t] Loomiss C[o]
Noah Beach	" "
Rich[d] Leech	" "

[Copy in Comptroller's Office.]

EIGHTEENTH REGIMENT—COL. PETTIBONE.

SIMSBURY MINUTE MEN.

[Simsbury men belonging to the 1st Company in the 18th Regiment of Militia, Abel Pettibone Captain, Jonathan Pettibone Colonel, who "inlisted to serve as Minute-Men for the Defence of this and the adjoining Colonies" June 11, 1776.]

Ehud Tuller
Ahijah Pettibone
Noah Humphry Jr
Isaac Alderman
Joel Tuller
Ozios Phelps
Joel Case
Isaac Willcocks
Richard Humphry
John Alderman
James Cornish Jun[r]
Aaron Willcocks
Sarrid Thomas
Elisha Willcok
Eli Alderman
Isak Allen
Elijah Tuller

[The following names found upon the back of the same paper appear to be a further record of inlistments.]

David Phelps
Sedose Willcoks
Jo[s] Foot
Jo[s] Goodwine
Dudly Pettibone
Caleb Case
Sam[ll] Goodwine
Peres Maskel
Moses Case
Jon[a] Case

[L. W. Bigelow, Simsbury.]

NINETEENTH REGIMENT—LIEUT.-COL. PITKIN.

[*See Record of Connecticut Men in the Revolution, page 450.*]

CAPT. FITCH'S COMPANY.

A Pay Roll of Capt James Fitch's Company Commanded by Maj^r. Nath^ll Terry to 1st of Octb^r Inclusive.

Names	Arrival in New York Aug. 1776	Days added on 144 Miles from N. Y.		Discharged	Days Service
Capt. James Fitch	24	7			46
Lieut Elisha Kibbe	24	7		Sepr 6th	27
Ensign Daniel Elsworth	24	7			46
Serj^t Ichabod Wadsworth	24	7			46
Serj^t Daniel Warner	24	7		6th	27
Serj^t Gurdon Elsworth	24	7			46
Serj^t Daniel Day	24	7			46
Clerk Daniel Porter	24	7		20th	41
Corp^l John Craw Jr.	24	7			46
Corp^l Silas Reed	24	7		20th	41
Corp^l Rufus Cleaveland	24	7			46
Corp^l Edward Paine	24	7			46
Drum^r Sam^ll Pierson Jr.	24	7			46
Fifer Eb^r Pinney	24	7			46
Eliphas Bartlet	24	7			46
Edmund Bragg	24	7			46
Saml Bartlet	24	7			46
Simeon Belknap Jr.	24	7			46
Joseph Campbell	24	7			46
Adonijah Day	24	7		3rd	24
Jonathan Damon	24	7		3rd	24
Jedediah Durphy or Durfy	24	7			46
John Damon	24	7			46
Nathan Hall	24	7			46
Elijah Farnam or Farmon	24	7			46
Thomas Kennedy	24	7		6th	27
Elijah Kingsbury	24	7			46
David McCray	24	7		3	24
Benja Lewis	24	7			46
John Lovett			Deserted		
James Lovett			Deserted		
William Kinney	24	7			46
James Kinney			Deserted		
William McCray	24	7			46
Nathan McQuavy or MCurthy	24	7			46
Thos McKnight	24	7			46
Isaac Newton	24	7			46
John Newhall	24	7			46
Andrew Pimber	24	7		3rd	24
John Parker	24	7		6th	27

Names	Arrival in New York Augt. 1776	Days added on 144 Miles from N. Y.		Discharged	Days Service
Jonathan Porter	24	7			46
Daniel Person	24	7			46
Ephraim Pierson	24	7			46
Lemuel Pinney			Deserted		
Hezekiah Russell	24	7		6th	27
Lothrop Shirtleff	24	7			46
Wiliam Spear Jr.	24	7			46
John Wallace	24	7		6th	27
James Wallace	24	7		3rd	24
William Wallace	24	7		6th	27
Lemuel West	24	7			46

[*Connecticut Historical Society.*]

TWENTY-FIRST REGIMENT—COL. DOUGLASS.

[*See Record of Connecticut Men in the Revolution, page 450.*]

CAPT. SMITH'S COMPANY.

Pay Role of Capt Wm Smiths Company in Co^ll J. Douglas Reg^t who joind the American army in the State of New York Sep^t. 1776

Mens Names	Miles to & from Camp		Entred Service		Dischargd
Capt Wm Smith			7th Sept^r		Novr 20
Ensi Peter Davison			"		Nov 9
Sarj Na^t Cogwell	272		"		Nov 20
Sarj John Stevens	272		"		Nov 10
Sarj Wm Cushman	160				
Cor. Deleno Peirce	272		"		Nov 20
Cor. Nathan Deans	272		"		Nov 20
Col. Walter Boman	272		"		Nov 10
Cor. John Baker	272		"		Nov 20
David Thayer	272		"		Nov 6
Jonathan Pike	272		"		Nov 8
Ward Woodard	272		"		Nov 9
John Ashcraft	272		"		Nov 20
Wm Foster	112		"	Dead	Nov 4
Wm Ashcraft	272	Absent Carting 1 month	"		Novr 20
Caleb Adams	272		"		Oct 10
Jonathan Copland	272		"		Oc^t 12
Eleazer Litchfield	272		"		Nov 20
Silas Adams	272		"		Sep^t 30
Increse Huit	272		"		Oc^t 10
Jonas Baker	272		"		Nov 20
Stephen Huit	272		"		Nov 20
Elisha Fitch	112		"	Enlisted	Sep^t 21
James Cleavland Ju	112		"	"	" 24
Uriah Holt	112		"	"	" 21

[*Connecticut Historical Society.*]

CAPT. CADY'S COMPANY.

A Pay Roll of Capt David Cady^s Company in Co^ll Douglass^s Rig^t Who Join'd The American Army In the State of Newyork Sep^t 1776.

Mens Names	Engag^d in Service	Miles to and From Camp	Deserted	Discharg^d	Time in Service m	d
Capt D : Cady	Sep^t 7th 1776			Nvo^r 20	2	21
Liu^t Co^l Day				"	2	21
Ens^n Na^t Spaulding				"	2	21
Serg^t Jo^n Roberts		288		"	2	21
" Willm Graves			Sep^t 26th	"		
" Jed^h Bennet			"			
" Jon^tn Day			"			
Clark Sil^s Huchans			"			

	Engag^{d} in Service	Miles to and From Camp	Deserted	Discharg^{d}	Time in Service m	d
Corp^{ll} Step^{n} Rude			Sep^{t} 26th			
" Abner Day				Sep^{t} 28	0	29
" Corn^{as} Whitney			"			
Fif^{r} Ros^{l} Fairman		288		Nov. 20	2	21
Willm Spaulding		288		Nov. 20	2	21
Uriah Kee		288		Nov. 9	2	10
Henry Sparks		288		Nov. 20	2	21
John Sparks		288		Nov. 20	2	21
Jam^{s} Dixson		288		Nov. 7	2	8
Step^{n} Grover		288		Sept. 27	0	28
John Bush		288		Sep 30	1	1
Icah^{d} Sparks		288		Nov. 20	2	21
John Moffitt		288		Nov. 20	2	21
And^{w} Moffitt		288		Oc^{t} 6th	1	7
Jo^{n} Stedman		288		Nov 20	2	21
Seth Short		288		Nov. 5	2	6
Elim Hulet		288		Nov. 9	2	10
Ezek^{l} Walan			"			
Joseph Whitney			"			
Ezra Huchans			"			
Shub^{l} Huchans						
Mathi^{s} Whitney			"			
Thos Bordon			"			
Joshua Eaton			"			

N. B. The Above Company Found Themselves 19 Guns 19 Blankets and 19 Knapsacks &c Test

David Cady Capt

[*Connecticut Historical Society.*]

CAPT. ANDREW BACKUS' COMPANY.

Travil Pay Role of Capt Andrew Backus Company in Co^{ll} John Douglas Rig^{t} Who Joind the Amarican army in the State of New York Sep^{t} 1776.

	When Engaged	Miles travil to & from Camp
Capt Andrew Backus		
Liu^{t} Joshua Dunlap		
Sarj^{t} Nathan Dean	Sep^{t} 7. 1776	280
Sarj^{t} Joseph Spaulding		"
Sarj^{t} John Cleavland		"
Sarj^{t} Silas Spalding		"
Q^{rm} Sarj^{t} John Peirce		"
Cor Robert Car		"
Cor Ezra Spalding		"
Fifer Stephen Backus		"
Squier How		"
David Atterton		"
Thomas Antrum		"
Joseph Robinson		"

	When Engaged	Miles travil to & from Camp
Abijah Dean		280
James Hawkins		"
Timothy Babcock		"
Ezra Warren		"
Nathaniel Barnet		"
Nathaniel Marsh		"
Daniel Spalding		"
David Carter		"
Andrew Herick		"
Moses Barnet		"
Henry Head		"
Lemuel Warren		"
Daniel Moredock		"
Joshua Hall		"
James How		"
William Thompson		"
James Stromthorn [?]		180
		8020

Premium for 33 men including Aaron Wheetor & Na[hl] Hewlet who marched with the Rig[t] & taken Sick & was not Returnd with the Rest of y[e] Rig[t]

Test Andrew Backus Captain

[*Connecticut Historical Society.*]

CAPT. TIMOTHY BACKUS' COMPANY.

Mileage Roll of Cap[t] Tim[o] Backus Company of Volunteers In Co[ll] Jn[o] Douglass's Reg[t] of Melitia From the State of Connecticutt

Mens Names	Miles to & from Camp	Mens Names	Miles to & from Camp
Cap[t] T. Backus		Jona[h] Downing	295
L[t] Jo[s] Raynsford		Tho[s] Dimmick	"
En[s] Jo[s] Leach		William Dyar	"
Serg[t] Sam[ll] Felch	295	James Durfee	"
" Josiah Dewey	"	Nathan Fish	"
" Caleb Faulkner	"	John Hough	"
Corp[l] Jn[o] Curtiss	"	Asa Leffingwell	"
Corp[l] Levi Adams	"	Abel Lyon	"
Drum[r] Jon[a] Davis	"	Josiah Munrow	"
Elihu Adams	"	Simeon Parke	"
Nehemiah Adams	"	John Simms	"
John Adams	"	Jo[s] Safford	"
Silas Allen	"	Zacheriah Waldo	"
Jo[s] Buth	"		
Nath[l] Clark	"	Total	7375

[*Connecticut Historical Society.*]

CAPT. BACON'S COMPANY.

A Travil Abstract of Capt Benja Bacon's Company in Col. Jn. Douglass Regiment North Castle Novr 1776.

Mans Names	Miles Travil to & from Camp	Mans Names	Miles Travil to & from Camp
Capt B. Bacon		Phinehas Lester	295
Lt J. Adams		Oliver Tyler	"
Sarg. D. Foster	295	Ebenezer Ransome	"
" J. Park	"	Thadeus Palmer	"
" B. Moore	"	Nathaniel Luce (?)	"
" S. Bacon	"	Ebenezer Smith	"
Corp. J. Bacon	"	John Brown	"
" J. Bradford	"	Ezekiel Park	"
" J. Clark	"	Roswell Parish	"
F. L. Bingham	"	Robert Stephens	135
F. W. Brown	"	Lemuel Stephens	"
George Austin	"	Joseph Rainsford	"
James Adams	"	Josiah Bradford	"

Premiums to Lt & Capt and 24 men £26.

[*Copy in Connecticut Historical Society.*]

LIEUT. PARKE'S COMPANY.

Pay Roll of Lt Robart Parke Company in Col Douglas Regt who Joind the American army in the Stat of Newyork Sept

Mens Names	Entered Service	Miles to and From Camp	Deserted	Discharged	Time in Service m	d
Lt Robart Parke	Sep 7. 1776			Nov. 7	2	8
Sargt David Eames		288		Nov. 9	2	10
Sargt Thomas Dixson		288		Nov. 20	2	21
Sargt John Eames		288		"	2	21
Corp John Gaston		288		Nov. 10	2	11
Corp Peleg Mateson		288		Nov. 9	2	10
Job Green		288		Nov. 10	2	11
Joshua Thrall		288		Nov. 20	2	21
Job Talbat		288		"	2	21
Moses Barret		120		Died Oct. 10	1	3
Reuban Marshal		288		" 10	2	11
David Hatch			Sept 26			
William Vaughn		288		Oct. 10	1	11
Isaac French		288		Nov. 9	2	10
Jonathan Chilson			Sept 26			
Amaziah Parke		288		Nov. 20	2	21
William Williams		288		Nov. 8	2	9
Archabel Dorranc		288		Nov. 20	2	21
Comfort Slack		288		Nov. 7	2	8

Payed the Above Deserters £1. 0. 0 Each

N. B: The Above Company Found themselves 17 Guns 17 Blankets 17 Knapseks Thos Dixson Sergt

Elisha Hall and Gideon Tower Recd 20s each & were left sick on the Road & Returnd home & nothing Drawn for them

Jany 31. 1777 Test Robert Parke Lieut

[*Connecticut Historical Society.*]

CAPT. PALMER'S COMPANY.

A Roal of Capt Palmer Company that march to Westchester September ye 7th those names as followeth that is intitled to a Premium

Capt Joseph Palmer
Sargt Pelik Randall
Sargt William Gallup
Sargt John Wylie
Sargt John Huston
Sargt Daniel Hopkins
Cor Nehemiah Parks
Cor Nicolas Randal
Cor Cyrus Keney
Joseph Egliston
Robart Wylie
William Stuard
Brintnell Robins
Daniel Fish
Henry Nuton
Jonathan Palmer
Stevene Ray
Seth Morgin
Ruben Babcock
Peter Morgin
Benjamin Rods
Christopher Randal

test by Joseph Palmer Capt
January ye 16 AD 1777

[Another copy adds the following to the names on the above roll:]

New Haven Sept 12th 1776

Phineas Edwards
Benjamin Palmer
Samuel Kinne Corporal
Jarius Palmer

These marched from Voluntown 9th Sept to New Haven and arrived on the 12 & to Strafford 14th Sept & to fairfield 15th Sept with our Packs I. E. we carried all our packs

[A receipt for wages adds the following names:]

Joseph Randall
Moses Fish
Matthew Newton
Thomas Stewart

[*Connecticut Historical Society.*]

CAPT. HEBBARD'S COMPANY.

A Ration Role of Capt Wm Hebbard Company in Col John Douglass Regment in the State of Connecticut Who marched to New London Sept the 2 day A D 1776

Mens Names	Number of days in Carvis	Mens Names	Number of days in Carvis
Capt. Wm Hebbard	5	Jams Butt	5
Leut. Joseph Burgus	5	Isaac Backes	4
Ens. Stephen Dowing	5	Paul Harris	4
Sar. Wm Foster	5	Samuel Harris	4
Sar. Ebenezer Deains	4	Joshua Ramond	4
Sar. Aleck Gorden	5	Lee Wodard	5
Corp. Joseph Dimack	5	Eliphet Farnam	5
Corp. Samuel Hovey	5	Joseph Dewey	5
Drumer John Brown	4	Joseph Botton	4
John Hebbard Jr.	5	Silus Glass	5
Wm Hebbard Jr.	4	John Hebbard	4
Ebenezer Butt	5	Samuel Parish	4
John Butt	5	Isaac Fuller	4
Cyrus Manard	5		

[*State Library, Revolution 6.*]

CAPT. HEBBARD'S COMPANY.

A Travel Abstract of Capt Wm Hebbards Company In Co^ll^ John Douglass Regt North Castle November 1 1776

Test Joseph Burgs Leu^t^.

	Miles to & From Camp		Miles to & From Camp
Capt Wil^m^ Hebbard		Eben^r^ Butt	295
Lt J. Burges		Steph^n^ Farnam	"
En^s^ S. Downing		Eliph^t^ Farnam	"
Seg^t^ M. Goodell	295	Sils Glass	"
Serg^t^ J. Dimock	"	Dani^l^ Herington	"
Co^p^ S. Hovey	"	Sir^s^ Manord	"
" J. Hebbard	"	Jason Rood	"
F^r^ Wil^m^ D. Foster	"	Lee Woodard	"
Jno Butt	"	Jo Dewa	"
Jams Butt	"		

[*Connecticut Historical Society.*]

CAPT. BUTT'S COMPANY.

A Return of a Company of Minute men Rais^d^ in May 1776 in the 21st Reg^t^ in the State of Connecticut and Commanded by Sherebiah Butt Capt of the 2^d^ Militia Company in 8^d^ Reg^t^

Mens Names	Days spent in Service	Mens Names	Days spent in Service
Capt She^b^ Butt	9	Warren Williams	2
Lt John Adms	4	Joshua Bradfoad	2
Lt Jos Burges	4	Jacob Staples	2
Ens P^t^ Davidson	5	John Cleaveland	2
S James Delop	2	Thos Herris	2
S Benj Morse	2	Rufus Downing	2
S Levi Downing	2	Eb^r^ Butt	7
S Jon^an^ Day	1	Solomon Adams Jr	2
S John Stevens	2	Rufus Hebbard	2
C Jos Adams	2	John Butt	2
C Corl^s^ Adams	2	Phineas Downing Jr	2
C Sam^ll^ Hovey	2	John Lilley	1
C Delino Pierce	2	Lee Woodward	1
F James Leach	2	John Stedman	1
Dan^ll^ Herrick	2	Amasa Hutchins	1
Elijah Parke	2	George Little	1
John Butt Jr	2	Ezra Hutchins	1
Gideon Butt	2	Stephen Hewit	2
Jesse Adams	2	Joshua Miles	2
Eb^r^ Berstow	2	Jesse Miles	2
Jo^s^ Adams 3^d^	1	Eb^r^ Simons	2
Oliver Tiler	2	Jo^s^ Gorum	1
John Bradford	2	Nathan Dean	1
Sim^l^ Benjamins	2	Jo^s^ Baker	1

[*State Library, Revolution 11.*]

MAJOR SHELDON'S REGIMENT.

[*See Record of Connecticut Men in the Revolution, page 480.*]

CAPT. BULL'S COMPANY.

Pay Rool for Capt Thos Bulls Company of Light Horse When Ordered to New York in July 1776

Mens Names & Rank	Time when marched	When Discharged or Returned home
Thos Bull Capt	July 4	July 20
James Judson Leut	"	"
Agur Curtis Cornet	"	"
Gideon Martin Qurr	"	"
Isaiah Gilbert Copl	"	"
John Edwards Copl	"	"
Solomon Hurd Copl	"	"
Thos Parmile Copl	"	"
James Karsen Clerk	"	"
Robert Clark Trumpt	"	"
Elezur Dudley Trumpt	"	"
Silas Hicok	"	"
Solomon Conisey	"	"
Solomon Robinson	"	"
Daniel Judd	"	"
Ichabod Stoddard	"	"
Matthew Loggan	"	"
Jeremiah Burton	"	"
Wait Curtis	"	"
Joseph Clark	"	"
David Leavit	"	"
Moses Hawley	"	"
John Clark	"	"
Nathan Dudley	"	"
Benjn Durkee	"	"
Simeon Cole	"	"
Timth Goodrich	"	"
Thos Thompson	"	"
Caleb Austin	6	"
David Judson	6	"
Walker Mallery	4	"
Danll Sherman	"	"
Elnathan Gilbert	"	"
Peter Walker	"	"
John Abernathey	"	"
Asa Curtis	"	"
Wm Robinson	"	"
Simeon Mitchel	6	"
Chapman Judson	"	"
Samll Woodman	"	"
Truman Hurlbut	"	"
Ezekiel Lewis	6	"

[*State Library, Revolution 27.*]

GROTON HILL FORT GUARD.

[*See Record of Connecticut Men in the Revolution, page 617.*]

CAPT. MOTT'S COMPANY.

A Pay Role of Capt Edward Mott's Company Stationed at Groton 1776

Mens Names	Time of Inlistment	Time when Discharged or turned over
Edward Mott Capt	Feb. 16	July 4
Oliver Coit 1 Lt	"	"
Wm Latham 2 Lt	"	"
Wm Whitney Ens.	"	"
Serj. John James	28	"
Serj. Lemuel Wethey	"	"
Serj. Elisha Perkins	Mar. 1	"
Serj. Benjn Hilliard	Feb. 27	"
Clark Jed^h Whitney	26	"
Corp. Levi Tracy	27	"
Corp. Peris Tracy	28	"
Corp. Joseph Bentley	Mar. 1	"
Corp. Ephraim Herrick	Feb. 27	"
Drum. Thos Leach	Mar. 1	"
Fifer Jn^a Averil	5	"
Fifer Robert Latimer	4	"
John Austin	1	"
Nathan Avery	4	"
Zebulon Button	Feb. 27	"
Danl Benit	28	"
Abiel Benjamin Jr.	Mar. 4	"
Silas Brewster	Feb. 26	"
Thos Brooks	Mar. 10	"
John Baley Jr	4	"
Paul Burrows	"	"
Elisha Burrows	May 13	"
Hugh Brown	Mar. 4	"
Richard Burnet	"	"
Joshua Baker	"	"
Isaac Coit	Feb. 29	"
Farwell Coit	28	"
Benjn Clark	Mar. 1	May 18
James Comstock	4	July 4
Fairbanks Church	"	"
James Culver	"	"
Charles Chester	"	"
Eldridge Chester	"	"
Joseph Davis	Feb. 28	"
David Edgcomb	Apr. 11	"
James Fish	Mar. 4	"
John Gates	1	"
Thos Giles	June 8	"
Lemuel Geer	Feb. 28	"
Oliver Gates	"	"

Mens Names	Time of Inlistment	Time when Discharged or turned over
Zephaniah Hartshorn	Mar. 4	July 4
Jonathan Hartshorn	"	"
Beriah Hartshorn	June 24	"
Thos Harris	Mar. 1	"
Danl Harris	"	"
Josiah Harris	Feb. 28	"
Asaph Jones	26	"
Luther Jones	"	"
George Jeffords	Mar. 4	"
Rober Langworthy	1	"
Joseph Latham 2nd	"	"
Daniel Latham	"	"
Joseph Latham 4th	4	Apr. 18
Cary Latham	Apr. 18	July 4
Jasper Latham	Mar. 4	"
Joseph Latham 5th	1	"
Amos Latham	Apr. 28	"
David Lamb	Mar. 4	"
Ephraim Morgan	2	"
Joshua Meech	Feb. 26	"
Jacob Meech	27	"
Pero Moody	Mar. 4	"
Moses Park	Feb. 26	"
Rufus Park	"	"
Levi Park	27	"
John Ray Jr.	Mar. 4	"
Richard Otis	Feb. 28	"
Ezekiel Rude	26	"
Benjn Richards	27	"
Rufus Rix	Mar. 9	"
Nathan Rix	"	"
Lemuel Smith	1	June 24
Ephraim Starkweather	2	July 4
David Stanton	"	"
Asa Stanton	"	"
Saml Sabin	1	"
Richmond Tracy	7	"
Cyrus Tracy	1	"
Bela Tracy	"	"
Absalom Thompson	"	"
Ephraim Wethey	7	"
Henry Walton	1	"
Adin Wilbur	4	"
Henry Wethey	1	"
Elijah Wethey	Feb. 28	"
Peter Williams	Mar. 4	"
Simeon William	3	"
John Wood Jr	"	"
Thos Wells	"	"
Wate Wells	"	"
John Whitney	"	"
Ezekiel Yarrington	Feb. 27	"
Elisha York	26	"
William Manning	Mar. 11	Apr. 28
Seth Frink	2	11

[*State Library, Revolution 6.*]

MILITIA REGIMENTS, 1777.

DANBURY RAID.

[*See Record of Connecticut Men in the Revolution, page 492.*]

OFFICERS.

The United States D^r To the State of Connecticut, for Services &c of Militia in the Danbury Alarm in April 1777. Viz.—

Bills & Accounts	Remarks
Capt D. Judson	13th Reg^t
Lt D. Phelps	Col. J. Humphries
Capt N. Gilbert	
Col. J. P. Cook	his Reg^t
Capt C. Raymond	
Col. J. Thomson	his Reg^t
Capt S. Morehouse	Col. J. Meads
Capt Thos Fenn	10th Reg^t
Capt N. Seeley	Col S Whitings
Capt Elijah Case	
Col. Saml Whiting	his Regt
En^s Jona. Filley	1st Reg^t
Capt A. Brimsmade	4th "
Capt E. Russell	Col Thomsons
Capt N. Wheeler	Col. S. Whitings
Capt E. Hinman	Col. J. Moseleys
Daniel Lyman	
John Crane	Col. T. Cooks
Col. E. Abel	

[*Comptroller's Office, Haskell's Receipts.*]

CAPT. PLATT'S COMPANY.

A pay Roll of Capt. Dan Plattses Company of the 7th Regiment in the State of Conetecut Commanded by Wm Worthington Esq Leut. Cornel who march^{t} in the Larram as far as New haven on April 27th A D 1777

Entered Sarvis Apriel 27 — Sarvis 5 Days

Capt. Dan Platts
Leut. Elijah Scovel
Ens. Saml Doty
Sar. Israel Done
Sar. Asa Pratt
Sar. Ruben Pratt
Sar. Jesse Pratt
Cor. James Comstock
Cor. Daniel Pratt
Cor. Saml Bushnel
Cor. Saml Parker
Benjamin Williams Jr.
Frances Bushnel
Jesse Pratt 2^{d}
Ashbel Clark
Zephemiah Pratt
Phinis Pratt
Abraham Pratt Jr.
Stephen Starkey
Joseph Glading
Ebenezar Williams
Noah Scovel Jr.
Jered Buckingham
Taber Pratt
Jorge Shaw
Bemond Clark
James Utter
William Buckley
Nathan Southard
David Beebe Pratt
James Hamblen
Marten Dibble
Josiah Post
Isaac Webb
William Southard
Gideon Pratt
John Williams 2d
James Shaw
Ezra Pratt
Abraham Buckley

[*State Library, Revolution 6.*]

CAPT. STARKEY'S COMPANY.

A Pay Roll of Capt Timothy Starkeys Company the 7th Company of the alarm List of the 7th Regiment of the State of Connecticut Commanded by Lieu^{t} Con^{l} William Worthington Esqr.

Marcht in the alarm to New haven april ye 27th A D 1777

Time of Service 5 Days

Capt. Timothy Starkey
Lieut. Noah Platts
Ins. John Bull
Sert. Simon Hough
Sert. Phinehas Bushnel
Sert. John Pratt
Sert. Edwd Bull
Clark Edmon Pratt
Cor. Jonth^{n} Pratt
Cor. John Platts
Cor. Daniel Bushnell
Cor. David Williams
Saml Pratt
Jacob Haydon
Daniel Chalker
Jno Handley Bushnell
Jeremiah Kelcy
Benjn Handy
Edmond Snow
Jno Williams
Abr^{m} Pratt
Et[ ] Pratt
Selden Chalker
Lem^{l} Bushnell
Job Buckley
Saml Steavens

[*State Library, Revolution 6.*]

SECOND REGIMENT—COL. THOMPSON.

ALARM LISTS.

A List of the Names of the Subaltins in the Alarm Lists in the 2[d] Reg[t]

Names	List	Names	List
Jonah Bradley Lieut John Austin Ens	1st	John Dibble Lieut Enoch Newton Ens	10th
Benj Freen Lieut John Fowler Junr Ens	2[d]	Ebenezer Trusedel Lieut Asel Harrison Ens	11th
Sam[ll] Hoadley Lieut Ferrington Harrison Ens	3[d]	Dan[ll] Chatfield Lieut David Woodrose Ens	13th
Joseph Loveland Lieut Abraham Smith Ens	4th	Isaac Sherman Kimberly Lt Timothy Hoadly Ens	14th
Henry Daggett Lieut John Pierpoint Ens	5th	Joel Bradly Lieut Alling Ives Ens	15th
John Smith Lieut John Powel Ens	6th	Jesse Beecher Lieut Jacob Hotchkiss Ens	16th
Jared Robertson Lieut Dan[ll] Smith Ens	7th	Elisha Booth Lieut Caleb Alling Ens	17th
Sam[ll] Smith Lieut Lemuel Humphrevile Ens	8th	Jabez Prechard Lieut Levi Tomlinson Ens	18th
Jonathan Dayton Lieut Thomas Humiston Ens	9th		

New Haven y[e] 24 of May 1777

[*State Library, Hebard Papers.*]

FOURTH REGIMENT—COL. WHITING.

[*See Record of Connecticut Men in the Revolution, page 514.*]

OFFICERS.

A Ration Bill of the Officers in Col. Saml Whitings Regiment of Guards being the 4th Regiment of Militia in the State of Connecticut and Raised for the defense of Said State in March 1777 And Stationed at Fairfield & Stratford &c By Order of Brigadier Genl Silliman

Names	Time of Entering into the Service	Time when Discharged
S. Whiting Esq Col.	Apr. 3	Aug. 2
Ab^{m} Gould Lt. Col.	Mar. 6	Apr. 7
Jonathan Dimon Major	7	22
P. Hendrick & Lewis Adjutant	7	Aug. 2
T. Smedley & Benedict Q^{r} master	7	2
Elijah Abel Capt.	6	Apr. 22
Saml Seelye Lieut.	7	Mar. 22
Nathan Seelye Lieut.	22	Apr. 22
Daniel Dimon Ens.	6	Mar. 22
Nathan Bennitt Ens.	22	Apr. 22
Zache^{h} Coe Capt.	7	9
William Thomson Lieut.	7	21
Solomon Booth Ens.	7	22
Eph^{m} Curtis Lieut.	23	22
Beach Tomlinson Capt.	6	Mar. 22
Eph^{m} Lyon Lieut.	6	22
Enoch Lewis Ens.	7	22
Eben^{r} Hill Capt.	7	Apr. 22
Lewis Goodsell Lieut.	7	22
D. Dimon Ens.	23	22
Jabez Wheeler Capt.	Apr. 7	22
Daniel Bennitt Lieut.	8	22
Seth Seelye Ens.	8	22
James Booth Capt & Company as per abstract		956 Days
Joseph Birdsey Capt.	5	11
Jedd^{n} Mills Ens.	5	11
Thom^{s} Nash Capt.	5	23
Eben Jesup Ens.	5	23
Jonath^{n} Squire Ens.	5	23
George Burr Capt.	4	22
David Williams Lieut.	4	22
Albert Sherwood Ens.	4	22
Steph^{n} Thorp Capt.	8	22
Job Bartram Lieut.	8	22
David Wheeler Ens.	8	22
Zalmon Reed Capt.	Mar. 7	Mar. 22
Daniel Duncan Lieut.	7	22
Danl Sanford Ens.	7	22
William Hawley Lieut.	Apr. 8	Apr. 22
Phin^{s} Sherman Lieut.	7	13
Steph Thorp Capt.	23	

Names	Time of Entering into the Service	Time When Discharged
Lewis Goodsell Lieut.	Apr. 23	July 22
Nathan Seelye Lieut.	23	22
Eliph[t] Thorp Capt.	Mar. 23	22
Stephen Wakeman Lieut.	23	22
John Olmsted Ens.	23	Apr. 22
Daniel Dimon Ens	Apr. 23	July 22
Edmond Leavenworth Capt	May 15	22
Sam[l] Patterson Lieut.	16	22
Solomon Booth Lieut.	22	June 17
Judson Burton Ens.	16	July 22
Abrah[m] Brinsmade Capt.	Apr. 7	Apr. 22
Steph[n] Bourroughs Capt	8	13
Woolcutt Hawley Serjt.	May 15	July 22
Capt. Dan[l] Godfrey as per abstract 1776	Dec. 5 76	Dec 17 '76.

[*State Library*, *Revolution 6.*]

CAPT. BOOTH'S COMPANY.

A Ration Role of Cap[t] James Booths Company of Guards Which were Detach[d] from the 4th Regiment of Melitia for that Purpose, Pursuant to Order From G. Sillick Silliman Brigadier General &c.

Mens Names	Number of Days in service	Mens Names	Number of Days in service
Capt. James Booth	15	John Sherman	18
Lieut. Samuel Patterson	18	Lewis Curtiss	15
Ens. Judson Burton	15	Nathan Osborn	18
Serg. David Thompson	15	James Coe	18
Serg. Elihew Curtiss	15	Abner Beers	15
Serg. Stephan Beers	15	Benjamin Wells	15
Serg. John Peck	18	Isaac Curtiss	18
Corpl. Abijah Booth	18	James Sherman	15
Corpl. Josiah Peck	15	Judson Peck	15
Corpl. David Curtiss	15	Ebenezer Curtiss	18
Corpl. Aaron Judson	18	Joseph Deforest	15
Fifer William Tomlinson	8	John Beardslee	15
Joel Judson	15	James Judson	18
Ephraim Willcockson	15	William Hilliard	15
Thomas Stratton	18	George Lewis	15
William Southworth	18	Benjamin Gorham	15
Edmund Curtiss	10	John Wells	18
Samuel Burritt	18	Abner Elgur	15
Robert Curtiss	15	Jeremiah Curtiss	18
John Booth	15	Samuel Ward	18
Elihew Judson	15	Ebenezer Hubbil	18
Abner Curtiss	15	Josiah Walker	15
Elnathan Wheeler	15	David Barlow	18
John M[c]Graw	13	Ephraim Burton	15
Nathan Beardslee	18	Josiah Beers	10
Samuel Osborn	18	John E. Olcott	10
Andrew Curtiss	15	John Wayland	10
Daniel Curtiss	18	Henry Beardslee	10
William Judson	18	Henry Curtiss	10
Jonathan Tongue	15	John Whiting	13
Jabes Curtiss	18	Joseph Frost	15

[Indorsed] Capt. James Booth's Ration Roll Company of Guards from the 11 Regiment Militia April 1777.

[*State Library*, ***Revolution*** *6.*]

TWELFTH REGIMENT—COL. MASON.

GUARD.

A Pay Abstract for a gard kept in Lebanon By order of Colonel Jeremiah Masen Col° of the 12th Rigment in the State of Conecticut Gard Began Augt 19, 1777

Mens Names	Number of Nights	Mens Names	Number of Nights
Jams Bayley	11	Jams Diskill	11
Thos Groos	11	Nehimh Payn	11
Isaac Gillit	11	Josh Hutchenson	10
Saml Gay	11	John Vaughan	10

[These men were guarding a building containing Continental stores.]

[*State Library, Revolution 11.*]

MAJ. WOODRUFF'S VOLUNTEERS.

[*See Record of Connecticut Men in the Revolution, page 514.*]

OFFICERS.

Retaind Rations Due to Major Woodruff Regt of Volunteers from Conecticut from October 13th to October 22th 1777

	Rations		Rations
Major Judah Woodruff	30	Ensn Nathaniel Lewis	3
Adjt Simean Newel	20	Capt John Porter	20
Q Master Elijah Lewis	10	Leut Elisha Scott	10
Capt Amos Barns	20	Ensn Joseph Woodford	10
Leut Samuel Adams	10	Capt Ambris Sloper	20
Capt Matthew Cowles	20	Leut Joel Potter	10
Leut Samuel Wiliams	10	Leut Simean Fullor	5
Capt Hezekiah Gridley	20	Ens John Clark	10
Leut Thomas Hungerford	10	Capt Abraham Pettibone	6
Capt Samuel Upson	6	Ensn Samuel Hotchkiss	10
Leut Isaac Cleavland	10		

[*Connecticut Historical Society.*]

MILITIA REGIMENTS, 1778.

COL. M^{c}CLELLAN'S REGIMENT.

[*See Record of Connecticut Men in the Revolution, page 543.*]

PETITION.

To the Honorable General Assembly of the State of Connecticut now sitting at Hartford Octo^{r} Sessions 1778. The Petition of the Commission Officers, Non Commission Officers and Soldiers in the Battallion under the Command of Col^{o} Samuel McClellan being one of the Battallions Included in the Two Brigades Raised by Order of the Genl Assembly at their Adjourned Sessions in Feb^{ry} 1778. Sheweth.

That Wee Were Raised while an Act of this State was Existing Regulating the Prices of Labour Produce &c and upon the Faith and Footing of said Act and had such Wages and Allowances as while s^{d} Act Continued were Just and Reasonable. But that since s^{d} Act has been Repeal'd the Prices of the Various Necessaries of Life are so Enhanced as that Our Wages and Allowances are by no means an Adequate Reward for Our services.

We Therefore Pray your Honors to take Our Case into your Wise Consideration and Grant such an Addition to Our Wages and Allowances as shall be adequate to the Reward we Expected when we Entered said service. Justice is all Wee Ask. Wee doubt not your Honors will Grant Our Reasonable Request, and wee as in Duty Bound Shall Ever Pray. Dated at New London Octo^{r}. 1778.

Elisha Chapman	Capt^{ns}	Daniel Larned Lt	
Daniel Tilden	Capt^{ns}	Saml Capron Lt	
Lee Lay	Capt^{ns}	Ambros Bawldwin Lt	
Abner Robinson	Capt^{ns}	Asahel Harrison Ens	
Squier Hills	Capt^{ns}	Joshua Gates Ens	
William Whitney	Capt^{ns}	George Gallup Ens	
Aron Hale	Lieut^{s}	Obad^{h} Child Ens	
Gam^{ll} Ripley	Lieut^{s}	Zechariah Parker Ens	
Phinehas Peck	Lieut^{s}	Benj^{a} Billins Serg^{t} Maj^{r}	
Nehemiah Smith	Lieut^{s}	Justis Johnson	Serjeants
Lem^{ll} Grosvenor	Lieut^{s}	John Arnold	Serjeants
Willm Morriss	Lieut^{s}	Eliakim Stannard	Serjeants
Aaron Cleaveland	Lieut^{s}	Joseph Baldwin	Serjeants
John Frink	Lieut^{s}	Moses Hyde	Serjeants
Ezra Root	Lieut^{s}	Aseph Goodale	Serjeants

Noah Day
Jabez Foster
Dan Lee
Silas Ackla
William Sheldon
John Colt
Serjeants

Jonathan Downning
James Clark
Jeremiah Durkee
Vaniah Palmer
Moses Amadown
Eben[r] Kindal
Benj[n] Carpenter
John Gilbart
Nehemiah Gallup
Rufus Brown
Pain Kinman
John Fox
Elisha Converce
Serjeants

Francis Clark D Major

Sam[ll] Wise
Darias Learned
Darias Fuller
Rementon Sears
Drummers

Rufus Parks
Jabez Brainard
Darias Leskomb
Jacob Holt
John Green
Rufus Felton
Fifers

Joseph Colbet
Amos Brainard
John Welch
Radireck Platts
Sam[ll] Beamont
Elisha Sabin
Issachar Graves
Thomas Peake
Elijah Bennet
Joseph Turner
Lemuel Clark
Amos Randol
Gamalel Huntington
Elisha Boman
Samuel Linchon
Amos Smith
Soloman Robins
Jabez Cheesebrook
James Fletcher
Woodbury Starkweather
Elias Babcock
Elkanah Huet
Jacob Meach
Corporals

Privates

Samuel Arnold
Felix Augru (?)
Jonathan Baldwin
David Bishop
Heman Balwin
Jonathan Bushnull
Zachariah Branaird
Ruben Bushnull
Richard Bialey
Ephiream Bushnull
John Benjamin
Senas Balwin
Robert Clark
Dimetrus Cook
Caleb Chapman
John Carter
Sam[ll] Church
Joseph Clark
Olive Clark
John Field
John Tuller
Elisha Goff
Ithial Harrison
Nathan Harrison
Eben[r] Hamistond
Jacob Hurd
Phileman Harrison
Rufus Harrison
Joel Houd
Asahel Hull
Dan[ll] Ingham
Stephen Johnston
Ruben Keley
Joel Keley
Christ[o] Masunall
Ithael Munson
James Nichols
Eben[r] Waid
James Utter
James Spencer
Daniel Ray
David Sears
Micahel Smith
Joathan Smith
Mat[w] Scofel
Jacob Savage
Jehial Tod
Nathan Wilcocks
William White

William Alton
Nath[ll] Allen
Joseph Boid
Samuel Burnall
Epheriam Barrit
Lyman Childs
Cyrus Chafee
Jonathan Converse
Elias Carpenter
Seth Cutler
Noah Davenport
David Hosmer
John Moffat
Joseph Russell

Moses Wylder
Ambermarle Stone

John Adams
Roswell Bennet
Abial Bill
John Burt
James Burnham
Joseph Carey
Phineas Downing
Solomon Durkee
Oliver Flint
Elijah Pharnum
George Goram
Robert Gager
Roswell Green
Elijah Huntington
Gershom Haill
Dan^{ll} Herrick
Asahel Herrick
Paul Harriss
Eben^{r} Kingsley
Eben^{r} Luce
Elijah Lilley
Roswell Manning
Asher Morgan
Banj^{a} Manning
Eliphalet Ormsby
William Parish
Oliver Parish
Roswell Parish
Chester Pool
Jon^{a} Robinson
Ebor Robinson
Richard Robinson
Eben^{r} Robins
Dan^{ll} Ringe
Lem^{ll} Stephens
Oliver Smith
James Smith
David Smith
Abnor Webb
William Wailes
Amos Woodward
Timothy Winter

Philarman Androus
Peter Ayres
Cherub Abel
Richard Bogue
Nhth^{ll} Baker
Cromell Bennet
Willm Butler
Abel Bennet
Cyrus Cone
Abel Edgerton
Dan^{ll} Ellis
Alpheus Foster
Amos Fox

Wm Foresider
Dan Gillit
Richard Greenfield
Asahel Harvey
Moses Huntly
Zadock Huntly
Amos Ingraham
Stephen Lee
John Manwaring
John Mitchel
Naman Mosher
Benj^{a} Peck
John Perigo
Joseph Ransom
Stephen Richenson
Richard Rogers
Gideon Rogers
Theo. Rathbone
David Shattock
Clemment Stebbens
Elijah Spencer
Ebenezer Staples
Emmon Spencer
Francis Smith
Joseph Steward
John Starling
Nath^{ll} Starr
Zebadiah Scott
Eleazer Tubbs
Asa Watson
Timo. Wright
Daniel Wright

Ezekiel Waterman
Abraham Warner
Ruel Woodworth
Thomas Anderson
Willm Anderson
Thomas Brag
Peter Button
James Brown
Sam^{ll} Brown
Robert Baker
Eli Brown
Rufus Barnard
Nath^{ll} Babcock
Elijah Carpenter
David Carpenter
Nath^{ll} Conant
Jeremiah Cunnil
Parly Dean
Humphrey Davenport
Asahel Eastman
Ebenezer Eaton
Ebenezer Eastman
Marvirick Eaton
Jedediah Fay
Elijah Fenton
Edward Holmes

Eliphlet Huntington
Bazalileen Hopkins
Christopher Huntington
Elijah Hunt
Ezeriah Hall
Ezekil Kellogg
Amisa Ladd
Dan[ll] Olds
Ebeneze Oen
Shubal Presson
Thomas Russell
William Rice
Jon[a] Rice
Abijah Smith
Phillip Squire
Elijah Squire
Levi Snow
Silas Snow
Rufus Tyler
Ebenezer Whiton
George Austin
Barthilmus Arthur
Jesse Brown
Walter Branch
John Billings
Asa Bawdish
David Bellus
Robart Crary
Joseph Crary
Peter Culver
Robort Dixon
Asahel Fish
David Fish
William Fagens
Robart Geer
Jacob Gallup
Levi Gallup
W[m] Hethe
Crandal Holley
Henrey Hewit
Azariah Hillard
Simeon Jones
Stephen Kimey
David Lewis
Tubal Moody
Elijah Meech
Hubbard Mason
Henrey Main
Jerimiah Main
Samuel Newton
Joseph Price
Daniel Ruff
Gilbart Tracy
Salmon Treat
John Tift
Ebenezer Witter
Ichabud Worden
Benjamin Williams
Icabud Palmer
Aden Swan

[*State Library, Revolution 13.*]

GUARDS.

HARTFORD GUARD.

A Pay Roll of the Guard in the Town of Hartford to Guard Sundry Offices in S[d] Town as p[r] Act of the General Assembly of the State of Connecticut in the Month of Fabruary Anno Dom 1778

	Time when Inlisted	Time in Service Months	Days
Lieut Tho[s] Sloan	March 12	2	24
Sarj W[m] Collyer	12	2	24
Sarj. Nath[n] Goodwine	12	2	24
Serj. Nathen Wadworth	16	2	20
Drummer Theoder Goodwine	19	2	17
Phifer James Cook	22	2	10
W[m] Pratt	12	2	24
George Pratt	14	2	22
George Wadsworth	14	2	22
Robert Waterman	14	2	22
Caleb Church	16	2	20
Joal Boyington	16	2	20
Frederick Lorde	16	2	20
Samuel Hall	16	2	20
W[m] Lord	16	2	20
Oliver Clapp	19	2	17
Mosses Dickinson	19	2	17
W[m] Watson	19	2	17
Jo[n] Pantrey Goodwine	19	2	17
David Peirce	19	2	17
Ashbel Dodd	20	2	16
Whiting Seymor	20	2	16
Neamiah Cadwall	20	2	16
Calvin Wooding	20	2	16
Dorus Warron	20	2	16
Timothy Church	20	2	16
Jason Howell	20	2	16
Levi Curtiss	22	2	14
Tho[s] Bunce	22	2	14
Jona[th] Olcott	22	2	14
Frederick Standly	22	2	14
Isrel Wadsworth	22	2	14
James Butler	22	2	14
Haz. Seymor	22	2	14
Daniel Sheldon	24	2	12
Sam[l] Church	24	2	12

[*State Library, Revolution 11.*]

OFFICE GUARD.

A pay Roll of the Garde for Garding the Treasurrs and Loan Offices Office of the Secretary and Pay Tabel Office Apointed by General Assembly of the Governer and Company of the State of Connecticut Holden at Hartford May 1778 — from June 1st to Novr 5 Inclusive

Leut. Thos Sloan
Ser^{t} Joseph Pratt
Ser Levi Curtis
Ser Fradrick Standley
Drummer Thos Bunce
Phif^{r} Freeman Seymour
David Parce
Wm Watteson
Ashbell Dodd
Timothy Church
Mosses Dickinson
Neamiah Cadwall
Normand Bunce
Isaac Oakes
Uriah Shippard
Normand Clapp
Richard Hood
John Bardwall
Saml Hall
Samu^{l} Chipman
Danniel Shaldon
Doris Warron
Fradrick Lord
James Mookler
Ebez^{r} Moor
Saml Church
Rodrick Larkim
David Goodwine
John Tiel
John Pan^{r} Goodwine
Robert Watterman
Neamiah Cadwall
Benjaman Townshand
Robert Nivens
Jonathan Olcott
Haz Seymor
Joseph Barnerd

[*State Library, Revolution 11.*]

CONVENTION TROOPS GUARD.

The United States D^{r} To the State of Connecticut for services &c. of Militia guarding the Convention Troops through said State in 1778, when they marched from Massachusetts to Virginia — viz —

Bills & Accounts	Remarks
Capt Moses Forbs	Guarding Convention Troops
Capt E. F. Bissell	"
Capt Lemuel Roberts	"
Capt Chester Wells	"
Capt W. Gibbs	"
Capt Isaac Pomeroy	"
Capt Wm Burrell	"
Capt Adon^{h} Griswold	"
Ens^{n} John Reynolds	"
Capt Hez^{h} Parsons	"
Col. Noah Phelps	"
Capt Ozias Pettibone	"
Lt Seth Smith	"
Capt N. Kellogg	"
Capt Jona. Wells	"

[*Comptroller's Office, Haskell's Receipts.*]

MILITIA REGIMENTS, 1779.

TRYON'S INVASION.

[*See Record of Connecticut Men in the Revolution, page 549.*]

CAPT. HOLBROOK'S COMPANY.

A Return of the Horses Employed for the Use of Capt Daniel Holbrook Junr Company of Melitia in Col^o^ Edward Russels Reg^t^ On A Larm from Derby to New Haven & from Derby to Fairfield in the Month of July A D 1779 Under Command of Maj^r^ Nathan Smith

Mens Names	No Miles	Mens Names	No Miles
Daniel Holbrook J^r^ Capt	76	Jonathan Hitchcock	28
Joseph Riggs Ju^r^ Lieut	38	Roberd Pope	28
Thadeus Baldwin Ens	48	Abel Peirson	28
Hezekiah Johnson Serj^t^	28	Enoch French	10
Dorman Coe Clark	28	Joseph Johnson Junr	28
Joseph Parson Corp^l^	28	Enos Bradley Junr	10
Moses Hotchkiss Corp^l^	28	Shelden Curtis	10
Abraham Peirson Corp^l^	10	Truman Loveland	10
Zepheniah Tucker Drm	28	Richard Mansfield	28
Ashel Johnson	10	Ethel Keeney	28
Nathanel Johnson J^r^	28	Leveret Hotchkis	28
Thadeus Kene	10	Ashbel Loveland	18
Gideon Johnson J^r^	28	Abraham Downs J^r^	28
Israel French J^r^	28	Abenezer Dagget	18
Moses Wheler	28	Ebenezer Chatfield	18
Samuel Allen	28	Micael Clark	18
Amos Johnson	28	Edmon Clark	28
Medad Keeney	10	Joseph Picket	18
John Wheler	10	Nathan Wheler	28
Amos Parson	28	Abel Wheler	10
Samuel Johnson	28	Charles French	18
Frances French	10	James Beard	10

[*State Library, Revolution 16.*]

CAPT. BIRDSEY'S COMPANY.

A pay Role of Capt Joseph Birdsey Company In Col Whiting Regiment in a tower; at the Alarm at New Haven and from Their to Fairfield which was five Days in Searvice July 9th 1779 Entred Service

Capt. Jo. Birdsey
Leut. Luke Sumner
Ens. Blackman
Clark Wooster
Ser. Eph Wooster
Ser. Lins (?) Thompson
Ser. Sam. Beard
Ser. M. Wheeler
Cor. N. Deforest
Cor Stepn Beardslee
Cor. Eber Beardslee
Cor. Wil Curtiss
Jo. Munson Drm
Lins (?) Beardslee
Ben Beardslee
Curtiss Fairchild
John Gilbart
Cal. Levans (?)
Sam. Hide
Eph. Mitchel
Edm. Thulford
David Wilson Jor
Abrh Thompson
Tho. Gilbart
Abijah Wells
Jo. Larkings
Joso. (?) Clark
Hez Curtiss
Nathan Blackman
Gideon Levensworth
Gideon Beard

[*State Library, Revolution 16.*]

CAPT. BENJAMIN'S COMPANY.

A Pay Abstract for horse hire of Captn John Benjamin's Company of the 4 Regiment of Alarm List of Militia, in the New Haven & Fairfield Alarms, also Pay & Subsistance for three Men Omitted in the Pay Abstract now on File in Pay Table Office, Hartford. Stratford December 8th 1779

Mens Names	Time entered service	Days in service	Number of miles out
Capt John Benjamin	July 5	4	26
Lieut Samuel Patterson	5	4	26
Sergt Ezra Elgar	5	4	10
Sergt Hezekiah Burritt	5	4	26
Corpl Samuel Ward	5	4	26
John Brooks Esq	5	4	26
Saml Burton	5	4	26
Nathanl Lamson Junr	5	4	26
Samuel Wells	7	2	10
Isaac Gorham	5	4	10
Samuel Curtiss	5	2	14
Josiah Curtiss	5	4	26
Abijah McCune	5	4	26
Darius Folsom	7	2	10
John Hubbil Junr	7	2	10
Stephen Porter	5	2	14
Samuel Burritt	6	3	26
Benjamin Brooks	7	2	10
John Hubbil	7	2	10
Nathaniel Lamson	7	2	10
Abijah Brooks	7	2	10
Joseph Prince	7	2	10
Isaac Brooks	5	4	10
Omitted before			
Solomon Plant	5	2	14
Stephen Cunningham	7	2	14
Nathan Dagget	7	2	10

[*State Library, Revolution 16.*]

LIEUT. PORTER'S COMPANY.

A Horse Mileage Roll of Lieu[t] Aaron Porter's Comp[y] in y[e] Sixth Reg[t] Ordered to N. Haven July 5th 1779.

Mens Names	N° Miles	Mens Names	N° Miles
Lieut Aaron Porter	30	Fifer Abijah Porter	30
Ens Solo. Dunham	"	William Kelsey	"
Corpl John Kelsey	"	Solo. Dunham Jr.	"
Corpl Sam[l] North	"		

[*State Library, Revolution 16.*]

CAPT. LANDON'S COMPANY.

Guilford State of Connecticut Dr
For horse hire for the 2[d] Compy Alarm list in the 7 Regt to New Haven on an Expedition July 5th 1779 Commd by Col W[m] Worthington

David Landon . . .	15 Miles	David Hull . . .	15 Miles
Daniel Norton . . .	"	Asher Seward . . .	"
Nathaniel Ruggles . .	"	Edward Benton . .	"
Pitman Collins . .	"	John Scovill . . .	"
Wilmot Goldsmith . .	"	Jared Grifling . . .	"
Elishua Reves . . .	"	Daniel Tuthill . . .	"
John Ingraham . .	"	Nathaniel Ingraham .	"
Demetius Cook .	"		

David Landon Capt.

[*State Library, Revolution 16.*]

CAPT. ROBINSON'S COMPANY.

A pay Roll for Horse Travel of Capt James Robinsons Company in Coll[o] Cooks Reg[t] of Militia when call'd for the Relief of New-Haven July 5th A D 1779 and also for the Releif of Fairfield July 8th 1779

Mens Names	N° Miles	Mens Names	N° Miles
Lt. Simeon Parsons . .	40	Benjamin Ames . .	20
Ens. John Johnsons . .	20	Elnathan Stevens . .	20
Serjt. Jeremiah Butler .	20	Rejoice Camp . .	20
Serjt. Joseph Parsons .	40	John Curtiss . . .	20
Serjt Jacob Clark . .	20	Richard Spelman . .	40
Corl. Asher Canfield . .	40	Ozias Picket . . .	20
Corl. Joseph Tibbals . .	20	William Chauncy . .	40
Daniel Coe	40	Titus Canfield . .	40
Timothy Coe . . .	40	Ebenezer Tibbals . .	20
Asher Coe	20	James Robinson . .	40
David Parsons . .	40	James Curtiss . .	20
Abial Baldwin . .	20		

[*State Library, Revolution 16.*]

CAPT. CAMP'S COMPANY.

A pay Roll for Horses Travel of Capt Sam[l] Camps Company Col Cooks Regt of Militia when Calld for the Relief of New Haven July 5th 1779 and also for the Relief of Fairfield July 8th 1779

Mens Names	N° Miles	Mens Names	N° Miles
Capt Sam[l] Camp	40	Elihu Goodrich	40
Lt Sam[l] Hart	40	Seth Graves	40
Ser Joseph Wright	40	David Graves	20
Ser Eli Crane	20	John Nois Wadsworth	20
Ser Abra[hm] Scranton	40	Wil[m] Wadsworth	20
Cor Gordon Hull	20	Enoch Henman	20
Cor James Hickcox	20	John Hull	20
Cor Charles Parmele	40	Charles Hull	20
Dr Nathaniel Hickcox	20	Gad Hall	20
Abram Bartlit	20	John Norton	20
Zebulon Bishop	20	Joel Parmele	20
Jabez Chalker	20	Selah Strong	20
Elihu Crane	20	Thomas Strong	40
Ozias Camp	20	Ichabod Scrantom	20
Sam[l] Camp	20	Steven Spencer	20
Jonathan Wells	20	Asher Wright	20
Gilbert Catlin	20	Reubin Bishop	20

[*State Library, Revolution 16.*]

CAPT. COLLINS' COMPANY.

A Milage Roll for The Horses in the New haven & Fairfield Alarms July 5th & 7th last For the 5th Company of the Alarm list in the 10th Reg[t].

Mens Names	N° Miles	Mens Names	N° Miles
Dan Collins Capt	38	W[m] Merriam	19
James Haugh Lt	38	Joseph Merriam	38
Brinton Hall Ens	19	Yale Bishop	38
Sam[l] Hall Serj	38	John Barns	38
Benjamin Merriam	38	John Ives	38
Amos Ives Serjt	19	Abel Curtiss	19
John Merriam Serjt	38	Timothy Ives	38
Daniel Janes Corpl	19	Timothy Foster	19
Ezra Rice Corpl	38	John Miles	19
Sanburn Ford fifer	38	Caleb Merriman	19
John Couch	38	Moses Hall	19
Bezaleel Ives	38	Elisha Scovil	38
Jesse Merriam	19	Jared Benham	38
Stephen Perkins	19	Moses Hall Ju[r]	19
James Cabon	38	Insign Haugh	19
Benj[a] Hart	38	Daniel Hall	19
Sam[l] Johnson	38	Isaac Hall	19
Titus Merriam	38		

[*State Library, Revolution 16.*]

CAPT. NORTON'S COMPANY.

A Pay Roll for Horse Travel of Capt Charles Nortons Company Col Thaddeus Cooks Reg[mt] being the 10th Regiment of Melitia in the State of Connecticut when Call'd for the Relief of Newhaven July 5th 1779, and also for the Relief of Fairfield July 8th A D 1779

Mens Names	No Miles	Mens Names	No Miles
Capt. Charles Norton	20	Joseph Chidsey	20
Ens. Joseph Smith	40	Timothy Hall	20
Serjt. John Jones	40	Heth Camp	20
Serjt. Phinehas Parmele	20	Israel Burritt	20
Serjt. Jonathan Cruttenden	20	Sylvanus Hull	20
Corpl. Stephen Norton	40	William Lucas	20
John Canfield	40	Thomas Lyman	20
John Curtiss	20	Daniel Meeker	20
Noadiah Grave	40	Noah Norton	20
Elnathan Norton	20	John Norton	20
John Newton	20	Burwell Newton	40
Joseph Southworth	20	Benjamin Pickett	20
Thomas Strong	20	Samuel Squire	20
James Arnold	40	Abel Tibbals	20
Samuel Bartlet	20	David Ward	20
Elnathan Camp	40	Job Camp	20
Jesse Crane	20	Reuben Bishop	20

[*State Library, Revolution 16.*]

CAPT. HOUGH'S COMPANY.

A Milage Abstract for Horse Travil in the Alarms at New Haven & Fairfield July 5th and 7th 1779 for the 6th Militia Company in the 10th Regiment.

John Hough Capt.
Nathaniel Merriam Lt.
Thos. Foster Ens.
Serj. Joseph Edwards
" Timothy Hall
" Jonth[n] Yale
" Comfort Butler
" Giles Griswould
Marshal Merriam
Elisha Merriman
Phinehas Hall
Phinhas Lyman
Edward Collins
Enos Hall
Daniel Mekye
Jn[o] Morgan
Caleb Merriman
Thos. Spencer
Amasa Merriam
Giles Foster
Ozius Foster
Jeremiah Ferrington
Simeon Perkins
Ameton Yale
Elijah Scovil
Elijah Yeomans
Elisha Curtis
Wyllys Mekye
John Yale
Moses Way
Jesse Merriman
Abner Way
Israel Hall
Wyllys Bishop
Daniel Yale
Nathaniel Yale
Asa Brown
David Scovil
Samuel Merriam
John Robinson
Samuel Rice

[*State Library, Revolution 16.*]

CAPT. STANLEY'S COMPANY.

A Pay Abstract of Capt Abraham Stanley's Company in Col Thaddeus's Reg^t^ for Horses Travel in two Alarms as far as New Haven Viz. One to New Haven on the fifth of July 1779, and the other for Fairfield on the Eighth of July 1779

Cap. Abraham Stanley
Lieu. Solomon Doolittle
Ens. Benjamin Preston
Serg. Charles Hull
Serg. Elihu Yale
Serg. John Davidson
Serg. Daniel Parker
Serg. Abner Rice
Corp. Jotham Gaylord
Corp. David Johnson
Corp. Joel Rice
Corp. Isaac Doolittle
Drum. Ebenezer Moss
Samuel Ives
Joseph Doolittle Jr.
John Doolittle
Jedediah Button
Charles Parker
Joel Hough
Joshua Parker
Oliver Doolittle
Lent Hough
John Lewis
Caleb Merriman
Ebenezer Hull
Eliakim Parker
Stephen Beach
William Atwater Jr
Nicholas Jones
Jonathan Johnson
Daniel Hitchcock
Abel Ward Atwater
Jehiel Rice Jr
Abijah Ives
James Prout
Levi Parker
Francis Wilcox

Abraham Stanley Ju^r^ Capt
Wallingford August 13, 1779

[*State Library, Revolution 16.*]

CAPT. CLARK'S COMPANY.

Pay Role for Horse travel Capt James Clarks Company 16th Reg^t^ Commanded by Nehemiah Beardsley Esqr Col^o^ on an Expedition to Fairfield Norwalk Danbury &c 16th July 1779

Names of Persons who Rode Horses

James Clark Capt
Elijah Wood Lieut
Thad^us^ Barnum Ens.
Aaron Stone Serg.
Nathan Starr Serg
Seth Crofoot Serg.
Daniel Hoyt Serg.
Benjn Wood Corp.
Elnathan Gregory Drum
Joshua Benedict
James Crary
Stephen Curtis
Joseph Crofoot

Names of Persons who Rode Horses

Amos Hoyt
Agur Hoyt
Stephen Peck
Stephen Scovil
Eli Sanford
Daniel Stone
William Stone
Joel Stone
Jonathan Taylor
Abraham Waring
Benjn S. Rockwell
Joseph Wood
James Lincoln

[*State Library, Revolution 16*]

CAPT. OLMSTED'S COMPANY.

Pay Roll for Horse travle of Cap[t] David Olmsted's Company in Col[n] Nehemiah Bardsleys Reg[t] Whilest on Alarm at Fairfield

David Olmsted Capt
Job Smith Leut
Jered Olmsted Ens
Abijah Benedict Serj
James Scott Serj
Jacob Nash Serj
Ebenezer Hauley Cl
Corp John Benedict
Corp Trowbridge Bennett
Corp Nathan Hoyt
Ezra Nash
Benjimin Keeler
John Gilbert
Jonathan Hoyt
Alexander Resseguie
Nathan Smith
Ezra Mead
Mathew Olmsted
Robert Wilson
Jesse Benedict
Hial Morris
Nathan Kellogg
Josiah Osbourn
Gamaliel Benedict
Mathew Keeler
Jonathan Nash
Jeremiah Dauchy
Josiah Northrop
Abijah Seymour
James Follet

[*State Library, Revolution 16.*]

CAPT. ABEL BOTSFORD'S COMPANY.

Pay Role for Hors travel Capt Abel Botsford Company Commanded by Abel Baldwin Let. in the 16th Rigment Commanded by Nehemiah Bardsle Esq. Colo on an Expedition to Fairfield Norrowolk and Canon Newtown July 8th 1779

Let. Abel Baldwin
Serj. Nirum Botsford
Serj. Ezekel Beers
Serj. Edward Blackman
Cor. Ely Whelor
Cor. Elijah Baldwin
Daniel Turrel
Zalmon Burret

[*State Library, Revolution 16.*]

CAPT. RICHARD SMITH'S COMPANY.

A Rool for Hors Travel, Capt Richard Smith's Company 16th Regt Commanded by Nehemiah Bardsley Esq Col[o] on an Expedition to Fairfield & Norwalk Newbury August y[e] 9th 1779

Lieut Dibbl
Ens Marwin
Segt Starr
Sergt Nearin
Sergt Bostwick
Corp Keeler
Corp David Keeler
Joshua Northrup
Benjamin A. Ruggles
Comfor Ruggles
Isaac Lockwood
Liverus Dunning
Joseph Nearin
Eli Smith
Bostwick Ruggles
Samuel Dunning
John Bostwick
George Clark
Ruben Taylor
Amiel Camp
Shermon Smith
John Peck
Jonathan Beacher
Peter Hubbell
Samuel Cobet

[*State Library, Revolution 16.*]

CAPT. JOSEPH SMITH'S COMPANY.

Pay Role for Horse travel of Capt Joseph Smith of ye 16th Reg^t^ Comanded by Nehemiah Beardley Col on an Expedition to Norwalk &c July 1779

Capt. Joseph Smith
Liut. Timothy Buggles
Ens. Marles Warner
Seg. Isaas Gray
Seg. Eli Trowbridg
Jcial Smith
Wll^m^ Nicols
Samuel Ruggles
Ashbel Ruggles
John Kimberley
Garshum Jackson
Nathan Camp
Ezra Duning
Jeremiah Lockwood
Job Bunnell
Joseph Thomblenson
Ruben Talor
Andrew Northrup
Joshua Northrup
Joel Judson
David Smith
Jered Baldwin
Thad Baldwin
Ager Stevens
Levi Murrwin (?)
Ebenezer Barnum
Caleb Stevens

[*State Library, Revolution 16.*]

CAPT. PENFIELD'S COMPANY.

A Pay Role for Horse Travel Capt Peter Penfield Company 16th Regiment Commanded by Nehemiah Beardsley Esqr Col. on an Expedition to Fairfield & Norwalk &c New fairfield July 17th 1779

Peter Penfield Capt
Sarj. Eliphalet Brush
" Joseph Bearse
" Janas Brush
Abel Trowbridge
Zadock Barnum Corp
Abel Corier
Abel Hodges Jr
Asa Disbrow
Elijah Bearse
Newcomb Bearse
Sam^ll^ Crane
Lem^ll^ Pardee
Oliver Trobridge
Gideon Beardsley Jr.
Gideon Hubbell
Asel Hambleton
Thos Brush
Wail Bull

[*State Library, Revolution 16.*]

CAPT. ELIJAH BOTSFORD'S COMPANY.

A Pay Roll for Horse Travel Capt Elijah Botsford Company 16th Regiment Commanded by Col Nehem^h^ Beardsley in an Expedition in the State of New York July 1779

Capt Elijah Botsford
Lieut Matth^w^ Curtis
Nathan Plats
Ezra Sherman
Moses Bardsley

A Pay Roll of a Corps Belonging to S^d^ Company in an Expedition to Fairfield Norwalk &c

Capt Elijah Botsf^d^
Lieut Math^w^ Curtis

[*State Library, Revolution 16.*]

CAPT. JABEZ BOTSFORD'S COMPANY.

Pay Role for Horse Travil Capt Jabez Botsfords Company 16 Redg^{t} Commanded by Nehemiah Bardsley Colonel on an Expedition to Fairfield and from there to Norwalk and Stamford

Jabez Botsford Capt
Henry Fairman Lt
Joshua Hatch Ens
Amos Barrett Serg
Asa Cogswell Serg
Abraham Bennett Cor
Enoch Hubble Cor
Silas Huble
Fitch Kimberly

[*State Library, Revolution 16.*]

CAPT. PARDEE'S COMPANY.

A Pay Role for Horse travel Belonging to the 6th Alarm List Company in New fairfield in the 16th Redgment of Connecticut Militia Commanded by Nehemiah Bardsley Col. at a Late Expedition to Fairfield Norwalk for the defence of this and the Rest of the United States of America July 7th 1779

Stephen Pardee Capt
Daniel Smith Lieut
Sarg. Seth Trobridg
Corp. Squier (?) Wakeman
Corp. Moses Gray
Pr Moses Knap
Abel Hodges
John Smith
Luis Hall
Thomas Brush
John Gorham
Elisha Hobbard
Eli Stevens
Benjamin Stevens
Josiah Bardsley

[*State Library, Revolution 16.*]

CAPT. GIDDINGS' COMPANY.

Pay Role for Horse travel Capt Wm Giddings Comp^{y} in 16th Regt Militia Commanded by Nehemiah Beardsley Esqr Col^{o} to Fairfield Norwalk Stamford New Fairfield July 8th 1779

Zephan^{h} Briggs Liut
Benjn Picket Ens
Joseph Phelps
Amos Hubbell
Thos Dunk
John Gorham
Hezekiah Bosworth
Joseph Eastman
Shadrack Hubbell
Aaron Smith
Josiah Hungerford
Noble Bennet
Nehemiah Seelye
Alexand^{r} Stewart
John Page
Isaiah Babcock

[*State Library, Revolution 16.*]

LIEUT. SEELEY'S COMPANY.

Pay Role for Horse Travil Liu[t] James Seelyes Company 16th Rig[t] Commanded by Nehemiah Bardsley Esq Colo on an Expedition to Fairfield Danbury Norwalk &c July 16th 1779

James Seelye Liut.
John Andrews Ens.
Nathaniel Hoyt Serj.
Oliver Benedict Serj.
Matthew Barnum Corp.
Nathaniel Barnum
Luke Roberds
Eliakim Starr
Silas Taylor
David Barnum
Benjami Martin
Joshua Starr

[*State Library, Revolution 16.*]

CAPT. WILDMAN'S COMPANY.

Pay Roll for horse Travel Cap Daniel Wildman's Company of Alarm List 16th Reg[t] commanded by Co[l] Neh[h] Beardsly on an Expedition to Fairfield Norwalk &c July 1779

Dan[l] Wildman Cap
Theop[s] Bened[t] Ens
Caleb Baldwin
Tim[o] Ketcham
Major Taylor
Benj[n] Crosby
Eleazer Bened[t]
Comfort Wildman
Sela Gregory
Jonas Benedict
Jon[h] Starr
Jacob Finch
Levi Stalker
Philip Corbin
Alex[r] Stuart
Lem[l] Wood Ju[r]
Obed Wildman
Sam[l] Baldwin
Abijah Starr
Comfort Hoyt
Eleazer Taylor
Daniel Wood

[*State Library, Revolution 16.*]

CAPT. SHUTE'S COMPANY.

A Pay Abstract for Capt Richard Shutes Company in Col. Bardsley Reg[t] of Militia of the State of Connecticut for hors travel in an Expedition to fairfield Norwalk &c A D 1779

Richard Shute Capt
Benja[n] Boughton Lieut
Jared Patchin Ens
David Peirce Sarj
Ely Boughton Sarj
Paul Hamelton Sarj
Samuel Stevens Corp
Eleazor Benedict Corp
John Barnum Drum
Ebenezer Nichols fifer
John Barnum Jr.
Judah Barnum Jr.
Asel Benedict
Nathan Barhan (?)
Abraham Benedict Jr.
William Comes
Samuel Cook
Nathan Gregory Jr
Enos Hoyt
Ezra Hobbol
Tho[s] Judd Jr.
Abner Judd
Jacob Judd
Silas Peirce
Peter Starr
Eleazer Starr
Forod Stevens
Eleazer Weed
Samuel Wildman Jr
David Wildman Jr
Daniel Boughton

[*State Library, Revolution 16.*]

CAPT. HUBBELL'S COMPANY.

Pay Role For Horse travil Capt[n] W[m] G. Hubbell's Comp in 16th Reg[t] Militia Commanded by Nehemiah Beardsley Esq[r] Col[o] in an Expedition to Fairfield Norwalk & Stamford New Fairfield July 8th 1779

W[m] G. Hubbell Capt
W[m] Phelps Ens
John Penfield Serj
Eben[r] Buck "
Berzilla Brown "
Sam[l] Stewart Corp
Benj[n] Bennet
David Gorham
Jeremiah Mead
Bennet Sill
Abel Page
James Gorham
Isaiah Hungerford
Ezra Hungerford
Joseph Eastman
Aaron Perry
Isaac Tripp
Stephen Stewart
Abel Lamphear
Sam[l] Richardson
George Higgins
John Sturdavant
Nath[ll] Squire
Obadiah Tibits
Silvenus Palmetur
Stephen Sherwood
Joseph Giddings
John Gould
Eph[m] Conger

[*State Library, Revolution 16.*]

CAPT. HICKOK'S COMPANY.

Pay Roll for Horse travel Capt Daniel Hickoks Company 16th Regiment Commanded by Nehemiah Beardsly Esq[r] Col on An Expedition to Fairfield Danbury 9th July A D 1779

Daniel Hickok Capt
Joseph Elmor Lieut
Mathew Starr Ens.
Benajah Benedict Serg
Eliphalet Ferry Serg
Moses Vail Serg
Daniel Platt Corp
Benjamin Peeck Fif
William Benedict
Moses Benedict
Seth Benedict
Daniel Crowfut
Samuel Hoyt
James Hoyt
Lazerus Barnum
Daniel Barnum
Eden Andrus
Eliphalet Peck
James Platt
Samuel Benedict
Ebenezer Judd
John Holcomb
Benajah Hoyt
Eliud Taylor
Samuel Taylor
John Taylor
Elihu Judd
Stephen Trowbridge
Amos Starr
Samuel Starr
Nathan Wallor

[*State Library, Revolution 16.*]

CAPT. BARNUM'S COMPANY.

A Pay Abstract for Horse travel Belonging to the 4 Alarm List Company in Danbury in the 16 Redgment of Militia in the State of Connecticut Commanded By Nehemiah Bardsley Col. In a Late Expidition to Farfield Norwalk &c for the Defence of this State and the Rest of the United States of Amaricah, July the 7 1779

Officers and Soldiers names That Rode on Horse Back

Richard Barnum Cap.
Nathaniel Barnum Lieut.
Serg. Thaddeus Mourhouse
Serg. Miles Boughton
Serj. Matthew Wilkee (?)
Clerk John Lindsley
Corp. Justus Hoyt
Corp. Lemuel Lindsley
Drum. Amos Knap
Priv. David Boughton
Matthew Boughton
Noble Benedict
Calub Church
Benjamin Curtis
Daniel Grigory
Nathan Grigory
Hezekiah Gray
John Hoyt
Noah Hoyt
Jonathan Hoyt
Jonathan Hays
Elnathan Knap
Matthew Lindsley
James Lindsley
David Picket
Noah Starr
John Starr
Ezra Stevens
Samuel Weed
Isaac Wildman

[*State Library, Revolution 16.*]

CAPT. HINE'S COMPANY.

A Pay Abstract of Capt. Isaac Hines Company in Col° Nehemiah Bardsley Regt: Militia in ye State of Connecticut for Horse Travil in Alarm to Fairfield Bedford & Norwalk

Dated Ridgefield July 1779.

Mens Names	Miles Travil
Capt Isaac Hine	20
Lieut David Scott	20
Ensn John Keeler	20
Clerk James Rockwell	20
Serj^t Hugh Cane	20
Serg^t Samuel Olmsted	20
Serj^t Abram Nash	20
Serj^t James Resseguie	20
Corpl Daniel Smith	20
Corpl Samuel Smith	20
Corpl Gabriel Bennet	10
David Hoyt	20
John Morris	20
Jacob Smith 2^d	20
Thomas Hauley	
Daniel Olmsted	20
Jehial Bouton	20
David Stjohn	20
Daniel Kellogg	
Amos Baker	20
Theodore Rockwill	20
Benjamin Sherwood	20
Robert Edmond	20
Ebenezer Price	20
John Benedict	20
Samuel Fairbanks	20
David Olmsted 2^d	
Stephen Hard	10
Aaron Northrup	10
Timothy Keeler	10
Ezekiel Wilson	10
Seth Lee	
Aaron Hull	20
Thadeus Sturgis	20
James Lusey	
Ebenezer Jones	
Elijah Kellogg	20
Silas Hall	10
Benjamin Smith	10
Timothy Keeler 2^d	20
Gideon Scott	20
John Baldwin	10
Daniel Dean	20
Elijah Weedg	10
Joseph Stebbins	10

[*State Library, Revolution 16.*]

CAPT. WAUGH'S COMPANY.

A Pay Abstract for the Horse Travel of Capt Alex[d] Waughs Company in the 17th Reg[t] of Militia of the State of Connecticut who March'd on a sudden emergency to oppose the Enemy; who were burning Fairfield & Norwalk on July 10th A D 1779

Mens Names	N° Miles	Mens Names	N° Miles
Alex[d] Waugh Capt	50	Andrew Woodruff	50
David Stoddard Lt	50	Sol. Woodruff	20
Abner Cone Ens	50	Sam[ll] Woodruff	50
Sergt. Benj. Webster	50	John Woodruff	50
Serj. Clark Royce		Reuben Webster	50
Serj. Solomon Linly	50	Elijah Webster	50
Serj. Friend Dickinson	50	John Waterbury	50
Corpl. Aaron Gibbs	50	Ezekiel Graves	50
Corpl. John Osborn	50	Seba Canfield	50
Corpl. Jeremiah Riggs	50	Joshua Hide	50
Corpl. James Griffis	50	Asa Page	50
Abner Baldwin	50	Jo. Barber	50
Samuel Bernard		Zadok Seelye	50
Stephen Brown	50	Abel Page	50
Benj. Baker	50	Moses Munson	50
Benj. Birge	50	Alex[d] M[c]Neil	50
Truman Beamon	50	Eliada Orton	50
Nathaniel Benton	50	Oliver Dickinson	50
Jesse Bartholomew	50	John Bissell	50
Reuben Page	50	Sam[ll] Catlin	50
Stephen Baldwin	50	Moses Barns	50
Daniel Clark	50	Abel Barns	20
Isaac Catlin	50	Serj. Nath[n] Munson	20
Levi Coe	50	William Lewis	20
Charles Collens	50	Benj. Throop	20
John Carter	50	Zach[y] Johnson	20
Oliver Churchill	50	Ezekiel Borden	20
Bradley Catlin	50	Hezekiah Agard	20
Simeon Gibbs	50	Ahijah Warren	20
Uri Goodwin	50	Reuben Landon	20
Jacob Green	50	Jeremiah Osborn	20
Oliver Gibbs	50	Jesse Stoddard	20
Solomon Harrison	50	Jarey Kilborn	20
John How	50	Benjamin Barns	20
Harris Jones	50	John Metcalf	20
Samuel Jones	50	Asa Morey	20
Helmont Kellogg	50	Aahel Dickinson	20
Griffin Kinnion	50	Stephen Judson	20
William Little	50	Zophar Beach	50
Samuel Little	50	John Russell	50
Timothy Linly	50	Isaac Thomson	50
James Landon	50	Isaac Horsford	50
Samuel Orton	50	Reuben Barns	50
Darius Orton	50	Seely Way	20
Isaac Osborn	50	Daniel Page	20
Amos Parmeley	50	David Wetmore	20
Moses Peck	50	Bela Graves	20
Joseph Sanford	50	Stephen Plant	20
Abel Saunders	50	Luther Mason	50
Ezekiel Trumbul	50	George Bull	50
Asher Thorp	50		

Stephen Plant 2 Days in Service John Bissell 4 Days in Service

[This company was in service at Horse Neck in July and August, 1779, under Andrew Adams, Lieut.-Colonel Commander.]

[*State Library, Revolution 16.*]

CAPT. PHELPS' COMPANY.

A Pay Abstract for the Horses that went in Service in Cap[t] Josiah Phelps[s] Comp[y] in Col. Phelps[s] Reg[t] of Militia Ordered by Co[l] Epaphras Sheldon in a Tour to Norwalk July 9th 1779

Horses Sent Back at Wilton Being 60 Miles Travel

Mens Names

Capt Josiah Phelps
Lieut Eph[m] Bancroft
Ens Jona[th] Kettell
Serjt Jacob Tyler
" Seth Lockwood
" Amos Webster
" Timothy Hale
Corp Thomas Skiner
" Solomon Moss
" Seth Meacham
" Amos Bush or Beech
Elijah Andrus
Levi Benedick
Jacob Benton
Francis Beech
Oliver Bissel
Elijah Bill
Hezekiah Bissel
Ichabod Brown
Russel Burr
William Brown
Asahel Barbur
Brewin Beech
Ambrose Blakesly
Eben[r] Johnson
Thom Cook
Ichabod Chapins
Will[m] Cook
Elisha Catlin
Gad Ely
John Frisbie
Silas Gridley
George Griswold
Andw Gleason
Asa Griswold
Simeon Humphry

Mens Names

Gideon Hurlbard
Noah Humphry
John Hurlbard
Benoni Johnson
Nathan Keley
Abraham Loomis
Epaphras Loomis
Eph[m] Loomis
Joseph Loomis
Grove Loomis
Brigadore Loomis
Joseph Wooden
Elisha Gaylord
Ens. Bissel
Isaiah Loomis
Oliver Loomis
Jonas Leech
Roswel Marshel
Israel Merriman
Benjamin Mills
Jesse Murrain
Remembrance North
Eber Norton
Elisha Norton
Gideon Peck
Noah Preston
Tim[th] Kay
Robert Rood
Ebenezer Smith
David Smith
Jesse Smith
Medad Taylor
Moses Wilcox
John Winchel
John Wilcox
Hervy Whiting

Horses Sent Back at New Milford Being 30 Miles

Mihael Bull
David Mansfield
Abner Perkins
Benj[n] Butler
Eliphalet Bristol
Moses Wilcox 2[d]
Elijah Catlin
Andw Austin
John Strong
Lieut Eli Wilson

[*State Library, Revolution 16.*]

FIFTEENTH REGIMENT—LIEUT.-COL. STANLEY.

CAPT. HALL'S COMPANY.

A Pay Abstract for Capt Asaph Halls Company in Col. Gad Stanlys Regt for Hors Travel Who Was ordered to Ride to Horse Neck by Col Epaphras Sheldon in August 1779 for the Defense of the State of Connecticut.

Capt Asaph Hall
Lt Nath^ll Bull
Ensn David Goff
Sergt Chancy Beech
Corpl Jonathan Miller
Alen Kellogg
Ira Phelps
Joseph Baley
Israel Smith
Oliver Wilcox
Ruben Barber
Sam^ll Tyler
Jonathan Cook
Sam^ll Phelps
Noah Gleason
Stephen Thomson
Sam^ll Weston
John Weston
Nathan Davis

[*State Library, Revolution 16.*]

EIGHTEENTH REGIMENT—COL. PHELPS.

CAPT. BATES' COMPANY.

September ye 7th A D 1779 to Joel Moor Clark of ye Second Company of Alaram List in Simsburey in the State of Connecticut Greting

Persuant to orders you are heareby Commanded to Deracte Richard Gay Ephram Adams Nath Winchil Ezekiel Phelps Juny Barnabus Meacham Jams Luis David Clark Obediah Moore Joseph Griswold Isaac Broker John Horskins Isaac Moor Ranc Cossit John Check Wm Shepard Adonijah Holcomb Silas Holcomb Mathew Griffin Juny Ephraim Holcomb Hezakiah Holcomb Joshua Holcomb Thomas Spring Josiah Toping Asa Hilyer Benjah Dibol David Holcomb John Vallants Elnathan Lamson Juda Hays Rebert Fields Aron Ducy Abijah Phelps Elijah Phelps Seth Viets Noah Phelps Silvanus Bartlet John Miller to Aquipt them Selves with arms and acounterments and hold them Selves in Readeynes to march at ye Shortest Notis for ye Defence of this this State

Lemuel Bates Capt

[*Charles W. Bates, East Granby.*]

DETACHED SERVICE.

LIEUT. HEPBURNE'S COMPANY.

This may certify that Peter Hepburne Command [ ]

Jos Davidson
Daniel Burn
James Goldsmith
Sam B Smith
John W[m] Gillit
Benajah Smith
David Miles
Jene Stow
Theoph[s] Smith
Garrit DeWitt
Henry Lenimey (?)
Tiret Bull
Eben[r] Oviat
Henry Bull
Jos. Whiting

Each of them served as Matrosses in the Fort at Milford A. D. 1779 and therefore have their Hea[ ] abated from their Lists Viz[t] Eighteen pounds from each of them James Goldsmith only excepted his Son being under 21 years of age

Milford 28th April 178[ ]

[*State Library, Revolution 16.*]

MIDDLETOWN GUARD.

A Pay Rolle for Guarding Six Brass Field Pieces in Middletown from the 3[d] of August 1779 to the 15th of September.

Elihu Cotton	20 Nights	John Hollit	15 Nights
Timothy Cornwell	14 "	Abel Sizer	15 "
Noah Higbe	8 "	Prince Winban	15 "
Andrew Bacon	15 "	Aaron Robards	15 "
George Adkins	15 "		

[*State Library, Revolution 16.*]

FIRST LIGHT HORSE REGIMENT—MAJ. HART.

[*See Record of Connecticut Men in the Revolution, page 442.*]

SECOND TROOP—CAPT. WOODRUFF.

A Pay Abstract of Capt Enoch Woodruff Troop of Horse while in State Service at Greenwich for Extra Expense A D 1779

Enoch Woodruff Capt
Andrew Clark, Express to Fairfield
Michael Taintor
Wilford Johnson
Isaac Lane, Express to Hartford
Timothy Gilbard
Eber Ward, Express to Stanford
Jonas Larence, Express to Fairfield
Solomon Stanton, Express to Fairfield
Lemuell Martin
John Ables
Lent Kough
Abner Tharp
Jacob Morgan
Jesse Cook
Daniell Willard
Nathan Basset, Express to Norwalk
Abram Buckley
Benj[a] Weeb, Express to Wilton Canon &c
Ozias Phelps
Sam[ll] Hays
Gabrel Flowers
Pineas Coe
David Giddins, Express to Fairfield

[*State Library, Revolution 16.*]

VARIOUS COMPANIES.

SERVICE WITH CONTINENTAL ARMY.

The United States Dr To the State of Connecticut, for the Service &c of Militia, ordered to joyn the Continental Army in 1779, Viz :—

Bills & Accts	Remarks
Capt Uriel Holmes	Col. B. Hutchins Regt
Capt Peter Curtis	15th Regt
Capt Aaron Keley	Majr N. Smiths
Capt J. Forward	Col. B. Hutchins
Capt Noble Hine	Col. S. Canfields
Capt Divan Berrys	Majr N. Smiths
Capt I. Lewis	"
Col. B. Hutchins	
Capt Joseph Dart	Col. A. Tylers Regt
Capt D. Olmstead	Col. S. Canfields
Capt E. Hinman	"
Genl A. Ward	
Capt J. Wright	Col. Gallops
Capt J. Johnson	"
Capt J. Wyllys	"
Capt Amos Woodward	Col. Gordons
Capt Caleb Handee	"
Capt John Swan	Col. Gallups
Capt O. Spicer	"
Col. N. Gallup	
Capt A. Waterman	Col. O. Johnsons
Capt Wm Frissel	Col. J. Gordons
Capt A. Loomis	Col. H. Wyllys
Col. H. Wyllys	
Capt E. Botsford	Col. S. Canfield
Capt R. Abbe	Col. H. Wyllys
Capt J. Converse	Col S. Chapmans.
Capt Charles Smith	Majr J. Davenports

[*Comptroller's Office, Haskell's Receipts.*]

SERVICE WITH COUNT D'ESTAING.

The United States Dr To the State of Connecticut, for the service &c of Militia orderd to Co-operate with Count De Estang in 1779—Viz.—

Bills & Accounts	Remarks
Col. James Gordon	
Capt J. Gray	Col. S. Canfields
Col. S Canfield	
Capt J. Burton	"
Capt J. Gillet	Col. R. Newbury
Capt E. Moseley	Col. J. Gordons

Bills & Accounts	Remarks
Capt D. Hitchcock	Col. Tylers
Capt Moses Gilbert	"
Capt N. Waterman	Col. Gallup
Capt B. Buell	Col. J. Mason
Capt J. Green	
Capt B. Buell	"
Capt C. Wells	Col. H. Wyllys

[*Comptroller's Office, Haskell's Receipts.*]

MILITIA SERVICE.

The United States Dr To the State of Connecticut for the service of State Troops & Militia [between the 1st April & 1 Novr] raised for the defence of the State & allowed by Act of Congress December 28th 1779 computed according to the Continental establishment of Pay [and rations as per resolution of Congress of 2 & 6 June 1778].

(The statements in brackets were added in pencil in a different hand. It is not stated for how long any of these companies served. A few of them also served before or after the period April 1,—Novr 1, 1779.)

Officers Pay Rolls	
Capt Lee Lay	[Guard Lyme]
Capt John Williams	[" Fort Griswold]
Capt William Howard	[coast guard Newbury Regt 1777]
Capt Isaac Howe	[Meads Regt]
Capt Odle Close	[Guard Horseneck May 1779]
Capt Charles Smith	[Compy Horseneck]
Capt Reuben Bostwick	[Horseneck Alarm]
Lt Colo Samuel Canfield	["]
Capt D. Leavenworth	[Coast guard]
Colo Roger Newberry	[field & staff N. London]
Capt George Terrill	[Coast guard Horseneck]
Capt Edward Payne	[Company at New London]
Capt John Porter	[Coast guard Horseneck]
Capt Samuel Bronson	[" "]
Colo Noadiah Hooker	[" " field & staff]
Capt Divan Berry	[" "]
Capt Judah Woodruff	[" "]
Capt Lemuel Bates	[" "]
Capt Giles Miller	[" "]
Capt N. Chapman	[Company Horseneck ——]
Capt Charles Norton	[Company N. Haven alarm]
" "	[" Fairfield alarm]
Capt J. Robinson	[" N. Haven "]
" "	[" Fairfield "]
Capt Samuel Camp	[" New Haven "]
" "	[" Fairfield "]
Ensign Joseph Smith	[Coast guards]
Colo Hezekiah Wyllys	[Coast guards]

Capt Josiah Phelps	Capt Roger Riley
Capt Amos Barnes	Capt John Hugh
Capt Timothy Clark	Capt Dan Collins
Capt Solomon Sage	Colo Andrew Adams
Capt Nathan Gilbert	Serjt James Payson
Capt Jared Shepperd	Capt James Stoddard
Capt Samuel Hart	Capt David Phelps

Officers Pay Rolls

Capt Elizur Hale
Capt Elizur Hubbard
Capt David Hitchcock
Capt Nathl Bunnell
Capt Miles Hull
Capt Robert Martin
Capt David Hitchcock
Capt Ephraim Cook
Lt Nathan Hurd
Capt Nathan Hine
Capt Amos Wetmore
Capt John Wetmore
Capt Joseph Kellogg
Capt Joseph Blague
Capt Jacob Witmore
Capt George Hubbard
Capt Jabez Brooks
Capt Othniel Williams
Capt George Phillips
Capt Daniel Stewart
Capt Daniel Clark
Capt Othniel Williams
Capt Thomas Giddings
Capt Elizur Hubbard
Capt Augustus Collins
Capt Oliver Stanley
Capt Caleb Hall
Capt Abraham Stanley
Capt Miles Johnson
Capt Thomas Shepard
Lt Daniel Holt
Capt Abraham Stanley
Capt Joseph Carew
Col^o Samuel Abbot
Maj^r Asa Bray
Capt Simeon Sheldon
Capt Hezekiah Gridley
Capt Job Case
Lt Thomas Phelps
Col^o Comfort Sage
Capt Enos Hawley
Col^o Comfort Sage
Capt Samuel Osborn
Lt Stephen Goodrich
Col^o Howel Woodbridge
Capt Nehem^h Laurence
Capt James Burton
Col^o N. Beardsley
Capt Richard Smith
Capt Elijah Botsford
Capt A. Botsford
Capt Jabez Botsford
Capt James Clark
Capt Isaac Hine
Capt Richard Barnum
Capt William Giddings
Capt Daniel Wildman
Capt Richard Shute

Officers Pay Rolls

Capt William G. Hubbell
Capt Stephen Pardee
Capt Knowles Sears
Capt Peter Penfield
Capt Daniel Hickock
Capt Joseph Smith
Lt James Seeley
Capt David Olmsted
Capt Timothy Judson
Capt Jonah Foster
Capt William Willson
Capt Ephraim Barnum
Capt Joseph Bottom
Capt Abel Burritt
Capt Elijah Hazen
Lt Abner Mosley
Capt Jesse Curtiss
Lt Abner Moseley
Ensign Enoch Scribner
Capt Nathl Gilbert
Capt Jonathan Farrand
Capt Jesse Curtiss
Ens^n Sol^o Martin
Capt Stephen Seymour
Capt Elijah Backus
Capt Nehemiah Tinker
Capt David Hinman
Capt Thomas Giddings
Capt Uriel Holmes
Capt John Williams
Capt Elijah Avery
Capt John Williams
Capt John Dixon
Capt Daniel Brainard
Capt Joseph Dart
Col^o John Penfield
Capt Jonathan Case
Capt Elias Bliss
Capt N. Bunnell
Capt Amos Wetmore
Capt Lemuel Roberts
Capt Elisha Chapman
Capt Eliphalet Curtiss
Capt Reuben Sikes
Capt Samuel Felt
Capt Israel Converse
Maj^r Abiel Pease
Capt Stephen Roberts
Capt Jedediah Amedown
Capt Ezra Kinney
Capt James Morgan
Capt Joseph Bordman
Capt Jonathan Bush
Capt Gilbert Dudley
Capt William Giddings
Capt Abraham Fuller
Capt Abner Mallery
Capt James Averill

Officers Pay Rolls

Capt N. Barber
Capt Lazarus Ruggles
Capt Benjamin Stone
Capt Abel Botsford
Capt Jotham Curtiss
Capt Nathl Barnes
Capt William Cogswell
Capt Ebenezer Couch
Capt Jotham Curtiss
Lt Barth^l Pond
Capt Noble Hine
Capt Joseph Isham
Capt Reuben Bostwick
Col^o Samuel Canfield
Capt Adam Hurlbut
Serj^t Ebenezer Thomas
Lt Reuben Blakesley
Ens^n James Porter
Capt Alex^r Waugh
Capt Jared Dudley
Capt Nathl Hall
Capt Benj^a Richards
Capt John Woodruff
Capt Phineas Castle
Lt Thomas Dutton
Capt Thomas Fenn
Capt Joseph Garnsey
Col^o Noah Phelps
Capt Arch. McNeal
Capt Elisha Edgerton
Capt Isaac Johnson
Capt Josiah King
Capt Aaron Horsford
Capt Reuben Stone
Capt Miles Beach
Capt Samuel Rockwell
Capt Reuben Rose
Capt David Barber
Capt Amasa Mills
Col^o Jonathan Dimon
Lieu^t Aaron Porter
Capt L. Hotchkiss
Capt Asa Yale
Capt Joseph Bacon
Capt Josiah Terrill
Capt Charles Wright
Capt Abijah Hall
Capt Jonathan Kilborne
Capt Elias Graves
Capt John Lewis
Capt Kezin Gridley
Capt Elisha Scott
Capt Peter Curtiss
Capt Abel Brace
Maj^r Elihu Kent
Lt Nathan Noble
Capt Nehemiah Brainard
Capt Samuel Hubbard

Officers Pay Rolls

Capt Samuel Brooks
Capt John Smith
Capt James Lusk
Capt Hezekiah Wells
Capt Chester Wells
Lt James Arnold
Col^o William Worthington
Capt Amos Barnes
Capt B. Stoddard
Capt Asaph Hall
Capt Zeb Taylor
Capt M. Smith
Capt A. Burr
Ensign Wright
Capt Jabez Wright
Capt Matthew Cole
Capt Zeb Taylor
Capt Seth Peirce
Capt Asaph Hall
Capt Benjamin Mills
Capt Ebenezer Fletcher
Capt Adonijah Burr
Capt Ambrose Sloper
Capt Roger Moore
Capt Jonathan Cady
Capt Nehemiah Waterman
Capt J. Raynsford
Capt Samuel Wheat
Capt Jonathan Cady
Capt Benj^a Mills
Capt N. Waterman
Capt Samuel Upson
Capt Daniel Cone
Capt Z. Hungerford
Capt N. Jewit
Capt Israel Spencer
Capt William Cone
Capt Phelps
Capt Jacob Hinsdale
Capt David Wood
Capt Odle Close
Lt James Austin
Lt Nathaniel Mead
Capt Odle Close
Capt Caleb Mead
Capt John Allyn
Capt John Deshon
Genl Selah Heart
Lt Thomas Powers
Serj^t John Colt
Capt Amos Barnes
Capt Amos Beecher
Lt Ezra Dibble
Capt Josiah Fowler
Lt John Thrall
Capt Benoni Smith
Capt Samuel Wells
Capt Samuel Peck

Officers Pay Rolls

Cap[t] Timothy Clark
Cap[t] Matthew Cole
Cap[t] Ambrose Sloper
Cap[t] John Langton
Cap[t] Joseph Forward
Cap[t] Thomas Bidwell
Cap[t] Samuel Williams
Cap[t] Elijah Hinman
Cap[t] Ziba Hunt
Cap[t] Asa Bray
Cap[t] John Perkins
Cap[t] Abraham Stanley
Cap[t] Caleb Hall
Cap[t] Oliver Stanley
Cap[t] Dan Collins
Cap[t] Samuel Hays
Cap[t] Daniel Lyon
Cap[t] Matthew Smith
Cap[t] Peter Mills
Cap[t] Lewis Mills
Cap[t] Lewis Mallett
L[t] Noah Porter
L[t] Asa Cooley
Cap[t] Jesse Curtiss
Col[o] Oliver Smith
Ens[n] Joseph Babcock
L[t] John Williams
Cap[t] Daniel Lankton
Cap[t] Josiah Baldwin
Cap[t] William Stanton
Cap[t] John Breed
Cap[t] Josiah Baldwin
Cap[t] Job Wright
Cap[t] Isaac Bronson
Col[o] Hezekiah Sabin
Cap[t] J. Bronson
Col[o] Seth Smith
Cap[t] Jed Chapman
Cap[t] Simeon Lay
Cap[t] Isaac Bronson
Cap[t] Benjamin Richards
Cap[t] Aaron Kelcey
Cap[t] Bez[a] Bristol
Maj. Gen[l] O. Wolcott
Cap[t] John Pennoyer
Cap[t] John Willey
Col[o] Gad Stanley
Col[o] E. Storrs
Cap[t] Dan Bouton
Cap[t] C. Raymond
Cap[t] N. Gilbert
Cap[t] Reuben Scofield
L[t] Eliphalet Seeley
L[t] Joel Hays
Col[o] Gad Stanley
Cap[t] Allen Cooper
Cap[t] Caleb Mix
Cap[t] Timothy Starkey

Officers Pay Rolls

Cap[t] Thomas Shepard
Cap[t] Timothy Munger
Cap[t] Stephen Palmer
Cap[t] Jesse Goodyear
Cap[t] Benjamin Baldwin
Cap[t] Bryan Stoddard
Cap[t] Jesse Billings
Cap[t] Nathaniel Harriss
Col[o] E. Worthington
Cap[t] Jabez Perkins
Cap[t] N. Hall
Cap[t] John Breed
Cap[t] Benjamin Clark
L[t] Ichabod Palmer
Cap[t] Christopher Leffingwell
Cap[t] David Hough
Cap[t] Chrs. Leffingwell
Cap[t] David Landon
Cap[t] Benajah Leffingwell
Cap[t] Ichabod Miller
Maj[r] N. Brown
Cap[t] Shubael Griswold
Col[o] Epa[s] Sheldon
Cap[t] Epa[s] Loomis
Lieut Miller
B. General And[w] Ward
Cap[t] Amos Smith
Maj[r] John Belding
L[t] Timothy Lockwood
L[t] Nathan Sloson
Cap[t] Jesse Bell
Cap[t] Ebenezer Ferris
Cap[t] Richard Deshon
Cap[t] Jeremiah Halsey
Cap[t] Ebenezer Witters
Cap[t] Jonathan Warring
L[t] Justus Buck
Ensign Allen Smith
Cap[t] James Barker
Cap[t] James Lindsley
Cap[t] Edward Shipman
L[t] Hoadley
Cap[t] Isaac Howe
Col[o] William Worthington
Cap[t] John Hills
Cap[t] Joseph Loveland
Cap[t] Thomas Horsey
Cap[t] Seth Pierce
Cap[t] Jabez Wright
Cap[t] Abraham Foot
Cap[t] Daniel Holbrook
Cap[t] Amos Barnes
Cap[t] Samuel Peck
Cap[t] Charles Smith
Col[o] John Mead
L[t] Elijah Bruster
Cap[t] Joshua Dunlap
Cap[t] Stephen Lyon

Officers Pay Rolls

Colo Dyer Throop
Capt Simeon Edgerton
Capt Joseph Whitmore
Capt Amaziah Rust
Colo Marshfield Parsons
Capt C. Allen
Capt Samuel Osborne
Capt Noah Kellogg
Capt Jesse Ford
Capt M. Gilbert
Colo William Worthington
Capt John Isham
Capt Bethuel Treat
Capt Ruluff Dutcher
Capt Jared Cone
Capt William Howard
Capt Joseph Sanford
Capt Ebenezer Smith
Capt Augur Curtiss
Colo Jonathan Wells
Majr Thomas Bull
Capt Silas Dunham
Capt Daniel Platt
Capt Silas Dunham
Capt John Wood
Capt Israel Seymour
Capt Joseph Woodford
Capt Thomas Giddings
Colo Samuel Mott
Capt Samuel Leffingwell
Capt Ebenezer Barnard
Capt Eliphalet Bulkley
Capt Samuel Brooks
Capt Samuel Gates
Capt Thomas Bidwell
Capt Ladwick Hotchkiss
Capt Elisha Toby
Capt Shubael Griswold
Capt Isaac Hall
Capt John Riggs
Capt Bradford Steel
Capt Daniel Chatfield
Capt David Phelps
Capt David Beecher
Capt Peter Perkins
Capt Amos Hallam
Capt Amos Main
Colo Nathan Gallup
Capt Benjamin Summer
Colo Joseph Abbott
Lieut Hughes
Capt Stephen Smith
Lt William Lay
Capt Issachar Bates
Capt Jeremiah Bradley
Serjt Giddeon Brockway
Colo Edward Russell
Capt Benoni Smith

Officers Pay Rolls

Lt Lawrence Clinton
Capt Noah Ives
Capt Elijah Hazen
Capt Samuel Jones
Capt Othniel Williams
Capt Elnathan Nichols
Capt Enoch Woodruff
Corpl Elisha Edgerton
Capt Jonathan Dayton
Colo Jonathan Dimon
Capt James Borton
Capt Robert Wells
Majr Ichabod Norton
Capt Warham Gibbs
Capt Samuel Wells
Capt Phineas Sherman
Ensign Ebeno Morehouse
Capt Stiles Judson
Capt Samuel Uffott
Capt Charles Churchill
Capt Richard Shute
Capt Nathaniel Copley
Capt Abel Burritt
Capt Dan Collins
Genl Erastus Wolcott
Corpl Nathan Goodspeed
Corpl Silvanus Cone
Capt Richard Wait
Lebbeus Beckwith
Lt Silvanus Smith
Capt Odel Close
Capt Samuel Wells
Majr John Davenport
Capt Benjn Peck
Capt Noah Fowler
Capt Thomas Wheeler
Lt Ichabod Brown
Capt William Whitney
Capt A. McNeal
Capt Peter Johnson
Capt John Mix
Serjt John Percival
Lieut John Crane
Capt Josiah Fowler
Capt Nathaniel Bunnell
Capt Miles Hull
Capt Lewis Mallett
Capt Jehial Bryan
Capt Benajah Holcomb
Capt N. Hutchins
Serjt James Davidson
Capt Aaron Hosford
Capt Hubbard Burrus
Corpl S Hartshorne
Samuel Wright
Capt Oliver Spicer
Capt John Waterhouse
John Munroe

Officers Pay Rolls

Peter Grant
Ephraim Kelley
Capt Elisha Graham
Capt Benjamin Clark
Capt Eliphalet Lockwood
Capt Jabez Gregory
Lt Isaac Foot
Lt Arnold Hazelton
Capt Jesse Starkweather
Capt Jesse Bell
Lt John Bean
Lt Justus Buck
Lt Col^o Jonath^n Baldwin
Capt J. Bronson
Col^o I. Baldwin
Capt Moses Seymour
Capt John Shipman
Capt Lemuel Lamb
Capt Amos Jones
Capt Daniel Bouton
Serj^t Henry Wood
Lt Jacob Bunnell
Lt Joseph Bennett
Serj^t William Hall
Capt C. St John
Capt David Hitchcock
Allen Lane
Ebenezer Coe
Capt Ezra Kinnee
Col^o Increase Moseley
Lt Peter Hepburne
Col^o Thomas Belden
Capt John Green
Serj^t Wolcott Hawley
Capt Oliver Stanley
Capt Nehemiah Tinker
Serj^t Solomon Stoddard
Capt Benjamin Stone
Capt Eli Butler
Capt Daniel Godfrey
Capt Benjamin Dean
Capt David Phelps
Capt Elijah Seymour
Cap^{ts} Smith & Kimberley
Capt Seth Demming
Capt Daniel Tyler
Capt Phineas Bradley
E. Ledyard
Capt Jesse Raymond
Lt Gamaliel Taylor
Capt O. Marvin
Capt Eliakim Smith
Capt Absalom Williams
Daniel Abbott
Isaac Tucker
Capt Benjamin Green
Capt Eben. Lathrop

Officers Pay Rolls

Capt Moses Stevens
Capt S. Marshall
Lt Isaac Abell
Capt Jared Cone
Capt E. Thorp
Capt R. Richards
Lt A. Porter
Capt Solomon Morehouse
Capt Knowles Sears
Capt E. Lathrop
Capt George Peck
Capt William Giddings
Capt Elijah Palmer
Ensign Simeon Hiscox
Col^o Samuel Whiting
Capt Reuben Scofield
Capt Uriah Raymond
Col^o Levi Wells
Capt I. Stanton
Capt James Smith
Capt Peter Perit
Capt Benjn Summers
Capt John Allen
Capt John Pettibone
Capt S. Keelor
Capt John Yeates
Col^o Matthew Mead
Lemuel Nichols
Corp^l Charles Buckley
Capt Enos Hawley
Capt Adam Shapley
Capt William Latham
Capt Daniel Tilden
Capt Briant Stoddard
Capt Everts
Capt Enos Hawley
Maj^r William Ledyard
Capt Andrew Hyllyer
Capt Josiah Bradley
Col^o Phineas Porter
Capt Nathan Hine
Noah Wells
Lt Achors Sheffields
Capt Absalom Williams
Billious Kirtland
Capt Benjamin Richards
Lt Eben. Whitney
Capt Benj^a Hickock
Maj^r Ezra Starr
Anthony Annable
Capt Jabez Beebe
Capt John Hempstead
Capt Abell Hall
Capt Caleb St John
Capt Daniel Allen
Lieu^t John Curtis

[*Comptroller's Office, Haskell's Receipts.*]

MILITIA REGIMENTS, 1780.

SIX MONTHS REGIMENT.

[Although noted as recruits for the Continental Army the men named in this and the two following lists appear to have been raised to serve as Militia rather than in the "Line" or State regiments. See the doings of the Council of Safety May 30, 1780.]

Account of Bounties paid to recruits raised for 6 mo. to join the Continental Army in the year 1780, by Col^o Increase Moseley. Viz^t

Elisha Noble
Daniel Ouer
Asahel Ives
Amos Booth
Hezekiah Whitney
Luman Brownson
Johnson Wheeler
Joseph Ferry
Amos Davis
Benj^a Buckingham
Nathaniel Beecher
Nathaniel Geer
Noah Smith Jr.
Agur Hinman
S. Tracy
G. Phillips
Reuben Hill
Elizur Wheeler
Enos Hinman
John Royce
Matthew Reynolds
Caleb Scott
Ezekiel Beeman
Joel Hinman

[*State Library, Revolution 17.*]

Account of Bounties paid to recruits raised for 6 mo. to join the Continental Army in the year 1780 by Colonel Jonathan Dimon. Viz^t

Lemuel Chatfield
Roman Negro
W. Hurd
Samuel French
Joseph Mitchel
Peter Roes
J. Colver
Jack Gregory
Josiah Burroughs
James Hurlburt
Alen (?) Smith
W^m (?) Ward
Joseph Lewis
William Sissen
J. Wheeler
Richard Bangs
N. Hinman
J. Dimon Jr
E. Sherwood
E. Seyley
Aby Batter
S. Downs
Benj. Bennet
Justus Whitlock
Joseph Battson

[*State Library, Revolution 17.*]

A Bounty Roll of the 6 mo. men who joined the Continental Army from Col° John Meads Reg^{t} of Mil^{n} in the Year 1780

Justus Hait

John Mead Col° and Muster Master of the Recruits & 3 months men from the 9th Reg^{t}

[*State Library, Revolution 17.*]

MILITIA AT WEST POINT.

☞ The United States D^{r} To the State of Connecticut for sundry Expenditures &c. of Militia, who served at West Point, in the Year 1780

Bills & Accounts	Remarks
Capt N. Smith	Col. E. Russell's Reg^{t}
Capt J. Lusk	Col. Hutchins
Capt C. Norton	J. Richards
Capt M. Mills	Hutchins
Capt D. Brainerd	
Maj^{r} J. Cooks	
Capt D. Clark	Sages
Col. B. Hutchins	
Capt N. Hayden	Wells
Col. J. Wells	
Capt A. Loomis	Wells
Capt R. Abbee	"
Capt J. Cooke	"
Capt Abel Brace	Hutchins
Capt C. Churchill	Wells
Capt Gansey	B. Richards
Col. B. Richards	
Capt A. Pettibone	Hutchins
Ens^{n} H. Hines	B. Richards
Capt W. Coggswell	Moseleys
Capt A. Griswold	
Capt J. Brian	Russells

[*Comptroller's Office, Haskell's Receipts.*]

MILITIA REGIMENTS, 1781.

FOURTH REGIMENT—LIEUT.-COL. COMD. DIMON.

ADJ. JUDSON'S COMPANY.

A Pay Abstract for a Guard Ordered from the 4 Reg[t] in Connecticut for the purpose of Colecting all the Delinctuants within S[d] Reg[t] and ware Commanded By Nathaniel Judson Adgt of S[d] Reg[t] who was apointed August the 24th 1781 to take Command of S[d] guard which Service continued By turns until Nov. 28th 1781

Mens Names	Number of Days in Service	Mens Names	Number of Days in Service
Nath[ll] Judson Adj . .	34	Philow Hird . . .	3
Edmund Pulford Srgt .	19	Othenial French . .	9
Edmund Curtiss Srgt .	14	Beach Lewis Junr . .	12
Isaac Beach . . .	17	James Duning . . .	14
Selah Burrouss . . .	16	Joel Gilbert . . .	3
James Bardslay . . .	9	Lemuel Judson . . .	11
Eph[m] B. Hubbert . .	9	Nathan Thompson . .	4
Nath[ll] Sherman . . .	8	Sam[l] F Mills . . .	8
Sirus Hawley . . .	9		

[*State Library, Revolution 25*]

EIGHTH REGIMENT—COL. SMITH.

[*See Record of Connecticut Men in the Revolution, page 577.*]

CAPT. MORGAN'S COMPANY.

A Pay abstract of Capt John Morgan's Company in Col. Oliver Smith's Reg^t who Marched upon Alarm on the 6th Day of Sep. 1781. [Invasion of New London.]

Mens Names	Days in service	Mens Names	Days in service
John Morgan Capt.	3	Ralph Williams	2
Wm Williams Lt.	3	Nathan Avery	3
Chris^r Morgan Ens.	3	Stephen Morgan	3
Benadam Gallup Sarj.	3	David Annew	3
Thos Morgan Sarj.	3	Amos Brown	3
Amos Allyn Sarj.	3	Jabez Perkins	3
Phineus Fanning Sarj.	3	Simeon Barnes	3
Jesse Gallup Clerk	3	Seth Williams	3
Ephraim Allyn Corp.	3	Simeon Brown	3
Wm Brown Corp.	3	Joseph Thomson	3
Isaac Morgan Corp	3	Elisha Brown	3
Daniel Nickerson	3	Silas Lamb Jr.	3
Wm Heath	3	Jacob Perkins	3
Abel Newton	3	Joshua Elderkin	3
Isaac Williams	3	Benjn Gray	3
Jedediah Morgan	3	Rufus Williams	3
Saml Williams 4	3	Benjn Stedman	2
Nathan^l Brown Jr.	3	John Dixson Jr	2
Stephen Park	3	Nehemiah Barnes	1
Joseph Williams	3	Ezekiel Brown	2
Wm Morgan	3	Robert Dixson	2
David Allyn	3	Elkanah Hewit	2
Henry Gallup Jr.	3		

[*State Library, Revolution 25.*]

MILITIA REGIMENTS, 1782.

CAPT. MARVIN'S COMPANY.

A Pay abstract of Cap[t] Ozias Marvins Company of Coast guard Ordered To Be Raised by the town of Norwalk for the Defence of S[d] Town in Feb[r] 18th 1782

Mens Names	Time when Entered service	Time when discharged
Ozias Marvin Cap.	Feb. 18	Aug. 1
John Byxbe Ens.	"	"
Thomas Hyatt Sarj.	19	"
Sam[l] Hyatt "	"	"
Nathan Fillow "	20	"
Daniel Eversley "	Mar. 3	"
Elijah Fitch Corp.	1	"
Nathaniel Benedict "	Apr. 1	"
Jacob Jinnings "	Mar. 8	June 20
Sam[l] Seymour "	1	Aug. 1
Will[m] Bouton Private	9	"
Daniel Seymour	19	"
Joseph Waring	Feb. 20	"
James Waring	"	"
Ozias Marvin Jr	19	"
Stephen Hyatt	20	"
Stephen Marvin	"	June 20
Mathew Hanford	"	"
Thomas Penneoyr	"	"
Azor Fillow	"	"
Peter Tuttle	"	Apr 21
John Rull	May 5	Aug. 1
James Jelleff	Feb. 20	May 15
Jesse Taylor	"	Apr. 25
Stephen Fillow	May 12	June 20
Will[m] Fitch	Feb. 21	"
Levi Taylor	"	Aug. 1
Noah Nash	"	"
Edmond Tuttle	"	June 20
Josiah Gregory	Apr. 3	"
Isaac Fillow	Mar. 4	Aug. 1
Huttun Smith	"	"
Will[m] Mott	"	"
David Comstock	"	"
Isaac Hyatt	"	"

Mens Names	Time when Entered service	Time when discharged
Enoch Benedict	Mar. 4	Aug. 1
James Fitch	"	"
Willm Smith	"	"
John Eversley	"	June 20
James Hoyt	12	"
John Betts Jr.	"	"
Levi Sherwood	18	"
Jesse Bennidict	"	"
Hopkins Byxbee	Feb. 20	Aug. 1
Elijah Jones	"	"
Saml Bowton	"	"
Enoch Wareing	"	"
John Byxbee	"	June 20
Daniel Hoyt	"	"
Saml Brown	"	"
Stephen Bowton	"	"
Jesse Waring	"	"
John Kellogg	Mar. 1	Aug. 1
Wolcut Downs	"	"
Isaac Raymond	"	"
Willm Salmas	5	"
Job Hoyt	1	"
John Raymond	"	"
Ira Bowton	6	"
Walter Hoyt	5	"
Peter Quinturd Jr	22	"
Jonathan Hoyt	21	"
Nathl Raymond Jr	9	June 20
Stephen Wood	"	"
Eleazor Bedient	1	"
Stephen Picket	10	"
Ezra Picket	"	"
David Seymour	1	Aug. 1
Calub Curtis	"	"
Ruben Olmsted	"	"
Mordica Bedient	3	"
David Bennet	1	June 20
Jiles Fitch	"	"
Saml Gregory	3	"
Jeremiah Will^{ms}	5	"
Abraham Hurlbat	"	"
John Seymour	Apr. 1	"
Uriah Raymond	"	"
Nathaniel Raymond	"	"
Nathan Benedict	"	Aug. 1
John Seymour Jr	"	"
James Seymour	"	"
Hezekiah Raymond	"	"
Hezekiha Sillik	Apr. 3	June 20
Charles Sillick	"	"
Evert Quintard	"	"
Mathew Betts	6	"
Lemuel Brooks	1	Aug. 1

[*State Library, Revolution 32.*]

MILITIA REGIMENTS.

FOURTH REGIMENT.

CAPT. BOOTH'S COMPANY.

A Ration Roll of Cap[t] Ja[s] Booths C[o] of guards which were detached from the 4th Reg[t] of Militia for that purpose pursuant to order from G. S. Silliman Brig[r] Gen[l].

Names	N[o] of Days in Service	Names	N[o] of Days in Service
Ja[s] Booth Cap[t]	15	John Sherman	18
Sam[l] Patterson Lieut	18	Lewis Curtiss	15
Judson Burton Ens[n]	15	Nath[n] Osborn	18
David Thompson Serg[t]	15	Ja[s] Coe	18
Elihew Curtiss "	15	Abner Beers	15
Stephen Beers "	15	Benj[n] Wells	15
John Peck "	18	Isaac Curtiss	18
Abijah Booth Corp[l]	18	Ja[s] Sherman	15
Josiah Pĕck "	15	Judson Peck	15
David Curtiss "	15	Ebenez[r] Curtis	18
Aaron Judson	18	Ja[s] Deforest	15
W[m] Tomlinson Fifer	8	John Beardslee	15
Joel Judson	15	Ja[s] Judson	18
Eph[m] Wilcockson	15	W[m] Hilliard	15
Tho[s] Stratton	18	George Lewis	15
W[m] Southworth	18	Benj[n] Gorham	15
Edmund Curtiss	10	John Wells	18
Sam[l] Burnet	18	Abner Elgur	15
Rob[t] Curtiss	15	Jerem[h] Curtiss	18
John Booth	15	Sam[l] Ward	18
Elihew Judson	15	Ebenez[r] Hubbil	18
Abner Curtiss	15	Josiah Walker	15
Elnath[n] Wheeler	15	David Barlow	18
John M[c]Graw	13	Eph[m] Burton	15
Nath[n] Beardslee	18	Josiah Beers	10
Sam[l] Osborn	18	John E. Olcott	10
Andrew Curtiss	15	John Wayland	10
Dan[l] Curtiss	18	Henry Beardslee	10
W[m] Judson	18	Henry Curtis	10
Jon[o] Tongue	15	John Whiting	13
Jabez Curtiss	18	Jo[s] Frost	15

[*Copy in Comptroller's Office.*]

VARIOUS REGIMENTS.

[The dates in the following lists are the dates when the bills were rendered, and do not necessarily show the time of service.]

HARTFORD GAOL GUARD.

The United States D^r To the State of Connecticut, for services &c of Militia, guarding Prisoners in Hartford Goal &c & Continental Stores in sundry Places &c. Viz —

Date			Bills & Accounts	Remarks
1778	Aug^t	14	Ens^n B. Hudson	Guard^g Hartford Goal
	Dec	5	"	"
1779	Feb^ry	12	"	"
	Aug^t	11	"	"
	"		Ens^n Wm Barnard	"
	Dec^r	14	"	"
1780	April	3	"	"
	June	12	Ens^n Wm Barnard	"
	Aug^t	30	"	"
1781	Feb^ry	5	"	"
	Nov^r	17	Ens^n Wm Barnard	"
1782	May	3	"	"
1784	July	26	"	"
1779	July	9	Serg^t E. Denslow	Guard^g Hospital Stores
	Aug^t	16	Ens^n Danl Haydon	"
	Sep^t	24	Capt John Lewis	Guard^g Stores in Waterbury
1780	April	5	Serg^t E. Stoughton	Guard^g Hospital Stores
	Sep^t	15	William Emmons	Guard^g Military Stores
1781	Jan^ry	1	Serg^t Levi Clark	"
		31	Lt H. Dwight	Guard^g Prisoners
	March	10	Ens^n Saml Hugins	"
	April	17	Serg^t E. Stoughton	Guard^g Hospital Stores
	May	19	Serg^t Josiah Smith	Guard^g Prisoners
1782	March	14	Lt Saml Lattimer	"
1781	Nov^r	16	Moses Willson	Guard^g Hospital Stores
	Dec^r	1	John Johnson	Guard^g Prisoners
		29	Serg^t Job Cooke	" Powder
1783	Feb^ry	11	Moses Willson	" Hospital Stores
	May	19	Capt Hamlin Dwight	" Prisoners
		30	Simeon Huntington	" Naval Prisoners

[*Comptroller's Office, Haskell's Receipts.*]

SERVICE AT THE NORTHWARD.

The United States D^r To the State of Connecticut for sundry Expenditures for Bounties, extra Allowances, Wages &c of Troops from said State who served at the Northward. Viz: —

Date			Bills & Acct^s	Remarks
1777	Dec^r	24	Capt Jona. Calkins	Col. J Lattimers Reg^t
		"	Capt Amos Jones &c	"

Date			Bills & Acct[s]	Remarks
1778	Jan[ry]	24	Cap[t] Tarbal Whitney	Col. T Cooks
		30	Cap[t] Elip[t] Curtis	Bennington Alarm
	Feb[ry]	5	Cap[t] Ichab[d] Norton	Gen[l] Wolcotts Brigade
		17	Cap[t] John Allen	Col. N. Hookers
		"	Cap[t] James Stoddard	"
		18	Col. Seth Smith	
		27	Cap[t] Edw[d] Shipman	Col. T. Cooks Reg[t]
		28	"	"
	March	5	Samuel Hays	Bennington Alarm
		12	Joel Hays	"
		19	Cap[t] Benj. Hutchins	"
		23	Col. N. Hooker	"
	April	7	Cap[t] Asahel Holcomb	"
		11	Cap[t] Giddings	"
		16	Cap[t] Adon[h] Burr	"
		28	Cap[t] Asa Bray	"
		30	L[t] Elijah Case	"
		"	Ens[n] Sam[l] Benning	"
	May	16	Col. Epa[s] Sheldon	Under Gen[l] Gates
		29	Cap[t] Joseph Forward	Bennington Alarm
		30	Cap[t] Tho[s] Bidwell	"
	June	9	Cap[t] Moses Seymour	Gen[l] Wolcotts Brigade
		25	Cap[t] Ich[d] Norton	"
	July	9	Maj[r] Thomas Bull	Sundry Acct[s]
	Aug[t]	12	Cap[t] Nathan Smith	Col. T. Cooks Reg[t]
	Sep[t]	7	Charles Kellogg P. M.	Col. J. Lattimers
	Oct[r]	15	L[t] Samuel Hart	Col. T. Cooks
1779	Jan[ry]	12	Jonah Scofield	Col. J. Lattimers
		22	Stephen Scott	Woosters '75
		29	Col. Joshua Porter	Gen[l] Wolcotts Brigade
	May	20	Derias Spalding	Col. J. Lattimers '77
1778	Mar.	23	Cap[t] Asa Bray	Gen[l] O. Wolcotts Brigade
1781	June	20	Col[o] Samuel Mott	"
1783	Mar	25	David Trumbull	"
1785	Dec	17	Noah Phelps	"
1787	Nov.	5	Lieut. Stephen Goodrich	Col[o] T Cooks Reg[t]
"	Sep[t]	24	Edward Mott	"

[*Comptroller's Office, Haskell's Receipts.*]

SERVICE IN RHODE ISLAND.

The United States D[r] to the State of Connecticut for sundry Expenditures for Bounties, Extra Allowances, Wages &c of Militia from said State, who served in the State of Rhode Island. Viz:—

Date			Bills & Acct[s]	Remarks
1789	Jan[y]	21	Col. Sam[l] M[c]Clellan	his Reg[t] in 1777
	Feb[y]	25	Col John Ely	"
	Ap[l]	6	L[t] Daniel Dee	
	Dec[r]	17	Cap[t] Moses Stevens	Col. Oliver Smiths Reg[t]
		"	Cap[t] Timo[y] Percival	"
		"	Cap[t] Richard Pitkin	"
		31	Cap[t] David Miller	"
1779	Jan[y]	7	Cap[t] Joseph Cutler	"
		"	Cap[t] John Arnold	"
		26	Col. W[m] Worthington	his Reg[t]
	April	9	Col. Oba[h] Johnson	"

Date			Bills & Acct[s]	Remarks
1779	June	5	Cap[t] J. Chamberlain	his C[o] Drogoons
	Aug[t]	24	Cap[t] J. Churchill	Worthingtons Reg[t]
	Sept[r]	29	Col. Sam[l] Chapman	his Reg[t]
1780	Jan[ry]	25	Cap[t] Elias Graves	Col. Tylers
1781	Jan[y]	4	Cap[t] Dan[l] Tyler	Matross C[o]
	March	16	Cap[t] W[m] Whitney	Col. Smiths Reg[t]
	May	22	"	"
		31	Cap[t] Caleb Hendee	Col. E. Storrs
	June	26	Col. James Gordon	
		27	L[t] Elias Palmer	Col. O. Smith
		4	Cap[t] Sam[l] Thomson	Col. E. Storrs
	Aug[t]	29	Cap[t] Peter Keith	Col. J. Gordons
	Sept[r]	20	Cap[t] Timo[y] Backus	Volunteers
		24	Cap[t] Amos Woodward	Col. J. Gordons
	Oct[r]	14	Cap[t] Abner Adams	Col. S. M[c]Clellans
	Nov[r]	8	Cap[t] Titus Bailey	Col J. Gordons

[*Comptroller's Office, Haskell's Receipts.*]

SERVICE AT PEEKSKILL.

The United States D[r] To the State of Connecticut for sundry Expenditures for Bounties, extra Allowances, Wages &c of Militia from said State who served with the Main Army at and near Peekskill in the State of New York — Viz :

Dates			Bills & Accounts	Remarks
1777	Sep[t]	10	John Robbins	
		17	David Little	
		29	Cap[t] Miles Johnson	Col. Noadiah Hookers Reg[t]
	Oct	24	Cap[t] Amasa Loomis	Col. Nath[l] Terrys Regt
	Nov[r]	1	Col. John Chester	
		5	Wethersfield S. Men	
		"	Cap[t] Oliver Stanley	
		12	S[t] John Cook	
		18	Glassenbury S. Men	
		25	Maj[r] Gad Stanly	Field & Staff, Cap[t] Nortons & Slopers C[o]
		26	Cap[t] Peter Vial	
	Dec[r]	3	Cap[t] John Allen	
		"	James Stoddard	
		5	Cap[t] Josiah Converse	Col. Hez[h] Wyllys Reg[t]
		8	John Hurlbutt Q. M.	"
		9	Col. Hez[h] Wyllys	"
		10	Cap[t] Benj. Allyn	
1778	Jan[ry]	8	Hanley Bushnel	
		9	Cap[t] Giles Pettibone	
		20	Cap[t] Eliz. Hubbard	Col. Thomas Beldings Reg[t]
		22	Col. Joseph Thomson	2[d] Regiment
		29	Cap[t] Oliver Stanley	Sundry Acc[t]
		30	Cap[t] Ab[m] Fuller	Col. Increase Moselys Reg[t]
		"	Col. Samuel Whiting	
		"	Cap[t] Elisha Hall	
	Feb[ry]	3[d]	Col. Hez[h] Wyllys	1st Reg[t]
		4	Col. Tho[s] Belding	
		26	Cap[t] Dan Collins	
		"	L[t] Jabez Hamlin	Col. Increase Moselys Reg[t]
		27	Col. Hez[h] Wyllys	1st Reg[t]

Dates		Bills & Accounts	Remarks
1778 Feb^{ry}	28	Col. Noadiah Hooker	
March	4	Capt Noah Webster	Col. Nathl Terrys Reg^{t}
		Lt John Hough	Col. Jona. Baldwins
	5	Col. Baz^{a} Ives	"
	6	Col. Nathl Terry	
	19	Capt Judah Woodruff	15th Reg^{t}
April	3	Maj^{r} Ab^{m} Tyler	
	6	Col. Wm Worthington	7th Reg^{t}
	9	Capt Thom^{s} Fenn	16th "
		Lt Thomas Dutton	"
	10	Capt Jonathan Bull	Governors guard
	17	Capt Timo^{y} Gaylor	
	24	Ens^{n} Lucius Tuttle	Col. Jona. Baldwins Reg^{t}
	"	Capt Nathl Bunnel	"
	"	Capt Eph^{m} Cook	"
	"	Capt Jesse Moss	"
	"	Capt Ambrose Hine	"
	"	Maj^{r} Wm Hart	His Lt Dragoons
	28	Col. Sylvanus Graves	
May	19	Capt Jared Shepard	Col. Beldens Reg^{t}
	21	Lt James Arnold	7th Reg^{t}
	22	Col. J. P. Cook	his Reg^{t} Oct. 1777
	"	"	" Aug^{t}
	"	"	" "
	27	Col. Charles Burrell	"
	29	Lt Thomas Dutton	Col. J. Baldwins Reg^{t}
June	1	Lt Hanford	Col. J. Meads
	2	Col. Increase Moseley	his Reg^{t} Oct. 1777
	"	"	" Danbury Al^{m} '77
	5	Maj^{r} Judah Woodruff	his Reg^{t}
	"	Ens^{n} Lem^{l} Hotchkiss	"
	"	Capt Nathl Wales	Wards
	10	Capt Paul Yates	Col. Increase Moseleys Reg^{t}
	20	Lt Woodruff & Cornet Griswold	Maj^{r} Harts Reg^{t} Lt Dragoons
July	6	Charles Kellogg P. M.	10th Reg^{t}
	22	Capt Saml Camp	"
Aug^{t}	10	Col. Roger Newberry	his Reg^{t}
	26	Capt Charles Norton	Col. Jona. Baldwins
	"	Capt James Robinson	"
	27	Charles Kellogg P. M.	18th Reg^{t}
	28	"	Col. J. Cooks Reg^{t}
Sept^{r}	3	Maj^{r} Thos Bull	his Reg^{t} Lt Dragoons
	"	"	"
	5	Charles Kellogg P. M.	Col. Comfort Sages Reg^{t}
	7	"	Col. Roger Newburys
	9	"	Capt Strongs C^{o}
	"	"	Col. John Humphrys Reg^{t}
	"	"	Maj^{r} Jabez Hills
	11	Serj^{t} Joseph Brace	
	17	Capt Josiah King	Col. Roger Newburys Reg^{t}
	19	Capt Nathan Chapman	Col. Increase Moseleys Reg^{t}
	23	Capt Dav^{d} Leavensworth	
Nov^{r}	4	Genl James Wadsworth	Sundry Bills
	"	Capt Phin^{s} Castle	
	5	Lt Elijah Cook	Col. Roger Newburys Reg^{t}
	6	Nathan Sloson	
	12	Capt Adon^{h} Burr	Col. Increase Moseleys Reg^{t}

Dates		Bills & Accounts	Remarks
1778 Nov^r	24	Col. Comfort Sage	his Reg^t Supernum^y
	"	"	"
Dec^r	22	Capt Jesse Curtis	Col. Jona. Baldwins Reg^t
		"	"
		Capt Jotham Curtis	"
		Capt Stephen Seymour	"
1779 Jan^{ry}	9	Charles Kellogg P. M.	"
		"	Col. Increase Moseleys
	21	Capt Zach. Case	Col. Thos Beldens Reg^t
		Col. Comfort Sage	his Reg^t
		Capt Josiah Converse	Col. N. Terrys
	22	Amos Ives	Col. Baldwins
	29	Col. Increase Moseley	13th Reg^t
		"	"
Feb^{ry}	2	Samuel Bishop	
		Capt Aaron Foot	Col. N. Hookers Reg^t
	4	Capt Miles Johnson	Col. J. Baldwins
	23	Capt Oliver Stanley	
	26	Lt Eaton Jones	17th Reg^t
March	10	Capt Elijah Hinman	13th Reg^t
		Capt Eben^r Smith	"
		Lt Asa Hinman	"
		Capt David Hinman	"
		Ens^n Joseph Sanford	"
		Capt Caleb Mix	"
April	3	Capt Asa Bray	Col. Hookers Reg^t
		Capt J. Norton	
	13	Capt Joseph Viall	17th Reg^t
		Capt John Osborn	"
		Capt Amos Barns	"
	14	Capt James Stoddard	Col. Increase Moseleys
May	18	Capt Wm Cogswell	"
		Col. Comfort Sage	his Reg^t
	21	Capt Eben^r Couch	Col. Increase Moseleys
	22	Capt Wm G. Hubbel	16th Reg^t
June	3	Capt Job Case	Guarding Cannon
April	9	"	"
June	3	"	"
	4	Capt Isaac Bronson	Col. J. Baldwins Reg^t
	10	Capt Judah Woodruff	15th Reg^t
	30th	Capt Nathan Hine	13th "
		Capt D. Leavensworth	Col. S. Whitings
		Capt Nathan Hine	13th Reg^t
July	31	Capt John Strong	17th "
Aug^t	11	Capt Nathan Chapman	13th "
	24	Capt Nathan Hine	Col. S. Whitings Reg^t
		Capt Abner Mallery	13th
	27	Capt Enos Hawley	"
		"	"
		Col. Comfort Sage	his Reg^t
	31	Capt Peter Penfield	Col. J. F. Cooks Reg
	"	"	16th
	"	Capt David Olmstead	"
	"	Capt James Clark	"
	"	Capt Danl Hickocks	"
	"	Capt Richd Shutes	"
	"	Capt Richd Smith	"
	"	Capt Elijah Botsford	"
	"	Capt A. Botsford	"

Dates		Bills & Accounts	Remarks
1779 Aug^t	31	Capt Wm G. Hubbel	16th
	"	Ens^n Henry Whitney	"
	"	Col. N. Beardsley	"
		"	"
Sept^r	1	Capt Jona. Farrand	13th
	"	Capt Elijah Hazen	"
	10	Capt Benj. Stones	"
	"	Capt Joseph Carter	"
	"	Capt Eben^r Couch	"
	"	Capt Noble Hine	"
	"	Lt Morgan Noble	"
	"	Capt Ab^m Fuller	"
	17	Capt Miles Beach	17th
	"	Capt Reuben Stone	"
	"	Capt Jabez Wright	"
	"	Col. Medad Hills	"
	21	Col. Jona. Dimon	4th
	22	Capt David Hinman	13th
	23	Maj^r Elijah Abel	4th
	24	Capt Abel Brace	18th
Oct^r	1	Capt Jacob Hinsdale	17th
	14	Capt Elijah Hinman	13th
	15	Capt Timothy Stanley	Col. Hills Reg^t
	16	Capt Adam Hurlbut	Col. Increase Moseleys Reg^t
	20	Ens^n Saml Carter	"
	"	Capt Peter Mills	"
	22	Genl O. Wolcott	
	"	Col. Benj Richards	
	27	Capt John Strong	17th Reg^t
	"	Corp^l John Whiting	Guard^s Military Stores
	29	Capt Abel Botsford	Col. P. Beardsleys Reg^t
	"	Genl James Wadsworth	
Nov^r	5	Capt Bethuel Treat	Col. Saml Whiting
	9	Capt Eben^r Smith	Col. Increase Moseleys Reg^t
	"	Capt Jos. Sanford	"
	10	Maj^r Thos Bull	
	"	Capt Augur Curtis	Maj^r T. Bulls Reg^t
Dec^r	7	Col. Jona. Dimon	
	20	Capt Benj. Nichols	Co Jona. Dimon's Reg^t
1780 Jan^{ry}	14	Capt Isaac Howe	Col. John Mead
Feb^{ry}	3	Col. Increase Moseley	his Reg^t
March	1	Capt Danl Holbrook	Col. Tylers Reg^t
	16	Capt Danl Godfrey	Col. Saml Whitings Reg^t
	30	Col. Thad^s Cooke	his Reg^t
May	25	Col. Saml Whiting	
June	6	Capt Noble Hine	Col. J. Moseleys Reg^t
1779 Jan^{ry}	23	Capt John Tomlinson	2^d Reg^t
	"	Jona. Bartholemew	
1781 March	7	Capt Benj. Hutchins	18th
May	9	Capt Abner Malley	Col. J. Moseleys
June	4	Capt Paul Yates	"
1783 Aug^t	12	Lt Benj. Seeley	
Oct	16	Col. Benj. Richards	
1784 May	7	Clark Roys	
1785 Jan^y	11	Capt A. Barns	
1782 June	15	Capt E. Sumner	
1787 June	29	Capt J. Stoddard	Col. N. Hookers '77
Aug^t	28	Suntry Acct^s	" '77

[*Comptroller's Office, Haskell's Receipts.*]

SERVICE IN WEST CHESTER.

The United States D^r To the State of Connecticut, for sundry Expenditures for Bounties, extra Allowances, Wages &c of Troops from said State who served with the Army in West Chester County in the State of New York. Viz:

Dates			Bills & Acc^t	Remarks
1778	May	21	Ens^n Nathl Weed	Col. Roots Reg^t
		29	Capt U. Raymond	Col. John Meads
	July	1	Capt Silv. Knapp	"
	Nov^r	4	Capt Mills Hull	Col. S Graves
1779	Jana^y	16	Capt C. Churchill	2^d Reg^t
		19	Capt Isaac Howe	Col. John Meads Reg^t
		26	Bouton J. Scofield	Maj^r John Davenport
		28	Capt Uriah Raymond	Col. John Meads
		"	Col. Stephen St John	
	Feb^ry	18	Capt John Smith	Col. Increase Moseleys
	March	10	Capt Robert Martin	"
	April	2	Capt Adam Hurlbut	Col. John Meads Reg^t
		3	Capt Asa Bray	Col. Roger Enos's
		8	Capt Joseph Smith	Col John Meads
		14	Capt Ozias Marvin	"
	May	22	Capt Adonijah Burr	Col. Increase Moseleys
		26	Capt Silvanus Knapp	Col. John Meads
		27	Capt John Ensign	Col. J. Moseleys
		28	Capt Caleb St John	Maj^r J. Hills Dragoons
	June	3	Capt Nathan Gilbert	Col. John Meads
		7	Capt Knowles Sears	"
	Sep^t	1	Capt Clap Raymond	"
		"	Capt Ozias Marvin	"
		21	Capt John Gray	Col. Samuel Whitings
		"	Capt David Olmstead	Col. Jona. Dimon
		"	Capt Joseph Birdsey	"
		"	Capt David Wood	"
		"	Capt Comfort Hoyt	"
	Oct	1	Lt N. Mead	Col. John Meads
		20	Capt Peter Mills	"
	Nov^r	3	Capt Silv^s Marshall	Rangers
		13	Capt El^m Smith	Col. John Meads
		16	Capt David Hitchcock	10th Reg^t
1780	May	8	Capt Stiles Judson	Col John Meads
		22	Capt George Peck	"
1778	Jan^y	28	Silvanus Mead	Rangers
1779	Ap^l	13	Capt Jona. Waring	Maj^r J. Davenports
1787	Sep^t	13	Capt John Skinner	his Command

[*Comptroller's Office, Haskell's Receipts.*]

SERVICE IN NEW YORK.

The United States D^r to the State of Connecticut for sundry expenditures for Bounties, extra Allowances, Wages &c of Troops from said State who served with the Main Army in New York and places Adjacent: Viz:

Dates			Bills & Acct^s	Remarks
1777	Sep^t	26	Col. Jona. Fitch	his Reg^t
	Oct	24	Capt Isaac Hall	

Dates		Bills & Acct^{s}	Remarks
1778	Jan^{ry} 10	Col. Nehe^{h} Beardsley	
	Mar. 19	Col. Roger Newbury	his Reg^{t}
	April 28	Capt Saml Thomson	Col. E. Storrs
	May 22	John Kellogg	Capt Tarboxs C^{o}
	25	Lt Jona. Whiting	
	29	Lt Saml Abbott	
	June 4	Capt Jona. Calkins	3^{d} Reg^{t}
	"	Capt John Morse	10th
	5	Col. Jona. Pettibone	his Reg^{t}
	6	Col. Hoel Woodbridge	Lexington Alarm
	24	Col. Saml Whiting	Militia to Maroneck
	"	"	Enos Battalion
	"	Col. Increase Moseley	Bradleys & Webbs Battalions 1776
	Augt 22	Col. Matthew Talcot	23^{d}
	27	Maj^{r} Simeon Strong	15th
	Oct 23	Eleazer Scripture	22^{d}
	Novr 6	Col. Eben^{r} Gay	his Reg^{t}
1779	Ap^{l} 3	Capt Asa Bray	Col. Thadd^{s} Cooks Reg^{t}
	12	Capt Seth Seymour	Col. John Meads
	13	Genl John Douglass	
1777	Novr 17	Capt John Watson	Col. Thadd^{s} Cooks Reg^{t}
1779	May 4	Capt Ama^{h} Wright	Col. Enos's
1783	Feby 7	Capt J. Chamberlain	Volunteers
	8	Genl John Mead	his Reg^{t}
	13	Col. Saml Chapman	"
	May 20	Col. Eben^{r} Williams	"
	30	Baz^{a} Beebe	
	"	Nehe. Lewis	
1784	June 2	Lt Col. Dyer Throop	his Reg^{t}
	"	Col. O. Hosford	"
	"	Maj^{r} John Ely	3^{d} Reg^{t}
1785	Jan^{ry} 19	Elijah Hide	his Dragoons
	Feb^{ry} 25	Jesse Root Esqr	Volunteers
	Decr 29	Col. Benj. Hinman	his Reg^{t}
1786	Jany 24	Col. Elizur Talcott	his Reg^{t}
1787	July 16	Col. George Pitkin	"
	30	Capt James Robinson	Baldwins
	"	Capt J. Hickoxs	"
	Augt 24	Col. Saml Coit	his Reg^{t}
	Sep^{t} 13	Capt M. Kirtland	

[*Comptroller's Office, Haskell's Receipts.*]

SERVICE AT WESTMORELAND.

The United States, To the State of Connecticut D^{r} for sundry Expenditures for extra Allowances, Wages &c. of Militia who served at Westmoreland. Viz.—

Date		Bills & Accounts	Remarks
1778	Octr 21	Capt Daniel Gore	Mil^{a} Westmoreland
	31	Col. Nathan Dennison	"
1779	May 22	Capt Wm H. Smith	"
	"	Lt Daniel Gore	"

[*Comptroller's Office, Haskell's Receipts.*]

SUNDRY SOLDIERS.

Names of Sundry Soldiers whose Rect[s] are on File 1778

Josiah Brinsmade	date unknown	Selah Griswold	1778
L[t] Phineas Grover . .	1778	A Taylor	1778
Luther Jones . . .	1778	Aaron D Wolf . . .	1778
Co[l] Roger Enos at Horseneck in	1778	Seth Eddy	1778
Ezekiel Rood . . .	1778	Reuben Taylor . . .	1778
Jacob Meach . . .	1778	Gershom Treat . . .	1778
Salmon Treat . . .	1778	George Trumbull . .	1778
Jo[s] Gladding . . .	1778		

[*Copy in Comptroller's Office.*]

NAVAL RECORD.

[*See Record of Connecticut Men in the Revolution, page 605.*]

BRIG "MINERVA".

CAPT. HALL'S MEN.

1775 A Muster Roll and Pay Roll for the Brigantine Minerva Fitted out on the Acc[t] of the Colony of Connecticut By Order of his Hon[r] the Gov[r] and Com[tee] of Safety for the Defence of said Colony Viz[t]

Names of Officers and Men	Quality	When Inlisted	When Discharged or Deserted
Giles Hall	Captain	Aug. 2	1776 Jan. 26
James Hopkins	1st Lt.	Aug. 14	Dec. 19
Thompson Phillips	2[d] Lt.	Sep. 14	Dec. 19
William Pluymert	Master	Aug. 22	Dec. 17
William Warner	1st Mate	Aug. 24	Dec. 26
John Cotton	2[d] Mate	Aug. 12	Dec. 26
Tho[s] Lamb	Clark	Sep. 4	1776 Jan. 26
Andrew Johonnot	Stewart	Sep. 11	1776 Jan. 20
Gregory Powers	Boaswain	Aug. 14	Dec. 26
Benj[n] Cranston	Gunner	Aug. 31	Dec. 19
William Miles	Gunners Mate	Aug. 15	Dec. 19
George Lewis	Carpenter	Sep. 10	Nov. 5
Richard Dickerson	Pilote	Sep. 16	Dec. 25
John Harris	Carpenters Mate	Aug. 15	Dec. 26
Jacob Gibson	Mariner	Aug. 14	Nov. 25
Will[m] Thomas	Marine	Aug. 15	Nov. 9
Tho[s] Dande	Mariner	Aug. 15	Nov. 20
William Warner	Cook	Aug. 16	Dec. 16
Jesse Higgins	Mariner	Aug. 17	Oct. 17
Jonathan Tinker	"	Aug. 17	Nov. 10
Jeremiah Branard	"	Aug. 22	Dec. 25
Giles Cone	"	Aug. 22	Dec. 16
John Russell	"	Aug. 24	Dec. 16
John Chipman	"	Aug. 22	Dec. 23
Aaron White	"	Aug. 27	Dec. 19
Jerediah Norton	"	Aug. 28	Dec. 25

Names of Officers and Men	Quality	When Inlisted	When Discharged or Deserted
George Pelton	Mariner	Sep. 4	Oct. 24
Joseph Burn	"	Sep. 12	Dec. 19
George Lucas	"	Sep. 15	Dec. 19
Sam[l] Johnson	"	Sep. 21	Dec. 18
Stephen Lee	"	Sep. 21	Dec. 23
James Griffin	"	Sep. 22	Nov. 17
Edward Tryon	"	Oct. 3	Dec. 19
Peter Granger	"	Oct. 3	Dec. 19
Dave Whittlecey	"	Oct. 7	Dec. 19
Giles Gill	"	Oct. 9	Dec. 26
Walter Spooner	"	Oct. 12	Dec. 19
Derny Butler	"	Aug. 26	Sep. 26
Zebediah Mix	Marine	Aug. 22	Dec. 25
Elisha Ward	"	Aug. 24	Dec. 19
Peter a Negro Man	"	Aug. 25	Dec. 23
Gift a Negro Man	"	Aug. 25	Dec. 19
John Theaf	"	Aug. 25	Oct. 17
William Casheen	"	Aug. 25	Nov. 18
Richard Hunt	"	Aug. 25	Nov. 10
Phillip Mahan	"	Aug. 26	Oct. 15
Ebenz[r] Savage	"	Aug. 27	Dec. 19
Philip Aspell	"	Aug. 27	Dec. 16
James McDavid	"	Aug. 30	Dec. 18
Edward Griswold	"	Aug. 31	Nov. 19
James Johnson	"	Aug. 31	Oct. 25
George Stow	"	Sep. 5	Dec. 19
Stephen Jordan	"	Sep. 5	Dec. 23
Joseph Graum	"	Sep. 5	Dec. 23
Sam[l] Torry	"	Sep. 6	Dec. 19
John Wright	"	Sep. 11	Nov. 18
John Coult	"	Sep. 18	Dec. 23
Jacob Hail	"	Sep. 12	Nov. 5
John Elderkin	"	Oct. 3	Dec. 19
John Allen	"	Oct. 3	Dec. 19
James Fisher	"	Oct. 11	Nov. 11
John Lucas	Boaswains Mate	Aug. 24	Suspended Nov. 8
David Hall	Mariner	Sep. 12	Suspended Nov. 8
James Johnson	"	Aug. 21	Ran away Oct. 14
Rouben Bailey	"	Aug. 26	Ran away Dec. 5
Timothy Bailey	"	Aug. 26	Ran away Dec. 5
Peter Gantly	Marine	Aug. 26	Ran away Sep. 10
George Spencer	"	Aug. 29	Ran away Dec. 5
Nath[l] Witmore	"	Aug. 30	Ran away Oct. 15
Philemon Roberts	"	Aug. 30	Ran away Oct. 15
John Nickolas	"	Sep. 5	Ran away Dec. 6
Moses Pelton	"	Sep. 12	Ran away Dec. 6

Capt Gills Halls Pay Roll of the Brig Minerva January 25th 1776.

[*State Library, Revolution 9.*]

BRIG "DEFENCE".

[*See Record of Connecticut Men in the Revolution, page 593.*]

CAPT. HARDING'S MEN.

A Pay List of Cap Harding^s men belonging to the Brigg Defence Colony Service

Time of Entry		Mens Names	Rank	Time of payment
1776				
May	24	Nathan Tupper	Marene	July 24
June	15	James Young	Seam	Nov. 15
Mar.	13	Benjn Gold	Boy	"
	"	Wm Burnett	"	"
	"	Eleazer Buckly	"	"
	"	Francis Swords	"	"
	"	Seth Bur	"	"
July	1	Anthony Manuel	Seam	"
May	29	Wm Hooks	"	"
	"	Jno Mitts	"	"
	"	Jon^a Alden	Sailm	"
	"	Vallintine Skiff	Seam	"
Aug.	9	Thos Menter	"	"
	18	Wm Murry	"	"
Nov.	8	Josiah Willey	"	"
	"	Jno Holms	"	"
	10	James Alden	"	"
Aug.	20	Prosper Brown	Q^r mas^tr	"
	"	Sam^ll Balden	Seam	"
	"	Robert Fowler	"	"
	"	Christopher Lewis	"	"
	"	Jno Davis	"	"
	"	Wm Shelden	"	"
	"	Abbe Spicer	"	"
	28	Pelatiah Peas	"	"
	"	Stephen Peas	"	"
July	1	Thos Morris	"	"
Aug.	20	John Bond	"	"
	"	Lebbeus Quy	"	"
May	29	Moses Cam	"	"
Aug.	20	James Davis	"	"
	"	Turner Harding		"
	28	West Daggett	Boy	"
	20	Jno Kazer	Seam	"
	"	Benj^a Rockwell	"	"
May	18	Thos Crandal	"	Aug. 15

[*State Library, Revolution 9.*]

A Pay List of Capt Harding^{s}. Men Belonging to the Brig Defence Colony Service

When Entered into the Service	Mens Names	Rank	Time of Payment	Time of Discharge
1776				
Mar. 6	Joseph Whitemore	Seaman	Nov. 15	
"	Jno May	"	"	
"	Guillam Veale	Cockswain	"	
"	Thomas Graystock	Seaman	"	
21	Martin Patchin	"	"	
17	Edward Brown	"	"	
May 7	George Moyer	"	"	
Apr. 10	George Negro	"	"	
Mar. 12	Gabril Allin	"	"	
"	Russil Disbrow	"	"	
May 1	Jon^{a} Poor	"	"	
21	Jon^{a} Colkins	"	"	
"	Jon^{a} Jervis	Qt^{r} Gun^{r}	"	
"	Nathaniel Jervis	Seaman	"	
June 25	Wm Bolton	"	"	
Mar. 6	Joseph Bartran	"	"	
June 7	David Norton	"		Nov. 8
Mar. 25	Henery Disbrow	Mareen		Oct. 18
"	James Judson	"		Aug. 29
6	Oliver Midelbrooks	Seaman		Nov. 8
21	Ezekiel Canfield	"		"
April 10	James Barton	"		July 22
May 26	Jno Connor	"		"
21	Ebinezar May	Qt^{r} Gun^{r}		Oct. 2
18	Zephaniah Hatch	Seaman		July 23
Mar. 21	Morris Griffin	"		June 22
"	Thomas Reed	"		27
Apr. 10	Richard Hunt	Mareen		July 29
Mar. 18	Josiah Walker	"		Oct. 15
May 24	Abraham Sturgis	Boy		Nov. 9
"	Abraham Cable	Mareen		8
29	Robert Crage	Gun^{r} M^{t}		Aug. 23
"	Isaac Cottle	Seaman		Nov. 8
Mar. 10	Israel Clefford	Mareen		Oct. 12
Aug. 21	James Greer	Seaman		Nov. 10
Mar. 10	Gideon Wells	Surgeon		Aug. 20
18	Richardson Minor	Arm^{r}		July 28

[*State Library, Revolution 9.*]

A Pay List of Capt Hardings Men Belong^{g} to the Brig Defence Colony Service

Time of Entry in the Service	Mens Names	Rank	Time of Payment
1776			
Mar. 6	Joseph Squire	Lieut Marmes	Nov. 15
10	Thomas Elwood	1st Serj^{t}	"
"	Nehemiah Whiting	2^{d} "	"
"	Joseph Minor	3^{d} "	"
"	James Jennings	4th "	"
"	Charles Mans	5th "	"

Time of Entry in the Service		Mens Names	Rank	Time of Payment	
1776					
Mar.	15	David Parret	Mareen	Nov. 15	
	21	Isaac Elwood	"	"	
	"	John Still	"	"	
April	11	Francoes Woodburn	"	"	
Mar.	16	Benjamin Darrow	Boy	"	
	"	George Battison	Mareen	"	
	"	Abraham Buckley	Seaman	"	
	13	Gideon Allin	Mareen	"	
	6	Nathan Squire	"	"	
	24	Samuel Taylor	"	"	
	"	Samuel Raymong	"	"	
	"	Stephen Hays	"	"	
	"	David Meaker	"	"	
	"	Giulbard Dudley	"	"	
	"	David Patchin	"	"	
	10	Joseph Battison	"	"	
Nov.	8	Francoes Butler	Seaman	"	
	9	Joseph L. Rowley	"	"	
	"	Peter Curtis	"	"	
	"	Wm Williams	"	"	
June	7	Silas Dagget	"		Discharged July 24
	"	Jno Hazelton	Q^{r} Gun^{r}		" "
	"	Cornelius Dunham	Seaman	"	
	"	Barzilla Luce	"	"	
	"	Samuel Norris	"	"	
June	15	Simeon Spencer	Arm^{r} M^{t}	"	
	5	Calob Dyar	Qt^{r} Gun^{r}	"	

[*State Library, Revolution 9.*]

A Pay List of Captn Hardings Officers & men belong^{g} to the Brigg Defence Collony Service

1776		Mens Names	Rank	Time of Payment	
Feb.	24	Seth Harding	Capt	Nov 15	
Mar	3	Eben^{r} Bartram	1st Lieut	"	
	10	Sam^{ll} Smedly	2^{d} Lieut	"	
Apr.	1	Josiah Burnham	Master	"	
Aug.	20	Henry Billings	3^{d} Lieut	"	
Mar.	4	Edward Bebe	1st Mate	"	
Apr.	12	Jesse Geacoks	2^{d} Mate	"	
Mar.	13	David Lewis	Boat^{sn}	"	
May	18	Thos Hutchenson	Gun^{r}	"	
Mar.	13	Justis Plum	Mate		Discharged Oct 15
"		Jon^{a} Darrow	Carpen^{tr}	"	
	6	Curtis Reed	Steward	"	
Aug.	20	Simon Calkins	Copper	"	
May	29	James Moor	Cook	"	
Mar.	13	John Warsan	Carp^{tm}	"	
"		Isaac Squires	Yeoman	"	
May	28	Laurance Martin	" B^{s}	"	
	3	Sam Asband	G^{r} "	"	
Mar.	10	John Chatfield	Pilote	"	
June	7	Nathan Daggett	"	"	

1776		Mens Names	Rank	Time of Payment
June	25	Eben[r] Nicholson	Capt Clark	Nov. 15
Mar.	13	Shearman Lewis	1st Q[r] M[t]	"
"		Jon[a] Silsby	2[d] Q[r] M	"
"		Andrew Thorp	3[d] "	"
"		David Jinings	4th "	"
June	8	George Newcomb	5th "	"
July	1	John Lewis	6th "	"
Mar.	10	Ezra Bushnal	Surg[n] Mate	"
	25	Henry Taylor	B Mate	"
	6	W[m] Higgins	1st Mate	"
Apr.	15	Asail Smith	1st p. Mast.	"
Mar.	10	Rial M House	Phifer	"
	12	Simon Desbrow	Sea m	"

[*State Library, Revolution 9.*]

1776 A List of the Dead & Desert[d] from Capt Harding in brigg Defence Collony Service

Time of Entry		Mens Names	R or Desert[d]		In Service Months	Days
March	6	James Young Copper	July	22	4	16
		George Gee	Aug	5	4	29
	17	John Steward		23	5	6
April	11	Richard Fry	July	14	3	3
May	8	Jared Ervin	Aug.	23	3	15
	24	Peter Thorp	"		2	29
	30	Edward Ingraham	"		2	23
	1	John Brown	"		3	22
		Solomon Brown	"		3	22
	12	Joseph Thomas	June	21	1	9
July	1	John Basson	Aug	1	1	0
		James Maden	"		1	0
March	6	W[m] Harrison	Died		3	17

[*State Library, Revolution 9.*]

NORTHERN DEPARTMENT.

CAPT. CHAPEL'S COMPANY.

Pay Roll of Captain Fredrick Chapels Company of Seamen, raised in the State of Connecticut, for the Naval Service on the Lakes in the Northern Department commencing on the day of their Inlistment & ending the 25 Day of Sept[r] [1776] Inclusive agreeable to encouragement of first M° advance wages, Including also Billeting Money, traveling Expenses, Premiums for entering the Service, Blankets, Guns, Cartouch Boxes, Knapsacks and Belts.

Names	When entered the service	Names	When entered the service
Fredrick Chapel Capt	Aug. 9	Ephraim Hotchkiss	Aug. 26
Ephraim Goldsmith Lt	18	Robert Hotchkiss	"
Stephen G. Thatcher Lt	"	Joseph Cooper	"
Samuel Little Seaman	"	Nathaniel Stacey	"
John Miller	"	Samuel Tharp	"
James Benham	"	Clement Tuttle	"
John Martin	"	Eliada Parker	"
Joseph Hosmer	25	Eliakim Parker	"
Stephen Willson	"	Joshua Parker	"
John Wilson	"	Levi Parker	"
Reuben Hadlock	"	Ebenezer Merry	"
Fredrick Standley	"	Reuben Judd	"
Benjamin Almstead	"	Samuel Holmes	"
Benjamin Kenney	"	Abraham Hays	"
John Wilcott	"	Nehemiah Knap	"
Joseph Wise	"	Samuel Morwin	23
Benjamin Osborn	"	John Gardner	26
Thomas Mix	"	James Taylor	"
Amos Potter	"	Edward Neile	"
William Ives	"	John Kelly	"
Benjamin Cook	"	William Briggs	"
Abraham Sugdon	"	John Knap	"
Elenozer Alling			

[*State Library, Revolution 32.*]

CAPT. HAWLEY'S COMPANY.

Pay Roll of Captain David Hawley's Company of Seamen raised in the State of Connecticut for the Naval Service of the American States in the Northern Department, commencing on the Day of their inlistment & ending the 25 Septem 1776 agreeable to encouragement of first M° advance wages, Including also Billeting money, Traveling Expences, Premiums for entering the Service, Blankets, Guns, Cartouch Boxes, Knapsacks & Belts.

Names	When entered the Service	Names	When entered the Service
David Hawley Capt	Aug 9	John Hayes	Aug 24
John Fairweather Lieut	19	William Duncomb	"
Ephraim Hawley "	"	Abner Hendricks	"
Michael Jennings Sea	"	John Lyon	"
Samuel Hawley "	"	Samuel Daniels	25
Andrew Patterson	24	Samuel French	"
Jesse Burr	"	Peter Butler	"
Joseph Mather	"	Levy Goodrick	"
William Brothwell	"	Sam[l] Freedswell	"
Mel Wahlee	"	Edmund Pulford	"
Samuel Hendricks	"	George Leemon	"
Enoch Lacey	"	Darius Fisher	"
Daniel Winifred	"	Squire Breadsley	"

[*State Library, Revolution 32.*]

GALLEY "TRUMBULL".

[*See Record of Connecticut Men in the Revolution, page 594.*]

CAPT. WARNER'S COMPANY.

A Pay Roll of Captain Seth Warners Company of Seamen raised in the State of Connecticut for the naval Service on the lake in the Northern department, commencing on the day of their enlistments and ending when they were discharged being Nov: 25, 1776 including Billiting money traveling expence premium for ent^{s} the Service Blanket Money, Gun, Cartouch box Knapsack &c &c agreable to encouragement.

Names		When entered the Service	When left the Service and for what reason
Seth Warner	Cap.	Aug. 12	Nov 17 Dischd.
Josiah Canfield	Seaman	13	Prom^{d} Sep. 9
"	2 Lt	Sep. 9	Disch^{d} wounded in Hospitl Nov. 25
Job Wheeler	Seaman	Aug. 15	Prom^{d} Sep. 9
"	Mate	Sep. 9	Disch^{d} Nov. 25
Giles Cone	Seaman	Aug. 25	Prom^{d} Sep. 9
"	Boatswain	Sep. 9	Disch^{d} Nov. 25
Simon Hough	Seaman	Aug. 15	Prom^{d} Sep. 9
"	Capt. clerk	Sep. 9	Disch^{d} Nov. 25
Samuel Ames	Seaman	Aug. 15	Prom^{d} Sep. 9
"	Carpenter	Sep. 9	Disch^{d} Nov. 25
Amos Bates	Seaman	Aug. 15	Prom^{d} Sep. 9
"	Carp^{ts} Mate	Sep. 9	Disch^{d} Nov. 25
Thomas Fitch	Seaman	Aug. 13	Prom^{d} Sep. 9
"	Steward	Sep. 9	Disch^{d} Nov. 25
Ebenezer Squires	Seaman	Aug. 15	"
David Warner	"	13	"
Joseph Barbee	"	15	"
Pascal Deangalis	"	13	"
Peter Negro	"	29	"
George Puffer	"	Sep. 1	"

[*State Library, Revolution 6.*]

SCHOONER "SPY".

[*See Record of Connecticut Men in the Revolution, page 593.*]

CAPT. NILES' MEN.

Schooner Spy Acc^t Wages Octr 8th 1776
Schooner Spy to Robert Niles for sund^y Persons wages by him paid Viz

Name	Rank	From	To
Robt Niles	Capt	from Jan. 8	Oct. 8
Timothy Parker	Lieut	"	"
Zebadiah Smith		"	"
Benjn Mortimore	Boatsw^n	"	"
Rct^n Moore	Clerk	"	"
John Lessieur	Cook	"	"
Eber Blakesley	Gun^r	"	"
Ezekle Sayers	Seaman	"	"
John Hall	"	"	"
Archibald Nails	"	"	"
John Tucker	"	"	"
Wm Rambow	Boats^n Mate	"	"
James Devenport	Seaman	"	"
John Johnson	"	"	"
John Gaylord	Marine	"	"
Wm Swan	"	"	"
Wm Devall	Seaman	"	"
Stephen Squire	"	"	"
Josiah Carew	Carpenter	"	"
Zephaniah Tapping	Seaman	"	"
David Hand	Marine	"	"
David Bowers	Seaman	"	"
Luther Hildreth	"	"	"
Wm Goldsmith	Off^r Marines	"	"
Caleb Brown	Marine	"	"
Lewis Chatfield	Seaman	"	"
John Gan	"	"	"
Ezekiel Miller	Marine	"	"
Wm Covel	Pilot	Aug. 13	"
John Tisaker	Seaman	"	Sep. 9
Joseph Hally	"	"	Oct. 8
Wm Sprigs	"	22	Sep. 14
John Nails	"	" 13	" 19
Hen^y Walker	"	"	"
Thom^s Coffin	"	"	Oct. 8
Manuel Swazey	"	"	Sep. 9
Wm Gardner	Marine	"	" 19
Jaquin Ferdenands		" 22	Oct. 8
Silas Clement		"	"
Richd Baxter		"	Sep. 8
James Gowdy		"	Oct. 8
Dan^ll Toomy		" 25	Sep. 18
Anthony Bonscourse		"	"
Thos Etherly		"	"

[*State Library, Revolution 9.*]

Schooner Spy to Robert Niles for Sundry Persons Wages by him paid Viz Jany 8 1777

			m	d
Robert Niles	Capt.	Oct. 8 to Jan. 8, 1777	3	
Timothy Parker	Lieut	" "	3	
Zebadiah Smith	Master	" "	3	
Benjn Mortimore	Boatswain	" Dec. 8	2	
Eben Blakesley	Gunner	" Jan 8	3	
Ret^{n} Moore	Clerk	" "	3	
Josiah Cary	Carpenter	" "	3	
John Lasseur	Cook	" "	3	
Wm Gold Smith	Serjant Marines	" "	3	
Wm Rumbow	Boatswains Mate	" "	3	
John Johnson	Seaman	" Nov. 29	1	21
Ezekle Sayers	"	" Nov. 13	1	2
Archibald Nails	"	" Jan. 8	3	
John Hall	"	" "	3	
James Davenport	"	" "	3	
Wm Swan	Boy	" "	3	
John Gaylord	Marine	" "	3	
Wm Davall	Seaman	" "	3	
David Hand	Marine	" Dec 26	2	18
Stephen Squire	Seaman	" Jan. 8	3	
Caleb Brown	Marine	" "	3	
Zephaniah Tapping	Seaman	" "	3	
David Bowen	"	" "	3	
Luther Hildreth	"	" "	3	
William Covel	Pilot	" "	3	
Thomas Coffin	Seaman	" "	3	
Joseph Holley	"	" "	3	
John Tucker	"	" "	3	
John Gan	"	" "	3	
Ezekle Miller	Marine	" "	3	
James Goudy	Seaman	" "	3	
Lewis Chatfield	"	" "	3	

[*State Library, Revolution 9.*]

Schooner Spy to Robert Niles For Sund^{y} persons wages by him paid Viz

Robert Niles	Capt	f^{m} Jany 8 to May 8 1777
Nath^{ll} Barns	Mate	March 26 to " 14
Thos Rice	2^{d} Mate	" 12 to Apr 12
Willm Higgins	. . . . . .	Feby 28 to " 28
Ezekiel Sayers	. . . . . .	March 5 to " 21
Stephen Squire	. . . . . .	" 5 to " 18
John Tucker	. . . . . .	Jany 8 to Feby 22
John Tucker	. . . . . .	Feby 22 to May 14
David Bowers	. . . . . .	March 5 to " 14
John Anthony	. . . . . .	" 5 to " 14
Richard Stewart	. . . . . .	" 12 to " 14
William Swan	. . . . . .	Jany 8 to Feby 21
William Swan	. . . . . .	Feby 21 to May 14
James Ford	. . . . . .	" 1 to " 14
Josiah Carey		
Jaquin Fernandes	. . . . . .	Jan 8 to Feby 8
Jaquin Fernandes	. . . . . .	Feby 8 to May 14
William Skinner	. . . . . .	March 15 to April 20

[*State Library, Revolution 9.*]

Schooner Spy to Robert Niles For Sund^y^ Persons Wages by him paid Viz

Robert Niles	Capt. . .	from May 8	to Sep 26 1777	
Zebadiah Smith	Lieut. . . .	23	"	
Willm Harris	Master . . .	23	"	
Michael Pepper	Mate . . .	27	"	
Richd Stewart	Gunner . . .	26	"	
David Lewis	B. Swain . . .	26	"	
Peter Jeffers	Carpenter . .	23	"	
John Robertson	Clark . . .	29	" 29	
Jonath. Rudd	Stuard . . .	"	Deserted	
Jacob Kingsbury	Serj^t^ . . .	23	"	
Willm Swan	Cook . . .	29	"	
Joseph Francis	B. Mate . . .	26	"	
Kingsbury Edgerton	. . . . .	23	"	
Thos Wood	Seaman . . .	24	"	
Harris Tinker	"	30	"	
Charles Turner	"	30	"	
David Rogers	"	30	" 24	
Thomas Dandec	"	June 4	"	
Anthony Wolf	"	June 6	"	
Thomas Reed	"	June 12	July 22	
Jacob Cooper	"	July 11	Aug. 12	
John Williams	"	July 20	Sep. 26	
Johan Leseur	"	Aug. 16	"	
Jooseph Webb	Boy	May 29	"	

[*State Library, Revolution 9.*]

CAPT. SMITH'S MEN.

Dr Schooner Spy to Zebadiah Smith for Sund^y^ wages by him paid Viz March 24 1778

Zebadiah Smith	Capt. . .	Oct. 16 1777	to March	24 1778
Asahel Smith	Leut. . .	Nov. 3	to Feb.	27
Benjn Mortimore	Master . .	Oct. 20	to	20
James Elderkin	Gunner . .	"	to	"
Jonathan Sachel	Boatswain .	"	to Nov.	20
Hen^y^ Boardman	Boatswains mate	"	to Feb.	22
John Johnson	Cook . . .	31	to	"
Thos Wood	Seaman . .	Nov. 3	to	"
Minor Elderkin	Seaman . .	"	to	"
Roger Avery	" . .	12	to	"
John Parsons	Boy . .	21	to	27
Wm Swan	Seaman . .	18	to	"
Nathl Swan	" . .	24	to	24
Jno Williams	" . .	12	to	22
John Masters	" . .	"	to	28
Willm Allen	Marine . .	30	to	20
Saml R Smith	Clerk . .	Dec. 20	to	22

[*State Library, Revolution 12.*]

The United States Dr To the State of Connecticut for the Wages &c of sundry on board the Schooner Spy while prisoners in the service of the United States.

Michael Pepper	Service on board the Schooner Spy
Capt Robert Niles	"
James Brown	"
Solomon Hatch	"
Zephaniah Hatch	"
Cyrus Fanning	"

[*Comptroller's Office, Haskell's Receipts.*]

SLOOP "DOLPHIN".

[*See Record of Connecticut Men in the Revolution, page 593.*]

MASTER NILES' MEN.

Sloop Dolphin to Robert Niles Dr for Sundry Persons Wages by him Paid Viz

Robert Niles Master	from Sep. 27 to Mar. 6, 1778
Frederick Calkins Mate	from Oct. 12 to Feb. 25
Peter Jeffers Capt	from Nov. 14 to Mar. 2
John Lescur	from Oct. 3 to " 5
John Paterson	from Nov. 15 to Feb. 24
Cornelius Savage	from Oct. 6 to Mar. 6
Zefeniah Hatch	from Nov. 14 to " 2
Abner Bebee	from " 13 to " 2
Joseph Webb	from " 26 to " 2
James Treet	from Dec. 26 to Feb. 24
Lawdin Higgins	from " 29 to " 18

[*State Library, Revolution 12.*]

SLOOP "GUILFORD".

CAPT. NOTT'S MEN.

A Pay Abstract for Capt Notts men on board the Sloop Guilford.

Mens Names	Time Rec from	Time Rec up to	
Capt Willm Nott	Feb. 25	June 29	
Lieut W^{m} McQueen	Apr. 15	"	
Lieut Danl Mallery	Mar. 21	"	
Sailing Mr Dan. Miles	"	"	
Doct Wm Fitch	Apr. 25	"	
Mate Wm Coggeshall	Mar. 24	"	
Clarke John Dewitt	17	"	
Gunner Timothy Andrews	Apr. 15	"	Disartd
Pilot Wm Stuart	May 10	"	
P Master Simeon Linley	"	"	
Armo^{r} Bela Stone	Mar. 20	"	
Harry Taylor Boats^{n}	May 26	"	
David Raymond Cook	"	"	Disartd
David Morris	Mar. 26	"	
David Baldwain	"	"	
Job Clarke	Apr. 4	"	
Sam. Burrell	May 10	"	
Peter Pond	21	"	
Wm Wolcott	15	"	Disartd
John Hall	17	"	
Willm Hall	15	"	Disartd
Acher Molthrop	June 3	"	Disartd
Jacob Molthrop	"	"	
Levy Mallery	May 10	"	Disartd
John Barns	June 17	"	
Joseph Wheaton	May 19	"	Disartd
James Goodrige	"		
Peter Gabriel	Mar. 5		
Thomas V^{n} Dosen	"		
Peter Sisco			
Peter Nostrand			
Stephen Row			

[An entry on the back of this Pay Abstract shows that it is for the year 1779 and that the vessel was lost during that year.]

[*State Library, Revolution 31.*]

CAPT. HAWLEY'S MEN.

A Pay Roll of Capt David Hawleys Company of Seamen on board the Sloop Guilford belonging to the State of Connecticut, 1779.

Officers and Mens Names		When Entered	When Discharged
David Hawley	Capt	June 18	July 8
and from the 16 Aug. to the 3 Sep. — Court Enquiry Ended			
Willm McQueen	1 Lieut	June 29	July 11
Danl Mallery	2 Lieut	"	"
Nathan Jackson	Lieut marines	21	"
Danl Miles	Sailing master	29	"
John Dewett	Clerk	"	"
Simeon Linsly	prise master	"	"
Willm Steward	"	"	"
Wm Coggswell	Mate	"	"
Danl Jackson	Pilot	22	6
John Hawley	Gunner	25	"
John Ritch	Carpenter	22	"
Henry Tayler	Boatswain	29	11
Seth Barker	Serj marines	25	6
Nathl Jennings	"	"	"
Reuben Bostwick	Steward	"	"
Jonathan Saymour	G mate	"	"
John Hall	Boatswains mate . . .	29	"
Benj Morrill	Carpenters mate . . .	25	"
Saml Siscoll	Cook	"	"
Jeffry Bur	Seaman	"	"
Peter Finch	"	"	"
Bela Stone	Armourer	29	11
John Meakor	"	25	6
Zebulon Wiscutt	"	"	"
Thomas Darrow	"	"	"
Richard Provost	"	"	"
John R Lockwood	"	"	"
Alvin Huatt	"	"	"
Wm Jarvis	"	"	"
John Duncomb	"	"	"
Wakemon Burrtt (?)	"	"	"
David Lacy	Seaman	"	"
Abijah Gilbert	"	"	"
Adner Henerdricks	"	"	"
Peter Pond	Marine	"	"
Billay Finch	"	"	"
Wm Holburton	"	"	"
Peter Rose	"	"	"
John Bostwick	"	"	"
John Barns	"	29	11

[*State Library, Revolution 31.*]

SHIP "OLIVER CROMWELL".

[*See Record of Connecticut Men in the Revolution, page 596.*]

CAPT. ROBARTS' MEN.

Account of men inlisted by Capt Elip^t^ Robarts [for the Ship Oliver Crómwell]

Mens Names	Capacites	Time of inlisting
Wm Robarts	Seaman	September 1, 1776
Wm Mosley	Clarke of marenes	2
Moses Butler	Gunners mate	2
Step^n^ Ward	Marine	25
Gurdin Burnham	Drummer	26
John Spencer	Sergnt	October 2
James Bidwell	Seaman	September 15
John Watkins	Marine	October 4
William Allyn	"	7
James Patterson	"	7
John Brownley	"	7
Richd Risley	"	7
Jon^t^ Arnold	"	7
Levi Risley	"	7
[ ] Robarts Junr	"	2
David Porter	"	7
Jacob Gibson	"	14
Aaron Robarts	"	14
David Mackintosh	Yoman	November 10
Benjamin Burnit	Marine	8
John Wilson	"	8
John Hale	"	12
Wm Johnson	"	7
[ ] Fulorton	"	October 3
Wm Powell	"	7
David Bagley	Seaman	December 23
Isaac Rogers	Marine	
Moses Porter	"	January 28, 1777
John Steuart	Seaman	February 8
Abel Davise	Marine	January 16

To Cash to men inlisted by others

Saml Stratton
John Williams
Solomon Lord
Saml Stodard
Adrial Simans
John Hartshorne
Heze Abbe Jr
Arad Simans
Steph^n^ Both
Isaiah Rogers
John Shoart
John Robinson
David Hawkins
Henery Arnold

[*State Library, Revolution 9.*]

CAPT. COIT'S MEN.

Feb. 1777 A List of Seamen on bord the Ship Oliver Cromwell D^{d} in Pr Capt Wm Coit

A List of Officers Seamen & Mareens

Wm Coit Esqr	Capt P
Micael Mullally	1 Lt P
John Chapman	2 " P
John Smith	3 " P
Elefelett Roberts	Capt Marines P
John Prentice	1 Lt P
Bela Elderkin	2 Lt P
Levi Young	Master P
Thos Chatfield	1 Mate
Nathl Wilson	2 " P
Allegence Waldo	Surgeon P
Thos Gray	Mate
Luther Elderkin	Midshipman P
Jno A Christophers	"
John Bailey	" P
Giles Hollester	" P
Selvenus Pinkham	" P
Robt Newson	Boatswain P
Robt Graige	Gunner P
Thos Williams	Carpenter P
Thos Winston	Capt Clerk P
Christopher Prince	Stewart P
Wm Howard	Cooper P
Hugh Mathews	Cook
Solomon Lord	Serg^{t} P
Jno Spencer	" P
Wm Moseley	Clerk Marines D
Thos Setchele	Boatswains Mate
Jno Dennice	2 " "
Jno Burns	Carpenters Mate P
Moses Butlers	Gunners "
Gurdon Burnham	Drummer R
David McIngtosh	Gunners Yeoman P
Thos Jones	Pilot P

Seamen

Saml Bassett
Jno Rogers
Ja^{s} Mathews
Jno Robins
Thos Roberts
Saml Stratton
Jno Smith R
Jno Adams R
Thos Bowen R
Hezekiah Baker R
Oliver Blossom R
Joseph Fisher P
Jotham Gardner R
Thos Holladay G
Elijah Loveland R
Jno Morrison P
Wm Palmer R
Nath^{n} Chase D
Stephen Ward R

Seamen

Jon^{n} Miner
Jno Woolf R
George Lord D
Edward Culver P
Ben Short P
Stephen D Woolf P
John Merrow D
Henry Cannady P
Ichabob Shifield R
Willm Fagands
John Heath P
John Tease P
Robt Alsop James R
Thomas Smith P
Thos Blin Harris R
Thos Hampton P
Paul Long
James Hill
Edward Crow P

Seamen

Reuben Godfrey P
Shubele Crowele D
Thos Etterly R
Stephen Blossom R
Joseph Frederick
William Dansey G
Ruben Smith
John Woobury
Ben Hussey P
Stephen Brooks R
Joseph King R
Geo Worthylake P
Bazaliel Beby P
Nathan Burrus
Wm Harris D
John Randolp
Eben^{r} Backus
James Bedwell D
Wm Roberts P
Wm Garrick Murdred
Cornelius McPerson P
Josiah Ware R
Silas Daggett
John Collings R
John Linstrum Run
Steph^{n} Booth
Daniel Waggs S
Ezekael Lyon P
Saml Fosdick R
Thos V^{n} Duson R
Joseph Bailey R
Silvenus Smith
Job Hanniball
John Williams
Nathaniel Cowett P
Solomon Capee S
Joseph Pornett
Thos Winston Clerk
Jonas Hultman
David Trueman

Marenes

Isaiah Rogers
John Spencer
Saml Robinson
Silas Flint
Thos Holbrook
Saml Stoddard
Abel Woodworth
Pheneus Carew
Jacob Sawer D
Jon^{n} Jennings D
Nath^{n} S Calkings
Ezekel Dunham
John Hartsorn
Henry Williams Drowned
David Folger D
Frederick Curtice
Saml Curtice

Seamen

John Williams
Peter Hanson P
Peter Harry P
Jonathan Whelding P
Judah P. Spooner P
Ceaser Niles D
Henry Burnsides P
Thos Nuchcold R
John Robinson R
Jarrus Alden R
Vollantyne Bunker D
Joseph Ewett R
Thos Sinemon
Saml Gyer R
John Short R
Saml Boston
Joseph Hannibale P
Joseph Thatcher P
George Potague P
Boston Boston P
James Lanphere D
Charles Clark G
Oliver Done P
Simeon Debago P
Solomon Perpener P
John Dunking R
Selvenus Simes P
Thos Shiverick P
Edwd Hatch P
Wm Bishop G
Timothy Weeks
Robinson Jones
John Lathergo R
Freeborn Bowes P
Moses Talmon P
Jonas Horsewett P
Zacceus Chase P
Abele Soppoosor
Job Bunker R

Marenes

Nathl Backus D
Jon^{n} Hubbard
Hezekiah Abby
Solomon Tracey
Elijah Shaford
Arad Simonds
Eleazer Welch
Adrial Simonds
John Williams R
Abner Follett D
Dearky Elderkin
Abijah Hutchingson S
John Dingley D
Abele Minor S
Wm Capp P
Stephen Ward
David Hawkins P

Marenes	Marenes
John Watkins D	Natha'l Fullerson D
Wm Allen R	Henry Arnold D
James Patteson P	John Wilson R
Willm Powell P	Ben Burnett
John Brownley P	John Hay
Richd Risley P	Hammond Sup
Jonn Arnould P	Thomas Williams
Levi Risley P	Wm Johnson R
Elifelet Roberts Junr D	Wm Marsh P
David Porter P	Abele Davis
Jacob Gibson D	Benn Fowler P
Boys	Boys
Duglass Chapman P	Thos Robins
Joseph Merrils R	Jno Baccus D
Asael Flint	Jonn Burnett
David Young	Jno Deming R
Aron Roberts P	Thos Doertes R
Elijah Ormsby	Joseph Fisher P
Charles Brown P	Jno Grant D
Vollantyne Chase P	Phineus Manfeld P Seaman
Wm Peat P	Thos Parseval
Benn Sinemon	Cornl Baxter Seaman
Jno Robins	Davis P
Seamen	Seamen
Henry Hunt P	David Bagley P
John Hill P	Jno Steward
Daniel Card P	Stephen Fox P
Frederick Murfey P	

Present	85
On Furlow	63
In Gaol	4
Run away	41
Discharged	20
Murdred	1
Drownd	1
Sick	4
	219
Not known	13
	232

[*State Library, Revolution 9.*]

List of Officers and Men formerly belonging to the Ship Oliver Cromwell, and still on board, viz

John Chapman	Lieut	Judah P. Spooner
John Smith	"	John Rees
David Mackintosh	Yeoman of Powder Room	Benjamin Hussy
		Frederick Curtis
Jonathan Setchell	Quarter Master	Samuel Curtis
Henry Kennedy	Coxwain	George Worthylake
Edward Culver		Abel Woodworth
William Marsh		Douglas Chapman
Barzaleel Beeby	Armourer's Mate	

[Indorsed] List of Men on Bord O. Cromwell who were in Capt Coits cruise.

[*State Library, Revolution 9.*]

A list of the Marines that have and do Belong to the Ship Oliver Cromwell William Coit Esq Commander

Elifelett Roberts	Captn	Furlow
John Prentice	1st Lieut	Present
Bela Elderkin	2 "	Furlow
Solomon Lord	Sergant	"
John Spencer	"	Present
Wm Moseley	Clerk	Dischargd
Gurdon Burnham	Drummer	Runaway
Isaih Rogers	Private	Present
John Spencer	"	Furlow
Saml Robinson	"	"
Silas Flint	"	"
Thos Holbrook	"	Present
Saml Stoddart	"	Furlow
Abel Woodworth	"	Small Pox
Phereus Carew	"	Furlow
Jacob Sawyer	"	Discharged
Nathl Calkings	"	"
Zekel Dunham	"	Furlow
John Hartshorn	"	Present
Henry Williams	"	Downed
Frederick Curtice	"	Present
Saml Curtice	"	"
Nathl Backus	"	Dischargd
Jonn Hebard	"	Furlow
Hezekiah Abby	"	"
Solomon Tracey	"	"
Elijah Sparford	"	"
Arad Simonds	"	Present
Eleazer Welch	"	Furlow
Adrial Simonds	"	"
John Williams	"	"
Abner Follet	"	Discharged
Diarky Elderkin	"	Present
Abijah Hutchinson	"	"
John Dingley	"	Discharged
Abel Minor	"	Furlow
Wm Copp	"	Present
Stephen Ward	"	"
David Hawkins	"	
John Watkins	"	Discharged
Wm Allen	"	Runaway
James Patterson	"	Present
Wm Powell	"	Runaway
John Brownley	"	"
Richd Risley	"	Present
Jonn Arnold	"	"
Levi Risley	"	"
Elifelett Roberts Junr	"	Discharged
David Porter	"	Present
Jacob Gibson	"	Drumd Out
Nathl Fullerton	"	Discharged
Henry Arnold	"	"
John Wilson	"	Runaway
Benn Burnett	"	Present
John Hale	"	Runaway
Ammon Seep	"	Present
Thos Persevall	"	

Wm Johnson	Private	
Wm Marsh	"	Present
Abel Davis	"	
Benn Fowler	"	Present
John Robins	"	Furlow
John Baccus	"	Discharged
Jonn Burnett	"	Furlow
Thos Doherty	"	Runaway
John Grant	"	Furlow
Pheneus Munsell	"	Discharged
Cornelius Baxter	"	
Jonn Jennings	Fifer	Discharged
Wm Roberts	Private	"

[*State Library, Revolution 9.*]

A List of Officers & Seamen Belonging & have Belong'd to the Ship Oliver Cromwell.

Wm Coit Esqr	Capt. & Commander	Present
Michail Millally	1 Lieut	"
John Chapman	2 "	"
John Smith	3 "	"
Levi Young	Master	"
Thos Chatfield	1 Mate	"
Nathaniel Wilson	2 "	"
Albegence Waldo	Surgeon	"
Thomas Gray	" Mate	"
Luther Elderkin	Midshipman	"
Allen Christophers	"	"
John Bailey	"	"
Giles Hollister	"	"
Selvenus Pinkham	"	"
Robt Graige	Gunner	"
Robt Newson	Boatswain	"
Thos Williams	Carpenter	"
Christopher Prince	Steward	"
Wm Howard	Cooper	"
George Lord	Clerk	Discharged
Hugh Mathews	Cook	
James Hill	Boatswains Mate	Present
Moses Butler	Gunners Mate	"
David Mackingtosh	Grs Yeoman	"
Thos Jones	Pilot	"
John Dennis	Bt 2d Mate	in Gaol for Murder
Jonn Setchell	Qutr Master	Present
Job Bunker	"	Runaway
John Smith	"	"
John Burns	Carpenters Mate	Present
Cornl McPerson	2 "	"
John Woolf	Boatsns Yeoman	Runaway
Stephen De Woolf	Carpenters "	Present
Henry Cannady	Coxswain	"
John Merrow	Armorour	Discharged
James Lanphere Junr	Steward	"
David Folger	Boatswain	"
Edward Culver	Seaman	Present
Benn Short	"	"

Ickebert Shiffield	Seaman	Runaway
Wm Fagons	"	Present
John Heath	"	"
John Pease	"	"
Robt Alsop James	"	Runaway
Thos Smith	"	Present
Thos Blin Harris	"	Runaway
Thos Hampton	"	Present
Paul Long	"	"
Edward Crow	"	"
Reuben Godfrey	"	"
Shubell Crowele	"	Discharged
Thos Etherly	"	Runaway
Stephen Blosson	"	"
Wm Dansey	"	Present
Reuben Smith	"	Discharged
John Woobury	"	"
Ben^n Hussey	"	Present
Steph^n Brooks	"	Runaway
Joseph King	"	"
Geo. Wetherlegs	"	Present
Baz^l Beby	"	"
Nathan Burrows	"	Sick in Small Pox
Wm Harris	"	Discharged
John Randol	"	Present
Eben^r Baccus	"	Discharged
James Biddell	"	"
Wm Garrick	"	Murdered
Josiah Ware	"	Runaway
Silas Daggett	"	
John Collings	"	Runaway
John Linston	"	"
Stephen Booth	"	
Danl Waggs	"	Sick and not fit for Duty
Ezekiel Lyon	"	Present
Saml Fosdick	"	Runaway
Thos V^n Duson	"	"
Jos. Baylye	"	"
Selevenus Smith	"	Present
Job Hanniball	"	
John Williams	"	Runaway
Solomon Corvett	"	
Solomon Capee	"	Runaway
Nathl Cowett	"	Present
Jos^h Porrutt	"	Runaway
Thos Winston	"	Present
Jonas Horswett	"	"
David Freeman	"	Runaway
John Williams	"	"
Peter Hanson	"	Present
Peter Harry	"	"
Jon^n Welding	"	"
Judah P. Spooner	"	Present
Ceasar Niles	"	Discharged
Henry Burnside	"	Present
Thos Nicholds	"	Runaway
James Alden	"	Discharged

Vallantyne Bunker	Seaman	Discharged
Saml Bunker	"	Runaway
Josh Hewett	"	"
Thos Cinnamon	"	Present
Saml Geer	"	Runaway
John Short	"	"
Saml Poston	"	"
Joseph Hanniball	"	
Joseph Thatcher	"	Present
Geo. Patague	"	"
Boston Boston	"	"
Chas Clerk	"	"
Oliver Done	"	"
Simon Debago	"	
Solomon Popenah	"	Present
Selvenus Simms	"	"
John Demking	"	"
Thos Shiverick	"	"
Edwd Hatch	"	"
Wm Bishop	"	Discharged
Timothy Weeks	"	Present
Robinson Jones	"	"
John Lathergo	"	Runaway
Freeborn Bowes	"	Present
Moses Talman	"	"
Zacceus Chace	"	"
Abel Sapposorn	"	
Samo Bassett	"	
John Mathews	"	
John Rogers	"	
Saml Stratton	"	Present
John Adams	"	Runaway
Thos Bowen	"	
Hezekiah Baker	"	Runaway
Joseph Fisher	"	Present
Jothan Gardner	"	Runaway
Thos Holladay	"	Present
Elijah Loveland	"	Runaway
John Morrison	"	Present
Wm Palmer	"	Runaway
Nathan Chase	"	Discharged
Stephen Ward	"	Runaway
Jonn Minor	"	"
Timothy Murphey	"	"
Henry Hunt	"	"
Danl Carr	"	"
John Hill	"	"
John Bagley	"	Present
John Steward	"	
Thos Jones	"	Present
Abner Ransom	"	"
Peter Swain		"
Maning Stubbs		"
Nathaniel Rowley		"
Robt Hatch		"
Seth Swift		"
	Boys	
John Deming		Runaway
Joseph Merrills		Runaway

Boys

Duglass Chapman	Present
Asael Flint	On Furlow
David Young	"
Aron Roberts	Present
Elijah Ormsby	On Furlow
Chas Brown	Present
Vollantyne Chase	"
Wm Peet	"
Ben^n Cinemon	"
Peter Darrow Junr	"

[*State Library, Revolution 9.*]

COMMANDER PARKER'S MEN.

Pay Roll of Officers & Men belonging to the Ship Oliver Cromwell 1777.

Names	Qualities	Time of Entry	Time of Discharge
Timothy Parker	Lieutenant	April 14	Oct. 14
John Chapman	"	"	"
John Smith	"	"	"
Caleb Frisbie	Master	April 24	"
Thomas Rice	Mate	May 3	"
Stephen Lee	"	May 31	"
Thomas Whelden	"	June 1	Sep. 22
David Pool	Boatswain	May 8	Oct. 14
David Mackentosh	Gunner	April 14	"
William Marbell	Carpenter	"	"
Jonathan Woodworth	Midshipman	"	"
Shirman Lewis	"	"	"
Curtis Reed	"	"	"
Ralph Hoadley	"	April 27	"
Andrew Morris	"	May 28	"
Robert Alsop James	"	June 9	"
Judah P. Spooner	Clerk	April 14	"
Benjamin Ellis	Surgeon	"	"
Timothy Rogers	Surgeon's Mate	April 28	"
John Craige	Boatswains Mate	May 8	"
William Higgins	"	May 3	"
James Elderkin	Gunner's Mate	April 14	"
Phinehas Chapman	Carpenter's "	May 17	Oct. 8
Jonathan Setchell	Quartermaster	April 14	Oct. 14
Prosper Brown	"	May 16	Sep. 22
Samuel Adams	"	May 26	Oct. 14
Benjamin Smith	"	"	Sep. 22
John Boyle	"	May 27	Oct. 14
William Baldwin	"	"	"
Peleg Hillman	"	June 1	"
David Norton	"	"	Sep. 22
Henry Parry	Cooper	May 26	Oct. 14
Epaphras Smith	Steward	April 14	Sep. 22
Henry Taylor	Cook	May 10	Oct. 14
Henry Kennedy	Coxswain	April 14	"
Frederick Curtis	Master at Arms	"	Sep. 22
Barzaleel Beebe	Armourer	"	Oct. 14
William Kimbalin	Sailmaker	June 1	"
John Negus	Arm^rs Mate	May 2	Sep. 22

Names	Qualities	Time of Entry	Time of Discharge
Ephraim Herrick	Steward's Mate	April 14	Oct. 14
Joab Alden	Gunner's Yeoman	April 24	Sep. 22
Henry Hunt	Yeoman	May 27	Sep. 22
Josiah Walker	"	April 18	"
Nathan Daggett	Pilot	May 19	Oct. 14
John Chatfield	"	April 14	Sep. 26
George Hillman	"	June 1	Sep. 22
John Rees	Seaman	April 14	Died Sep. 1
Edward Culver	"	"	Oct. 14
Benjamin Hussey	"	"	"
George Worthylake	"	"	"
James N. Griffin	"	"	"
Samuel Silliman	"	"	"
Abel Woodworth	"	"	"
Timothy Teal	"	"	Sep. 22
Zephaniah Hatch	"	"	"
Abel Lewis	"	"	"
Samuel Curtis	"	"	"
Arnold Kinyon	"	"	"
Philip Driscoll	"	"	"
James Hilliard	"	"	"
William Holmes	"	April 20	"
Archelaus Barker	"	April 28	Oct. 14
Stephen Smith	"	"	"
Isaac Sharpe	"	May 2	"
Theophilus Whaley	"	May 3	"
Azariah Hilliard	"	"	"
Isaac Frisbie	"	May 5	Sep. 22
Teleman Cuyler	"	May 7	Oct. 14
Turtle Hunter	"	May 8	"
Justus Harrison	"	"	Sep 22
Butler Harrison	"	"	"
John Jacobs	"	May 10	Oct. 14
Henry Bowman	"	May 18	Sep 22
James Brown	"	May 26	Oct. 14
John Manuel	"	"	"
Charles Kenney	"	"	"
Felix Quin	"	"	"
Peter Grant	"	"	"
James Everett	"	"	"
William Odell	"	"	"
William Ingraham	"	"	"
William Hall	"	"	Sep. 22
James Morris	"	"	"
Timothy Murphy	"	"	"
Robert Gordon	"	"	"
James McVey	"	"	"
James Ford	"	"	"
James Anderson	"	"	"
James Wall	"	"	"
William Harris	"	"	"
Joab Scranton	"	"	"
John Willard	"	"	"
Thomas Groundwater	"	"	"
Benjamin Rockwell	"	"	
Rosamus Laurence, Extra	"	May 31	Oct. 14
Anthony Swasey	"	June 6	Sep 22
William Teleder	"	"	"

Names	Qualities	Time of Entry	Time of Discharge
Michael Moore	Seaman	June 6	Sep 22
Richard Lillie	"	"	Oct. 14
Patrick Conner	"	June 10	Sep. 22
John Taylor	"	July 8	Oct. 14
Boston Swain	"	June 13	"
William Ellis	"	June 6	Oct. 14
William Lamb	"	July 26	"
James Wimberley	"	July 22	"
David Rogerson	"	"	"
John Mortimer	"	"	"
Thomas Burke	"	"	"
Robert Marks	"	"	"
Nathaniel Swan	Boy	April 14	Oct. 14
John Parsons	"	"	"
Douglas Chapman	"	"	"
Theophilus Fitch	"	April 20	"
John Setchell	"	April 14	"
Darius Brewster	"	May 11	Sep 22
Philo Lewis	"	May 1	Oct. 14
George Edwards	"	May 27	"
Ivory Snow	"	May 26	Sep. 22
Sylvanus Daggett	"	June 6	"
West Daggett	"	"	"
Thomas Jones	"	July 22	Oct. 14
John Cleverly	"	"	"
Run			
Thomas Wilson	Seaman	April 14	
Thomas Graystock	"	"	
James Murray	"	May 27	
Peleg McGuire	"	May 26	
Thomas Aaron	"	May 3	
James Goging	"	May 27	
Alpheus Johnson	"	April 27	
Henry Pierce	"	May 30	
Obadiah Sears	"	May 8	
Thomas Keney	"	April 20	
Ebenezer Smith	"	May 5	
John Rosson	"	May 26	
Samuel Webster	"	April 20	
Francis Jackson	"	"	
Nicholas Taaffe	"	April 22	
Thomas Knowlton	"	April 24	Disc[d] June 7
William Russell	"	May 3	"
James Day	Lieut. Marines	April 14	Oct. 14
William Marsh	Serjeant	"	Sep. 27
Samuel Holt	"	May 13	Sep. 22
Henry Walton	Drummer	April 14	"
John Walton	Fifer	May 13	"
Nathaniel Jennings	Marine	April 14	Oct. 14
Nathan Jennings	"	"	"
John Easton Olcott	"	April 26	"
Josiah Beers	"	"	Sep 22
Richard Kimball	"	April 27	"
Elijah Spencer	"	"	"
Hendrick Pickle	"	April 14	Oct. 14
James Beers	"	May 1	"
George Stilken	"	May 13	Sep. 22
Elihu Cook	"	May 2	"

Names	Qualities	Time of Entry	Time of Discharge
John Linslie	Marine	May 2	Oct. 14
Timothy Huffman	"	"	Sep. 22
Oliver Gates	"	May 13	"
Robert Geer	"	May 9	"
Noah Stevens	"	May 2	"
Heli Foot	"	May 6	"
John Mouterdier	"	May 26	"
Timothy Hebbard	"	April 27	"
Josiah Wolcott	"	May 27	"
John Pullman	"	May 8	"
Elnathan Dexter	"	May 2	"
Jepthah Curtis	"	May 17	"
Charles Dana	"	June 2	"
Edmund Morris	"	May 7	"
Samuel Bartholomew	"	May 13	"
Asaph Pease	Yeoman	June 1	"
James Calkins	Marine	May 5	"
Henry Hunt	Seaman	May 27	"
Samuel Foy	"	Aug 22	"
Daniel Green	"	"	"
Alexander Wood	Marine	April 14	Oct. 14
Thomas Rogers	"	May 5	Sep. 22
Josiah Frisbie	"	"	"
Thomas Holbrook	Seaman	May 13	"

Seth Harding

[*State Library, Revolution 9.*]

Pay List for Ship Oliver Cromwell Timothy Parker Esqr Commander from 10th December 1777 to Sept 10th 1778

Names	Capacities	Time of Entry	When Discharged
Timothy Parker Esqr	Commander	6 Dec. 1777	22 Sep. 1778
John Chapman	first Lieutenant	6th Decr 1777	10 Sep. 1778
Caleb Frisbie	2d "	10th Decr 1777	10th
John Tillinghast	3d "	2nd Feby 1778	10th Sep 1778
Benjn Jones	Master	12th March	11 June
Andrew Morris	1st mate to 12th June	10 Dec. 1777	11 June 1778
	& then master	12th June 1778	10th September
Joseph Hubbard	2d mate	6th Dec. 1777	10th
Curtis Reed	3d " to 12th June and then first	15th	10th
Ralph Hoadly	Midshipman to 12th June	10th Dec. 1777	11th June 1778
	& then 2d Mate	12 June	10th Sept.
Samuel Stow	Midshipman to 12th June	5th Jany. 1778	12th June
	& then 3d mate	12th June	10th Sept.
William Higgins	midshipman	10th Dec. 1777	10th "
Samuel Bidwell	"	6th Dec. 1777	10th "
Isaiah Cahoon	"	5th Feby. 1778	10th
Samuel Buffam	"	10th "	10th Sep.
John Crage	Boatswain	10th Decr 1777	10th
Thomas Tillinghast	" mate	14th Dec. 1777	Run 25th June 1778
Samuel Lollard	2d "	2nd Feby 1778	10th Sep.
Thomas Wait Foster	Gunner	9th Jany.	10th "
Peter John Forrsster (?)	" mate	12 Feby	10th
Edward Brasier	Yeoman	18th Feby.	Run 1st June
Jacob Chandlor	Carpenter	10th Jany.	10th Sept
Amos Ranny	" mate	6th decr 1777	20th June Run.
Timothy Boardman		5th Jany. 1777	10th Sep. 1778
James Day	Capt Mariens	6th Dec. 1777	died 18th Apl.
Azeriah Hillyard	Sergt Mariens	15th	10th Sepr 1778
Abel Woodworth	"	20th	10th "
Jabez Perkins 3d	Captain's Clark	19th	22d Sepr
Turtle Hunter	Coxswain (Say Sailmaker)	18th Feby.	10th Sepr
Samuel Holman	Steward	6th Decr 1777	10th
Thomas Smith	Qr Master	11th Feby. 1778	10th Sepr
John Essex	"	13th March.	1st June Run

Douty Randol	"	16th		10th Sepr
Thomas Waples	"	10th		1st June Run
Chace Rogers	Cooper	1st Jany.		10th Sepr
Gideon Chapman	Doctrs Mate	3rd		10th Sepr
Edmond Morris	Seman	12th Decr	1778	10th "
Richard Rose	Marien	"		"
Jurden Smith	"	22d "		"
Caleb Smith	Cook	14th Jany		"
Archelus Barker	Seman	"		"
Samuel Andrus	marien	14th Dec.	1777	"
Joseph Smith	Seman	23d "		"
Hutchins Bowden	"	16th Jany.	1778	"
Charles Bordman	Marien	26th		"
Ebenezer Baldwin	"	14th		"
Eliphalet Roberts Junr	(") Seman	23rd Decr	1777	deserted
John Henry	Marien	29th		"
Levy Darling	"	29th		"
Cruttenden Ward		3rd Jany		10th September
Jeremiah Ward	Marien	3rd		10th Sepr
Daniel Sandeforth	"	3rd		10th Sepr
John Rogers 5th	Drummer	3rd		10th Sepr
Chapman Simmons	Marien	4th		10th
Thomas Croman	"	20th		10th
Jeremiah Thorp	"	20th		10th
Jonathn Waterhouse	"	20th		10th
Daniel Hillyard	" to ye 12 June. & then Gunners yewman	10th		12th June & then Enter'd as Yewman
John Wittlesey	Marien	20th		10th Sepr
John Welman	"	10th		10th
Roswell Lamphear	"	20th		10th
Nathl Riley	"	20th		10th
John Batt	"	30th		Deserted
Roger Dyer	Seman	20th		10th Sepr
Joseph Miller	"	20th		10th Sepr
Anthony Woolf	"	20th		10th
Samuel Mackentash	"	17th		Deserted

Names	Capacities	Time of Entry		When Discharged
John Drisco	Seman	17th		Deserted
John Slattury	"	26th		"
Jonas Park	Marien	30th		deserted 24th June.
Levy Park	"	30th		10th Sep^{r}
Pirum Ripley	"	3rd Feby.		10th Sep^{r}
Joseph Starkweather	"	3^{d}		10th
Giles Tracy	"	3^{d}		deserted 24th June
James Starkweather	"	31st Jany.		10th Sep^{r}
Amasa Waterman (negro)	"	9th Feby.		9th Sep^{r}
Chancy Smith	Seman	15th Dec.	1777	1 July died at Boston.
Hezekiah Goff	Marien	6th Dec.		7th June
John Rogers Junr		6th Dec.		10th Sep^{r}
Stephen Ward Junr	Marien	6th		10th
Philemon Roberts	"	6th		10th
Charles Plum	"	6th		Run 9th June
Stephen Ward	Marien	6th		10th Sep^{r}
Benjn Gardnor	Stewards Mate.	9th Jany	1778	9th Sep.
Moses Butlor		6th Dec^{r}	1777	10th Sep^{r}
John Griffin	Marien	6th "		10th
Tombo Dea	"	6th		10th
Daniel Lee	"			Deserted
Daniel Starr	"	6th Dec^{r}	1777	Run 9th June.
John Lamb	"	5th Jany	1778	10th Sep^{r}
John Blasdell	Seman	3rd March		Run 1st June.
Thomas Ridgway	Seman	3rd		10th Sep^{r}
Benjn Woodruff	Master of Arms.	6th Dec^{r}	1777	10th
Wilson Rowlandson	Marien	25th Feb^{y}	1778	10th
Edmond Dorr	"	25th		10th
William Bunce	Seman	25th		10th
Ebenezer Tolcut	Marien	25th		10th
Michael Dwire	Seman	9th March		Run 3rd June.
George Runey	"	5th "		9th Sep^{r}
Samuel Johnson	Marien	5th		15th April killed
John Baker		6th		10th Sep^{r}
Elkenah Elmes	Seman	6th		Deserted

Peter Gilbert	"	7th March 1778	"
Benjm Shetten	Marien	24th Feby.	Sept 9th
Nathl Oliver	"	5th March	9th
John Hedge	Seman	26th Jany	9th
Benjm Wyett	"	"	Run
Thomas Mathews	"	1st Feby.	"
Jotham Gardnor	"	2nd Feby	"
Joseph Hovey	"	2nd	9th Sepr
Samuel Chace	Marien	3rd	9th
Boston Swain	Seman	11th	9th
Samuel Coombs	"	11th	Run
James Mathews	"	9th	9th Sepr
Thomas Brimblecom	"	19th	9th
Enoch Crowell	"	7th	10th
Samuel Addams	" Qr Master	10th Jany	Run 3rd July
Simeon Post	Marien	25 Decr 1777	Sepr 10th
Abraham Low	"	31st "	Run 2d July
William Jones	Seman	10th Feby 1778	10th Sepr
Samuel Williams	Marien	10th "	10th
Stephen Payn	"	10th	10th
William Waterman	"	13th	9th
William Swan	Seman	26th	10th
John Setchel	"	26th	10th
John Parsons	"	26th	10th
Wm Henry Wattles		12th Decr 1777	10th
Thomas Goodman	Seman	23ed "	Run
Thomas Revers	"	23ed "	"
Chandlor Wattles	Marien	10th Jany. 1778	10th Sept
Jabez Palmer	"	25th	Run
Eliphalet House Junr	"	27th	10th Sept
Asa Lyman	"	27th	10th
Joseph Allen	"	10th	10th
Jesse Loomis	"	10th	10th
Derias Waterman	"	17th	10th
Jerard Allen	"	3rd Feby.	10th
Timothy Goodwin	"	4th	10th

Names	Capacities	Time of Entry	When Discharged
Neal Lathrop (Negro)	Marien	7th	10th
Ezekiel Fitch Junr	"	20th Decr 1777	10th
Abijah Hutchinson	"	25th "	10th
Walter Hunt	"	1st Jany. 1778	10th
Gladden Waterman	"	10th Jany.	10th Sepr
John Bliss	"	10th	10th
Josiah Woodworth	"	10th	10th
John Coatney	"	20th Feby.	10th
Samuel Wattles	(" Corporal)	10th Jany.	10th
Daniel Rockwell	Marien	15th	10th
John Brichel	"	29th	10th
Joshua Boyinton	"	20th	10th
Benona Dick	"	17th Feby.	10th
Richard Hendrick (Negro)	Marien	18th	10th
Peter Molbone	Seman	Deserted	
Cato Tyng (Negro)	Marien	17th March.	9th
Francis Jarvis	Seman	11th Feby 1778	Deserted
Bosaleel Beebie	Armorer	22d Decr 1777	10th Sepr 1778
Benjn Jones Junr		12th March	11th June
Dominique Tawsin	Surgen	1st "	10th Sepr
Wm Byrnes	Seman	19th	10th
Hugh McMannes	Landman	19th	9th
Thomas Williams	Seman	22d	Run 3d June
John Wood	"	"	" "
John Killey	"	"	" "
William Lamb	Volunteer	"	8th June
George Lamb	"	"	10th Sepr
Daniel Malcolm	"	"	10th
Isaac Frisbie	Cockswain	14th Jany.	10th
George Jacobson	doctrs Mate	17th July	10th
Amos Harding	Seman	8th	10th
Alexander McLain	Boatswain's Mate	10th	10th
John Coatney Entered Charles-town	Seman	10th	10th

Name	Station		Entered		Discharged
Solomon Siles "	"		10th		Run & did not Repair on board
Wm Petty	"		10th		10th Sepr
William Davis			10th		Deserted & did not Repair on board
William Raymond	Seman		11th		10th Sepr
Israel Smith	"		13th		10th
Peter Parker	5th Midshipman		15th		10th
John Knowles	4th "		10th June		10th
John H. Green	"	deserted	15th July		Deserted & did not Repair on board
Charles Howard	Seman		10th		10th Sepr
Thomas Smith Shipt in Charlestown	Marien		14th		10th
Seth Higgins	Seman		10th		10th
Richard Nowlan	"		18th		10th
Joseph Tee	"		11th		Deserted & did not Repair on board
James Risley	"		26th June		10th
Isrel Dyer	"		21st July		9th
Timothy Woodbridge	Midshipman		20th		"
Daniel Hillyard	Gunners Yewman from		12th June	to	10th Sepr
James Hanscum	Seman		14th July		Deserted Ship
Philemon Roberts	Landsman was in the Brig from		10 Inst.	to	23rd Inst. Dischargd
John Whittlesey	"	"	"		"
James Starkweather	"	"	"		"
Joseph Starkweather	"	"	"		"
Josiah Woodworth	"	"	"		"
Daniel Rockwell	"	"	"		"

Hartford Sepr 25th 1778 Personally appeared Timothy Parker Esqr Commander of the Ship Oliver Cromwell, & made Oath that according to his best knowledge & Belief the Pay Abstract by him exhibited & Subscribed of the Officers & Men belonging to Ship is Justly and truly made Out

Sworn before James Church one Comtee P. Table.

[*State Library, Revolution 31.*]

Pay List for Ship Oliver Cromwell, Timothy Parker Esqr Commander from 22^{d} Sepr 1778 to ye Augt 1779.

Names	Capacities	Time of Entry	Time of Discharge
Timothy Parker	Captain	Sep. 11th 1778	11th Sep. 1779
John Chapman	First Lieut.	" 11th	23rd Aug. 1779
Zebadiah Smith	2nd "	Decemb^{r} 1st	"
Andrew Morris	3^{d} "	Sep. 11th	"
Curtis Reed	Sailing Master	Sep^{t} 11th	"
Jabez Perkins ye 3rd	Capt Mariens	Sep^{t} 11th	"
Peter Lingdyon	Gunnor	March 15th 79	"
John Crage	Boatswain	" 15th 79	"
John Smith	Carpentor	" 15th 79	"
Dominique Tawzin	Surgeon	Sep. 11th 1778	"
Samuel Stowe	First Mate	11th Oct.	"
William Palmer	2^{d} "	10th April 1779	10th July died
John Knowles	3^{d} "	15th Feb^{y}	6th June Killed
Wm Howard	Midshipman	10th May	23^{d} Aug.
Nath^{ll} Stanton	"	10th Decemb^{r} 1778	"
John Smith	"	"	"
Gideon Chapman	"	11th Sep^{t}	"
Joshua Palmer	"	10th April 1779	"
Joseph Champlin	"	10th May	1st June
Robert Niles Junr	Captain's Clerk	25th Dec. 1778	23^{d} Aug.
Jeremiah Chapman	Steward	14th Dec 1778	"
John Hunt	Cooper	13th March 1779	"
Jonathan Setchel	Sail Maker	21st	"
Joseph King	Boatswains Mate	May 1st 1779	"
Nathan Burch	Gunnors Mate	31st March	"
John Lesure	Cook	1st Feb^{y}	"
Jesse Lester	Cockswain	Novr 25th 1778	"
Able Woodworth	Serg^{t} Mariens	May 1st 1779	"
Norman Morrison	"	10th April	"
Abraham Acker	Carpentors Mate	27th	"
Jasper Smith	Armourer	May 1st 1779	"
Timothy Lynch	Seaman	Jany 10th 1779	"
George George	"	10th Feb^{y}	"
Walter Bottom	Stewards Mate	15th April	"
Charles Millenor	Landsman	March 29th 1779	"
John Setchel	Seaman	28th	"
William Waterman	Landsman	1st	"
Paul Bunn	Seaman	April 3^{d}	deserted
Henry Calleway	Seaman	21st	"
Solomon Dunham	Landsman	21st	deserted
Samuel Thrasher	"	21st	"
Daniel Butler	"	21st	"
Allen Bidwell		21st	"
Levy Mallery	Seman	22^{d}	"
Edmond Morriss	"	19th	"
Valentine Rockester	"	22^{d}	deserted
Daniel Robbins	Landsman	Jany 17th	"
Asa Bellows	"	22^{d}	"
Ebenezer Allen	Landsman	April 19th 1779	"
Calvin Davison	Seaman	March 26th	"
James Ash	Landsman	17th	"
Alexander Young	Q^{r} Master	May 1st	deserted
John Webb	Seaman	March 1st	"
Eph^{m} Pumham	Landsman	27th	"
Robert Field	Seaman	Ap^{l} 15th	"

Names	Capacities	Time of Entry	Time of Discharge
A Francics	Seaman	Ap[l] 19th	deserted
Cull Cobus	"	1st	33[d] Aug.
Joseph Cutler	Master at Arms	April 20th	deserted
Joseph Keenne	Corperal Mariens	20th	"
Frederick Andrus	Seaman	20th	"
William Tyack	"	25th	"
Alexand[r] Lowry	"	25th	deserted
Peleg Sanford	"	25th	deserted
Thomas Scott	Quarter Master	27th	"
Hezekiah Meach	Landman	27th	"
Israel Durfey	"	27th	"
Christopher Brown	"	28th	"
Abijah Fisk	Seaman	29th	"
Philip Covel	Landman	May 1st	"
Micael Knox (?)	Seaman	April 25th	deserted
Benj[n] Unchous	Seaman	27th	"
Joseph Squib	Landman	28th	"
Bimeleck Uncas	"	30th	"
James Bottom 3[d]	"	7 Dec. 1778	"
Joseph Walker	Seaman	14 Jan[y] 1779	deserted
Martin Ford	Landman	14 "	deserted
Jonathan French Jun[r]	"	20th "	"
Eliphalet Coburn	"	20th "	"
Jabez Kingsley	"	30 "	deserted
John Cary	"	1 March	"
Jonathan Hill	"	1 "	"
Benjamin Shelden	"	15 Feb[y]	"
Benony Dick	Seaman	15 "	"
Philip Chuish	Landsman	3 May	"
Charles Freeman	"	6 "	deserted
James French	Seaman	15 Feb[y]	"
Jeremiah Bailey	"	7 May	"
John Baldwin	"	7 "	"
Samuel Ovit	"	7 "	"
Jonah Wells	"	7 "	"
William Buggee	Landsman	6 "	deserted
Jonah Malbone	"	11 "	"
Richmond Crandel	"	15 April	"
James Burnham	Seaman	15 "	"
Jacob Fobs	"	1 May	"
Charles White	Boatswains Mate	9 "	"
Willet Carpender	Landsman	9 "	"

Carried to another sheet.
[The other sheet is missing.]

[*State Library, Revolution 31.*]

Pay List for Ship Oliver Cromwell Tim[o] Parker Esq[r] Commander

John Richards	Seaman	9 May 1779	to 26 July	died
Zebulon Cooper	Landsman	10 "	to 23 Aug	
Cruttendon Ward	Seaman	15 Feb[y]	to "	
Benj[n] Fuller	Landsman	20 Jan[y]	to "	
William Satterlee	Seaman	14 May	to "	
Thomas Stanton	Quarter-master	28 April	to 7 June	killed
Daniel Stanton 2[d]	Landsman	10 May	to 23 Aug.	
Daniel Stanton 3[d]	"	10 "	to "	

Charles Cheeseborough	Quarter-master	12 May	to 20 July died
William Billings	Landsman	12 "	to 23 Aug.
Daniel Curtis	Seaman	10 "	to "
Isaac Frisbee	"	1 Dec^{r}	to "
John Wellman	Landsman	15 Feby.	to "
Eben^{r} Robinson	Surgeons-Mate	5 May	to "
William Malone	Quarter-Master	15 "	to "
Benjn Dickerson	Landsman	15 "	to "
Abner Beebe	Seaman	15 "	to "
Michael Ewen	Quarter-master	16 "	to 6 June killed
Simon Pembleton	Landsman	16 "	to 23 Aug
John Pembleton	"	16 "	to "
Jedediah Morton	Seaman	1 April	deserted
Edward Barrett	"	26 May	to 23 Aug^{t}
John Moan	"	26 "	to "
Jabez Luce	Landsman	28 "	to "
William Aborn	Quarter Gunner	28 "	deserted
Frederick Niles	Seaman	28 "	to 23 Aug.
Simeon Starkweather	Landsman	28 "	to "
Rufus Gardener	"	28 "	to "
Retrieve Moore	Seaman	26 "	to "
Eliphalet Covel	"	29 "	to "
Michael Holland	"	29 "	to "
Joseph Curtis	Landsman	25 "	to "
John Walton	Seaman	29 "	to "
Thomas Larkam	"	29 "	to "
Norman Bunce	"	29 "	to "
Daniel Clark	"	29 "	deserted
William Young	Landsman	29 "	"
Conklin Shadin	"	21 "	to 23 Aug^{t}
William Otis	"	31 "	to "
Pharoh Sharper	"	31 "	to "
Thomas Sprigs	"	31 "	deserted
Isaac Heard	"	31 "	to 23 Aug^{t}
Guardin Wyyaung	Seaman	31 "	to "
Daniel Winfield	"	31 "	deserted
Simon Ray Ward	Midshipman	20 "	to 23 Aug^{t}
Eben^{r} Colfax	"	1 June	to "
John Chatfield	Pilote	30 May	to "
Thomas Hancock	Seaman	1 June	to "
Guy Palms	"	1 "	died 10 July
James Jeffery	Landsman	1 "	to 23 Aug^{t}
Thomas Bolles 3^{d}	"	1 "	to "
William Fuller	"	20 Jany.	to "
Bristow Palmer	"		deserted
Clement Miner	"	15 May	to 23 Aug^{t}

[*State Library, Revolution 31.*]

The following persons signed receipts for wages for service on board the Ship of War Oliver Cromwell.

William Lamb
John Chatfield
Hutchins Boden
Daniel Hillard
John Whittelsey

Dominioque Tawzin was taken prisoner and put on board prison ship at New York.

[*Connecticut Historical Society.*]

PENSIONERS.

HALF PAY.

[This and the following list are condensed from several lists by omitting all but a single reference to each name.]

The United States D^r To the State of Connecticut for disbursements for half pay for Troops wounded in the service of the United States Agreeably to Act of Congress August 26th 1776.

Bills & Accounts	Remarks
Serj^t Thomas Farnham	Col. C. Webbs Reg^t
Serj^t Nathan Smith	Col. S. Sheldons " Dragoons
John Rood	Col. G. S. Sillimans "
Joel Ives Jr.	Col. Andrew Wards "
Benj^a Denslow	Col. Thad^s Cooks "
Stephen Fellows	Col. Burrells "
Simeon Mills	Col. Burrells " '76
Lt Elnathan Nichols	Danbury Alarm
Joseph Matson or Mattison	Col. Thad^s Cooks Reg^t
Salmon Buell	Danbury Alarm
Serj^t Lothrop Davis	Col. Starrs Reg^t, 1st Conn.
Artemas Johnson	Col. Woosters "
Justus Johnson	Danbury Alarm
William Edmonds	"
Stephen Everts	Col. Warners Reg^t
John Hutchinson	1st Conn "
Seth Boardman	Col. Thad^s Cooks "
Lemuel Demming	Col. Huntingtons "
Moses Raymond	Col. Saml Whitings "
Lt Thomas Avery	Col. Huntingtons "
Elijah Lincoln	Col. Swifts "
John Chilson	Col. Charles Webbs "
William Lucas	Col. Meigs "
Lt David Williams	Danbury Alarm
Nathaniel Church	Col. G. S. Sillimans Reg^t
William Tarball	Col. Durkees "
Ransford A. Ferris	Danbury Alarm
James St John	Col. Bradleys Reg^t
William Burrus	Col. S. B. Webbs "
Stephen Fellows	Col. Burrells " '76

Bills & Accounts	Remarks
William Edmonds	Danbury Alarm
Isaac Richards	Col. Stephen St Johns Reg^t
Ozias Goodwin	Express Danbury Al^m
Lieu^t Aaron Kelcey	Col. Thad^s Cooks Reg^t
Isaac Trowbridge	Danbury Alarm
John Crane	"
Ezra Willcox	Col. Thad^s Cooks Reg^t
Amos Gray	Danbury Alarm
Nathaniel Austin	Col. Thad^s Cooks Reg^t
Seth Johnson	"
Serj^t Jeremiah Markham . . .	"
Roswell Franciss	"
Jonathan Bowen	"
E. & J. Sheldon	"
Levy Peck	Danbury Al^m Sheldons Reg^t
Asa Tyler	Col. John Chesters "
Joseph Mix for his son . . .	5th Connec^t "
Richard Watrous	6th " "

[*Comptroller's Office.*]

The United States D^r To the State of Connecticut for disbursements for half pay for Troops Wounded in the service of the State of Connecticut agreeably to Act of Assembly passed May 1777

Bills & Accounts	Reg^ts to which they belonged
Josiah Smith . .	Col. N. Hookers Reg^t
Thomas Bristol . .	Col. Thad^s Cooks "
Lent Ives . . .	Col. M. Meads " or Col. John Meads
Constant Webb . .	Col. M. Meads "
George Lord . . .	Col. M. Meads " or Col. John Meads
Zacheus or Zachariah Fargo	Militia N. London; Col. J. Lattimer's Reg^t
Lemuel King . . .	Col. Wells's Reg^t
Wait Hinkley . .	Capt Miels C^o
David Squier . . .	Fairfield Battery
William Osborne . .	Capt D. Leavensworths C^o
Justin Jennings . .	Brig Defence
Ens^n And^w Mead . .	Capt Fitchs C^o
Benj^a Close . . .	Capt Fitchs C^o
William Hodge . .	Col. N. Hookers Reg^t
Tim^y Bassett . . .	2^d Militia "
Amos Mix . . .	Col John Meads "

[*Comptroller's Office.*]

CIVIL LIST.

Names &c. of Connecticut soldiers entitled by reason of wounds or disabilities recieved in service to be placed upon the pension list

[The names here given are those not found in the pension list printed in Record of Connecticut Men in Revolution.]

	Town from	Served in
John Williams		
Nathan Ellis		1st Conn. Reg.
Lewis Hurd		3d Conn. Reg.
Sherman Gardner		Invalid Corps.
Benoni Conel		"
Richard P. Hallow		"
Aaron Wilder		"
Albert Bowman		5th Conn. Reg.
Lemuel Rich		Invalid Corps.
John Kelly		"
Theophilus Mead		8th Conn. Reg.
Jirah Carter		2d Conn. Reg.
Edward Benton		Invalid Corps.
Richard Finney		3d Conn. Reg.
Benjamin Denslow	Suffield	Militia under Col. Thaddeus Cook [lass
Roswell Parish	Canterbury	Militia under Col. John Doug-
Lent Ives	Bristol	Col. Matthew Mead's Reg.
Lemuel Deming Jr.	East Hartford	Col. Huntington's Reg.
Isaac Finch	Stratford	Col. Samuel B. Webb's Reg.
Wiat Hinckley	Stonington	Gen. Waterbury's Brigade.
Stephen Hemstead	New London	Col. Webbs Reg.; Militia, 1781.
Benjamin Close	Greenwich	Independent Co.
Stephen Everts	Salisbury	Col. Warner's Reg.
William Edmond	Woodbury	Col. Increase Moseley's Reg.
Elnathan Nichols	Stratford	Gen. Arnold's Horse
Selah Scofield	Stamford	Col. Charles Webb's Reg.
Thomas Avery	Groton	1st Conn. Reg.
John Rood	New Milford	Col. Silliman's Reg.
Grant Johnson	Stratford	Col. Heman Swift's Reg.
John Herren or Herron	Lyme	1st Conn. Reg.
Park Avery Jr.	Groton	Militia
Robert Gallup	Groton	Fort Griswold
John Starr	Groton	Militia
Solomon Stark	Groton	Col. Lattimers Militia
Jabez Pembleton	Groton	Militia [Reg.
Joseph Waterman	Norwich	Gen. Jedediah Huntington's
Elisha Burrows	Groton	Col. John Ely's Reg.
Samuel Mills Jr.	Norfolk	Col. Charles Burrall's Reg.
William Barrows	Killingley	Col. Samuel B. Webb's Reg.
Lemuel Deming	East Hartford	
Oliver Bennitt		Invalid Corps
John Starr		

[*Comptroller's Office.*]

SCHEDULE OF PENSIONERS.

[Copied from a "Letter from the Secretary of War, communicating a transcript of the pension list of the United States —— June 1, 1813 —— Washington. 1813."]

No. on the Roll	Names	Rank or Quality	Annual Stipend
1	Thomas Avery	lieutenant	$200
2	Park Avery, Junior	"	60
3	Ebenezer Avery	corporal	30
4	David Atkins	private	60
5	Gad Asher	"	60
6	Abner Andruss	"	60
7	Daniel Avery	"	36
8	Amos Avery 2d	"	30
9	Theodore Andruss	"	60
10	Samuel Andrus	corporal	45
11	Smith Ames	private	60
12	Nathaniel Austin	"	45
13	Daniel Bouton	captain	180
14	Oliver Bostwick	ensign	120
15	Daniel Bushnell	private	60
16	Simeon Bishop	"	60
17	Salmon Buell	"	(dead)
18	William Burrows	"	60
19	Daniel Bill	"	60
20	Isaiah Bunce	"	45
21	Stephen Barnum	"	60
22	Samuel Burdwin	"	60
23	Benjamin Bennett	"	24
24	John Beardsley, junior	"	60
25	Jedediah Brown	"	20
26	Elisha Burrows	"	15
27	Isaiah Beaumont	"	15
28	Walter Burdick	"	30
29	Edward Bassett	"	30
30	William Bailey	"	30
31	Robert Bailey	"	15
32	Enos Blakesley	"	(dead)
33	David Blackman	"	40
34	Jonathan Bowers	corporal	60
35	Aner Bradley	sergeant	30
36	Oliver Burnham	"	15
37	Isaiah Buell	private	45
38	Joseph Button	"	60
39	Seth Boardman	"	40
40	William C. Beebe	"	60
41	Ebenezer Coe	captain	240
42	Richard Chamberlain	private	44
43	John Clark	"	60
44	Matthew Cadwell	"	60

No. on the Roll	Names	Rank or Quality	Annual Stipend
45	Benoni Connell	private	$60
46	Jirah Carter	"	60
47	Timothy Ceasar	"	60
48	Benjamin Close	"	48
49	Amariah Chappell	"	24
50	Elisha Clark	"	30
51	Jonah Cook	"	60
52	Henry Cone	"	60
53	Simon Crósby	"	40
54	Nathaniel Church	"	30
55	Ebenezer Duran	"	60
56	George Dixon	"	60
57	Lemuel Denning, junior	"	20
58	Lothrop Davis	sergeant	60
59	Israel Dibble	private	30
60	Gershom Dormon	"	60
61	Joseph Dunbar	corporal	45
62	John Daboll	private	7.50
63	Stephen Everts	"	40
64	William Edmonds	"	40
65	Eliphalet Easton	"	60
66	Gideon Edwards	"	60
67	Stephen Fellows	sergeant	60
68	Thomas Farnham	"	36
69	John Fountaine	private	60
70	Aaron Farmar	"	60
71	Isaac Frink	"	60
72	Ransford A. Ferris	"	60
73	Zaccheus Fargo	"	30
74	Henry Filmore	"	30
75	Samuel French	"	60
76	Andrew Griswold	lieutenant	160
77	Sherman Gardner	private	60
78	Henry Gilner	"	60
79	Andrew Gallup	"	40
80	Robert Gallup	"	15
81	Richard P. Hallow	"	60
82	Jazaniah How	"	60
83	Stephen Hull	corporal	30
84	Joseph Harrup	private	60
85	Stephen Hempstead	"	45
86	Nero Hawley	"	40
87	Isec Hayt	"	30
88	John Herron	"	30
89	Eleazer Hudson	"	45
90	Ashbel Hosmer	corporal	(dead)
91	Nathan Hawley	"	48
92	Daniel Hewitt	sergeant	20
93	Isaac Higgins	private	(dead)
94	Thurston Hilliard	"	20
95	John Horsford	"	(dead)
96	Benjamin Howd	"	45
97	Elijah Hoyt	"	30
98	David Hubbell	"	60
99	Nathaniel Hewitt	"	45
100	Joel Hinman	"	60
101	David Hurd	"	60

No. on the Roll	Names	Rank or Quality	Annual Stipend
102	Charles Jones	private	$60
103	Justus Johnson	"	40
104	Johuel Judd	"	48
105	Lent Ives	"	30
106	Caleb Jewett	"	20
107	William Johnson	"	30
108	Jared Knapp	sergeant	60
109	Lemuel King	private	60
110	Elisha Lee	captain	240
111	Peter Lewis	private	60
112	Phinehas Lake	"	60
113	William Leach	"	60
114	Christopher Latham, junior	"	45
115	John Ledyard	"	45
116	Naboth Lewis	"	40
117	Nathaniel Lewis	"	15
118	Samuel Lewis	corporal	45
119	Lee Lay	captain	80
120	Elijah Lincoln	corporal	60
121	Timothy Mix	lieutenant	60
122	Andrew Mead	ensign	80
123	Dan Mansfield	private	(dead)
124	Samuel Mitchell	"	60
125	Samuel Mills, junior	"	30
126	John Morgan 3d	"	40
127	Jacob Meach	"	20
128	James Morgan, junior	"	30
129	Joseph Moxley	"	30
130	Jeremiah Markham	sergeant	60
131	Allyn Marsh	corporal	30
132	Stephen Miner	qr. gunner	30
133	Elnathan Norton	private	(dead)
134	Mark Noble	"	60
135	David Orcutt	"	60
136	Joseph Otis	"	30
137	Thomas Picket	"	60
138	Alexander Phelps	"	60
139	David Pool	"	60
140	Thomas Parmelie	sergeant	7.50
141	Chandler Pardie	private	52.50
142	Daniel Preston	"	20
143	Obadiah Perkins	lieutenant	96
144	Enos Petott	private	24
145	John Rood	"	48
146	Jeremiah Ryan	"	60
147	Lemuel Rich	"	(transfd)
148	Moses Raymond	"	60
149	Oliver Rogers	"	24
150	David Ranney	"	60
151	Solomon Reynolds	"	60
152	Samuel Rossetter	"	60
153	Elijah Royce	"	45
154	Josiah Smith	"	60
155	Edward Stanton	"	60
156	Josiah Strong	"	40
157	John Starr	"	40
158	Selah Scoffield	"	30

No. on the Roll	Names	Rank or Quality	Annual Stipend
159	William Seymour	private	$240
160	Benjamin Seely	"	15
161	William Starr	qr. master	45
162	Elihu Sabin	private	40
163	Samuel Sawyer	"	30
164	Thomas Shepherd	"	15
165	Amos Skeel	"	60
166	Heber Smith	sergeant	60
167	Aaron Smith	private	15
168	Edmund Smith	"	30
169	Samuel Stillman	"	30
170	Aaron Stephens	captain	120
171	Peter Smith	private	48
172	Elijah Sheldon	"	(dead)
173	John Smith	"	48
174	Moses Tracy	sergeant	60
175	William Tarball	corporal	36
176	Solomon Townsend	private	60
177	Aaron Tuttle	"	40
178	Jabez Tomlinson	"	15
179	Enoch Turner, junior	"	60
180	Levi Tuttle	"	15
181	Samuel Woodcock	sergeant	60
182	Constant Webb.	"	36
183	William Wilson	private	60
184	John Waklee	"	60
185	Joseph Waterman	"	40
186	Benjamin Weed, junior	"	60
187	Joseph Woodmansee	"	60
188	Thomas Williams	"	20
189	Jacob Williams	"	15
190	Richard Watrous	"	45
191	Jonathan Whaley	"	15
192	Ezra Wilcox	"	15
193	Azel Woodworth	"	60
194	Seth Weed	lieutenant	72
195	James Wayland	private	40
196	William Woodruff	corporal	60
197	Hezekiah Bailey	ensign	60
198	Isaac Durand	private	30
199	Joel Fox	"	30
200	Luke Guyant	"	60
201	Aaron Peck	"	40
	Total of annual stipends		9778.50

APPENDIX

[Here are included several rolls received too late for insertion in their proper place, one that was omitted in arranging the material at hand, and a few individual records and miscellaneous items.]

THIRD BATTALION—COL. ENOS.

See Page 141.

[*See Record of Connecticut Men in the Revolution, page 424.*]

CAPT. GRISWOLD'S COMPANY.

The Marching Roll of Capt. Griswold's Company, March 4, 1777.

From Torrington

John Burr
Seth Coe
Charles Roberts
Ambrose Fyler
Jonathan Miller
Asaph Atwater
John Birge
Isaac Filley
Timothy Loomis
Ebenezer Bissell
Return Bissell

From Litchfield

Stephen Smith
Gideon Philips
Abel Catlin
Simeon Ross
Timothy Gibbs
Benjamin Stone
Ashbel Catlin
Calvin Bissell
Benjamin Palmer
John Way
Abner Baldwin
Philemon Wilcox
Solomon Linsley

From Torrington

Daniel Winchell
Frederick Bigelow
Cotton Mather
Benjamin Frisbie
Thomas Skinner
Nathaniel Barber
Timothy Kelsey
Thomas Matthews
Stephen Rossiter
Elisha Kelsey

From Litchfield

John Woodruff
Enoch Sperry
Dyer Cleaveland
Enos Bains
Solomon Harrison
Harris Hopkins
Timothy Linsley
Joel Taylor
John Bissell
Solomon Woodruff
Philo Woodruff
Simeon Gibbs
Bela Benton

From Cornwall
John Mebbins
Samuel Burton
Josiah Hopkins
Asahel Leet
Solomon Johnson
Henry Philemor
Samuel Emmons
Israel Dibble

From Cornwall
Thomas White
Elisha Demmen
James Wadsworth
Joshua Hartshorn
Noah Harrison
Asa Emmons
Jonathan Bell
Simeon North

[*Dwight C. Kilbourne, Litchfield.*]

FIRST REGIMENT—MAJ. NEWBERRY.

See Page 149.

[*See Record of Connecticut Men in the Revolution, page 449.*]

FOURTH COMPANY—LIEUT. SEYMOUR.

August 14 1776. Received of Maj^r^ Newbury for advance money Towards wages £67 : 0 :

15 : Marcht with 58 men including officers towards New York
16 Set sail from New Haven upon our way to New York
16 Arived att Newyork late 7 o'clock.

Hartford August 15, 1776.

Ebenezer Belding	£1.00	Gideon Butler J^un^	£1.00
Willm Hopkins	1.00	Ruben Judd	1.00
Jon^th^ Sidgwick	1.00	Sam^ll^ Merrill	1.00
Elizer Merrill	1.00	Ashbel Hosmer	1.00
Peter King	1.00	Ashbel Wells	1.00
Rosseter Belding	1.00	Jon^th^ B. Balch	1.00
Elisha Mix	1.00	Joseph Brown	1.00
Oliver Kellogg	1.00	Ashbel Shepard	1.00
Noah Butler J^r^	1.00	Asa Goodman	1.00
Jon^th^ Gilbert	1.00	Gideon Merrill	1.00
Ebenezer Seymour	1.00	Nath^ll^ Braman	1.00
Richard Chapley	1.00	James Wadsworth	1 00
Francis Smith	1.00	Moses Brace	1.00
Ebenezer Merry	1.00	Ichabod Lyman	1.00
Willm Whiting	1.00	Sam^ll^ Stanly	1.00
Joel Lord	1.00	John Nott	1.00
Richard Goodman	1.00	Elihu Olmsted	1.00
Ens^n^ George Kellogg	1.00	Thos Olmsted	1.00
Isaac Webster	1.00	Sam^ll^ Holmes	1.00
Joseph Butler		Henry Brace	1.00
Aaron Seymour	1.00	John Nash	1.00
John Spencer	1.00	Isaac Flower	1.00
Aaron Cadwell J^un^.	1.00	Eben^r^ Faxon	1.00
George Bidwell	1.00	Eben^r^ Crosby	1.00
Enos Kellogg	1.00	Zach Kelsey	1.00
Stephen Skiner	1.00	John Wells J^un^	1.00
Jeduthan Cadwell	1.00	Moses Gaylord	1.00
Joseph Cadwell	1.00	Thos Faxon	1.00
Aaron Cadwell	1.00	Solomon Ensign	1.00

[There is an attestation in the book, signed by Sally S. Mills, stating that the within Document was a Journal and Roll of 58 men who served under her deceased Father, Charles Seymour, who was a Lieutenant in the army of the Revolution, and was found by her among his papers—dated January 26, 1837.]

[*Mary K. Talcott, Hartford.*]

TENTH REGIMENT—COL. COOK.

See Page 183.

CAPT. NORTON'S COMPANY.

List of those going to R. I under Command of Capt Charles Norton Aug 23 1778

Nathan Chittenden Serg[t]
Joseph Hall
Peter Peck
Liut James Peck
Jonathan Bartholomew
Benj Chittenden
John Lewis
Ward Johnson
Josiah Tuttle
Oliver Doolittle
Saml Barns
Saml Mattoon
Asahel Hull
Joseph Curtes Jr
Giles Cook

[*George M. Curtis, Meriden.*]

TENTH REGIMENT—COL. COOK.

See Page 203.

LIST OF MEN DETACHED.

Appraizal of Guns &c belonging to Cap Oliver Stanley Comp. for those detached June 13 1779

Roswell Beach
Moses Bartholomew
Ens Saml Culver
Dowey Daily
in the Room of Dan Peck

Of those belonging to Cap Miles Johnsons Company Same time

Isaac Kirtland
Leml Cook
Giles Churchill
Hine (?) Munson
Jesse Rice
Saml Barns
went in Rices Room

Appointment of Horses Arms & Acq. of a Number draughted from Cap Isaac Halls Compy of Troop Hill Hall 2d Master

Lent Hough — David Morgan

Appraizal of Guns &c belonging Capt Abraham Stanleys Company for those detached to go to Greenwich 13th June 1779

Reuben Horsford — Beri Tuttle
Ichabod Barns — Charles Johnson
Joel Doolittle — Enos Benham Jr
Chas Preston — in room of Wm Atwater

Of those belonging to Capt Thos Shephards Company Same time

Amos Johnson — Jacob Curtis
Amos Merriman — Thos Andrus
Edw. Fenn Jr

Of those belonging to Capt Caleb Hall Same time

Danl Merwin — Enos (?) Benham
Stephen Johnson — Saml Rice
David Barns — in room of Josiah Mix

Recd of the Selectmen out of the Town Stock each of us half a pound Powder & sixteen Balls being detached to go to Greenwich 16th June 1779

P us Simon Frances
Buller Ives

Wallingford

Appraisment of Arms &c Carried by men detached Aug 20 1779 from Capt John Houghs 2 Months Men

Jonathan Blakesley hired by Abner Way — Simeon Perkins
Ens Thos Foster — Osias Foster in the room of Tim Foster
Asahel Yale in the room of Noah Yale — Enos Hall
Isral Hall

Capt Thos Shepards Company

Robert Grannis — Jonth Francis

Capt Ephraim Cooks Company

Elisha Wilmot — Josiah Talmadge Jr
Gideon Curtes — Thos Gaylord
Robert Hotchkiss

Capt Abraham Stanleys Comp

Joel Hough — Zebulon Dudley hired by Cabb Merriman

Capt Divan Berrys Comp

Daniel Baldwin

[*George M. Curtis, Meriden.*]

SEVENTH REGIMENT—COL. WORTHINGTON.

See Page 215.

SECOND COMPANY—LIEUT. LEE.

[Guilford men summoned to serve as Sea Coast Guard at Sachem's Head, Guilford.]

Guilford February the 19th 1781

According to the within Writ I Have Summonsed the Following men to Guard under Lieut Saml Lee Viz Thelus Ward Jur Caleb Everts for Six Days Friend Collins Wm Barker John Leet Nehemiah Bradley Levy Lee Jared Bishop Nathan Redfield Wilmot Goldsmith Saml Everts Jur Isaac Parmele Thomas Griswold Jur John Wick Sineus Dibble Reuben Shelley James Davis Jur Joel Collens For three Days Each

John Starr Constable of Guilford

In addition to the Above I have summonsd the following Persons to guard Namely Asael Murry Timothy Lee Eber Hall James Davis Junr Russel (?) Stone James Bradley Joel Johnson Benjamin Hall Jur Joel Parmele Isaac Parmele Thomas Griswold Jur Levy Lee Treat Demming Reuben Shelly Medad Shelly John Leet Samuel Cruttenden Reuben Fowler John Stone Samuel Roberson Jur John Johnson Jur James Bradley William Barker Caleb Evarts Each of these garded three Days A Peace & James Bradley Six Days

[*E. C. Starr, Cornwall.*]

SHORT LEVIES, 1782.

The following names appear in account and receipt books among many names already in print:

Names	Service	Regiment
Rufus Hide	July 1 to Nov. 8	
Neal McClean . . .	May 21 to Dec. 6	
John Miller	June 8 to Dec. 3	3d
Phineas Perkins . . .	Apr. 30 to Sep. 21	
Mark Hamlin . . .		1st Conn.
Thomas Binge . . .		"
Joel Buckley . . .		Baldwins Artificers
Phineas Platt . . .		"

[*Comptroller's Office.*]

MISCELLANEOUS.

Justice Warner, Josiah Warner, Mark Warner & Timothy Scouval, where all Disafected Persons in Confinment, and Inlisted into the Service During the War, and Remaining disafected twas thought most Proper, for the good of the Service, they should procure Good men in their Stead, and Accordingly they Procured, William Heacock, Samuel Pribble, Patrick Snow, and Tabor Smith, and where accordingly Discharged.

[*State Library, Hebard Papers.*]

Rec[d] March 15th 1779 of Silvanus Starling one of the Select men of Stratford Fifty seven Pounds 12/ Shillings Lawful money which is in full for my Services and the persons under my Command in keeping Guard at North Fairfield In april 1777 Rec[d]

P Stephen Middlebrook

[*Louis F. Middlebrook, Hartford.*]

To whom concern[d] permit the bearer Thomas Sharp of Newtown to pass unmolested to Stamford or Hors Neck and there joyn the Company Detached from Colo[l] Bordleys Regt

pr Jabez Botsford J of peace

Newtown January ye 9 1781

[*William C. Sharpe, Seymour.*]

ADDITIONS FROM RECORD OF CONNECTICUT MEN IN THE REVOLUTION.

[The following is taken from the official copy in the Adjutant-General's office.]

Page 9 For Thomas Tuder, read Daniel Tudor.
" 45 Ambrose Church died in service Aug. 22.
" " Stephen Ackley died Oct. 1.
" " Bethuel Fuller died Sep. 23.
" " Timothy Fuller died Oct. 17.
" 46 For John Mash, read John Mack.
" " Giles Gilbert died Sep. 22.
" " Moses Olmsted died Sep. 26, of East Haddam.
" 48 For William Ston (?), read William Stowe.
" 85 Phineas Lyman Tracy died Aug. 22.
" 89 For Abraham Filer, read Abraham Tyler.
" 109 Robert Sumner of Ashford in Capt. Daniel Allen's Co., Col. Ward's Regt.
" 326 Capt. Billings' Company; add, Caleb Bailey, Haddam, enlisted June 24, 1781, for 6 months.
" 345 For John Mash, read John Mack.

Page 471 Eli Moore also served as a private and Adjutant in Col. Roger Enos' regiment. His name appears on an abstract of rations due for the period from Oct. 3 to Nov. 15, 1777—served as Adjutant 1st Connecticut regiment, commanded by Col. Roger Enos, joined June 25, 1778, name borne on the roll dated at Fort Clinton, Sept. 5, 1778.

" 501 Capt. Camp's Company; for Time of Marching, April 29, read March 29.

" " Capt. Stoddard's Company; for Time of Marching, May 30, read March 30. Also same correction on the following page.

" 553 Hezekiah Bassett and Medad Atwater were both members 17th New Haven Company State Militia, British Invasion of New Haven, 1779.

" 611 Capt. Amos Smith, Washington, Conn., Captain of Artillery Co., State Militia, carpenter and farmer.

" 636 Absolom Pride, private Capt. Ebenezer Brewtsers Co., Col. Parsons Regt., from Oct. 1775 to Dec. 1776, in battles of Long Island, New York Island and Harlem Heights.

" 663 For John Mash, read John Mack.

" 664 For David Shepard, read Daniel Shepard.

ERRATA.

Page 12. Transpose lines 12 and 13, beginning with word Officers.

Page 66. For Simcom Robertson, read Simeon Robertson.

Page 87. Line 13, for May 13, 1779, read May 13, 1777; line 17, for Michael Jenson, read Michael Jerison; line 19, for Oct. 6, read Oct. 1.

Page 165. For Wllliam Kinney, read William Kinney.

INDEX.

Alderman, Eli, 142, 164.
Alderman, Ephriem, 27.
Alderman, Isaac, 164.
Alderman, John, 164.
Alderman, Jonathan, Jr., 142.
Aldich, John, Jr., 1.
Alexander, James, 51.
Alford, Eliphelet, 36.
Alford, John, 36.
Alford, Peletiah, 119.
Alger, Asa, 65.
Allen, Amasa, 25.
Allen, Benjamin, 152.
Allen, C., 211.
Allen, Daniel, 14, 46, 88, 212, 278.
Allen, Daniel, Jr., 14.
Allen, David, 14, 55.
Allen, Ebenezer, 28, 262.
Allen, Eliphalet, 69, 99.
Allen, Isak, 164.
Allen, Jared, 143, 159.
Allen, Jerard, 259.
Allen, John, 212, 221, 222, 230.
Allen, Jonathan, 88.
Allen, Joseph, 105, 259.
Allen, Joseph, Jr., 105.
Allen, Martin, 39.
Allen, Moses, 54, 127.
Allen, Nathaniel, 184.
Allen, Phineas, 19.
Allen, Robert, 45.
Allen, Samuel, 57, 163, 189.
Allen, Silas, 169.
Allen, Thomas, 99.
Allen, Timothy, 161.
Allen, Titus, 43.
Allen, William, 14, 66, 240, 247, 248.
Allien, Benjamin, 1.
Allien, Christopher, 1.
Allin, Daniel, 57.
Allin, Gabril, 232.
Allin, Gideon, 233.
Allin, William, 14.
Alling, Caleb, 179.
Alling, Elenzoer, 235.
Allyn, 123.
Allyn, Amos, 216.
Allyn, Benjamin, 222.
Allyn, Chester, 23.
Allyn, David, 216.
Allyn, Elisha, 80.
Allyn, Ephraim, 216.
Allyn, John, 121, 209.
Allyn, Moses, 95, 117.
Allyn, Thomas, 146, 147.
Allyn, Timothy, 50.
Allyn, Titus, 41.
Allyn, William, 244.
Almey, John, 63.
Almstead, Benjamin, 235.
Almy, William, 82.
Alton, William, 184.
Alvord, Huet, 61.
Amadown, Moses, 184.
Ambler, Jonathan, 68.
Amedown, Jedediah, 208.
Amedown, Jonathan, 55.
Ames, 56.
Ames, Alvin, 28.
Ames, Arcules, 125.
Ames, Benjamin, 191.
Ames, Ezra, 58, 59, 60.
Ames, John, 64.
Ames, Nicholas, 134.
Ames, Samuel, 29, 82, 237.
Ames, Samuel, Jr., 31.
Ames, Smith, 268.
Ames, Zebulon, 74.
Amidown, Jedidiah, 14.
Ammidown, Jedediah, 14.
Ammit, John, 54.
Anderson, George, 14.
Anderson, James, 122, 253.
Anderson, Stephen, 14.
Anderson, Steven, 14.
Anderson, Thomas, 14, 45, 185.
Anderson, Timothy, 78.
Anderson, William, 68, 185.
Andras, Joseph, 59.
Andras, Obadiah, 59.
Andress, Samuel, 1.
Andrews, Andrew, 71.
Andrews, David, 115.
Andrews, James, 46.
Andrews, Jeremiah, 85.
Andrews, John, 198.
Andrews, John, Jr., 152.
Andrews, Joseph, 153.
Andrews, Samuel, 95, 153.
Andrews, Timothy, 242.
Andrews, William, 7.
Andrews, William, Jr., 142.
Androus, Philarman, 185.
Androus, Samuel, 117.
Andrus, Asahel, Jr., 142.
Andrus, David, 99.
Andrus, Eden, 199.
Andrus, Eli, 36.
Andrus, Elijah, 127, 128, 202.
Andrus, Frederick, 263.
Andrus, James, 155.
Andrus, John, 138.
Andrus, Jonathan, 142.
Andrus, Joseph, 80.
Andrus, Nathan, 32.

Andrus, Samuel, 127, 155, 257, 268.
Andrus, Thomas, 19, 276.
Andrus, Timothy, 9.
Andruss, Abner, 268.
Andruss, Asa, 20.
Andruss, Benjiman, 157.
Andruss, Charles, 157.
Andruss, David, 157.
Andruss, John, 157.
Andruss, Stephen, 157, 158.
Andruss, Theodore, 268.
Andruss, Timothy, 77.
Andruss, William, 27, 88.
Anger, George, 68.
Annable, Anthony, 212.
Annew, David, 216.
Annibal, David, 16.
Answorth, Ahial, 66.
Anthony, John, 88, 239.
Antony, James, 80.
Antrum, Thomas, 168.
Apley, Josiah, 98.
Armstrong, Peter, 34.
Armstrong, William, 100.
Arnold, 267.
Arnold, Benedict, 23.
Arnold, Henery, 244.
Arnold, Henry, 247, 248.
Arnold, James, 17, 18, 19, 20, 22, 193, 209, 223.
Arnold, John, 162, 183, 221.
Arnold, Jonathan, 244, 248.
Arnold, Josiah, 22.
Arnold, Samuel, 184.
Arnould, Jonathan, 247.
Arons, Benedick, 150.
Arrabas, Jack, 115.
Arthur, Barthilmus, 186.
Arthur, Bartholemew, 80.
Arvin, William, 27.
Asband, Sam, 233.
Ash, James, 262.
Ashcraft, John, 167.
Ashcraft, William, 167.
Asher, Gad, 268.
Ashford, 25, 55, 57, 65, 66, 79, 82, 88, 89, 104, 114, 130, 278.
Ashley, John, 69, 99.
Ashley, Joseph, 143.
Ashley, Samuel, 143.
Aspell, Philip, 230.
Aspenwall, Caleb, 39.
Atkins, David, 112, 268.
Atkins, Ira, 113.
Atkins, Isaac, 134.
Atkins, Isaiah, 113.
Atkins, Jabez, 107.
Atkins, Joel, 134.
Atterton, David, 168.
Atwater, 55.
Atwater, Abel W., 194.
Atwater, Asaph, 273.
Atwater, Caleb, 55.
Atwater, Medad, 279.
Atwater, William, 276.
Atwater, William, Jr., 194.
Atwell, Ozias, 27.
Atwood, John, 27.
Atwood, Joseph, 80.
Augru, Felix, 184.
Augur, Philemon, 9.
Ausborn, John, 56.
Austin, Aaron, 36.
Austin, Amos, 16, 17, 22.
Austin, Andrew, 202.
Austin, Benjamin, 20.
Austin, Caleb, 63, 173.
Austin, George, 170, 186.
Austin, James, 36, 209.
Austin, John, 174, 179.
Austin, Joseph, 46, 82.
Austin, Nathaniel, 266, 268.
Austin, Richard, 53.
Austin, Usebius, 36.
Austin, William, 94.
Averil, Daniel, 73.
Averil, Jacob, 64.
Averil, Jonathan, 174.
Averill, Jacob, 18.
Averill, James, 208.
Averill, Nathaniel, 18.
Averill, Thomas, 19, 23.
Avery, 50.
Avery, Amos, 2d, 268.
Avery, Benjamin, 38.
Avery, Christopher, 124.
Avery, Daniel, 82, 268.
Avery, Ebenezer, 120, 268.
Avery, Elijah, 208.
Avery, Frederick, 95.
Avery, Jabez, 17, 22.
Avery, John, 40, 53, 102, 130.
Avery, Jonathan, 14, 143.
Avery, Nathan, 174, 216.
Avery, Park, Jr., 267, 268.
Avery, Roger, 240.
Avery, Simeon, 45.
Avery, Sylvanus, 82.
Avery, Thomas, 88, 265, 267, 268.
Ayer, John, 94.
Ayers, John, 150.
Ayres, Peter, 185.

Babbit, Benjamin, 141.
Babcock, 150.

Babcock, Benjamin, 16.
Babcock, Elias, 184.
Babcock, Ephraim, 94.
Babcock, Isaiah, 197.
Babcock, John, 25.
Babcock, Jonathan, 105.
Babcock, Joseph, 210.
Babcock, Nathaniel, 185.
Babcock, Ruben, 171.
Babcock, Timothy, 169.
Baccus, Ebenezer, 250.
Baccus, John, 247, 249.
Back, Elisha, 114.
Backes, Isaac, 171.
Backus, Andrew, 168, 169.
Backus, Ebenezer, 246.
Backus, Elijah, 74, 208.
Backus, Nathaniel, 246, 248.
Backus, Stephen, 168.
Backus, Timothy, 169, 222.
Backus, Whighting, 149.
Bacon, 50, 64.
Bacon, Abner, 88.
Bacon, Andiew, 204.
Bacon, Asa, 142.
Bacon, Benjamin, 170.
Bacon, Ebenezer, 141.
Bacon, Henry, 69.
Bacon, J., 170.
Bacon, Joseph, 105, 209.
Bacon, Joseph, Jr., 141.
Bacon, Nathaniel, 67.
Bacon, S., 170.
Bacon, William, 28, 88, 107.
Badcock, 12.
Badcock, Beriah, 5.
Badcock, Daniel, 3, 4, 143, 161.
Badcock, Jonathan, 161.
Badger, Bezelial, 149.
Badger, Jonathan, 14.
Bagdon, Cesar, 71, 112.
Bagley, Bernard, 94.
Bagley, David, 244, 247.
Bagley, John, 251.
Baile, Hondrick, 121.
Bailey, Aaron, 74.
Bailey, Caleb, 98, 278.
Bailey, Ebenezer, 3, 4.
Bailey, Elijah, 115, 116.
Bailey, Gideon, 48, 88.
Bailey, Hezekiah, 46, 271.
Bailey, Ichabod, 114.
Bailey, Jeremiah, 263.
Bailey, John, 81, 245, 249.
Bailey, Joseph, 246.
Bailey, Louden, 68.
Bailey, Robert, 88, 268.
Bailey, Rouben, 230.
Bailey, Timothy, 230.
Bailey, Titus, 222.
Bailey, Uriah A., 35.
Bailey, William, 115, 268.
Bains, Enos, 273.
Bajcom, Abiel, 162.
Baker, Abel, 64.
Baker, Amos, 200.
Baker, Asa, Jr., 140.
Baker, Benjamin, 201.
Baker, Bristol, 108.
Baker, Edward, 108.
Baker, Eldad, 136.
Baker, Hezekiah, 245, 251.
Baker, John, 53, 140, 167, 258.
Baker, Jonas, 167.
Baker, Joseph, 172.
Baker, Joshua, 174.
Baker, Lemuel, 12.
Baker, Nathaniel, 185.
Baker, Palsey, 140.
Baker, Phinehas, 136.
Baker, Robert, 185.
Baker, Stephen, 64.
Baker, William, 57, 83.
Balcam, Nathaniel, 39.
Balch, Jonathan B., 274.
Balcom, Elias, 68.
Balden, Samuel, 231.
Baldwen, David, 35.
Baldwin, 224, 227, 277.
Baldwin, A., 142.
Baldwin, Aaron, 9.
Baldwin, Abel, 77, 81, 195.
Baldwin, Abial, 191.
Baldwin, Abner, 201, 273.
Baldwin, Benjamin, 210.
Baldwin, Caleb, 49, 88, 97, 198.
Baldwin, Daniel, 276.
Baldwin, David, 242.
Baldwin, Ebenezer, 257.
Baldwin, Eleazer, 97.
Baldwin, Eli, 38.
Baldwin, Elijah, 195.
Baldwin, Elisha, 74.
Baldwin, Henry, 88.
Baldwin, I., 212.
Baldwin, Isaac, 77.
Baldwin, J., 223, 224.
Baldwin, Jacob, 6.
Baldwin, Jered, 196.
Baldwin, John, 38, 200, 263.
Baldwin, Jonathan, 184, 212, 223, 224.
Baldwin, Joseph, 183.
Baldwin, Josiah. 210.
Baldwin, Levi, 9.
Baldwin, Nathaniel, 81.

Barnum, Ephraim, 208.
Barnum, Ezra, 85.
Barnum, John, 85, 121, 198.
Barnum, John, Jr., 198.
Barnum, Joseph, 86.
Barnum, Judah, Jr., 198.
Barnum, Lazerus, 199.
Barnum, Matthew, 98, 198.
Barnum, Nathaniel, 198, 200.
Barnum, Noah, 121.
Barnum, Richard, 200, 208.
Barnum, Samuel, 49.
Barnum, Stephen, 208.
Barnum, Thaddeus, 194.
Barnum, Zadock, 196.
Barret, Bartholomew, 41, 43.
Barret, Moses, 170.
Barrett, Amos, 197.
Barrett, Edward, 264.
Barrit, Epheriam, 184.
Barrit, Jeremiah, 68.
Barritt, Hilderick, 97.
Barrows, Caleb, 94, 127.
Barrows, Ethan, 143.
Barrows, Isaac, 57.
Barrows, Josiah, 59.
Barrows, Lemuel, 57.
Barrows, William, 267.
Barstow, Joseph, 6.
Barstow, Michael, 4.
Bartholemew, Jonathan, 225.
Bartholomew, Benjamin, 9.
Bartholomew, Gideon, 9.
Bartholomew, Isaac, 164.
Bartholomew, Jesse, 201.
Bartholomew, Jonathan, 275.
Bartholomew, Moses, 164, 275.
Bartholomew, Samuel, 255.
Bartholomew, William, 140.
Barthrong, Abraham, 37.
Bartlet, Edmond, Jr., 1.
Bartlet, Eliphas, 1, 165.
Bartlet, John, 160.
Bartlet, Joseph, Jr., 160.
Bartlet, Samuel, 1, 165, 193.
Bartlet, Silvanus, 203.
Bartlet, Stephen, 1.
Bartlit, Abram, 192.
Barton, James, 232.
Barton, Joseph, 87.
Barton, William, 87.
Bartram, Ebenezer, 233.
Bartram, Job, 180.
Bartram, Joseph, 232.
Bartrum, John, 32.
Bascomb, Elias, 105.
Basset, Nathan, 205.
Basset, William, 53, 102.
Bassett, Edward, 268.
Bassett, Hezekiah, 279.
Bassett, Isaac, 118.
Bassett, Samuel, 245.
Bassett, Samo, 251.
Bassett, Timothy, 266.
Bassett, William, 129.
Basson, John, 234.
Bassul, Hannibal, 64.
Bateman, Jacob, 68.
Bates, Amos, 237.
Bates, David, 76.
Bates, Ephraim, 103, 131.
Bates, Ezra, 69, 95.
Bates, Issachar, 211.
Bates, Lemuel, 203, 207.
Bates, Reuben, 22.
Bates, Waker, 84.
Bates, Zephaniah, 58.
Batt, John, 257.
Batter, Aby, 213.
Batterson, Abijah, 126.
Batterson, William, 152.
Battison, George, 233.
Battison, Joseph, 233.
Battson, Joseph, 213.
Bawdell, Benjamin, 57.
Bawdish, Asa, 186.
Bawldwin, Ambres, 183.
Baxter, Aaron, 94.
Baxter, Alexander, 119.
Baxter, Corn^{l}, 247.
Baxter, Cornelius, 249.
Baxter, David, 81.
Baxter, Francis, 58.
Baxter, Richard, 238.
Bayley, James, 182.
Bayley, Jeremy, 140.
Baylye, Joseph, 250.
Beach, Abijah, 127.
Beach, Agur, 85.
Beach, Asa, 32.
Beach, Ashbel, 20.
Beach, David, 48.
Beach, Eber, 21.
Beach, Elijah, 135.
Beach, Elisha, 159.
Beach, Elnathan, 55.
Beach, Isaac, 215.
Beach, Miles, 209, 225.
Beach, Nathaniel, 54, 121.
Beach, Noah, 164.
Beach, Reuben, 102, 129.
Beach, Reubin, 121.
Beach, Roswell, 94, 275.
Beach, Ruben, 54.
Beach, Stephen, 194.
Beach, Zophar, 201.

Beacher, Jonathan, 195.
Beacher, Joseph, 115.
Beacher, Nathan, 115, 116.
Beamis, John, 143.
Beamon, Truman, 201.
Beamont, Jonathan, 106, 127.
Beamont, Samuel, 3, 184.
Beamont, William, 38, 75.
Bean, John, 212.
Bearce, William, 23.
Beard, Elijah, 127.
Beard, Gideon, 190.
Beard, James, 189.
Beard, Samuel, 190.
Beardslee, Ben, 190.
Beardslee, Ebenezer, 190.
Beardslee, Henry, 181, 219.
Beardslee, John, 181, 219.
Beardslee, Lins, 190.
Beardslee, Nathan, 181, 219.
Beardslee, Stephen, 190.
Beardsley, Curtis, 151.
Beardsley, Gideon, Jr., 196.
Beardsley, John, Jr., 268.
Beardsley, N., 208, 225.
Beardsley, Nehemiah, 21, 23, 24, 25, 85, 194, 195, 196, 197, 198, 199, 200, 227.
Beardsley, P., 225.
Beardsley, Phinchas, 88.
Beardsly, 50.
Bearse, Elijah, 196.
Bearse, Joseph, 21, 196.
Bearse, Newcomb, 196.
Beaumont, Isaiah, 268.
Beaumont, William, 49.
Bebe, Edward, 233.
Bebee, Abner, 241.
Beby, Bazaliel, 246, 250.
Beckwith, Ezra, 57.
Beckwith, Guy, 28.
Beckwith, John, 55.
Beckwith, Lebbeus, 211.
Bedford, 200.
Bedient, Eleazor, 218.
Bedient, Mordica, 218.
Bedwell, James, 246.
Beebe, Abner, 140, 264.
Beebe, Asa, 134.
Beebe, Barzaleel, 252.
Beebe, Bazaliel, 227.
Beebe, Boanerges, 88.
Beebe, Christopher, 28.
Beebe, Ephraim, 28.
Beebe, Gideon, 28.
Beebe, Jabez, 212.
Beebe, James, 46.
Beebe, Joseph, 17.
Beebe, Paul, 28, 71.
Beebe, Reuben, 17.
Beebe, Thaddeus, 28.
Beebe, William C., 268.
Beebee, 123.
Beebie, Bosaleel, 260.
Beeby, Barzaleel, 247.
Beech, Ambrose, 39.
Beech, Amos, 202.
Beech, Brewin, 202.
Beech, Chancy, 203.
Beech, Francis, 202.
Beech, Israel, 39.
Beech, William, 22.
Beech, Zerah, 33.
Beecher, Amos, 209.
Beecher, Ashbel, 19.
Beecher, David, 211.
Beecher, Jesse, 179.
Beecher, John, 68.
Beecher, Jonathan, 19, 32.
Beecher, Joseph, 116.
Beecher, Nathaniel, 66, 213.
Beegbe, Moses, 66.
Beeman, Ezekiel, 213.
Beeman, Friend, 88.
Beeman, Jonathan, 88.
Beemas, Eph, 161.
Beemon, Samuel, 162.
Beers, Abner, 181, 219.
Beers, David, 86.
Beers, Elnathan, 85.
Beers, Ezekel, 195.
Beers, James, 254.
Beers, Jonathan, 152.
Beers, Johon, 151.
Beers, Joseph, 141.
Beers, Josiah, 181, 219, 254.
Beers, Nathan, 126.
Beers, Phineas, 152.
Beers, Riab, 152.
Beers, Stephan, 181.
Beers, Stephen, 219.
Belden, 223.
Belden, Moses, 153.
Belden, Thomas, 212, 224.
Belding, Abraham, 100.
Belding, Ebenezer, 274.
Belding, John, 109, 210.
Belding, Moses, 155.
Belding, Rosseter, 274.
Belding, Simeon, 47.
Belding, Thomas, 222.
Belknap, Francis, 1.
Belknap, Simeon, Jr., 165.
Bell, Asariah, 161.
Bell, Jesse, 210, 212.
Bell, John, 41, 43.

Bigelow, Eben, 153.
Bigelow, Eli, 58, 59.
Bigelow, Frederick, 273.
Bigelow, John, 33.
Bigelow, Joshua, 159.
Bigelow, Otis, 160.
Biggelow, Eli, 88.
Bigsby, Elias, 69.
Bill, 50.
Bill, Abial, 185.
Bill, Azariah, 41, 43.
Bill, Beriah, 63, 88.
Bill, Daniel, 16, 268.
Bill, Eleazer, 163.
Bill, Elijah, 202.
Bill, Gideon, 16.
Bill, John, 74.
Bill, Jonathan, 59.
Bill, Judah, 34.
Bill, Jude, 16.
Bill, Oliver, 162.
Bill, Reuben, 161.
Bill, Thomas, 2, 3, 40.
Billing, Sanford, 150.
Billings, 150.
Billings, Ebenezer, 60.
Billings, Henry, 233.
Billings, Jesse, 210.
Billings, John, 186.
Billings, Roger, 17.
Billings, Stephen, 49, 278.
Billings, William, 264.
Billins, Benjamin, 183.
Binge, Thomas, 277.
Bingham, Abisha, 88.
Bingham, Adam, 161.
Bingham, Chester, 39.
Bingham, F. L., 170.
Bingham, John, 74.
Bingham, Levi, 74.
Bingham, Nathaniel, 142.
Bingham, Rial, 37.
Bingham, Thomas, 149.
Birck, Elenezar, 37.
Bird, Daniel, 95, 127.
Bird, Isaac, 37.
Birdsey, Ebenezer, 151.
Birdsey, Joseph, 180, 190, 226.
Birdsey, Nathan, 151.
Birg, John, 159.
Birge, Benjamin, 201.
Birge, Beriah, 23.
Birge, Hosea, 162.
Birge, John, 273.
Bishop, 50.
Bishop, David, 184.
Bishop, Elisha, 112.
Bishop, Jared, 277.
Bishop, Jesse, 37.
Bishop, Joel, 71.
Bishop, John, 107.
Bishop, Lenard, 55.
Bishop, Moses, 37.
Bishop, Nathaniel, 88.
Bishop, Reuben, 193.
Bishop, Reubin, 192.
Bishop, Richard, 126.
Bishop, Samuel, 39, 65, 224.
Bishop, Simeon, 108, 268.
Bishop, William, 246, 251.
Bishop, Wyllys, 193.
Bishop, Yale, 192.
Bishop, Zebulon, 192.
Bissel, Abel, 162.
Bissel, Asahel, 38.
Bissel, Benjamin, 113, 164.
Bissel, Ensign, 202.
Bissel, Hezekiah, 202.
Bissel, Joseph, 149.
Bissel, Joseph W., 160.
Bissel, Oliver, 202.
Bissell, Benjamin, 116.
Bissell, Calvin, 273.
Bissell, Daniel, 68.
Bissell, E. F., 188.
Bissell, Ebenezer, 273.
Bissell, Ebenezer F., 27.
Bissell, George, 79.
Bissell, John, 201, 273.
Bissell, John P., 6.
Bissell, Jonathan, 163.
Bissell, Jonathan T., 162.
Bissell, Return, 273.
Bixbee, Solomon, 114.
Bixbey, Daniel, 65.
Bixby, Moses, 65.
Black, Thomas, 53.
Blackman, 190.
Blackman, David, 268.
Blackman, Edward, 195.
Blackman, Elijah, 88, 141.
Blackman, Ichabod, 94.
Blackman, Jeremiah, 76.
Blackman, Jonathan, 5, 88, 149.
Blackman, Nathan, 78, 190.
Blackman, Nehemiah, 94.
Blackman, William, 161.
Blackwell, Thomas, 153.
Blague, Joseph, 134, 208.
Blake, Christopher, 99.
Blake, Ebenezer, 88.
Blake, Jeremiah, 141.
Blake, Reuben, 110.
Blakeley, Isaac, 136.
Blakeley, Samuel, 136.
Blakesley, Asa, 19.

Brechin, Thomas, 41.
Breed, John, 210.
Brester, Jonathan, 60.
Brewer, Thomas, 122.
Brewster, Darius, 254.
Brewster, Ebenezer, 279.
Brewster, Jonathan, 6.
Brewster, Samuel, 94.
Brewster, Silas, 18, 174.
Brian, J., 84, 214.
Briant, John O., 108.
Briant, Straton, 152.
Brichel, John, 260.
Bricks, John, 111.
Briggs, Joseph, 81.
Briggs, William, 235.
Briggs, Zephaniah, 197.
Brigham, Paul, 49, 75, 161.
Brimblecom, Thomas, 259.
Brind, Edward, 88.
Brimsmade, A., 177.
Brinsmade, Abraham, 181.
Brinsmade, Josiah, 228.
Brister, Jonathan, 58.
Bristol, 267.
Bristol, Abel, 139.
Bristol, Aron, 139.
Bristol, Benjamin, 111.
Bristol, Bezaleel, 210.
Bristol, Eliphalet, 202.
Bristol, Samuel, 110, 116.
Bristol, Thomas, 266.
Bristoll, John, Jr., 39.
Bristoll, Peter, 75.
Britain, Samuel, 10.
Brockett, Titus, 21.
Brockway, Giddeon, 211.
Broker, Isaac, 67, 203.
Bronson, Isaac, 210, 224.
Bronson, J., 210, 212.
Bronson, Samuel, 207.
Brook, Josiah, 139.
Brook, Thomas, 139.
Brookline, 19.
Brooks, Abijah, 190.
Brooks, Benjamin, 190.
Brooks, David, 126.
Brooks, Elizur, 19.
Brooks, Isaac, 190.
Brooks, Jabez, 134, 208.
Brooks, John, 190.
Brooks, Jonathan, 153, 155.
Brooks, Joseph, 22, 81, 110, 117, 137.
Brooks, Josiah, 137.
Brooks, Lemuel, 218.
Brooks, Levi, 157.
Brooks, Michael, 37.
Brooks, Samuel, 209, 211.
Brooks, Solomon, 94.
Brooks, Stephen, 20, 246, 250.
Brooks, Thomas, 3, 4, 18, 73, 137, 174.
Brooks, Thomas, Jr., 19.
Brooks, Wickham, 17.
Brooks, William, 151.
Brothwell, William, 236.
Brown, 50.
Brown, Aaron, 145, 147.
Brown, Abell, 51.
Brown, Amasa, 57, 58.
Brown, Amos, 216.
Brown, Asa, 193.
Brown, Austin, 118.
Brown, Azariah, 4.
Brown, Benajah, 56.
Brown, Berzilla, 199.
Brown, Caleb, 238, 239.
Brown, Charles, 28, 32, 60, 88, 247, 252.
Brown, Christopher, 263.
Brown, D., 84.
Brown, Daniel, 16, 20, 38, 110.
Brown, David, 161.
Brown, Ebenezer, 58, 60.
Brown, Edward, 232.
Brown, Eli, 185.
Brown, Elisha, 58, 216.
Brown, Ezekiel, 216.
Brown, F. W., 170.
Brown, Henry, 58, 60, 64, 153, 155.
Brown, Hugh, 174.
Brown, Ichabod, 202, 211.
Brown, Isaac, 23.
Brown, James, 81, 185, 241, 253.
Brown, Jedediah, 268.
Brown, Jeremiah, 163.
Brown, Jessa, 40.
Brown, Jesse, 160, 186.
Brown, John, 28, 58, 170, 171, 234.
Brown, Jonathan, 1, 88, 110, 123.
Brown, Joseph, 10, 274.
Brown, Jude C., 69.
Brown, N., 210.
Brown, Nathan, 53.
Brown, Nathaniel, 107.
Brown, Nathaniel, Jr., 216.
Brown, Obadiah, 57.
Brown, Oliver, 65, 88.
Brown, P., 45.
Brown, Prosper, 231, 252.
Brown, Reuben, 71.
Brown, Rufus, 184.
Brown, Samuel, 10, 12, 34, 45, 70, 71, 85, 112, 185, 218.

Brown, Simeon, 216.
Brown, Solomon, 234.
Brown, Stephen, 201.
Brown, Thaddeus, 14.
Brown, Thomas, 61, 134.
Brown, William, 77, 202, 216.
Browning, Daniel, 51.
Brownley, John, 244, 247, 248.
Brownson, Asa, 24.
Brownson, Luman, 213.
Bruester, James, 34.
Brumon, Stephen, 58.
Brun, Isaac, 30.
Brune, Charles, 62.
Brunson, Beriah, 18.
Brunson, Michael, 133, 134.
Brunson, Stephen, 59.
Brush, Eliphalet, 196.
Brush, Janas, 196.
Brush, Jonas, 21.
Brush, Thomas, 196, 197.
Bruster, Cumfort, 149.
Bruster, Elijah, 210.
Bryan, Elijah, 109.
Bryan, Jehial, 211.
Buck, Abner, 34.
Buck, Ebenezer, 199.
Buck, Elijah, 55.
Buck, Frank, 130.
Buck, Joel, 19, 24.
Buck, Justus, 210, 212.
Buckingham, 114.
Buckingham, Benjamin, 213.
Buckingham, Gideon, 113.
Buckingham, Jered, 178.
Buckingham, Stephen, 117.
Buckland, Alexander, 1.
Buckland, Stephen, 88.
Buckley, Abraham, 178, 233.
Buckley, Abram, 205.
Buckley, Charles, 212.
Buckley, Job, 178.
Buckley, Joel, 277.
Buckley, Seth, 75.
Buckley, William, 178.
Buckly, Eleazer, 231.
Buel, John, 47.
Buell, B., 207.
Buell, Isaiah, 268.
Buell, John, 140.
Buell, John H., 2, 3.
Buell, Josiah, 46.
Buell, Levi, 161.
Buell, Nathaniel, 19, 20, 21, 25, 33.
Buell, Salmon, 265, 268.
Buffam, Samuel, 256.
Bugbe, Abihel, 14.
Bugbe, Amos, 14.
Buggee, William, 263.
Buggles, Timothy, 196.
Bucknel, Thomas W., 155.
Bulkley, Edward, 100, 101, 153, 155.
Bulkley, Eliphalet, 134, 211.
Bulkley, Fras, 153.
Bulkley, Francis, 155.
Bulkley, Jack, 60.
Bulkley, Levy, 80.
Bull, Edward, 178.
Bull, Epaphras, 33, 34, 35, 36, 37, 38, 39.
Bull, George, 201.
Bull, Henry, 24, 204.
Bull, Jeremiah, 24.
Bull, John, 178.
Bull, Jonathan, 223.
Bull, Michael, 202.
Bull, Nathaniel, 19, 203.
Bull, T., 225.
Bull, Thomas, 173, 211, 221, 223, 225.
Bull, Tirct, 204.
Bull, Wail, 196.
Bullen, Benjamin, 58.
Bullen, David, 121.
Bullin, David, 53.
Bullock, Jonathan, 100.
Bumpus, Edward, 34.
Bunce, David, 133.
Bunce, Isaiah, 268.
Bunce, Jered, 155.
Bunce. Norman, 264.
Bunce, Normand, 188.
Bunce, Thomas, 187, 188.
Bunce, William, 258.
Bundy, William, 78.
Bunker, Job, 246, 249.
Bunker, Samuel, 251.
Bunker, Vallantyne, 251.
Bunker, Vollantyne, 246.
Bunker Hill, 17, 24.
Bunn, Paul, 134, 262.
Bunnel, Abraham, 10.
Bunnel, John, 9, 25.
Bunnel, Nathaniel, 223.
Bunnell, Abraham, 16.
Bunnell, Jacob, 212.
Bunnell, Job, 196.
Bunnell, N., 208.
Bunnell, Nathaniel, 208, 211.
Bunnell, Noah, 85.
Bur, Jeffry, 243.
Bur, Seth, 231.
Buratt, Joseph, 127.
Burch, Ebenezar, 37.

Burch, Nathan, 262.
Burdain, Samuel, 74.
Burdick, Walter, 268.
Burdwin, Samuel, 268.
Burges, J., 172.
Burges, Jos, 172.
Burgess, Ephraim, 103, 131.
Burgess, Joshua, 27.
Burghes, Edward, 121.
Burghes, Ephraim, 124.
Burgiss, Lothrop, 97.
Burgoyn, John, 68.
Burgs, Joseph, 172.
Burgus, Joseph, 171.
Burham, Wolcott, 61.
Burk, John, 88.
Burke, Thomas, 254.
Burley, Aseph, 14.
Burley, Jacob, 14.
Burn, Daniel, 204.
Burn, James, 32.
Burn, Joseph, 230.
Burnall, Samuel, 184.
Burnam, Joseph, 143.
Burnap, Benjamin, 88.
Burnap, Josiah, 161.
Burnes, William, 78.
Burnet, Richard, 174.
Burnet, Samuel, 219.
Burnett, Ben, 247.
Burnett, Benjamin, 248.
Burnett, Jonathan, 247, 249.
Burnett, Thomas, Jr., 152.
Burnett, William, 231.
Burnham, Asa, 88.
Burnham, Eliphalet, 95.
Burnham, Eliphas, 127.
Burnham, Freeman, 66.
Burnham, Gurdin, 244.
Burnham, Gurdon, 245, 248.
Burnham, James, 185, 263.
Burnham, Joseph, 88.
Burnham, Josiah, 233.
Burnham, O., 153.
Burnham, Oliver, 268.
Burnham, Orrin, 155.
Burnham, Roswell, 79.
Burnham, Stephen, 80.
Burnham, William, 57.
Burnham, Wolcott, 95.
Burnit, Benjamin, 143, 244.
Burnit, Jonathan, 143.
Burns, Benjamin, 109.
Burns, Edward, 63.
Burns, John, 245, 249.
Burns, Orange, 67.
Burnside, Henry, 250.
Burnsides, Henry, 246.
Burr, A., 209.
Burr, Adonijah, 209, 221, 223, 226.
Burr, Asa, 95.
Burr, Daniel, 69, 117.
Burr, George, 180.
Burr, Jehial, 35.
Burr, Jesse, 236.
Burr, John, 273.
Burr, Russel, 202.
Burr, Salem, 145, 147.
Burr, Salmon, 142.
Burr, Sturges, 152.
Burrall, Charles, 33, 267.
Burrell, 265.
Burrell, Charles, 34, 35, 36, 37, 38, 39, 223.
Burrell, Samuel, 242.
Burrell, William, 188.
Burret, Charles, 48.
Burret, Elihu, 19.
Burret, Elishia, 19.
Burret, Zalmon, 195.
Burrill, James, 127.
Burrit, Charles, 69.
Burritt, Abel, 208, 211.
Burritt, Hezekiah, 190.
Burritt, Israel, 193.
Burritt, Joseph, 141.
Burritt, Samuel, 181, 190.
Burrough, Charles, 141.
Burroughs, Abner, Jr., 1.
Burroughs, Josiah, 213.
Burroughs, Stephen, 1.
Burroughs, William, 63.
Burroughs, Zebulon, 1.
Burrous, Hubbard, 122.
Burrous, Joseph, 124.
Burrous, William, 124.
Burrouss, Selah, 215.
Burrows, Caleb, 105, 117.
Burrows, Elisha, 174, 267, 268.
Burrows, George, 105.
Burrows, Josiah, 88.
Burrows, Nathan, 250.
Burrows, Paul, 174.
Burrows, William, 268.
Burrtt, Wakemon, 243.
Burrus, Hubbard, 211.
Burrus, Nathan, 246.
Burrus, William, 103, 131, 265.
Burt, John, 185.
Burt, William, 160.
Burton, Daniel, 21.
Burton, Ephraim, 181, 219.
Burton, J., 206.
Burton, James, 208.
Burton, Jeremiah, 173.
Burton, Joseph, Jr., 135.

Calleway, Henry, 262.
Cam, Moses, 231.
Cambell, Robert, 149.
Cambridge, 4, 17, 134.
Camp, Aaron, 17.
Camp, Amiel, 195.
Camp, Elnathan, 193.
Camp, Heth, 193.
Camp, Isaac, 19, 24.
Camp, Job, 193.
Camp, John, 17.
Camp, Nathan, 196.
Camp, Ozias, 192.
Camp, Phinehas, 88.
Camp, Rejoice, 191.
Camp, Samuel, 134, 192, 207, 223, 278.
Camp, Sharp, 108.
Camp, Sharper, 71.
Campbell, Joseph, 165.
Campbell, Mathew, 1.
Campbell, Samuel, 143.
Camron, John, 32.
Canaan, 20, 21, 22, 23, 52, 55, 76, 83, 195, 205.
Canada, David, 28.
Canada, James, 110.
Canada, 12, 13, 23, 43.
Cande, Theophilus, 135.
Cane, Hugh, 200.
Canfield, Asher, 191.
Canfield, Ezekiel, 232.
Canfield, Ezeriah, 97.
Canfield, Ichabod, 23, 152.
Canfield, John, 193.
Canfield, Josiah, 237.
Canfield, S., 206.
Canfield, Samuel, 84, 207, 209.
Canfield, Seba, 201.
Canfield, Thomas, 136.
Canfield, Titus, 191.
Canida, David, 60.
Cannady, Henry, 245, 249.
Cannon, Ira, 95.
Canterbury, 54, 58, 65, 78, 88, 89, 90, 102, 103, 104, 114, 118, 267.
Cape Ann, 69.
Capee, Solomon, 246, 250.
Capen, Timothy, 37.
Capp, William, 246.
Capron, Samuel, 183.
Car, Robert, 168.
Card, Daniel, 247.
Card, Elisha, 81.
Carew, Joseph, 208.
Carew, Josiah, 238.
Carew, Phereus, 248.
Carew, Phineus, 246.
Carey, Joseph, 185.
Carey, Josiah, 239.
Carey, Roger, 64.
Carlton, Derias, 56.
Carpender, Willet, 263.
Carpenter, Allen, 119.
Carpenter, Benjamin, 184.
Carpenter, David, 95, 185.
Carpenter, Eli, 1.
Carpenter, Elias, 124, 184.
Carpenter, Elijah, 66, 185.
Carpenter, Eliphalet, 103, 124.
Carpenter, Eliphelet, 131.
Carpenter, Ephraim, 159, 162.
Carpenter, James, 105.
Carpenter, Joshua, 162.
Carpenter, Nathan, 18, 22.
Carpenter, Uriah, 66.
Carr, Clement, 108.
Carr, Daniel, 251.
Carr, Ebenezer, 108.
Carr, Robert, 107.
Carr, William, 71, 107.
Carrell, Elisha, 96.
Carrier, Benjamin, 138.
Carrier, John, 81.
Carrier, Thomas, Jr., 160.
Carter, Aaron, 60.
Carter, David, 169.
Carter, Eleazer, 160.
Carter, J., 84.
Carter, James, 88.
Carter, Jirah, 267, 269.
Carter, John, 184, 201.
Carter, Jonah, 97.
Carter, Joseph, 225.
Carter, Nathan, 37.
Carter, Reuben, 88, 102.
Carter, Reubin, 130.
Carter, Samuel, 225.
Cartwright, Jonathan, 17.
Carty, Asher, 59.
Carver, David, 162.
Cary, John, 263.
Cary, Joseph, 143.
Cary, Josiah, 239.
Cary, Oliver, 143.
Case, Abel, 145, 147, 148.
Case, Asahel, 39.
Case, Caleb, 164.
Case, Dan, 145, 147, 148.
Case, Elihu, 145, 147, 148.
Case, Elihu, 2d, 142.
Case, Elijah, 177, 221.
Case, Elisha, 27.
Case, Hosea, 147.
Case, Hosea, Jr., 145, 148.
Case, Israel, 145, 146, 147, 148.

Chapman, Phinehas, 252.
Chapman, R., 142.
Chapman, Reuben, 110.
Chapman, S., 206.
Chapman, Samuel, 57, 70, 109, 222, 227.
Chapman, Silas, 28, 31.
Chapman, Thomas, 14.
Chappel, Alpheus, 28.
Chappel, Caleb, 160.
Chappel, Comfort, 88.
Chappel, Curtis, 37.
Chappel, Curtiss, 88, 111.
Chappel, Elijah, 163.
Chappel, Hiram, 65.
Chappel, James, 67.
Chappel, John, 28, 31.
Chappel, Joshua, 88.
Chappel, Joshua, Jr., 5.
Chappel, Noah, 41, 43.
Chappell, Amariah, 269.
Chaps, John, 69.
Chariey, John, 59.
Charles, Nicholas, 62.
Charlestown, 260, 261.
Charter, George, 1.
Charter, John, Jr., 1, 25.
Chase, Jeremiah, 23.
Chase, Jonathan, 14.
Chase, Nathan, 245, 251.
Chase, Vollantyne, 247, 252.
Chase, Walter, 88.
Chase, Zacceus, 246.
Chatfield, Caleb, 21.
Chatfield, Dan, 85.
Chatfield, Daniel, 179, 211.
Chatfield, Ebenezer, 189.
Chatfield, John, 233, 253, 264.
Chatfield, Lemuel, 213.
Chatfield, Lewis, 238, 239.
Chatfield, Thomas, 245, 249.
Chatham, 58, 59, 60, 61, 62, 69, 74, 80, 81, 82, 88, 89, 118.
Chauncy, William, 191.
Check, John, 203.
Cheeney, Ebenezer, 57.
Cheeseborough, Charles, 264.
Cheeseborough, Thomas, 22, 23.
Cheesebrook, Jabez, 184.
Cheever, Ezekiel, 87.
Cheevers, Ezekiel, 87.
Cheney, Joseph, 10, 124.
Cheney, Thomas, 63.
Cheney, William, 14.
Cheshire, 82, 111.
Chester, Charles, 174.
Chester, David, 124.
Chester, Eldridge, 174.
Chester, John, 18, 19, 23, 153, 155, 222, 266.
Chester, Lemuel, 118.
Chick, John, 142.
Chidester, Andrew, 98.
Chidester, Jonathan, 41, 43.
Chidester, William, 41, 43.
Chidsey, Ephraim, 10.
Chidsey, Joseph, 193.
Chidsey, Street, 10.
Child, Obadiah, 183.
Childs, 50.
Childs, Charles, 66.
Childs, Harba, 105.
Childs, Jesse, 64.
Childs, Lyman, 184.
Childs, Stephen, 67.
Chilson, John, 265.
Chilson, Jonathan, 170.
Chipman, John, 229.
Chipman, Jonathan, 37.
Chipman, Samuel, 188.
Chitingdon, Solomon, 55.
Chittenden, Benjamin, 275.
Chittenden, Cornelius, 97.
Chittenden, Nathan, 275.
Chittenden, Solomon, 97.
Chittendon, Gideon, 107.
Chittenton, Abraham, 19.
Chorse, Ephraim, 69.
Christophers, Allen, 249.
Christophers, John A., 245.
Chubbuck, Ebenezer, 127.
Chuish, Philip, 263.
Church, Abner, 143.
Church, Ambrose, 278.
Church, Caleb, 187.
Church, Calub, 200.
Church, Ebenezer, 88.
Church, Elihu, 51.
Church, Fairbanks, 174.
Church, James, 261.
Church, Joseph, 28, 31.
Church, Josiah, 141.
Church, Nathaniel, 265, 269.
Church, Oliver, 37.
Church, Samuel, 98, 184, 187, 188.
Church, Timothy, 187, 188.
Church, Uriah, 12, 41.
Churchel, Charles, 155.
Churchel, Jesse, 137.
Churchel, Joseph, 137, 157.
Churchel, Moses, 78.
Churchell, Hezekiah, 38.
Churchell, Joseph, 81.
Churchell, Josiah, 38.
Churcher, John, 34, 54.
Churchill, C., 214, 226.

Clemmonds, Abijah, 67.
Clemons, John, 23.
Clerk, Charles, 251.
Clerk, John, 140.
Cleveland, Eliphas, 64.
Cleveland, Garner, 122.
Cleveland, Johnson, 78.
Cleveland, Jonas, 35.
Cleveland, Josiah, 35.
Cleveland, Tracey, 105.
Cleverly, John, 254.
Clift, Samuel, 47.
Clift, Wills, 46.
Climet, Robert, 108.
Clinton, Allen, 55.
Clinton, Joseph, 53, 121.
Clinton, Lawrence, 211.
Close, Benjamin, 266, 267, 269.
Close, Odel, 211.
Close, Odle, 207, 209.
Cluff, Isaac, 111.
Clumb, Amariah, 21.
Coatney, John, 260.
Coats, 150.
Coay, Moses, 56.
Coban, James, 112.
Cobb, John, 73.
Cobet, Samuel, 195.
Cobuck, Ebenezer, 95.
Coburn, Edward, 58.
Coburn, Eliphalet, 263.
Coburn, Samuel, 64.
Cobus, Cull, 263.
Coc, Jedediah, 95.
Cochecks, Peter, 18.
Cochram, 16.
Cockcel, Joseph, 124.
Codner, John, 82, 107.
Codnor, John, 116.
Coe, Asher, 191.
Coe, Daniel, 191.
Coe, Dorman, 189.
Coe, Ebenezer, 212, 268.
Coe, James, 181, 219.
Coe, Jeddiah, 117.
Coe, Jedediah, 127.
Coe, Levi, 201.
Coe, Pineas, 205.
Coe, Samuel, 21, 58.
Coe, Seth, 273.
Coe, Timothy, 191.
Coe, Zacheriah, 180.
Coffin, Christopher, 73.
Coffin, Thomas, 238, 239.
Coggeshall, William, 242.
Coggswell, W., 214.
Coggswell, William, 243.
Cogins, David, 69.
Cogswell, Asa, 197.
Cogswell, William, 209, 224.
Cogwell, Nat, 167.
Cohorse, Ephraim, 99.
Coit, Farwell, 174.
Coit, Isaac, 174.
Coit, Nathaniel, Jr., 140.
Coit, Oliver, 174.
Coit, Samuel, 227.
Coit, William, 25, 245, 247, 248, 249.
Colbct, Joseph, 184.
Colburn, Daniel, Jr., 18.
Colburn, Eliphalet, 63.
Colchester, 57, 58, 59, 60, 61, 65, 69, 78, 81, 82, 87, 88, 89, 90, 103, 118.
Cole, Abner, 20.
Cole, Alben, 77.
Cole, Asa, 16.
Cole, David, 97.
Cole, Gideon, 59.
Cole, Job, 117, 127.
Cole, John, 73, 88.
Cole, Jonathan, 162.
Cole, Josiah, 114.
Cole, Leonard, 115.
Cole, Marcus, 88.
Cole, Matthew, 209, 210.
Cole, Samuel, 94.
Cole, Simeon, 173.
Cole, Solomon, 117, 127.
Coleman, Ebenezer, 160.
Coleman, Edward S., 47.
Coleman, Noah, 46, 88.
Coley, Nathan, 69.
Colfax, Ebenezer, 140, 264.
Colfax, William, 45.
Colkins, Jonathan, 232.
Collat, Thomas, 58.
Collens, Charles, 201.
Collens, Edward, 136.
Collens, Joel, 277.
Collings, John, 246, 250.
Collins, Ambrous, 37.
Collins, Augustus, 208.
Collins, D., 84.
Collins, Dan, 192, 207, 210, 211, 222.
Collins, Edward, 193.
Collins, Eleazer, 163.
Collins, Elijah, 37.
Collins, Friend, 277.
Collins, John, 87.
Collins, Josiah, 143.
Collins, Pitman, 191.
Collins, Rufus, 163.
Collins, Samuel, 95, 111.

Cook, T., 177, 221.
Cook, Thaddeus, 191, 192, 193, 194, 227, 265, 266, 267, 275.
Cook, Thomas, 1, 28, 71, 113, 202.
Cook, Timothy, 1.
Cook, Warren, 112.
Cook, William, 58, 60, 108, 202.
Cooke, J., 214.
Cooke, Job, 220.
Cooke, Thaddeus, 225.
Cooke, William, 106.
Cooks, J., 214.
Cool, Himan, 111.
Cool, Isaac, 111.
Cooley, Asa, 210.
Cooley, Paul, 132.
Coombs, Samuel, 259.
Coon, J., 97.
Cooper, 41.
Cooper, Abraham, 108.
Cooper, Allen, 210.
Cooper, Jacob, 240.
Cooper, James, 71, 112.
Cooper, Joseph, 235.
Cooper, William, 112.
Cooper, Zebulon, 263.
Copland, Jonathan, 167.
Copley, Nathaniel, 211.
Copp, Joseph, 58, 60.
Copp, William, 248.
Copper, James Y., 234.
Corbett, James, Jr., 19.
Corbin, Philip, 198.
Corby, James, 139.
Cordrick, John, 69.
Corier, Abel, 196.
Cornelius, John, 83.
Cornell, Benjamin, 134.
Cornell, Richard, 69.
Corning, Allyn, 121.
Cornish, George, 146, 147, 148.
Cornish, James, Jr., 164.
Cornish, Joel, 147.
Cornwall, 23, 55, 56, 74, 82, 90, 91, 274.
Cornwell, Ashbel, 141.
Cornwell, Timothy, 204.
Corvett, Solomon, 250.
Corwin, Jonathan, 88.
Corwin, Selah, 88.
Cossit, Rane, 203.
Cottle, Isaac, 232.
Cotton, Elihu, 204.
Cotton, Elisha, 135.
Cotton, John, 229.
Cottrill, Nathan, 51.
Couch, 133.
Couch, Abraham, 54, 126.
Couch, Amos, 57.
Couch, Benjamin S., 152.
Couch, Daniel, 110.
Couch, E., 84.
Couch, Ebenezer, 209, 224, 225.
Couch, Elisha, 157.
Couch, Gideon, 152.
Couch, James, 59.
Couch, John, 134, 192.
Couch, Stephen, 137.
Couch, Steven, 137.
Couch, Thomas N., 152.
Coult, John, 230.
Coval, Abraham, 36.
Covel, Elijah, 137.
Covel, Eliphalet, 264.
Covel, Jonathan, 137, 139.
Covel, Philip, 263.
Covel, William, 238, 239.
Coventry, 16, 31, 58, 64, 65, 66, 74, 75, 78, 79, 81, 82, 87, 88, 114.
Covill, Philip, 157.
Covill. Samuel, 157.
Cowen, Daniel, 126.
Cowen, John, 126.
Cowett, Nathaniel, 246, 250.
Cowle, John, 35.
Cowles, Joseph, 37.
Cowles, Matthew, 182.
Cowles, Timothy, 161.
Coy, David, 57.
Coy, Ephraim, 103.
Coy, Moses, 100.
Coye, Joseph, 143.
Coye, Thomas, 143.
Cox, Jedediah, 95.
Cradock, William, 27.
Crage, John, 256, 262.
Crage, Robert, 232.
Craige, John, 252.
Crain, Joseph, 153.
Cramer, William, 64.
Crammer, Bishop, 119.
Crammer, John, 79.
Crampton, Benjamin, 71.
Crandal, Thomas, 231.
Crandel, Hazel, 159.
Crandel, Richmond, 263.
Crandle, Abiel 133.
Crane, Adonijah, 78.
Crane, Elihu, 192.
Crane, Elijah, 24.
Crane, James, 102, 124, 130.
Crane, Jesse, 193.
Crane, John, 177, 211, 266.
Crane, Jonathan, 14.
Crane, Joseph, 155.

Curtiss, Eleazer, 110, 116.
Curtiss, Eleazer, Jr., 18, 23, 24.
Curtiss, Eli, 49.
Curtiss, Elihew, 181, 219.
Curtiss, Eliphalet, 208.
Curtiss, Giles, 48, 71, 133.
Curtiss, Henry, 181.
Curtiss, Hezekiah, 190.
Curtiss, Isaac, 181, 219.
Curtiss, Jabes, 181.
Curtiss, Jabez, 219.
Curtiss, James, 153, 191.
Curtiss, Jeremiah, 181, 219.
Curtiss, Jesse, 208, 210.
Curtiss, John, 23, 169, 191, 193.
Curtiss, Jonathan, 106.
Curtiss, Joseph, 153.
Curtiss, Josiah, 190.
Curtiss, Jotham, 209.
Curtiss, Levi, 187.
Curtiss, Lewis, 181, 219.
Curtiss, Peter, 209.
Curtiss, Robert, 181, 219.
Curtiss, Samuel, 190.
Curtiss, William, 153, 190.
Cushman, Benjamin, 93.
Cushman, Jonah, 54.
Cushman, William, 167.
Cutler, Joseph, 76, 221, 263.
Cutler, Seth, 184.
Cutting, Hezekiah, 159.
Cutting, Zebedee, 159.
Cuyler, Teleman, 253.

Daboll, John, 269.
Dagget, Abenezer, 189.
Dagget, Henry, 49.
Dagget, Nathan, 190.
Dagget, Silas, 233.
Daggett, Henry, 179.
Daggett, Nathan, 233, 253.
Daggett, Silas, 246, 250.
Daggett, Sylvanus, 254.
Daggett, West, 231, 254.
Dailey, John, 105.
Daily, Dowey, 275.
Dale, Richard, 38.
Daley, Joseph, 87.
Daman, Edmund, 3, 4.
Dammorg, Richard, 124.
Damon, Aaron, 1.
Damon, John, 165.
Damon, Jonathan, 165.
Damon, Jonathan, Jr., 1.
Dana, Charles, 135, 255.
Danaty, Francies, 32.
Danbury, 56, 57, 65, 67, 69, 78, 81, 89, 90, 103, 104, 110, 118, 177, 194, 198, 199, 200, 223, 265, 266.
Dande, Thomas, 229.
Dandee, Thomas, 240.
Daniel, Anthony M., 70, 108.
Daniel, Ezekiel, 57.
Daniel, Joel M., 70.
Daniels, David, 68.
Daniels, Ezekiel, 58, 60, 74.
Daniels, Nehemiah, 57, 58, 60, 118.
Daniels, Samuel, 137, 236.
Danolds, Samuel, 139.
Dansey, William, 246, 250.
Darbee, Benjamin, 160.
Darby, William, 159.
Darens, Daniel, 138.
Darga, Asa, 12.
Darling, Benjamin, 41, 43.
Darling, Levy, 257.
Darrow, Benjamin, 233.
Darrow, Christopher, 45.
Darrow, Jonathan, 233.
Darrow, Peter, Jr., 252.
Darrow, Thomas, 243.
Dart, Joseph, 206, 208.
Dart, Samuel, 119.
Dart, Stephen, 60.
Daskomb, William, 54.
Daten, S., 84.
Datton, John, 12.
Dauchy, Jeremiah, 195.
Daurough, James, 83.
Davall, William, 239.
Davenport, Humphrey, 185.
Davenport, J., 206.
Davenport, James, 239.
Davenport, John, 110, 211, 226.
Davenport, Noah, 184.
Davidson, 114.
Davidson, Asa, 79.
Davidson, Daniel, 99.
Davidson, Isaac, 110.
Davidson, John, 110.
Davidson, James, 211.
Davidson, John, 194.
Davidson, Joseph, 204.
Davidson, Pt. 172.
Davinson, Robert, 88.
Davis, 59, 69, 247.
Davis, Abel, 249.
Davis, Abele, 247.
Davis, Amos, 71, 110, 213.
Davis, Daniel, 122.
Davis, David, 1, 87.
Davis, Jacob, Jr., 7.
Davis, Jacob, 3d, 142.
Davis, James, 231.

Dunham, Solomon, Jr., 191.
Dunham, Zekel, 248.
Duning, Ezra, 196.
Duning, James, 215.
Dunk, Thomas, 197.
Dunking, John, 246.
Dunlap, Joshua, 168, 210.
Dunning, Gideon, 21.
Dunning, Liverus, 195.
Dunning, Samuel, 195.
Dunning, Silas, 86.
Dunwell, Stephen, 74.
Dupe, Simeon, 35.
Duran, Ebenezer, 269.
Durand, Ebenezer, 110.
Durand, Isaac, 271.
Durfee, Benjamin, 122.
Durfee, James, 169.
Durfey, Israel, 263.
Durfey, Thomas, 61.
Durffee, Ebenez, 106.
Durffee, Elijah, 106.
Durfy, Jedediah, 1, 165.
Durfy, Joseph, Jr., 1.
Durham, 22, 70, 80, 81, 104, 107, 108, 133.
Durkee, 50, 265.
Durkee, Benjamin, 89, 173.
Durkee, Jeremiah, 32, 66, 89, 184.
Durkee, John, 47, 63, 64, 65, 93.
Durkee, Solomon, 143, 185.
Durkee, William, 143.
Durphee, Ephraim, 63.
Durphy, Jedediah, 165.
Dutcher, Ruluff, 211.
Dutton, Amos, 24.
Dutton, Moses, 99.
Dutton, Thomas, 209, 223.
Dutton, Titus, 88.
Dwight, H., 220.
Dwight, Hamlin, 220.
Dwire, Michael, 258.
D Wolf, Aaron, 228.
D Woolf, Stephen, 245.
Dyar, Calob, 233.
Dyar, William, 169.
Dyer, Elisha, 96.
Dyer, Isrel, 261.
Dyer, Juba, 114.
Dyer, Roger, 257.
Dykeman, Jonathan, 69.

Eadee, Amor, 75.
Eagleston, David, 108.
Eaglestone, Josiah, 35.
Eagliston, Jonathan, 127.
Eames, David, 170.
Eames, John, 170.
Eams, Everet, 89.
Eansworth, Jedediah, 49, 78.
Earl, William, 58.
Easmon, Eli, 139.
East Chester, 159, 160, 161, 162, 163.
East Haddam, 23, 57, 58, 59, 82, 89, 90, 114, 278.
East Hartford, 58, 60, 87, 267.
East Haven, 25.
East Windsor, 1, 54, 55, 57, 58, 78, 87, 88, 89, 103, 104.
Eastman, Asahel, 185.
Eastman, Azariah, 136.
Eastman, Benjamin, 136.
Eastman, Deliverance, 79.
Eastman, Ebenezer, 185.
Eastman, Joseph, 197, 199.
Eastman, Timothy, 15.
Easton, Eliphalet, 269.
Easton, Julan, 75.
Eaton, Ebenezer, 185.
Eaton, Joshua, 168.
Eaton, Marvirick, 185.
Eaton, Aron, 103, 131.
Eaton, Daniel, 105.
Eaton, Josiah, 15.
Eaton, Stephen, 57.
Eberhard, John, 70, 112.
Eccleston, Jonathan, 138.
Eddy, Seth, 74, 228.
Edgcomb, David, 174.
Edgcomb, Ezra, 36, 89.
Edgcomb, Jabez, 123.
Edgcomb, Preserve, 32.
Edgerton, Abel, 80, 185.
Edgerton, Elisha, 209, 211.
Edgerton, Jedediah, 160.
Edgerton, Jonathan, 162.
Edgerton, Kingsbury, 240.
Edgerton, Simeon, 211.
Edmond, Robert, 200.
Edmond, William, 267.
Edmonds, William, 265, 266, 269.
Edson, Caleb, 93.
Edwards, Ceasar, 53.
Edwards, Daniel, 120.
Edwards, George, 254.
Edwards, Gideon, 269.
Edwards, Henry, 27.
Edwards, John, 173.
Edwards, Jonathan, 103, 130.
Edwards, Joseph, 193.
Edwards, Phineas, 171.
Edwards, Samuel, 135.
Edwards, Thomas, 37.
Edy, Charles, 160.
[ ]eed, 85.

Eells, Edward, 46, 60.
Eells, Samuel, 76, 60.
Egeton, Joshua, 7.
Eggleston, 123.
Eggleston, Benedict, 123.
Egglestone, Jonathan, 95.
Egleston, Joseph, 60.
Eglestone, Bennit, 141.
Egliston, Joseph, 171.
Elderkin, Bela, 245, 248.
Elderkin, Dearky, 246.
Elderkin, Diarea, 29.
Elderkin, Diarky, 248.
Elderkin, James, 240, 252.
Elderkin, Jedidiah, 136.
Elderkin, John, 28, 230.
Elderkin, Joshua, 216.
Elderkin, Luther, 245, 249.
Elderkin, Minor, 240.
Elderkin, Vine, 89.
Eldredge, Daniel, 25.
Eldredge, William, 111.
Eldridge, Daniel, 14.
Eldridge, James, 114.
Eldridge, Thomas, 66.
Eldridge, Zoeth, 133.
Elgar, David, 58.
Elgar, Ezra, 190.
Elger, Abner, 136.
Elger, David, 60.
Elgur, Abner, 181, 219.
Eli, Edward, 59.
Eli, King, 78.
Eli, Tuller, 131.
Eliot, Joseph, 17.
Ellis, Benjamin, 252.
Ellis, Daniel, 185.
Ellis, Nathan, 267.
Ellis, William, 254.
Elliss, Carpenter, 51.
Ells, Edward, 134.
Ells, Samuel, 130.
Ellsworth, Charles, 23.
Ellsworth, Moses, 54.
Elmer, Daniel, Jr., 38.
Elmes, Elkenah, 258.
Elmor, Joseph, 199.
Elmore, Daniel, 69.
Elmore, Samuel, 16, 17, 41, 43.
Elswood, Abijah, 126.
Elsworth, Charles, 55.
Elsworth, Daniel, 165.
Elsworth, Daniel, 3d, 1.
Elsworth, Gurdon, 165.
Elsworth, Hezekiah, 1.
Elsworth, Moses, 103, 130.
Eluzzad, Nathan, 81.
Elwell, Ebenezer, 127.
Elwell, Ozias, 76.
Elwell, Samuel, 127.
Elwood, Isaac, 152, 233.
Elwood, Joseph, 109.
Elwood, Nathan, 54.
Elwood, Thomas, 232.
Ely, Elisha, 48.
Ely, Gad, 202.
Ely, John, 142, 150, 221, 227, 267.
Ely, S., 84.
Emerson, Joseph, 119.
Emerson, Nathaniel, 141.
Emerson, Stephen, 65.
Emmes, John B., 91.
Emmons, Asa, 274.
Emmons, Noadiah, 20.
Emmons, Samuel, 274.
Emmons, William, 220.
Emorson, Nathaniel, 111.
Enfield, 53, 54, 58, 88, 89, 90, 103.
Eno, Isaac, 67.
Enos, 227.
Enos, David, 59.
Enos, Roger, 18, 24, 141, 142, 226, 228, 273, 278.
Ens, David, 63.
Ensign, Daniel, 67.
Ensign, John, 226.
Ensign, Jonathan, 37.
Ensign, Otis, 126.
Ensign, Solomon, 274.
Ensworth, Edward, 78.
Ervin, Jared, 234.
Essex, John, 256.
Etherly, Thomas, 238, 250.
Etterly, Thomas, 246.
Europe, 118.
Evans, Abiather, 102.
Evans, Benjamin S., 119.
Evans, Henry, 58, 60.
Evans, Isaac, 89.
Evans, Jonah, 60.
Evans, Josiah, 58, 118.
Evans, Samuel, Jr., 89.
Evans, Thomas, 94.
Evans, Willard, 64.
Evarts, Caleb, 277.
Evarts, Charles, 37.
Evarts, Ebur, 37.
Evens, Abiather, 53, 129.
Evens, Allyn, 122.
Evens, Cotton, 66.
Evens, John, 35.
Evens, Stacey, 128.
Evens, Stacy, 127.
Everest, Benjamin, 37.
Everest, Daniel, 35.
Everest, Elisha, 37.

Gibbs, W., 188.
Gibbs, Warham, 211.
Gibson, Jacob, 229, 244, 247, 248.
Giddens, Richard, 89.
Gidding, Benjamin, 41.
Giddings, 221.
Giddings, Benjamin, 43.
Giddings, Joseph, 199.
Giddings, Thomas, 208, 211.
Giddings, William, 197, 208, 212.
Giddins, David, 205.
Gideon, Niles, 126.
Gift, 230.
Gilbard, Timothy, 205.
Gilbart, John, 184, 190.
Gilbart, Thomas, 190.
Gilbert, Abijah, 243.
Gilbert, Allen, 135.
Gilbert, Amos, 21.
Gilbert, Ashel, 163.
Gilbert, Burr, 75.
Gilbert, Elnathan, 173.
Gilbert, Gardiner, 59.
Gilbert, Giles, 278.
Gilbert, Isaiah, 173.
Gilbert, Jedediah, 66.
Gilbert, Jesse, 68, 114.
Gilbert, Joel, 152, 215.
Gilbert, John, 75, 162, 195.
Gilbert, Jonathan, 274.
Gilbert, Joseph, 42, 43.
Gilbert, M., 211.
Gilbert, Moses, 77, 207.
Gilbert, N., 177, 210.
Gilbert, Nathan, 207, 226.
Gilbert, Nathaniel, 208.
Gilbert, Peter, 259.
Gilbert, Samuel, 19.
Gilbert, Thomas, 35.
Gilbert, Williams, 135.
Gilbertson, Edward, 83.
Gilburt, Daniel, 27.
Giles, Thomas, 174.
Gill, Giles, 230.
Gill, John, 141.
Gillet, Abraham, 99.
Gillet, Adney, 81.
Gillet, Asa, 145.
Gillet, Charles, 34.
Gillet, Charles, Sr., 34.
Gillet, Ebenezer, Jr., 3.
Gillet, Garshom, 3.
Gillet, Gershom, 4.
Gillet, J., 206.
Gillet, Jacob, 3, 4, 123.
Gillet, Joab, 67.
Gillet, John, 76, 162.
Gillet, Jonah, Jr., 138.
Gillet, Joseph, 139.
Gillet, Lemuel, 21, 105.
Gillet, Othniel, Jr., 20.
Gillet, Rufus, 80.
Gillett, Benoni, 106, 126.
Gillett, Zacheus, 106, 126.
Gillit, Dan, 185.
Gillit, Ebenezer, Jr., 2.
Gillit, Isaac, 182.
Gillit, John, 39.
Gillit, John W., 204.
Gillit, William, 39.
Gilner, Henry, 10, 269.
Gilson, Eleazar, 69.
Gilson, Jacob, 107.
Ginnings, Daniel, 28.
Ginnings, Stephen, 28.
Gipson, John, 81.
Gladding, Joseph, 74, 228.
Glading, Joseph, 178.
Glasgow, Silas, 76.
Glass, Samuel, 58.
Glass, Silas, 124.
Glass, Sils, 172.
Glass, Silus, 171.
Glastenbury, 22, 58, 59, 60, 61, 74, 81, 88, 89, 90, 91, 103, 137, 222.
Gleason, Andrew, 202.
Gleason, Noah, 203.
Godale, Silas, 46.
Godard, Levi, 146.
Goddard, Edward, 110.
Goddard, Schuyler, 107.
Goddard, Skylor, 70.
Godfrey, C., 84.
Godfrey, Christopher, 152.
Godfrey, D., 84.
Godfrey, Daniel, 152, 181, 212, 225.
Godfrey, Reuben, 246, 250.
Goff, David, 36, 203.
Goff, Elisha, 184.
Goff, Gideon, 100.
Goff, Hezekiah, 258.
Goff, Jonathan, 61.
Goff, Richard, 56.
Goff, Samuel, 61, 118.
Goff, Solomon, 114.
Goff, Squire, 82.
Goging, James, 254.
Gold, Benjamin, 231.
Gold, David, 41, 43.
Goldsmith, Ephraim, 235.
Goldsmith, James, 109, 204.
Goldsmith, Joseph, 109.
Goldsmith, William, 109, 238.
Goldsmith, Wilmot, 191, 277.
Goodale, Aseph, 183.

Goodale, Elezr, 137.
Goodale, Joseph, 157.
Goodell, M., 172.
Goodluck, London, 76.
Goodman, Asa, 274.
Goodman, Richard, 274.
Goodman, Thomas, 259.
Goodrich, Abner, 34.
Goodrich, Asahel, 58.
Goodrich, Bethuel, 61.
Goodrich, David, Jr., 34.
Goodrich, Elihu, 192.
Goodrich, Elisha, 38.
Goodrich, Ephraim, 89.
Goodrich, Ichabod, 121.
Goodrich, Hosea, 154.
Goodrich, Hozea, 156.
Goodrich, Isaac, 154, 156.
Goodrich, Jeha, 154.
Goodrich, Jesse, 34.
Goodrich, John, 41, 43, 154, 156.
Goodrich, Levi, 61.
Goodrich, Michael, 38.
Goodrich, Philer, 81.
Goodrich, Roswell, 133.
Goodrich, Samuel, 34.
Goodrich, Simeon, 81.
Goodrich, Stephen, 145, 208, 221.
Goodrich, Timothy, 173.
Goodrick, Levy, 236.
Goodrige, James, 242.
Goodsell, Lewis, 180, 181.
Goodsell, Samuel, 10.
Goodspeed, Nathan, 211.
Goodwin, Charles, 99, 142.
Goodwin, Hezekiah, 77.
Goodwin, John, 135.
Goodwin, Ozias, 266.
Goodwin, Samuel, 5.
Goodwin, Solomon, 23.
Goodwin, Stephen, 139.
Goodwin, Stephen, Jr., 39.
Goodwin, Timothy, 259.
Goodwin, Uri, 201.
Goodwin, Zebedee, 4.
Goodwine, David, 188.
Goodwine, John P., 187, 188.
Goodwine, Joseph, 164.
Goodwine, Nathan, 187.
Goodwine, Samuel, 164.
Goodwine, Theoder, 187.
Goodwine, Zebedee, 3.
Goodyear, Edward, 73.
Goodyear, Jesse, 210.
Gookins, Samuel, 53, 121.
Goram, George, 185.
Goram, Jonah, 38.
Gorden, Aleck, 171.
Gorden, William, 32.
Gordon, 206.
Gordon, J., 206, 222.
Gordon, James, 206, 222.
Gordon, Robert, 253.
Gore, Daniel, 227.
Gore, Obadiah, 46.
Gorham, Benjamin, 181, 219.
Gorham, David, 199.
Gorham, Isaac, 190.
Gorham, James, 199.
Gorham, John, 197.
Gorham, Phineas, 98.
Gorham, Samuel, 89.
Gorum, Joseph, 172.
Gosard, Levi, 148.
Goshen, 22, 23, 67, 68, 90, 91, 102.
Goslee, Timothy, 157.
Gosse, Aron, 157.
Gossord, Levi, 66.
Gossord, Rufus, 66.
Goudy, James, 239.
Gould, Abraham, 180.
Gould, John, 68, 199.
Gould, William, 69.
Gowdy, James, 238.
Grace, Matthew, 115.
Graham, Andrew, 85.
Graham, Cyrus, 113.
Graham, Daniel, 146, 147, 148.
Graham, Daniel, Jr., 145.
Graham, Elisha, 212.
Graham, Jesse, 113.
Graham, John, 61, 85.
Graham, Jonathan G., 46.
Graham, Joseph, 61, 89.
Grahom, Danel, Jr., 146.
Graige, Robert, 245, 249.
Grandey, Edmund, 37.
Grandey, Jesse, 37.
Granger, Peter, 230.
Granger, Phineas, 54.
Granger, Phinehas, 89, 123.
Granger, Samuel, 75.
Grannis, Isaac, 10.
Grannis, Robert, 276.
Grant, 12.
Grant, Abiel, 120.
Grant, Azariah, 89.
Grant, Hamilton, 15.
Grant, Hezekiah, 105.
Grant, Isaac, 69.
Grant, James, 15, 113.
Grant, Joel, 39.
Grant, John, 118, 247, 249.
Grant, Joshua, 150.
Grant, Matthew, 84.

Griswold, Andrew, 47, 269.
Griswold, Asa, 36, 202.
Griswold, Edmond, 127.
Griswold, Edmund, 95, 117.
Griswold, Edward, 55, 230, 273.
Griswold, Elijah, 93.
Griswold, George, 202.
Griswold, John, 97, 164.
Griswold, Joseph, 203.
Griswold, Moses, 100, 154, 156.
Griswold, Selah, 228.
Griswold, Shubael, 18, 19, 20, 21, 24, 210, 211.
Griswold, Thomas, Jr., 277.
Griswold, White, 36.
Griswould, Giles, 193.
Griswould, Selah, 74.
Groas, Thomas, 149.
Grogan, John, 62.
Groos, Thos., 182.
Gross, Jonah, 3, 4.
Gross, Samuel, 89.
Grosvenor, L., 142.
Grosvenor, Lemuel, 183.
Grosvenor, Thomas, 46, 101, 118.
Groton, 31, 55, 74, 78, 80, 82, 88, 89, 90, 113, 174, 267.
Groundwater, Thomas, 253.
Grover, Phineas, 49, 228.
Grover, Stephen, 168.
Grow, Ambros, 143.
Growse, David, 66.
Gudeahn, Dick, 21.
Guile, Samuel, 163.
Guilford, 18, 23, 24, 25, 55, 56, 70, 88, 89, 104, 113, 191, 277.
"Guilford," 242, 243.
Guinea, 104.
Gurnsey, Joel, 117, 127.
Gustin, Amos, 106, 126.
Gutherie, Abel, 123.
Guthrie, Abraham, 80.
Guy, John, 10.
Guyant, Luke, 271.
Gyer, Samuel, 246.

H[ ], Nehemiah, 80.
Hackensack, 139.
Hackley, Arunah, 101.
Hackly, Abel, 5.
Haddam, 56, 66, 68, 69, 81, 88, 89, 115, 278.
Hadley, Samuel, 70.
Hadlock, Reuben, 77, 235.
Hadlock, Stephen, 12.
Hagar, Simeon, 89.
Hail, Jacob, 230.
Haill, Gershom, 185.
Hait, Elijah, 85.
Hait, H., 84.
Hait, Joel, 103, 130.
Hait, John, 23.
Hait, Joseph, 53, 54.
Hait, Justus, 214.
Hait, Samuel, 47, 78, 85.
Hait, Stephen, 77.
Haladay, Jacob, 103, 131.
Halbisk, Preston, 38.
Hale, 50.
Hale, Aaron, 89.
Hale, Aron, 183.
Hale, Benjamin, 135, 137.
Hale, Elizur, 208.
Hale, Frary, 157.
Hale, Isaac, 157.
Hale, John, 36, 244, 248.
Hale, Jonathan, 133.
Hale, Joseph, 142.
Hale, Moses, 112.
Hale, Nathan, 28, 29, 30, 31.
Hale, Nathaniel, 80.
Hale, Robert, 15.
Hale, Samuel, 15.
Hale, Timothy, 202.
Halel, Kaswell, 145.
Hall, 97.
Hall, Abell, 212.
Hall, Abijah, 209.
Hall, Abner, 117, 127.
Hall, Asahel, 81, 117, 127.
Hall, Asaph, 203, 209.
Hall, Barnabus, 81.
Hall, Benjamin, 119.
Hall, Benjamin, Jr., 277.
Hall, Brinton, 192.
Hall, Caleb, 208, 210, 276.
Hall, Charles, 18, 19.
Hall, Daniel, 192.
Hall, David, 85, 230.
Hall, Ebenezer, 16.
Hall, Eber, 23, 113, 277.
Hall, Elisha, 170, 222.
Hall, Enos, 193, 276.
Hall, Ezeriah, 186.
Hall, Gad, 192.
Hall, Gilbert, 13.
Hall, Giles, 229.
Hall, Gills, 230.
Hall, Hiland, 20.
Hall, Hill, 2d, 276.
Hall, Isaac, 192, 211, 226, 276.
Hall, Israel, 193.
Hall, Isral, 276.
Hall, John, 1, 34, 238, 239, 242, 243.
Hall, Jonah, 17, 19.

Hall, Joseph, 275.
Hall, Joshua, 169.
Hall, Jotham, 112.
Hall, Levi, 106, 127.
Hall, Luis, 197.
Hall, Moses, 18, 192.
Hall, Moses, Jr., 192.
Hall, N., 210.
Hall, Nathan, 1, 165.
Hall, Nathaniel, 89, 209.
Hall, Philemon, 49.
Hall, Phinehas, 193.
Hall, Robert, 57.
Hall, Samuel, 13, 24, 27, 41, 43, 89, 187, 188, 192.
Hall, Silas, 200.
Hall, Stephen, 28, 48, 69, 109.
Hall, Street, 17, 20, 23.
Hall, Talmadge, 49.
Hall, Talmage, 25.
Hall, Timothy, 135, 193.
Hall, William, 89, 212, 242, 253.
Halladay, Jacob, 125.
Halladay, Simeon, 146.
Hallam, 64.
Hallam, Amos, 211.,
Hallam, Robert, 47.
Halley, Jesse, 27.
Halley, Silas, 31.
Hallow, Richard P., 267, 269.
Hallows, Samuel, 74.
Hally, John, 38.
Hally, Joseph, 36, 238.
Halsey, Jeremiah, 210.
Hambden, William, 89.
Hamblen, James, 178.
Hamblen, Joel, 39.
Hambleton, Asel, 196.
Hambleton, James, 34.
Hambleton, John, 32, 57.
Hambleton, Joshua, 34.
Hambleton, Seth, 43.
Hamblin, Mark, 94.
Hamblin, William, Jr., 23.
Hamelton, Paul, 198.
Hamilton, John, 118.
Hamilton, Seth, 41.
Hamistond, Ebenezer, 184.
Hamlin, Daniel, 134.
Hamlin, Jabez, 222.
Hamlin, Joel, 122.
Hamlin, Joseph, 85.
Hamlin, Mark, 277.
Hamlin, Thomas, 138.
Hamlin, William, 21, 22.
Hamlinton, Duke, 22.
Hammon, Isaac, 29.
Hammond, David, 103, 125, 131.
Hammond, Robert, 94.
Hampton, Thomas, 245, 250.
Hanchet, 12.
Hanchet, Oliver, 18, 19, 20, 21, 23.
Hanchin, 13.
Hancock, Abner, 164.
Hancock, John, 70.
Hancock, Thomas, 264.
Hand, David, 238, 239.
Hand, John, 29.
Hand, Joseph, 122.
Hand, Josiah, 29.
Hande, Caleb, 15.
Handee, Caleb, 206.
Handy, Benjamin, 178.
Hanfield, Benjamin, 15.
Hanford, 223.
Hanford, Mathew, 217.
Hanford, Timothy, 77.
Hanks, Consider, 119.
Hanmon, Japhet, 82.
Hannabal, Joseph, 89.
Hannah, James, 38.
Hannibale, Joseph, 246.
Hanniball, Job, 246, 250.
Hanniball, Joseph, 251.
Hanscum, James, 261.
Hanson, Peter, 246, 250.
Hard, Stephen, 200.
Harden, Frederick, 89.
Harden, James, 79.
Harding, Amos, 260.
Harding, Seth, 231, 232, 233, 234, 255.
Harding, Turner, 231.
Haridon, Daniel, 32.
Haris, Champlin, 57.
Harlem, 279.
Harman, John, 47.
Harmon, Jaquess, 54.
Harmon, John, 63.
Harp, Elias, 79.
Harrap, Joseph, 54.
Harrard, Sedeman, 85.
Harrey, Ephraim, 122.
Harrington, John, 35.
Harrington, Ruben, 56.
Harrington, William, 65.
Harris, Amos, 54.
Harris, Benjamin, 32.
Harris, Champlin, 89.
Harris, Daniel, 138, 175.
Harris, George, 65.
Harris, John, 61, 229.
Harris, Joseph, 135.
Harris, Josiah, 175.
Harris, Paul, 171.
Harris, Samuel, 171.

Hewit, Benjamin, 35.
Hewit, Elkanah, 216.
Hewit, Epheram, 35.
Hewit, Henrey, 186.
Hewit, John, 35.
Hewit, Randol, 35.
Hewit, Stephen, 172.
Hewitt, Daniel, 269.
Hewitt, Nathaniel, 269.
Hewlet, Nahl, 169.
Heydon, Benajah, 139.
Hibbard, Jedediah, 114.
Hibberd, Andrew, 64.
Hickcox, James, 192.
Hickcox, Nathaniel, 192.
Hickock, Benjamin, 212.
Hickock, Daniel, 208.
Hickocks, Daniel, 224.
Hickok, Daniel, 199.
Hickoxs, J., 227.
Hickum, Elisha, 127.
Hicock, Nathan, 19.
Hicock, Samuel, 46.
Hicok, Silas, 173.
Hide, Andrew, 162.
Hide, Clark, 82.
Hide, Elijah, 227.
Hide, James, 54, 121.
Hide, Joel, 124.
Hide, Joshua, 37, 201.
Hide, Oliver, 5.
Hide, Rufus, 277.
Hide, Samuel, 190.
Higbe, Noah, 204.
Higbee, John, 17.
Higgans, Isaac, 102.
Higgins, Benjamin, 132.
Higgins, Cornelius, 48, 89.
Higgins, George, 199.
Higgins, Isaac, 109, 130, 269.
Higgins, Jesse, 229.
Higgins, John, 59.
Higgins, Lawdin, 241.
Higgins, Seth, 261.
Higgins, William, 47, 50, 59, 234, 239, 252, 256.
Higley, Carmi, 27.
Higley, Eber, 142.
Higley, Obed, 27, 142.
Higley, Seth, 7.
Hildreth, Luther, 238, 239.
Hill, 55, 114.
Hill, Abraham, 38.
Hill, Bela, 67.
Hill, David, 10.
Hill, Ebenezer, 180.
Hill, Eliphalot, 81.
Hill, Henry, 45.
Hill, Isaac, 115, 117.
Hill, James, 245, 249.
Hill, John, 63, 247, 251.
Hill, Jonathan, 58, 120, 263.
Hill, Philip, 103, 131.
Hill, Phinhas, 38.
Hill, Reuben, 79, 213.
Hill, Russell, 81.
Hill, Samuel, 113.
Hill, Seth, 39.
Hill, Squier, 14.
Hill, Squire, 14.
Hill, Thomas, 58.
Hillard, Azariah, 186.
Hillard, Daniel, 264.
Hilleyer, Theodore, 145.
Hilliard, Azariah, 253.
Hilliard, Benjamin, 174.
Hilliard, James, 253.
Hilliard, Thurston, 269.
Hilliard, William, 181, 219.
Hillman, George, 253.
Hillman, Peleg, 252.
Hills, 225.
Hills, Ebenezer, 48, 73.
Hills, Elisha, 157.
Hills, Ephrm, 163.
Hills, Erastus, 41, 43.
Hills, George, 145, 146, 147, 148.
Hills, Israel, 157.
Hills, J., 226.
Hills, Jabez, 223.
Hills, James, 148.
Hills, John, 25, 210.
Hills, Joseph, 157.
Hills, Libbius, 160.
Hills, Medad, 225.
Hills, Phillip, 125.
Hills, Samuel, 116.
Hills, Samuel, Jr., 137.
Hills, Seth, 37.
Hills, Squier, 183.
Hills, Thomas, 160.
Hillyard, Azeriah, 256.
Hillyard, Daniel, 257, 261.
Hillyer, Theodore, 147.
Hilyer, Asa, 203.
Hinckley, Ichabod, 46, 54.
Hinckley, Wiat, 267.
Hindman, Benjamin, 83.
Hine, Ambrose, 223.
Hine, Isaac, 200, 208.
Hine, Nathan, 208, 212, 224.
Hine, Noble, 206, 209, 225.
Hine, Titus, 109.
Hines, H., 214.
Hines, Patrick, 54.
Hinkley, Gershom, 134.

Hinkley, Thomas. 32.
Hinkley, Wait, 266.
Hinman, 12, 136.
Hinman, Agur, 213.
Hinman, Asa, 224.
Hinman, Benjamin, 16, 18, 19, 20, 21, 22, 23, 24, 25, 227.
Hinman, David, 208, 224, 225.
Hinman, E., 177, 206.
Hinman, Elijah, 85, 210, 224, 225.
Hinman, Enos, 213.
Hinman, Hughn, 71.
Hinman, Joel, 213, 269.
Hinman, Joseph, 52.
Hinman, Justus, 85.
Hinman, Lewis, 37.
Hinman, N., 213.
Hinman, Nathan, 98.
Hinman, Samuel, 122.
Hinman, Wait, 85.
Hinsdale, Abiel, 105.
Hinsdale, Jacob, 209, 225.
Hinsdale, Samuel, 139.
Hinsdale, William, 37.
Hird, Philow, 215.
Hiscox, Simeon, 212.
Hiscox, Thomas, 89.
Hitchcock, Abel, 109.
Hitchcock, Benjamin, Jr., 85.
Hitchcock, D., 207.
Hitchcock, Daniel, 194.
Hitchcock, David, 24, 71, 208, 212, 226.
Hitchcock, Jared, 109.
Hitchcock, Jonathan, 189.
Hitchcock, Lemuel, 89.
Hitchcock, Levi, 76.
Hitchcock, Samuel, 138.
Hoadley, 210.
Hoadley, Ralph, 252.
Hoadley, Samuel, 112, 179.
Hoadly, Ralph, 256.
Hoadly, Samuel, 10.
Hoadly, Timothy, 179.
Hobart, John, 76, 104, 129, 131.
Hobart, Mason, 10, 24.
Hobbard, Elisha, 197.
Hobbol, Ezra, 198.
Hobby, Thomas, 21.
Hodg, Gulielmas, 79.
Hodge, Asahel, 36, 75, 119.
Hodge, David, 70, 103, 109, 130.
Hodge, William, 266.
Hodges, Abel, 197.
Hodges, Abel, Jr., 196.
Hodges, Asahel, 49.
Hodges, Thomas, 86.
Hodgkiss, Ladwick, 59.
Hodnett, Richard, 12.
Hoit, Samuel, 85.
Holabird, Timothy, Jr., 37.
Holaday, Jonathan, 27.
Holaday, Simeon, 146.
Holbrook, Daniel, 210, 225.
Holbrook, Daniel, Jr., 189.
Holbrook, John, 163.
Holbrook, Pelatiah, 3.
Holbrook, Peletiah, 162.
Holbrook, Thomas, 246, 248, 255.
Holburton, William, 243.
Holcom, Jedidiah, 146.
Holcomb, Adonijah, 203.
Holcomb, Amos, 67.
Holcomb, Asahel, 221.
Holcomb, Benajah, 211.
Holcomb, Benjamin, 147.
Holcomb, Carmi, 142.
Holcomb, David, 203.
Holcomb, Dosa, 67.
Holcomb, Ebenezer, 146, 148.
Holcomb, Elijah, 146, 148.
Holcomb, Ephraim, 203.
Holcomb, Hezekiah, 203.
Holcomb, Increase, 117, 127.
Holcomb, Jachish, 95.
Holcomb, Jed, 147.
Holcomb, Jedediah, 147.
Holcomb, Jedidiah, 145, 146.
Holcomb, John, 199.
Holcomb, John G., 123.
Holcomb, Joseph, Jr., 142.
Holcomb, Joshua, 203.
Holcomb, Nathaniel, 142.
Holcomb, Peter, 146.
Holcomb, Peter, Jr., 148.
Holcomb, Phineas, 67, 146, 147.
Holcomb, Phinehas, 147.
Holcomb, Seth, 146.
Holcomb, Silas, 203.
Holcomb, Timothy, 21.
Holcomb, Zacheus, 67.
Holden, Amos, 94, 103, 131.
Holdrath, William, 157.
Holdridge, Hezekiah, 48.
Holdridge, Robert, 123.
Holdridge, Rufus, 113.
Holebrook, Peletiah, 2.
Holiday, Jacob, 57.
Holladay, Simeon, 67.
Holladay, Thomas, 245, 251.
Hollady, Simeon, 146.
Holland, Michael, 264.
Hollenbeak, John, 37.
Hollester, Giles, 245.
Holley, Abraham, 76.
Holley, Crandal, 186.

Hough, John, 18, 169, 193, 223, 276.
Hough, Lent, 194, 276.
Hough, Samuel, 16.
Hough, Simon, 113, 178, 237.
Houghton, Lebbeus, 29.
House, Abner, 157.
House, Alexander, 161.
House, Daniel, 157.
House, Eleazer, 27.
House, Elijah, 4.
House, Eliphalet, Jr., 259.
House, Israel, 157.
House, James, 161.
House, Lazarus, 157.
House, Rial M., 234.
House, Simon, 2, 3.
House, William, 157.
Hovey, Jonathan, 143.
Hovey, Joseph, 259.
Hovey, Nathan, 105, 120.
Hovey, S., 172.
Hovey, Samuel, 171, 172.
Hovey, Zacheus, 114, 116.
How, Elisha, 157.
How, James, 169.
How, Jazaniah, 269.
How, John, 137, 201.
How, Squier, 168.
How, Zachariah, 110, 116.
Howard, Benjamin, 137.
Howard, Charles, 261.
Howard, Elijah, 95.
Howard, Hiram W., 99.
Howard, John, 64, 140.
Howard, Richard, 74.
Howard, Solomon, 95.
Howard, William, 207, 211, 245, 249, 262.
Howd, Benjamin, 269.
Howd, Joel, 10.
Howe, Isaac, 207, 210, 225, 226.
Howe, Jaazmah, 68.
Howe, Joseph, 96.
Howell, Jason, 187.
Howell, Nicholas, 102, 108, 130.
Howes, Jos., 2.
Howes, Joseph, 3.
Howis, Zenas, 4.
Hoyt, Agur, 194.
Hoyt, Amos, 85, 194.
Hoyt, Benajah, 199.
Hoyt, Comfort, 198, 226.
Hoyt, Daniel, 194, 218.
Hoyt, David, 200.
Hoyt, Elijah, 269.
Hoyt, Enos, 198.
Hoyt, James, 199, 218.
Hoyt, Job, 218.
Hoyt, John, 200.
Hoyt, Jonathan, 195, 200, 218.
Hoyt, Justus, 200.
Hoyt, Nathan, 195.
Hoyt, Nathaniel, 198.
Hoyt, Noah, 200.
Hoyt, Samuel, 199.
Hoyt, Walter, 218.
Hozard, Samuel, 142.
Huatt, Alvin, 243.
Hubard, George, 53.
Hubbard, Aaron, 137.
Hubbard, Abner, 61.
Hubbard, Asa, 145.
Hubbard, Daniel, 98.
Hubbard, David, 127, 128, 137.
Hubbard, Elihu, 89.
Hubbard, Elijah, 137.
Hubbard, Eliz., 222.
Hubbard, Elizer, 137.
Hubbard, Elizur, 22, 208.
Hubbard, George, 208.
Hubbard, Hezekiah, 46, 61.
Hubbard, John, 49.
Hubbard, Jonathan, 107, 246.
Hubbard, Joseph, 256.
Hubbard, Matthew, 98.
Hubbard, Samuel, 56, 209.
Hubbart, John, 41.
Hubbart, Simon, 51.
Hubbel, Nathan, 77.
Hubbel, Salmon, 49, 77, 78.
Hubbel, William G., 224, 225.
Hubbell, Amos, 197.
Hubbell, David, 120, 269.
Hubbell, Egbon, 75.
Hubbell, Gideon, 196.
Hubbell, Isaac, 85.
Hubbell, Seth, 77.
Hubbell, Peter, 195.
Hubbell, Shadrack, 197.
Hubbell, William G., 199, 208.
Hubbert, Ephraim B., 215.
Hubbert, Gideon, 135.
Hubbert, John, 43.
Hubbil, Ebenezer, 181, 219.
Hubbil, John, 190.
Hubbil, John, Jr., 190.
Hubble, David, 106, 126.
Hubble, Enoch, 197.
Hubble, William G., 16, 17, 20, 21.
Hubburd, David, 157.
Hubburd, Joseph, 157.
Huble, Silas, 197.
Huchans, Ezra, 168.
Huchans, Shubl, 168.

Huchans, Silas, 167.
Hudson, B., 220.
Hudson, Eleazer, 269.
Hudson, George, 39.
Hudson, John, 89.
Hues, John, 141.
Huet, Elkanah, 184.
Huffman, Timothy, 255.
Hugg, Isaac, 37.
Hugh, John, 207.
Hughes, 211.
Hughs, John, 62.
Hugins, Samuel, 220.
Huit, Increse, 167.
Huit, Stephen, 167.
Hulbert, Lucius, 57.
Hulet, Aaron, 63.
Hulet, Elim, 168.
Hulet, Nehemiah, 65.
Hulett, Joseph, 135.
Hulett, Phineas, 95.
Hull, Aaron, 200.
Hull, Andrew, 19.
Hull, Asael, 95.
Hull, Asahel, 127, 184, 275.
Hull, Charles, 192, 194.
Hull, Daniel, 111.
Hull, David, 48, 61, 70, 110, 191.
Hull, David, 2d, 94.
Hull, Ebenezer, 194.
Hull, Eli, 97, 110.
Hull, Ephraim, 98.
Hull, Gordon, 192.
Hull, Henry, 21, 37, 102, 111.
Hull, Henery, 129.
Hull, James, 89.
Hull, Jehiel, 20.
Hull, John, 192.
Hull, Jonathan, 111.
Hull, Joseph, 32.
Hull, Miles, 134, 208, 211.
Hull, Mills, 226.
Hull, Robart, 97.
Hull, Samuel, 103, 131.
Hull, Stephen, 89, 269.
Hull, Sylvanus, 193.
Hull, Wakeman, 69.
Hultman, Jonas, 246.
Humiston, Thomas, 179.
Hummiston, David, 119.
Humphrevile, Lemuel, 179.
Humphrey, 147.
Humphrey, David, 36.
Humphrey, Elihu, 20.
Humphrey, Erastus, 27.
Humphrey, Joel, 27.
Humphrey, John, 27.
Humphrie, J., 177.
Humphry, Asher, 145, 146, 147, 148.
Humphry, Benoni, 146, 147, 148.
Humphry, Charles, 145, 147, 148
Humphry, David, 48.
Humphry, Elihu, 24.
Humphry, Elijah, 48.
Humphry, Giles, 146, 148.
Humphry, John, 223.
Humphry, Jonathan, 145, 146, 147, 148.
Humphry, Joseph, 7.
Humphry, Noah, 142, 202.
Humphry, Noah, Jr., 164.
Humphry, Richard, 164.
Humphry, Simeon, 202.
Humphy, Jonathan, 147.
Humphy, Martin, 145, 147.
Humphy, Solomon, 145.
Hungerford, David, 70.
Hungerford, Ezra, 199.
Hungerford, Isaiah, 199.
Hungerford, John, 139.
Hungerford, Josiah, 197.
Hungerford, Thomas, 182.
Hungerford, Uri, 114.
Hungerford, Z., 209.
Hunt, Edmon, 34.
Hunt, Eldad, 163.
Hunt, Elijah, 105, 186.
Hunt, Henry, 247, 251, 253, 255.
Hunt, John, 262.
Hunt, Richard, 89, 230, 232.
Hunt, Russell, 2d, 37.
Hunt, Simeon, 105.
Hunt, Walter, 260.
Hunt, Ziba, 210.
Hunter, Turtle, 253, 256.
Huntington, 265, 267.
Huntington, Andrew, 161.
Huntington, Christopher, 186.
Huntington, Ebenezer, 67, 122.
Huntington, Elijah, 185.
Huntington, Eliphlet, 186.
Huntington, Gamalel, 184.
Huntington, Jedediah, 16, 17, 18, 19, 22, 23, 24, 25, 27, 51, 267.
Huntington, Robert, 79.
Huntington, Simeon, 220.
Huntley, Amos, 1.
Huntley, Phineas, 132.
Huntly, Moses, 185.
Huntly, Zadock, 185.
Hurd, Abner, 136.
Hurd, Adam, 136.
Hurd, Asahel, 38.
Hurd, Curtis, 136.
Hurd, Daniel, 136.

Ives, Noah, 211.
Ives, Samuel, 194.
Ives, Timothy, 192.
Ives, William, 235.

Jack, Andrew, 71.
Jacklin, Thaddeus, 110.
Jacklin, Thadeus, 116.
Jackson, Daniel, 106, 127, 243.
Jackson, David, 123.
Jackson, Elijah, 34.
Jackson, Ephraim, 32.
Jackson, Francis, 254.
Jackson, Garshum, 196.
Jackson, John, 69.
Jackson, John, Jr., 34.
Jackson, Nathan, 243.
Jackson, Nathan P., 89.
Jackson, Nathaniel, 49.
Jackson, Salah, 146, 147.
Jackson, Samuel, 78.
Jackson, William, 69, 99.
Jackways, William, 69.
Jacobs, John, 253.
Jacobs, M., 89.
Jacobs, Zebulon, 10.
Jacobson, George, 260.
Jacques, Launcelot, 49.
James, John, 174.
James, Robert A., 245, 250, 252.
Janes, Daniel, 192.
Janeways, Daniel, 35.
Jaquies, William, 138.
Jarvis, Francis, 260.
Jarvis, William, 243.
Jeffers, Peter, 240, 241.
Jeffery, James, 264.
Jeffords, George, 175.
Jelleff, James, 217.
Jellits, 138.
Jemson, John, 54.
Jenkins, Calvin, 68.
Jenkins, Samuel, 103.
Jennings, Charles, 38.
Jennings, D., 3d, 84.
Jennings, Elnathan, 89.
Jennings, Isban, 69.
Jennings, James, 232.
Jennings, Jonathan, 246, 249.
Jennings, Justin, 266.
Jennings, Lyman, 16.
Jennings, Michael, 236.
Jennings, Nathan, 23, 254.
Jennings, Nathan, Jr., 18.
Jennings, Nathaniel, 243, 254.
Jerison, Michael, 87.
Jermain, Charles, 19.
Jermain, Peter, 19.
Jerry, Ephraim, 74.
Jervis, Jonathan, 232.
Jervis, Nathaniel, 232.
Jesup, Eben, 180.
Jewell, Joshua, Jr., 37.
Jewett, Caleb, 270.
Jewett, Caleb, Jr., 34.
Jewett, Joseph, 22, 23.
Jewit, N., 209.
Jinings, David, 234.
Jinkens, Samuel, 130.
Jinnings, Jacob, 217.
Jinnings, Joseph, 74.
Johns, William, 119.
Johnson, 59, 146.
Johnson, Abraham, 109.
Johnson, Alpheus, 254.
Johnson, Amos, 189, 276.
Johnson, Artemas, 10, 24, 265.
Johnson, Asa, 32.
Johnson, Ashel, 189.
Johnson, Benoni, 202.
Johnson, Charles, 82, 276.
Johnson, D., 84.
Johnson, Daniel, 18, 23.
Johnson, David, 194.
Johnson, Ebenezer, 202.
Johnson, Eliakim, 58.
Johnson, Elias, 98.
Johnson, Elijah, 56.
Johnson, Gideon, Jr., 189.
Johnson, Grant, 267.
Johnson, Hamlin, 67.
Johnson, Henry, 112.
Johnson, Hezekiah, 189.
Johnson, Isaac, 135, 146, 147, 209.
Johnson, Israel, 58.
Johnson, J., 206.
Johnson, James, 141, 230.
Johnson, James A., 59.
Johnson, Joel, 113, 277.
Johnson, John, 71, 134, 147, 220, 238, 239, 240.
Johnson, John, Jr., 277.
Johnson, Jonathan, 47, 194.
Johnson, Joseph, 122, 146, 147.
Johnson, Joseph, Jr., 189.
Johnson, Justis, 183.
Johnson, Justus, 265, 270.
Johnson, Miles, 208, 222, 224, 275.
Johnson, Nathaniel, 53.
Johnson, Nathaniel, Jr., 189.
Johnson, O., 206.
Johnson, Obadiah, 221.
Johnson, Peter, 54, 211.
Johnson, Phinehas, 109.
Johnson, Prince, 114.
Johnson, Robert, 29, 31.

Keeler, Thaddeus, 48.
Keeler, Thomas, 69.
Keeler, Timothy, 200.
Keeler, Timothy, 2d, 200.
Keeler, Uriah, 78, 103, 130.
Keelor, Aaron, 50.
Keelor, Ebenezer, 73.
Keelor, S., 212.
Keeney, Benjamin. 5.
Keeney, Ethel, 189.
Keeney, Isaac, 157.
Keeney, James, 58.
Keeney, Medad, 189.
Keeney, Theodore, 133.
Keenne, Joseph, 263.
Keith; Peter, 222.
Kelcey, Aaron, 210, 266.
Kelcey, Jeremiah, 178.
Kelcey, Samuel, 21.
Kelcy, Aaron, 206.
Kelcy, Daniel, 36.
Keley, Joel, 184.
Keley, Nathan, 202.
Keley, Ruben, 184.
Kelley, Ephraim, 212.
Kelley, John, 53.
Kellogg, Aaron, 94.
Kellogg, Alen, 203.
Kellogg, Asahel, 37.
Kellogg, Bradford. 67, 139.
Kellogg, Charles, 221, 223, 224.
Kellogg, David, 160.
Kellogg, Daniel, 200.
Kellogg, Eldad, 35.
Kellogg, Elijah, 200.
Kellogg, Enoch, 77.
Kellogg, Enos. 274.
Kellogg, Ezekil, 186.
Kellogg, George, 274.
Kellogg, Grove, 77.
Kellogg, Helmont, 105, 201.
Kellogg, John, 159, 218, 227.
Kellogg, Joseph, 36, 208.
Kellogg, Leveret, 36.
Kellogg, Martin, 36.
Kellogg, N., 188.
Kellogg, Nathan, 195.
Kellogg, Noah, 36, 211.
Kellogg, Oliver, 274.
Kellogg, Phinihas, 27.
Kellogg, Samuel, 22, 39.
Kellogg, Stephen, 154, 156.
Kellogg, Thomas, 86.
Kelly, John, 235, 267.
Kelsey, Elisha, 273.
Kelsey, John, 191.
Kelsey, Nathan. 71.
Kelsey, Noah, 106.
Kelsey, Presto, 113.
Kelsey, Preston, 116.
Kelsey, Samuel, 37.
Kelsey, Timothy, 273.
Kelsey, William, 191.
Kelsey, Zach, 274.
Kelsey, Zechariah. 133.
Kelsy, Noah, 69.
Kene, Thadeus, 189.
Kenedy, Andrew, 1.
Keney, Cyrus, 171.
Keney, Thomas, 254.
Kennedy, Henry, 247, 252.
Kennedy, James, 95.
Kennedy, Thomas, 1, 165.
Kenney, Benjamin, 235.
Kenney, Charles, 253.
Kenny, Benjamin, 118.
Kensington, 79.
Kent, Elihu, 209.
Kent, Samuel, 80.
Kent, Zenas, 63.
Kent, 73, 89, 90, 103.
Kesley, Noah, 126.
Ketcham, Ezra, 110.
Ketcham, Timothy, 198.
Kettell, Jonathan, 202.
Kettle, Thomas, 55.
Keyes, Marshall, 124.
Kibbe, Elisha, 165.
Kibbee, Elijah, 128.
Kibbee, Frederick, 120.
Kibbee, Phillip, 120.
Kibby, Samuel, 139.
Kilbey, Ebenezer, 154.
Kilborn, Charles, 23.
Kilborn, Jarey, 201.
Kilborne, Araunah. 93.
Kilborne, Jonathan. 209.
Kilby, Ebenezer, 133, 156.
Kilby, Elijah, 127.
Killam, Cyrus, 74.
Killey, John. 260.
Killingley, 6, 55, 57, 58, 59, 64, 65, 66, 78, 79, 82, 90, 103, 104, 267.
Killington, 67.
Killingworth, 53, 55, 56, 88, 89, 113.
Kimbal, Charles, 15.
Kimbal, Jesse, 64.
Kimbalin, William, 252.
Kimball, Jared, 124.
Kimball, Jedediah, 103, 121, 131.
Kimball, Jesse, 35.
Kimball, John, 124.
Kimball, Richard, 254.
Kimball, Samuel. 105.

Ladd, Jesse, 1.
Ladd, Oliver, 64.
Lade, John, 56.
La Fayette, Marquis de, 121.
Laflen, John, 15.
Laflin, Abraham, 15.
Lain, Allen, 55.
Lain, John, 57.
Lake, Phinehas, 270.
Lake Champlain, 18.
Lamb, Benjamin, 74.
Lamb, David, 175.
Lamb, George, 260.
Lamb, Isaac, 34.
Lamb, John, 258.
Lamb, Joseph, 19.
Lamb, Lemuel, 212.
Lamb, Rufus, 163.
Lamb, Silas, Jr., 216.
Lamb, Thomas, 229.
Lamb, William, 254, 260, 264.
Lambart, Samuel, 55.
Lamberton, Nathaniel, 27.
Lamberton, Obed, 138.
Lamberton, Obediah, 68.
Lament, William, 110.
Lamphear, Abel, 199.
Lamphear, Roswell, 257.
Lamphear, William, 38.
Lamphere, Roswell, 128.
Lamson, Elnathan, 203.
Lamson, Nathaniel, 190.
Lamson, Nathaniel, Jr., 190.
Landers, Samuel, 27.
Landon, David, 191, 210.
Landon, Hazia, 81.
Landon, James, 201.
Landon, Reuben, 201.
Landor, Gael, 91.
Lane, Allen, 82, 212.
Lane, Allin, 141.
Lane, Daniel, 81.
Lane, Isaac, 205.
Lane, Joel, 79.
Lane, John, 135.
Lane, William, 89.
Lanford, James, 73.
Langton, John, 210.
Langworthy, Rober, 175.
Lankton, Daniel, 210.
Lanphere, James, 246.
Lanphere, James, Jr., 249.
Lansing, Jacob J., 72.
Larence, Jonas, 205.
Larkam, Thomas, 264.
Larkim, Rodrick, 188.
Larkin, John, 79.
Larkings, Joseph, 190.
Larned, Daniel, 183.
Larrabee, Seth, 74.
Larrabee, Willet, 89.
Larrance, James, 147, 148.
Larrenc, James, 145, 146.
Lary, Luman, 154.
Lasseur, John, 239.
Latham, 124.
Latham, Amos, 175.
Latham, Cary, 175.
Latham, Christopher, Jr., 270.
Latham, Daniel, 175.
Latham, Jasper, 175.
Latham, Joseph, 2d, 175.
Latham, Joseph, 4th, 175.
Latham, Joseph, 5th, 175.
Latham, William, 174, 212.
Lathergo, John, 246, 251.
Lathrop, E., 212.
Lathrop, Ebenezer, 212.
Lathrop, Neal, 260.
Latimer, John, 145, 146, 147.
Latimer, Robert, 140, 174.
Lattimer, 267.
Lattimer, J., 220, 221, 266.
Lattimer, Samuel, 220.
Lattimer, Solomon, 154, 156.
Lattimore, John, 147.
Laughlane, James, 34.
Laurence, Nehemiah, 208.
Laurence, Rosamus, 253.
Law, James, 5.
Law, Nathan, 113, 127.
Lawrance, James, 27.
Lawrence, Aaron, 35.
Lawrence, Amos, 68.
Lawrence, James, 147.
Lawrence, John, 32.
Laws, Thomas, 162.
Lawson, Joseph, 123.
Lawson, Samuel, 154, 156.
Lawson, Thomas, 32.
Lay, Asa, 48, 50, 71.
Lay, John, 113.
Lay, Lee, 132, 183, 207, 270.
Lay, Simeon, 210.
Lay, William, 211.
Leach, Caleb, 20.
Leach, James, 172.
Leach, Jonas, 164.
Leach, Joseph, 169.
Leach, Joshua, 20.
Leach, Lewis, 65.
Leach, Thomas, 174.
Leach, William, 105, 270.
Leaming, Judah, 18.
Learned, Darias, 184.
Leatch, William, 66.

McDavid, James, 230.
McDonald, John, 89.
McDowal, 89.
McDowel, Alexander, 47.
McDowell, Alexander, 58.
McFall, William, 56.
McFee, Angus, 22, 25.
McGeer, Gilbert, 126.
McGoon, John, 35.
McGraw, John, 181, 219.
McGregier, John, 63.
McGreigur, John, 47.
McGuire, Peleg, 254.
McHood, Joseph, 60.
McIngtosh, David, 245.
Macintire, Benjamin, 34.
Mack, 50.
Mack, Abner, 60.
Mack, Benjamin, 24.
Mack, Joel, 96.
Mack, John, 278, 279.
Mack, Josiah, 163.
Mack, Orlando, 90.
Mackarel, James, 160.
Mackaul, Jacob, 160.
McKee, Michael, 34.
McKenney, Andrew, 2.
McKenney, Wiliam, 2.
McKensey, James, 90.
McKenstry, Ezekiel, 2.
Mackentash, Samuel, 257.
Mackentosh, David, 252.
Mackhall, William, 89.
Mackinborough, Jedediah, 90.
Mackingtosh, David, 249.
McKinney, James, Jr., 1.
McKinney, James, 3d, 2.
McKinsey, John, 75.
Mackintosh, David, 244, 247.
McKilliss, Abraham, 12.
Macknel, Alexander, 15.
McKnight, Thomas, 2, 18, 55, 165.
Macksun, Robert, 39.
Mackswell, John, 149.
McLain, Alexander, 260.
McLean, Henry, 113.
McLean, Jacob, 110.
McLean, John, 21, 110.
McMann, John, 1st, 67.
McMann, John, 2d, 67.
McMannes, Hugh, 260.
McMullin, John, 62.
McNaal, James, 147.
McNall, James, 145, 146, 148.
McNally, John, 53.
McNe[ ], Mical, 61.
McNeal, A., 211.
McNeal, Arch., 209.
McNeal, Neal, 127, 128.
McNeil, Alexander, 201.
McNeil, Neil, 13.
McNiel, Niel, 37.
McPerson, Cornelius, 246, 249.
McPharson, Erie, 79.
McQuavy, Nathan, 165.
McQueen, William, 242, 243.
McRowe, Daniel, 78.
McRowe, John, 78.
McVey, James, 253.
McWavy, Ephrim, 2.
McWavy, Nathan, 2.
Maden, James, 234.
Maggott, Zebulon, 156.
Mahan, Phillip, 230.
Main, Amos, 211.
Main, Ezekiel, 80.
Main, Henrey, 186.
Main, Jerimiah, 186.
Main, John, Jr., 90.
Main, Stephen, 150.
Malbone, Jonah, 263.
Malbury, 69.
Malcolm, Daniel, 260.
Mallery, Abner, 208, 224.
Mallery, Amos, 108.
Mallery, Daniel, 242, 243.
Mallery, David, 10, 17.
Mallery, John, 10.
Mallery, John, Jr., 136.
Mallery, Jonah, 75.
Mallery, Levi, 16.
Mallery, Levy, 242, 262.
Mallery, Nathan, 123.
Mallery, Walker, 173.
Mallett, Lewis, 210, 211.
Malley, Abner, 225.
Malone, William, 264.
Maloney, Michael, 107, 116.
Malsby, John, 164.
Maltbie, Zaccheus, 10.
Man, Andrew, 162.
Man, Zadock, 163.
Manard, Cyrus, 171.
Mandwill, Ira, 79.
Maney, John, 116.
Manfeld, Phineus, 247.
Manley, Abner, 42, 43.
Manley, John, 42.
Manly, John, 43.
Mann, Elijah, 59.
Manning, 50.
Manning, Banjamin, 185.
Manning, David, Jr., 34.
Manning, Eleazer, 161.
Manning, Elijah, 64.
Manning, Joel, 64.

Mawwee, Elihu, 136.
Maxum, Jacob, 34.
May, Ebinezar, 232.
May, John, 232.
May, Joseph, 153, 155.
Maynard, Jabez, 29.
Maynard, Lemuel, 28.
Maynard, Samuel, 29, 30.
Mazuzen, Mark, 9.
Meach, Hezekiah, 263.
Meach, Jacob, 74, 184, 228, 270.
Meacham, Barnabus, 203.
Meacham, Seth, 36, 202.
Mead, 207.
Mead, Andrew, 266, 270.
Mead, Caleb, 209.
Mead, Ezra, 195.
Mead, Isaac, 98.
Mead, J., 177, 223.
Mead, Jasper, 48.
Mead, Jeremiah, 199.
Mead, John, 210, 214, 225, 226, 227, 266.
Mead, Joseph, 98.
Mead, M., 266.
Mead, Matthew, 23, 212, 267.
Mead, N., 226.
Mead, Nathaniel, 209.
Mead, Reuben, 85.
Mead, Reuben, Jr., 85.
Mead, Samuel, 69.
Mead, Silvanus, 226.
Mead, Theophilus, 77, 267.
Mead, Uriah, 77.
Meaker, David, 233.
Meaker, Ebenezer, 69.
Meaker, Hezekiah, 69.
Meakor, John, 243.
Meason, Elias, 123.
Mebbins, John, 274.
Meech, Elijah, 186.
Meech, Elkanah, 29.
Meech, Elkenah, 31.
Meech, Jacob, 175.
Meech, Joshua, 175.
Meeker, Daniel, 193.
Meeker, J., 84.
Meeker, John, 71, 107.
Meeker, Stephen, 54, 89, 121.
Meeks, Levi, 66.
Megraugh, John, 136.
Meigs, 97, 265.
Meigs, Phineas, 71.
Meigs, Return J., 17, 48, 70, 71.
Meigs, Simeon, 111.
Meigs, Stephen, 104, 113, 130.
Mekye, Daniel, 193.
Mekye, Wyllys, 193.
Melony, Matthew, 29.
Menter, Thomas, 231.
Meranda, Peter, 127.
Merchant, Thomas, 17.
Mercy, Thomas, 89.
Meriden, 68.
Merifield, Abraham, 149.
Meriman, Enoch, 53.
Merrel, Titus, 35.
Merrell, Cyperan, 20.
Merrell, Isaac, 27.
Merrells, Elias, 36.
Merrells, Nehemiah, 36.
Merrett, William, 66.
Merrey, Frances, 27.
Merriam, Amasa, 193.
Merriam, Benjamin, 192.
Merriam, Edmund, 111.
Merriam, Ephraim, 111.
Merriam, Ichabod, 16.
Merriam, Jesse, 192.
Merriam, John, 192.
Merriam, Joseph, 192.
Merriam, Marshal, 193.
Merriam, Nathaniel, 193.
Merriam, Samuel, 193.
Merriam, Titus, 192.
Merriam, William, 192.
Merrill, Elizer, 274.
Merrill, Gideon, 274.
Merrill, Samuel, 274.
Merrills, Cyprian, 89.
Merrills, Joseph, 251.
Merrills, Medad, 111.
Merrills, Nathaniel, 59.
Merrills, Noah, 124.
Merrils, Joseph, 247.
Merrils, Meade, 71.
Merriman, Amos, 276.
Merriman, Cabb, 276.
Merriman, Caleb, 192, 193, 194.
Merriman, Charles, 112.
Merriman, Elisha, 193.
Merriman, Israel, 202.
Merriman, Jesse, 193.
Merrit, Thomas, 29, 31.
Merritt, Ebenezer, 79.
Merrow, Elisha, 132.
Merrow, John, 245, 249.
Merry, Ebenezer, 235, 274.
Merwin, Daniel, 276.
Messenger, David, 145, 146, 147.
Messenger, Elisha, 27.
Messenger, Lemuel, 67.
Metcalf, Andrew, 149.
Metcalf, Dan, 149.
Metcalf, David, 162.
Metcalf, Ebenezer, 149.

Moffat, John, 184.
Moffitt, Andrew, 168.
Moffitt, John, 168.
Moger, Joseph, 69.
Molatto, Dick, 60.
Molbone, Peter, 260.
Molthrop, Acher, 242.
Molthrop, Jacob, 242.
Molton, Benjamin, 143.
Molton, Gurdon, 127.
Moltrop, John, 29.
Moltroup, Eli, 10.
Moltroup, Elihu, 10.
Moltroup, Joseph, 10.
Monroe, Joshua, 141.
Monson, Theophilus, 78.
Montague, Richard, 154.
Montigou, Bryon, 121.
Montigue, Richard, 156.
Moodus, 81.
Moody, Ebenezer, 85.
Moody, John, 42, 43.
Moody, Pero, 175.
Moody, Pichol, 19.
Moody, Tubal, 186.
Mookler, James, 188.
Moon, Isaac, 12.
Moor, Andrew, 39.
Moor, Ebenezer, 188.
Moor, Eber, 142.
Moor, Isaac, 203.
Moor, James, 233.
Moore, B., 170.
Moore, Eli, 278.
Moore, Michael, 254.
Moore, Obediah, 203.
Moore, Retrieve, 204.
Moore, Return, 238, 239.
Moore, Roger, 209.
Moore, William, 123.
Moorhouse, Ephraim, 119.
Moory, 55.
Morando, Peter, 117.
Morce, William, 15, 24.
Mordock, William, 161.
More, Caleb, 2.
More, William, 15.
Moredock, Daniel, 169.
Morehouse, David, 69, 152.
Morehouse, Ebenezer, 211.
Morehouse, James, 136.
Morehouse, Jesse, 152.
Morehouse, N., 84.
Morehouse, S., 177.
Morehouse, Solomon, 212.
Moretrup, David, 21.
Morey, Asa, 201.
Morey, Joseph, 64.
Morey, Reuben, 97.
Morgain, James, 60.
Morgan, Amos, 150.
Morgan, Asher, 185.
Morgan, Bemmir, 94.
Morgan, Christopher, 216.
Morgan, Daniel, 61.
Morgan, David, 276.
Morgan, Ephraim, 175.
Morgan, Isaac, 29, 216.
Morgan, Jacob, 205.
Morgan, James, 93, 208.
Morgan, James, Jr., 270.
Morgan, Jedediah, 216.
Morgan, Jesse, 82.
Morgan, John, 193, 216.
Morgan, John, 3d, 270.
Morgan, Jonathan, 150.
Morgan, Joseph, 95.
Morgan, Nathan, 74.
Morgan, Stephen, 216.
Morgan, Thomas, 216.
Morgan, William, 216.
Morgin, Peter, 171.
Morgin, Seth, 171.
Moriner, Henry, 81.
Morley, John, 137.
Morley, Thomas, 137.
Morrel, John, 85.
Morrill, Benjamin, 243.
Morris, Andrew, 252, 256, 262.
Morris, David, 19, 242.
Morris, Edmond, 257.
Morris, Edmund, 255.
Morris, Hial, 195.
Morris, Henry, 66.
Morris, James, 47, 50, 253.
Morris, John, 64, 200.
Morris, Thomas, 231.
Morris, William, 142.
Morrison, John, 245, 251.
Morrison, Norman, 262.
Morriss, Edmond, 262.
Morriss, Nathaniel, 52.
Morriss, William, 183.
Morse, Benjamin, 172.
Morse, James, 96.
Morse, Jesse, 134.
Morse, John, 227.
Morse, Joshua, Jr., 20.
Morse, Solomon, 139.
Morten, Jabez, 122.
Mortimer, John, 254.
Mortimore, Benjamin, 238, 239, 240.
Morton, Jedediah, 264.
Morwin, Samuel, 235.
Moseley, 214.

Patchers, Samuel, 126.
Patchin, David, 233.
Patchin, James, 128.
Patchin, Jared, 198.
Patchin, Martin, 232.
Pater, Shelden, 53.
Paterson, John, 241.
Paterson, William, 37.
Patten, Israel, 90.
Patterson, Andrew, 90, 236.
Patterson, Ansel, 114.
Patterson, James, 244, 247, 248.
Patterson, John, 23.
Patterson, Matthew, 35.
Patterson, Robert, 15.
Patterson, Samuel, 141, 181, 190, 219.
Patterson, William, 13.
Pauridge, Ananias, 35.
Paylon, Andrew, 141.
Payn, Benjamin, Jr., 6.
Payn, Dan, 6.
Payn, Nehemiah, 6.
Payn, Nehimiah, 182.
Payn, Stephen, 6, 259.
Payn, Stephen, Jr., 6.
Payne, Barnabas, 41.
Payne, Barnebas, 43.
Payne, Edward, 207.
Payne, Eleazer, 105.
Payne, Nehemiah, 149.
Payne, Rufus, 87.
Payne, Stephen, 149.
Payson, James, 207.
Peak, Samuel, 2.
Peake, Thomas, 184.
Pearce, Benjamin, 17.
Pearce, John, 16.
Pearle, John, 122.
Pearson, Daniel, 2.
Pearson, Ephrim, Jr., 2.
Pearson, Samuel, Jr., 2.
Peas, 133.
Peas, Pelatiah, 231.
Peas, Peter, 90.
Peas, Stephen, 231.
Pease, Abiel, 208.
Pease, Alpheus, 55.
Pease, Asaph, 255.
Pease, Benjamin, 32.
Pease, Daniel, 94.
Pease, David, 17, 94.
Pease, Eli, 23.
Pease, John, 2, 32, 250.
Pease, Joseph, 101.
Pease, Nathaniel, 159.
Pease, Silas, 57, 58, 60.
Pease, Sylvanus, 96.
Peat, James, 139.
Peat, William, 247.
Peck, Aaron, 17, 271.
Peck, Augustus, 108.
Peck, Benjamin, 98, 185, 211.
Peck, Dan, 275.
Peck, Daniel, 127.
Peck, Darius, 45, 90.
Peck, David, 101.
Peck, Eliphalet, 85, 199.
Peck, George, 212, 226.
Peck, Gideon, 202.
Peck, James, 18, 19, 151, 275.
Peck, Jesse, 95, 114, 116.
Peck, John, 71, 109, 181, 195, 219.
Peck, Josiah, 181, 219.
Peck, Judson, 181, 219.
Peck, Levy, 266.
Peck, Moses, 201.
Peck, Peter, 275.
Peck, Phinehas, 183.
Peck, Samuel, 25, 32, 127, 128, 209, 210.
Peck, Samuel, Jr., 16, 17, 19, 22, 24.
Peck, Silas, Jr., 90.
Peck, Stephen, 194.
Peck, Thomas, 93.
Peck, Ward, 108.
Peck, Zebulon, 90.
Peeck, Benjamin, 199.
Peck, Job, 151.
Peck, Josiah, 151.
Peck, Judson, 151.
Peekskill, 222.
Peepoon, Timothy, 5.
Peet, Benjamin, 38.
Peet, Daniel, 117.
Peet, Gideon, 135.
Peet, Samuel, 38.
Peet, William, 252.
Peirce, David, 187, 198.
Peirce, Deleno, 167.
Peirce, John, 168.
Peirce, Seth, 209.
Peirce, Silas, 198.
Peirson, Abel, 189.
Peirson, Abraham, 189.
Pelton, Daniel, 118.
Pelton, David, 90.
Pelton, George, 230.
Pelton, Jonathan, 135.
Pelton, Joseph, 134.
Pelton, Moses, 230.
Pember, Andrew, 2.
Pember, John, 40.
Pember, Samuel, 2.
Pember, Thomas, 2.

Phelps, Oliver, 20.
Phelps, Ozias, 205.
Phelps, Ozios, 164.
Phelps, Reuben, 51, 52, 139.
Phelps, Roger, 134, 162.
Phelps, Roswell, 162.
Phelps, Samuel, 162, 203.
Phelps, Seth, 47.
Phelps, Silas, 53, 121.
Phelps, Solomon, 160.
Phelps, Thomas, 59, 208.
Phelps, Thomas, Jr., 7.
Phelps, Timothy, Jr., 162.
Phelps, William, 67, 199.
Pheney, Joseph, 131.
Philemor, Henry, 274.
Philips, Eliphilet, 75.
Philips, Gideon, 273.
Philips, James, 51.
Phillips, G., 213.
Phillips, George, 208.
Phillips, Giddeon, 80.
Phillips, James, 29.
Phillips, Thomas, 110.
Phillips, Thompson, 229.
Phinney, Joseph, 104, 125.
Pick, Daniel, 95.
Picket, Benjamin, 197.
Picket, David, 200.
Picket, Ezra, 218.
Picket, Joseph, 189.
Picket, Ozias, 191.
Picket, Stephen, 218.
Picket, Thomas, 90, 270.
Pickett, Benjamin, 193.
Pickle, Hendrick, 254.
Picksley, Elijah, 76.
Pieno, Zenus, 81.
Pierce, Daniel, 93.
Pierce, Delino, 172.
Pierce, Henry, 254.
Pierce, John, 126, 127.
Pierce, Samuel, 35, 61, 133.
Pierce, Seth, 210.
Pierce, William, 13.
Pierpoint, John, 179.
Pierpoint, Thomas, 11.
Pierpont, Thomas, 16.
Pierson, Ephraim, 166.
Pierson, Samuel, Jr., 165.
Pike, James, 36.
Pike, Jonathan, 167.
Pike, Samuel, 36.
Pilgrim, Thomas, 61.
Pillias, A., 84.
Pimber, Andrew, 165.
Pineo, James, 159, 163.
Pineo, Jeams, Jr., 5.
Pinkham, Selvenus, 245, 249.
Pinneo, James, 4.
Pinneo, Jeams, Jr., 6.
Pinney, Ebenezer, 165.
Pinney, Elezer, 2.
Pinney, John, 2.
Pinney, Joseph, Jr., 2.
Pinney, Lemuel, 1, 166.
Pitcher, Ebenezer, Jr., 22.
Pitkin, George, 18, 165, 227.
Pitkin, Richard, 221.
Pitts, Benjamin, 15.
Pitts, Richard, 110.
Placey, William, 74.
Plainfield, 65, 66, 74, 79, 82, 118.
Plank, Isaih, 79.
Plant, Ethiel, 140.
Plant, Solomon, 190.
Plant, Stephen, 164, 201.
Plats, Nathan, 196.
Platt, Dan, 178.
Platt, Daniel, 199, 211.
Platt, Ebenezer, 104, 131.
Platt, James, 85, 199.
Platt, Jonas, 84.
Platt, Jonathan, 85.
Platt, Joseph, 84.
Platt, Phineas, 277.
Platts, John, 178.
Platts, Noah, 178.
Platts, Radireck, 184.
Plum, Charles, 258.
Plum, Justis, 233.
Plumb, Amariah, 25.
Plumb, Jesse, 135.
Plumbe, Daniel, 29.
Plumley, Joseph, 21.
Pluymert, William, 229.
Pogheegh, Thomas, 125.
Pollard, Isaac, 76.
Polley, Alpheus, 90.
Polley, Amasa, 87.
Pomeroy, Benjamin, 90.
Pomeroy, Isaac, 188.
Pomeroy, Medad, 63.
Pomeroy, Ralph, 46.
Pomfret, 58, 66, 69, 79, 90, 101, 104, 118.
Pomp, Jacob, 90.
Pomroy, Peletiah, 57.
Pond, Bartholomew, 209.
Pond, Peter, 242, 243.
Pond, Timothy, 22.
Pond, Wiram, 69.
Ponds, Henry, 122.
Pool, Chester, 185.
Pool, David, 252, 270.
Poole, John, 55.

Pooley, Henery, 87.
Poor, Jonathan, 232.
Pope, Roberd, 189.
Popenah, Solomon, 251.
Pornett, Joseph, 246.
Porrage, Ananias, 139.
Porrutt, Joshua, 250.
Porter, A., 212.
Porter, Aaron, 27, 191, 209.
Porter, Abijah, 191.
Porter, Alexander, 59.
Porter, Amos, 162.
Porter, Ashbel, 20.
Porter, Benjamin, 79, 82.
Porter, Daniel, 2, 68, 165.
Porter, David, 244, 247, 248.
Porter, Elijah, 119, 133.
Porter, Eliot, 163.
Porter, Gideon, 138.
Porter, Increas, 162.
Porter, James, 209.
Porter, Joel, 162.
Porter, John, 2, 67, 80, 182, 207.
Porter, Jonathan, 166.
Porter, Jonathan, Jr., 2.
Porter, Joseph, 54, 133.
Porter, Joshua, 221.
Porter, Moses, 244.
Porter, Nathaniel, 6, 110.
Porter, Noah, 210.
Porter, Phineas, 17, 19, 22, 24, 25, 212.
Porter, Stephen, 190.
Porter, T., 84.
Porter, William, 105.
Porter, Zachariah, 35.
Post, Abraham, 136.
Post, David, 163.
Post, John, 163.
Post, Josiah, 178.
Post, Simeon, 259.
Post, Stephen, 55.
Poston, Samuel, 251.
Potague, George, 246.
Pottage, Jabez, 74.
Potter, 50, 112.
Potter, Amos, 235.
Potter, Benjamin, 71.
Potter, Daniel, 54, 138.
Potter, David, 162.
Potter, Edward, 137.
Potter, Joel, 70, 112, 182.
Potter, John, 15, 85.
Potter, Lemuel, 61.
Potter, Levi, 11.
Potter, Medad, 108.
Potter, Moses, 108.
Potter, Nathan, 106.
Potter, Sheldon, 121.
Potter, Stephen, 48, 70.
Poughkeepsie, 23.
Powel, Daniel, 59.
Powel, John, 179.
Powell, William, 244, 247, 248.
Powers, Asa, 85.
Powers, Cyrus, 66.
Powers, Gregory, 229.
Powers, James, 27, 79, 115.
Powers, James, Jr., 116.
Powers, Lawrence, 159.
Powers, Thomas, 138, 209.
Prat, Cary, 5.
Pratt, Abijah, 59.
Pratt, Abraham, 178.
Pratt, Abraham, Jr., 178.
Pratt, Asa, 178.
Pratt, Benjamin, 11.
Pratt, Daniel, 178.
Pratt, David, 96, 100.
Pratt, David B., 178.
Pratt, Edmond, 178.
Pratt, Et[ ], 178.
Pratt, Ezra, 67, 178.
Pratt, George, 187.
Pratt, Gideon, 178.
Pratt, Isaiah, 123.
Pratt, James, 81, 162.
Pratt, Jasper, 61.
Pratt, Jesse, 178.
Pratt, Jesse, 2d, 178.
Pratt, John, 178.
Pratt, Jonathan, 178.
Pratt, Joseph, 93, 188.
Pratt, Peter, 138.
Pratt, Phinis, 178.
Pratt, Ruben, 178.
Pratt, Russell, 105.
Pratt, Samuel, 63, 178.
Pratt, Taber, 178.
Pratt, William, 187.
Pratt, Zephemiah, 178.
Prechard, Jabez, 179.
Prentice, John, 245, 248.
Prentice, Jonas, 20, 48, 90.
Prentice, Samuel, 17.
Prescott, Titus, 57.
Presson, Joseph, 142.
Presson, Shubal, 186.
Preston, Benjamin, 194.
Preston, Charles, 276.
Preston, Daniel, 270.
Preston, David, 35.
Preston, Jacob, 143.
Preston, John, 139.
Preston, Jonathan, 76.
Preston, Joseph, 39, 101.

Preston, Noah, 202.
Preston, Zera, 15.
Preston, 22, 24, 52, 55, 58, 60, 66, 74, 88, 89, 90, 103, 104.
Prevett, John, 37.
Pribble, Samuel, 278.
Price, Ebenezer, 200.
Price, Joseph, 186.
Price, Levi, 90.
Price, Nathaniel, 101.
Price, Paul, 69.
Price, Rufus, 90.
Price, Samuel, 65.
Pride, Absolom, 279.
Pride, Reuben, 46.
Primas, Japhura, 75.
Prince, Christopher, 245, 249.
Prince, Joseph, 190.
Prince, Zeckry, 59.
Prindle, Abiel, 86.
Prindle, Abijah, 77.
Prindle, Ezra, 16.
Prindle, Zalmon, 77.
Prior, Abner, 47, 133.
Prior, Allen, 114.
Prior, Ebenezer, 23.
Prior, Jesse, 135.
Prior, Josiah, 81.
Prissnear, Asa, 55.
Pritchard, Benjamin, 109.
Pritchard, Ebenezer, Jr., 22.
Prout, James, 194.
Prout, William, 111.
Providence, R. I., 55, 103, 118.
Provost, Daniel, 76.
Provost, Richard, 243.
Prudden, John, 142.
Prunwugh, Joseph, 141.
Pryor, Rozll, 139.
Puffer, Daniel, 114, 116.
Puffer, George, 237.
Puffer, Lazarus, 90.
Puffer, Simeon, 160.
Pulford, Edmund, 215, 236.
Pulford, Elisha, 76.
Pulford, Samuel, 122.
Pullman, John, 255.
Pulman, John, 52.
Pumham, Ephraim, 262.
Punderson, Ahimz, 108.
Purkines, Charles, 70.
Purple, Elias, 82.
Putnam, 16, 18.
Putnam, Israel, 14, 16, 17, 20, 22, 23, 24, 25.
Putnam, Israel, Jr., 20.
Putnam, William, 29.
Putney, Jonathan, 64.
Quakenbush, Abraham, 99.
Quebec, 40.
Quecheats, Peter, 17.
Quin, Felix, 253.
Quinley, Thomas, 140.
Quintard, Evert, 218.
Quinturd, Peter, Jr., 218.
Quirk, William, 53.
Quochecks, Peter, 18.
Quy, Lebbeus, 231.

R[ ]l, Joshua, 66.
Racke, William, 118.
Rainsford, Joseph, 170.
Rambow, William, 238.
Ramond, Joshua, 171.
Ramsdale, Ezra, 19.
Randal, Christopher, 171.
Randal, Nicholas, 171.
Randall, David, 34.
Randall, Jedediah, 150.
Randall, Joseph, 171.
Randall, Pelik, 171.
Randol, Amos, 184.
Randol, Douty, 257.
Randol, John, 250.
Randolp, John, 246.
Ranney, Amos, 82.
Ranney, Comfort, 58, 61.
Ranney, David, 270.
Ranney, Solomon, 128.
Ranney, Stephen, 61, 77.
Ranny, Amos, 256.
Ranny, Comfort, 141.
Ranny, Nathaniel, Jr., 141.
Ranny, S., 84.
Ranny, Simo, 141.
Ranny, Solomon, 127.
Ransom, Abner, 251.
Ransom, Elijah, 46.
Ransom, Joseph, 185.
Ransome, Ebenezer, 170.
Rathbone, Theodore, 185.
Rathburn, Ashley, 105.
Rawland, Sherman, 68.
Rawles, Aaron, 107.
Rawlinson, Bartholomew, 113.
Rawlinson, Reuben, 113.
Ray, Daniel, 184.
Ray, Stevene, 171.
Raymond, Abraham, 85.
Raymond, Amaziah, 79.
Raymond, C., 177, 210.
Raymond, Clap, 226.
Raymond, D., 84.
Raymond, David, 152, 242.
Raymond, Elijah, 84.
Raymond, Hezekiah, 218.

Raymond, Isaac, 218.
Raymond, James, 104, 131.
Raymond, Jesse, 212.
Raymond, John, 218.
Raymond, Moses, 265, 270.
Raymond, Nathaniel, 218.
Raymond, Nathaniel, Jr., 218.
Raymond, Samuel, 90.
Raymond, Seth, 35.
Raymond, Uriah, 85, 212, 218, 226.
Raymond, William, 85, 261.
Raymong, Samuel, 233.
Raymont, William, 16.
Raynsford, J., 209.
Raynsford, Joseph, 169.
Read, Jonathan, 85.
Read, Philip, 2.
Read, Richard, 32.
Read, Silas, 2.
Read, Zalmon, 19, 22, 23, 24, 25.
Reading, 110.
Redding, 54, 69, 80, 89, 90.
Redfield, Nathan, 277.
Redfield, Samuel, 135.
Redfield, William, 73.
Reed, 114.
Reed, Amas, 55.
Reed, Curtis, 233, 252, 256, 262.
Reed, Enoch, 45, 51.
Reed, Jonathan, 63, 135.
Reed, Joseph, 74.
Reed, Reuben, 90.
Reed, Silas, 165.
Reed, Stephen, 85.
Reed, Thomas, 69, 99, 232, 240.
Reed, William, 95, 117, 127.
Reed, Zalmon, 180.
Reen, John, 34.
Rees, John, 247, 253.
Remington, Josiah, 23.
Renner, Samuel, 164.
Resseguie, Alexander, 195.
Resseguie, James, 200.
Revers, Thomas, 259.
Reves, Elishua, 191.
Rexford, Isaac, 117, 127.
Reymond, Aaron, 53.
Reymond, Abraham, 54.
Reymond, Benjamin, 85.
Reymond, Isaac, 85.
Reymond, John, 85.
Reymond, William, 54.
Reynalds, Justice, 78.
Reynold, Samuel, 85.
Reynolds, David, 77.
Reynolds, Hezekiah, 136.
Reynolds, James, 136.
Reynolds, James B., 136.
Reynolds, John, 188.
Reynolds, Jonathan, 21.
Reynolds, Joshua, 124.
Reynolds, Matthew, 213.
Reynolds, Solomon, 270.
Rhode Island, 16, 31, 59, 64, 65, 66, 143, 221, 275.
Rice, Abner, 194.
Rice, Archibald, 19.
Rice, Asa, 34.
Rice, Charles, 94, 117, 127.
Rice, David, 18, 42, 43, 90.
Rice, Ezra, 192.
Rice, Jehiel, Jr., 194.
Rice, Jesse, 275.
Rice, Joel, 194.
Rice, John, 82.
Rice, Jonathan, 186.
Rice, Jotham, 111.
Rice, Nehemiah, 49, 76.
Rice, Samuel, 193, 276.
Rice, Thomas, 239, 252.
Rice, William, 186.
Rich, Amos, 96, 117, 127.
Rich, Lemuel, 267, 270.
Richards, 133.
Richards, B., 84, 214.
Richards, Benjamin, 133, 134, 175, 209, 210, 212, 225.
Richards, Isaac, 266.
Richards, J., 214.
Richards, Jacob, 85.
Richards, John, 263.
Richards, Nathaniel, 38, 69.
Richards, R., 212.
Richards, Samuel, 46, 47.
Richards, William, 45.
Richardson, Andrew, 3.
Richardson, Ephraim, 87.
Richardson, Roswell, 163.
Richardson, Samuel, 199.
Richenson, Stephen, 185.
Richmernd, Edward, 34.
Richmond, Abner, 105.
Richmond, Jonathan, 37.
Richmond, Oziel, 126.
Richmond, Samuel, 37.
Ridgefield, 67, 68, 69, 83, 90, 110, 200.
Ridgway, Thomas, 258.
Riggs, Jeremiah, 201.
Riggs, John, 211.
Riggs, Joseph, Jr., 189.
Riggs, Laban, 90.
Riley, 124.
Riley, Ashbell, 156.
Riley, Ashbil, 153.
Riley, Charles, 74.

Riley, Jonathan, 19.
Riley, Nathaniel, 257.
Riley, Roger, 207.
Rily, John, 39.
Rindge, Thomas, 95.
Rindge, William, 143.
Ringe, Daniel, 185.
Ripley, Charles, 74, 114.
Ripley, Gamaliel, 183.
Ripley, John, 20, 24, 25.
Ripley, Pirum, 258.
Ripton, 115.
Risley, James, 261.
Risley, Levi, 244, 247, 248.
Risley, Richard, 133, 244, 247, 248.
Risley, Ruben, 157.
Risley, Samuel, 157.
Ritch, John, 243.
Rix, Nathan, 175.
Rix, Rufus, 175.
Roach, John, 90.
Roads, Joseph, 156.
Roads, William, 156.
Robards, Aaron, 204.
Robarts, [ ], Jr., 244.
Robarts, Aaron, 244.
Robarts, Eliphalet, 244.
Robarts, Nathaniel, 82.
Robarts, William, 244.
Robartson, William, 37.
Robbarts, David, 122.
Robberds, Daniel, 141.
Robberds, Ebenezer, 141.
Robberds, Stephen, 141.
Robberts, Isaac, 70.
Robbin, Michael, 38.
Robbins, Ammi R., 33.
Robbins, Benoni, 106, 126.
Robbins, Daniel, 262.
Robbins, Frederick, 153, 155.
Robbins, Jacob, 124.
Robbins, John, 135, 222.
Robbins, Joseph, 74.
Robbins, Richard, 80.
Robbins, Samuel, 80.
Robbinson, Samuel, 160.
Roberds, Luke, 198.
Roberds, Noah, 163.
Roberson, Reuben, 101.
Roberts, Abial, 90.
Roberts, Amos, 17.
Roberts, Aron, 247, 252.
Roberts, Charles, 273.
Roberts, Clark, 69.
Roberts, Elefelett, 245.
Roberts, Elifelet, Jr., 247.
Roberts, Elifelett, 248.
Roberts, Elifelett, Jr., 248.
Roberts, Eliphalet, Jr., 257.
Roberts, Gideon, 55.
Roberts, Hiram, 87.
Roberts, Isaac, 107.
Roberts, John, 57, 167.
Roberts, Lemuel, 188, 208.
Roberts, Nathan, 57.
Roberts, Philemon, 230, 258, 261.
Roberts, Rosel, 34.
Roberts, Samuel, 101.
Roberts, Stephen, 208.
Roberts, Thomas, 245.
Roberts, William, 146, 147, 148, 246, 249.
Robertson, 31, 50.
Robertson, Arthur, 29.
Robertson, Eleazer, 74.
Robertson, Jared, 179.
Robertson, John, 123, 240.
Robertson, Peter, 28, 46.
Robertson, Samuel, Jr., 277.
Robertson, Simeon, 66.
Robins, Brintnell, 171.
Robins, Ebenezer, 185.
Robins, Enos, 114.
Robins, John, 245, 247, 249.
Robins, Solomon, 143, 184.
Robins, Thomas, 247.
Robinson, 71.
Robinson, Abner, 143, 183.
Robinson, Cato, 113.
Robinson, Chandler, 11.
Robinson, Charles, 13.
Robinson, Ebenezer, 264.
Robinson, Eber, 143.
Robinson, Ebor, 185.
Robinson, Eleazer, 114.
Robinson, Elias, 47, 50.
Robinson, Elijah, 18.
Robinson, Eliphalet, 30.
Robinson, J., 207.
Robinson, James, 143, 191, 223, 227.
Robinson, Jared, 9, 90.
Robinson, John, 90, 95, 117, 127, 193, 244, 246.
Robinson, Jonathan, 185.
Robinson, Joseph, 162, 168.
Robinson, Levi, 112.
Robinson, Ms, 71.
Robinson, Moses, 65, 66.
Robinson, Nathan, 143.
Robinson, Reuben, 143.
Robinson, Richard, 65, 185.
Robinson, Samuel, 90, 246, 248.
Robinson, Simeon, Jr., 90.
Robinson, Solomon, 173.

Rowlison, Reuben, 20.
Roxbury, 18, 136.
Roy, John, Jr., 175.
Royce, Asa, 143.
Royce, Clark, 201.
Royce, Elijah, 61, 270.
Royce, John, 213.
Roys, Clark, 225.
Rucket, Samuel, 97.
Rudd, Jonathan, 240.
Rude, Ezekiel, 175.
Rude, Rufus, Jr., 3, 4.
Rude, Simeon, 138.
Rude, Stephen, 168.
Ruff, Daniel, 186.
Ruggles, Ashbel, 196.
Ruggles, Benjamin, 110, 116.
Ruggles, Benjamin A., 195.
Ruggles, Bostwick, 195.
Ruggles, Comfor, 195.
Ruggles, Joseph, 24.
Ruggles, Lazarus, 209.
Ruggles, Nathaniel, 191.
Ruggles, Samuel, 196.
Rull, John, 217.
Rumbow, William, 239.
Rumsey, David, 85, 136.
Rumsey, Jeremiah, 126.
Rumsy, David, 139.
Rundalls, Timothy, 98.
Runey, George, 258.
Runnell, David, 38.
Runnels, Edward, 68.
Runo, Simeon, 34.
Rus, Benjamin, 15.
Rusco, David, 34.
Russ, Daniel, 13.
Russ, James, 21.
Russ, Jonathan, 21, 68.
Russel, Alpheus, 120.
Russel, Benjamin, 14.
Russel, Cornelius, 48.
Russel, Edward, 189.
Russel, Giles, 49.
Russel, Josiah, 36.
Russel, William, 76.
Russel, William, Jr., 23.
Russell, 214.
Russell, Benjamin, Jr., 14.
Russell, Cornelius, 27.
Russell, E., 177, 214.
Russell, Edward, 211.
Russell, Elezer, 57.
Russell, Gideon, 127, 128.
Russell, Hezekiah, 2, 166.
Russell, James, 66.
Russell, John, 154, 156, 201, 229.
Russell, Jonathan, 63.
Russell, Joseph, 184.
Russell, Nathan, Jr., 2.
Russell, Stephen, 1.
Russell, Thomas, 186.
Russell, William, 18, 254.
Rust, Amaziah, 211.
Ruston, William, 42, 43.
Ryan, Jeremiah, 270.
Rymond, David, 54.
Rynes, T., 84.
Ryon, John, 69.

Sabin, Elihu, 271.
Sabin, Elisha, 184.
Sabin, Hezekiah, 210.
Sabin, Samuel, 175.
Sabins, Nathaniel, 93.
Sachel, Jonathan, 240.
Sachem's Head, 277.
Safford, Joseph, 169.
Sage, 214.
Sage, Comfort, 208, 223, 224.
Sage, Francis, 28.
Sage, Michael, 135.
Sage, Solomon, 207.
St. John, Aaron, 53.
St. John, C., 212.
St. John, Caleb, 212, 226.
St. John, Daniel, 123.
St. John, David, 200.
St. John, James, 265.
St. John, Jesse, 54, 102, 130.
St. John, John, 47.
St. John, Justin, 53, 103, 122, 130.
St. John, Mathew, 13.
St. John, Stephen, 226, 266.
St. Johns, 17, 22, 25.
Salem, 54.
Sales, James, 108.
Salisbury, 21, 52, 55, 83, 88, 89, 102, 110, 111, 267.
Sally, James, 90.
Salmas, William, 218.
Salmon, Asahel, 108.
Salter, Francsis, 145.
Saltonstal, Nathaniel, 141.
Saltonstall, Gurdon F., 140.
Saltonstall, Nathaniel, 140.
Sandeforth, Daniel, 257.
Sanders, Amos, 77.
Sanders, William, 32.
Sandford, Ezekiel, 90.
Sandy Cruse, 102.
Sanford, Daniel, 180.
Sanford, Eli, 194.
Sanford, Elihu, 76.

Skeel, John, 85.
Skiff, Vallintine, 231.
Skiner, Adenijah, 163.
Skiner, Isarel, 163.
Skiner, Stephen, 274.
Skiner, Thomas, 202.
Skinner, Abraham, 3d, 160.
Skinner, Abram, 63.
Skinner, David, 159.
Skinner, Eleazer, 63.
Skinner, Enos, 18.
Skinner. Ezekiel, 158.
Skinner, John, 120, 134, 226.
Skinner, Richard, 98.
Skinner, Thomas, 78, 273.
Skinner, William, 239.
Skinner. Zamri, 36.
Slack, Comfort, 170.
Slade, Aaron, 2.
Slade, Abner, 2, 139.
Slade, Daniel, 2.
Slafter, Moses, 2.
Slarter, Amos, 142.
Slarter, James, 142.
Slate, Ezekal, 38.
Slater, Joel, 145, 146, 147, 148.
Slater, John, 24.
Slattury, John, 258.
Slitwell, Thomas, 34.
Sloan, Thomas, 187, 188.
Slooman, Thomas, 149.
Sloper, 222.
Sloper, A., 84.
Sloper, Ambris, 182.
Sloper, Ambrose, 209, 210.
Sloper, Ambrus, 138.
Sloson, Nathan, 210, 223.
Smalley, Daniel, 149.
Smedley, T., 180.
Smedly, Samuel, 233.
Smith, 19, 84, 212, 222.
Smith, Aaron, 197, 271.
Smith, Abijah, 15, 57, 124, 186.
Smith, Abner, 132.
Smith, Abraham, 179.
Smith, Alen, 213.
Smith, Allen, 210.
Smith, Ambrose, 108.
Smith, Amos. 184, 210, 279.
Smith, Asa, 138.
Smith, Asahel, 240.
Smith, Asail, 234.
Smith, Asher, 37.
Smith, Benajah, 55, 204.
Smith, Benjamin, 20, 200, 252.
Smith, Benoni, 209, 211.
Smith, Caleb, 11, 25, 257.
Smith, Chancy, 258.
Smith, Charles, 206, 207, 210.
Smith, Chauncey, 16.
Smith, Cuff, 97.
Smith, Dan, 19, 34.
Smith, Daniel, 15, 22, 51, 56, 197, 200.
Smith, David, 18, 23, 49, 76, 133, 185, 196, 202.
Smith, David, 2d, 134.
Smith, Ebenezer, 170, 202, 211, 224, 225, 254.
Smith, Edmund, 271.
Smith, Elezer, 57.
Smith, Eli, 105.
Smith, Eliakim, 212.
Smith, Eliakim, Jr., 85.
Smith, Elihu, 137.
Smith, Elijah, 63.
Smith, Elisha, 81.
Smith, Elkanah, 111, 117.
Smith. Elm, 226.
Smith, Epaphras, 252.
Smith, Ephraim, 119.
Smith, Ezra, 29, 31, 47.
Smith, Francis, 185, 274.
Smith, Fred, 94.
Smith, George, 90.
Smith, George C., 25.
Smith, Graves, 2.
Smith, Heber, 75, 271.
Smith, Heman, 22.
Smith, Henry, 65, 68.
Smith, Huttun, 217.
Smith, Isaac, 37, 77, 85.
Smith, Isaiah, 122.
Smith, Israel, 203, 261.
Smith, Ithamer, 63.
Smith, Jacob, 2d, 200.
Smith, James, 38, 90, 154, 156, 185, 212.
Smith, James G., 70.
Smith, Jared, 117, 127.
Smith, Jasper, 262.
Smith, Jeddidiah, 35.
Smith. Jedediah, 57.
Smith, Jehiel, 34, 86, 112.
Smith, Jeial, 196.
Smith, Jeremiah, 22.
Smith, Jesse, 99, 108, 202.
Smith, Jonathan, 184.
Smith, Job, 48, 90, 142, 195.
Smith, John, 27, 57, 81, 99, 101, 179, 197, 209, 226, 245, 247, 249, 252, 262, 271.
Smith, Jordan, 71, 112.
Smith, Joseph, 19, 21. 22, 23, 24, 84, 122, 193, 196, 207, 208, 226. 257.

Smith, Josiah, 15, 20, 138, 220, 266, 270.
Smith, Jurden, 257.
Smith, Justus, 152.
Smith, Landon, 32.
Smith, Lemuel, 175.
Smith, M., 209.
Smith, Matthew, 210.
Smith, Micahel, 184.
Smith, Moses, Jr., 2.
Smith, N., 206, 214.
Smith, Nathan, 189, 195, 221, 265.
Smith, Nehemiah, 138, 183.
Smith, Noah, Jr., 213.
Smith, O., 222.
Smith, Oliver, 185, 210, 216, 221.
Smith, Peter, 57, 271.
Smith, Phineas, 98.
Smith, Reuben, 21, 38, 250.
Smith, Reubin, 125.
Smith, Richard, 15, 137, 195, 208, 224.
Smith, Ruben, 246.
Smith, S., 84.
Smith, Sam B., 204.
Smith, Samuel, 62, 90, 158, 179, 200.
Smith, Samuel R., 240.
Smith, Solevenus, 250.
Smith, Seth, 188, 210, 221.
Smith, Shermon, 195.
Smith, Silvanus, 211.
Smith, Silvenus, 246.
Smith, Stephen, 38, 211, 253, 273.
Smith, Tabor, 278.
Smith, Theophilus, 204.
Smith, Thomas, 9, 245, 250, 256, 261.
Smith, William, 19, 48, 69, 110, 115, 167, 218.
Smith, William G., 239.
Smith, William H., 227.
Smith, Zebadiah, 238, 239, 240, 262.
Smith, Zebina, 67.
Smithers, William, 90.
Snow, Edmond, 178.
Snow, Isaac, 94, 105.
Snow, Ivory, 254.
Snow, Joseph, 14.
Snow, Joseph, Jr., 14.
Snow, Levi, 186.
Snow, Patrick, 278.
Snow, Salvanus, 15.
Snow, Shubal, 95.
Snow, Silvanus, 16, 24.
Snow, Silas, 186.
Solland, Joseph, 163.
Solomon, Amos, 150.
Somers, 17, 53, 55, 56, 69, 87, 118.
Soppoosor, Abele, 246.
Southard, Nathan, 178.
Southard, William, 178.
Southington, 115.
Southward, Thomas, 15.
Southworth, Joseph, 193.
Southworth, Lemuel, 87.
Southworth, Samuel, 34.
Southworth, Thomas, 15.
Southworth, William, 181, 219.
Soutice, Solomon, 109.
Sowers, William, 109.
Spafford, Elijah, 118.
Spalding, Daniel, 169.
Spalding, Derias, 221.
Spalding, Ephraim, 82.
Spalding, Ezra, 168.
Spalding, Silas, 168.
Sparford, Elijah, 248.
Sparks, Henry, 168.
Sparks, Icahd, 168.
Sparks, John, 168.
Sparks, Ruben, 157.
Spary, Stephen, 38.
Spaulding, John, 35.
Spaulding, Joseph, 168.
Spaulding, Nat, 167.
Spaulding, William, 168.
Spear, Elihue, 54.
Spear, Elijah, 54.
Spear, William, Jr., 2, 166.
Spears, John, 74, 90.
Spears, Nathaniel, 12.
Spears, States, 90.
Spelman, Richard, 133, 191.
Spencer, 50.
Spencer, Abner, 35.
Spencer, David, 90, 122.
Spencer, Elijah, 185, 254.
Spencer, Emmon, 185.
Spencer, Ezra, 36.
Spencer, George, 230.
Spencer, Ichabod, 45, 51.
Spencer, Israel, 209.
Spencer, James, 36, 184.
Spencer, Joel, 97.
Spencer, John, 94, 244, 245, 246, 248, 274.
Spencer, Joseph, 17, 18, 19, 20, 21, 22, 23, 24, 25.
Spencer, Noah, 95, 117, 127.
Spencer, Obadiah, 90.
Spencer, Samuel, 41, 43.
Spencer, Seth, 36.
Spencer, Simeon, 233.
Spencer, Steven, 192.

Spencer, Thomas, 76, 193.
Sperry, Chauncey, 90.
Sperry, Enoch, 69, 273.
Sperry, Jabez, 32.
Sperry, Silas, 12.
Spicer, Abbe, 231.
Spicer, Abel, 82.
Spicer, Nathan, 140.
Spicer, O., 206.
Spicer, Oliver, 211.
Spicer, Samuel, 90.
Spink, Asa, 28.
Spooner, Judah P., 246, 247, 250, 252.
Spooner, Walter, 230.
Sprage, John, 4.
Sprague, 50.
Sprague, Benjamin, 161.
Sprague, Beriah, 3, 5, 162.
Sprague, Elisha, 161.
Sprague, James, 90.
Sprigs, Thomas, 264.
Sprigs, William, 238.
Spring, Thomas, 203.
Springer, John, 99.
Springfield, 115.
Springger, Whala, 97.
Spurr, William, 77.
"Spy," 238, 239, 240, 241.
Squib, Joseph, 263.
Squier, Daniel, 14, 85.
Squier, David, 266.
Squier, John, 35.
Squier, Justus, 39.
Squier, Samuel S., 90.
Squire, Abiather, 72.
Squire, Asa, 100.
Squire, Asher, 107.
Squire, Daniel, 14.
Squire, Dudley, 107.
Squire, Elijah, 186.
Squire, Ephraim, 15.
Squire, J., 84.
Squire, Jonah, 152.
Squire, Jonathan, 180.
Squire, Joseph, 232.
Squire, Nathan, 233.
Squire, Nathaniel, 199.
Squire, Phillip, 186.
Squire, Phineas, 19.
Squire, Samuel, 193.
Squire, Sorel, 106.
Squire, Stephen, 238, 239.
Squires, Charles, 126.
Squires, Ebenezer, 237.
Squires, Isaac, 16, 99, 233.
Squires, Phinehas, 70, 107.
Squires, Sarel, 126.
Squires, Sariel, 104.
Stacey, Nathaniel, 235.
Stafford, 53, 54, 56, 114.
Stalker, Levi, 198.
Stalker, Peter, 102, 129.
Stamford, 53, 54, 55, 56, 68, 69, 70, 76, 77, 78, 79, 83, 89, 103, 104, 197, 199, 205, 267, 278.
Stanard, Seth, 39.
Stanbrough, Lemuel, 107.
Stanbrough, Silas, 107.
Stanclift, John, 36.
Stanclift, Lemuel, 122.
Standley, Fradrick, 188.
Standley, Fredrick, 235.
Standley, Lewis, 27.
Standly, Frederick, 187.
Stanley, Abraham, 194, 208, 210, 276.
Stanley, Abraham, Jr., 194.
Stanley, Gad, 203, 210.
Stanley, Oliver, 208, 210, 212, 222, 224, 275.
Stanley, Salmon, 22.
Stanley, Thomas, 100.
Stanley, Timothy, 225.
Stanliff, Samuel, 97.
Stanly, Gad, 138, 203, 222.
Stanly, Salmon, 20.
Stanly, Samuel, 274.
Stannard, Eliakim, 183.
Stannard, Jasper, 90.
Stannard, Limbo, 72.
Stannard, Peter, 140.
Stannard, Samuel, 69, 139.
Stannard, Seth, 122.
Stanton, 12, 13.
Stanton, Asa, 175.
Stanton, Daniel, 2d, 263.
Stanton, Daniel, 3d, 263.
Stanton, David, 175.
Stanton, Edward, 270.
Stanton, I., 212.
Stanton, James, 69.
Stanton, Nathaniel, 262.
Stanton, Solomon, 205.
Stanton, Thomas, 263.
Stanton, William, 210.
Staples, Ebenezer, 185.
Staples, Jacob, 172.
Stark, Diah, 159.
Stark, Solomon, 207.
Stark, Stephen, 90.
Stark, Timothy, 90.
Starkey, Stephen, 178.
Starkey, Timothy, 178, 210.
Starkweather, Amos, 96.
Starkweather, Asa, 90.

Stocking, Eber, 69, 135.
Stocking, Jonathan, 61.
Stocking, Marshall, 135.
Stockwell, Abel, 108.
Stodard, Cyrenus, 38.
Stodard, Eli, 76.
Stodard, Samuel, 244.
Stoddard, Abijah, 38.
Stoddard, Anthony, 75.
Stoddard, B., 209.
Stoddard, Briant, 212.
Stoddard, Bryan, 210.
Stoddard, Daniel, 82.
Stoddard, David, 6, 201.
Stoddard, Elisha, 74.
Stoddard, Enoch, 154, 156.
Stoddard, Ichabod, 173.
Stoddard, J., 225.
Stoddard, James, 207, 221, 222, 224, 278.
Stoddard, Jesse, 201.
Stoddard, John, 154, 156.
Stoddard, Jonathan, 153, 155.
Stoddard, Luther, 37.
Stoddard, Nathan, 38.
Stoddard, Samuel, 154, 156, 246.
Stoddard, Simeon C., 119.
Stoddard, Solomon, 212.
Stoddard, Thaddeus, 38.
Stoddart, Samuel, 248.
Stokes, Richard, 113, 117.
Ston, William, 278.
Stone, Aaron, 194.
Stone, Ambermarle, 185.
Stone, Bela, 242, 243.
Stone, Benjamin, 209, 212, 273.
Stone, Daniel, 194.
Stone, David, 90.
Stone, Joel, 194.
Stone, John, 277.
Stone, Joseph, 135.
Stone, Josiah, 90, 164.
Stone, Reuben, 209, 225.
Stone, Russel, 277.
Stone, Samuel, 111.
Stone, William, 194.
Stones, Benjamin, 225.
Stonington, 31, 56, 60, 64, 65, 68, 74, 88, 89, 90, 91, 113, 118, 267.
Store, 17.
Storrs, Amaziah, 143.
Storrs, E., 210, 222, 227.
Storrs, Experience, 22, 24.
Story, John, 135.
Story, Solomon, 33, 40.
Stoughton, E., 220.
Stoughton, James, 89.
Stow, George, 230.
Stow, Jene, 204.
Stow, Samuel, 256.
Stow, William, 141.
Stow, Zacheus, 107.
Stowe, Samuel, 262.
Stowe, William, 278.
Stowel, Abel, 101.
Stowel, Elisha, 90.
Stowel, Nathaniel, 101.
Stowel, Samuel, 101.
Stowell, Nathan, 63.
Stratford, 53, 54, 58, 69, 75, 76, 77, 78, 82, 88, 89, 102, 103, 104, 109, 135, 136, 141, 171, 180, 190, 267, 278.
Stratton, Lemuel, 158.
Stratton, Samuel, 244, 245, 251.
Stratton, Thomas, 181, 219.
Strickland, Stephen, 135.
Stricklin, Jonah, 80.
Stricland, Jonathan, 32.
Stromthorn, James, 169.
Strong, 223.
Strong, Adonijah, 33, 160.
Strong, Asahel, 9.
Strong, Benajah, 90.
Strong, Benjamin, 66.
Strong, David, 34, 47, 50, 160, 162.
Strong, Eliakim, 71.
Strong, Israel, 46.
Strong, Jacob, 122.
Strong, Jedediah, 50.
Strong, John, 49, 58, 60, 75, 202, 224, 225.
Strong, Josiah, 270.
Strong, Olliver, 160.
Strong, Phinehas, 111, 162.
Strong, Roger, 5.
Strong, Samuel, 105.
Strong, Selah, 192.
Strong, Seth, 71.
Strong, Simeon, 227.
Strong, Thomas, 192, 193.
Stronge, Josiah, 34.
Stuard, Daniel, 34.
Stuard, William, 171.
Stuart, Alexander, 198.
Stuart, William, 69, 242.
Stubbs, Maning, 251.
Stubbs, Samuel, 23, 24, 74.
Sturdavant, John, 199.
Sturdevant, Nathaniel, 90.
Sturdivant, Samuel, 99.
Sturges, Elias, 84.
Sturgis, Abraham, 232.
Sturgis, Aquilla, 77.
Sturgis, David, 16.
Sturgis, Thadeus, 200.

Stwart, Charles, 54.
Suffield, 53, 54, 57, 58, 59, 60, 75, 78, 80, 81, 82, 87, 89, 267.
Sugden, Abraham, 108.
Sugdon, Abraham, 235.
Summer, Benjamin, 211.
Summers, Benjamin, 212.
Summit, Prince, 90.
Sumner, E., 225.
Sumner, John, 47.
Sumner, Joshua, 63.
Sumner, Luke, 190.
Sumner, Robert, 66, 278.
Suncheman, Nathaniel, 90.
Sunderlin, Pheleg, 135.
Suntsimons, Aaron, 90.
Sup, Hammond, 247.
Surdan, Peter, 99.
Sutliff, Jannah, 98.
Sutton, Edward, 33.
Swain, Boston, 254, 259.
Swain, Peter, 251.
Swan, Aden, 186.
Swan, Christopher, 78.
Swan, John, 206.
Swan, Nathaniel, 240, 254.
Swan, William, 238, 239, 240, 259.
Swasey, Anthony, 253.
Swazey, Manuel, 238.
Sweet, Benjamin, 79.
Sweet, Isaac, 64.
Sweet, John, 36, 79.
Sweet, Jonathan, 37.
Sweet, Josiah, 38.
Sweetland, Ebenezer, 161.
Swetland, Aaron, 161.
Swift, 265.
Swift, Charles, 161.
Swift, Heman, 48, 73, 74, 97, 99, 135, 267.
Swift, Isaac, 33.
Swift, Jeriah, 33.
Swift, Robert, 90.
Swift, Seth, 251.
Swift, William, 3d, 4.
Swords, Francis, 231.
Sydleman, John, 90.
Syzer, Jabez, 22.

Taaffe, Nicholas, 254.
Tack, Andrew, 108.
Taft, Silas, 65.
Taintor, Michael, 205.
Talbat, Job. 170.
Talbott, Jonathan, 98.
Talcot, Matthew, 227.
Talcott, Elizur, 227.
Tallcot, Isaac, 157.
Tallcott, Abraham, 137.
Tallcott, Gad, 163.
Tallcott, George, 137.
Tallcott, William, 163.
Tallmadge, Jeremiah, 29, 30, 31.
Talmadge, Josiah, Jr., 276.
Talmage, Ichabod, 79.
Talmage, Solomon, 11.
Talman, Moses, 246, 251.
Talor, Ruben, 196.
Tankerd, George, 68.
Tanner, Joseph A., 35.
Tanner, Trial, 12, 41, 49.
Tanner, Tyral, 21, 49.
Tapping, Zephaniah, 238, 239.
Tarball, William, 265, 271.
Tarbox, 227.
Tarbox, Benjamin, 69, 99.
Tarbox, David, 159.
Tarbox, Jonathan, 162.
Tarbox, Solomon, 134, 159.
Tarbox, Zenas, 159.
Tarry, 111.
Tawsin, Dominique, 260.
Tawzin, Dominioque, 264.
Tawzin, Dominique, 262.
Tayler, Henry, 243.
Tayler, Jonathan, 107.
Taylor, 22.
Taylor, A., 228.
Taylor, Augustine, 49.
Taylor, Azariah, 74.
Taylor, Baruck, 69.
Taylor, Daniel, 38, 80.
Taylor, David, 123.
Taylor, E., 142.
Taylor, Eleazer, 198.
Taylor, Elijah, 77.
Taylor, Eliud, 109.
Taylor, Elizer, 86.
Taylor, Gad, 73.
Taylor, Gamaliel, 212.
Taylor, Harry, 242.
Taylor, Henry, 234, 252.
Taylor, James, 73, 235.
Taylor, Jesse, 85, 217.
Taylor, Joel, 273.
Taylor, John, 2, 56, 68, 74, 90, 99, 159, 199, 254.
Taylor, John, Jr., 2.
Taylor, Jonathan, 194.
Taylor, Josiah, 77.
Taylor, Justus, 110.
Taylor, Levi, 217.
Taylor, Major, 198.
Taylor, Medad, 202.
Taylor, Micha, 65.
Taylor, Nathaniel, 16.

Taylor, Phineas, 98.
Taylor, Reuben, 74, 195, 228.
Taylor, Salmond, 19.
Taylor, Samuel, 199, 233.
Taylor, Silas, 198.
Taylor, Simeon, 38, 76.
Taylor, Theodore, 74.
Taylor, Timothy, 46.
Taylor, William, 36, 53.
Taylor, Zeb, 209.
Teacomwaus, Isaac, 17.
Teal, Timothy, 253.
Teal, Titus, 140.
Teale, Samuel, 72.
Teall, Nathan, 97.
Tease, John, 245.
Tee, Joseph, 261.
Telcder, William, 253.
Temple, Amos, 75, 104, 130.
Ten Eyck, Henry, 46, 54.
Terrell, Hezekiah, 106.
Terrey, Dan, 149.
Terril, Thomas, 161.
Terrill, Caleb, 119.
Terrill, George, 207.
Terrill, Josiah, 209.
Terry, Jesse, 127.
Terry, Josiah, 93.
Terry, N., 224.
Terry, Nathaniel, 165, 222, 223.
Teuky, Jared, 58.
Thaires, Asa, 78.
Tharp, Aaron, 54.
Tharp, Abner, 11, 205.
Tharp, Amasa, 70.
Tharp, Amos, 70.
Tharp, Elias, 79.
Tharp, Jeremiah, 98.
Tharp, Nathaniel, 55, 140.
Tharp, Samuel, 235.
Thatcher, Joseph, 246, 251.
Thatcher, Stephen G., 235.
Thayer, David, 167.
Theaf, John, 230.
Thomas, 59.
Thomas, Absalom, 90.
Thomas, Caleb, 120.
Thomas, Daniel, 55.
Thomas, David, 145, 146, 147, 148.
Thomas, Ebenezer, 209.
Thomas, Ebenezer, Jr., 136.
Thomas, Elihu, 160.
Thomas, Enoch, 77.
Thomas, Ephraim, 108.
Thomas, Gregory, 69.
Thomas, Isaac, 136.
Thomas, James, 90.
Thomas, Jesse, 127, 128.
Thomas, John, 11, 85, 133, 136.
Thomas, Jonah, 82.
Thomas, Joseph, 85, 234.
Thomas, Josiah, 163.
Thomas, Malachi, 5.
Thomas, Malicha, 162.
Thomas, Samuel, 108.
Thomas, Sarrid, 164.
Thomas, William, 229.
Thomblenson, Joseph, 196.
Thompson, Abraham, 190.
Thompson, Absalom, 175.
Thompson, David, 113, 123, 151, 181, 219.
Thompson, Jabez, 17.
Thompson, James, 2, 123.
Thompson, John, 139.
Thompson, Joseph, 69, 179.
Thompson, Lins, 190.
Thompson, Nathan, 215.
Thompson, Nathaniel, 75.
Thompson, Nehemiah, 151.
Thompson, Samuel, 118.
Thompson, Stephen, 78, 104.
Thompson, Thomas, 173.
Thompson, William, 169.
Thomson, 177.
Thomson, Alexander, 27.
Thomson, Ebenezer, 20.
Thomson, Edward, 55.
Thomson, Elihu, 21.
Thomson, Isaac, 201.
Thomson, J., 177.
Thomson, James, 20.
Thomson, John, Jr., 37.
Thomson, Joseph, 17, 216, 222.
Thomson, Joshua, 36.
Thomson, Justus, 18, 23.
Thomson, Samuel, 222, 227.
Thomson, Stephen, 130, 203.
Thomson, William, 180.
Thorp, Aaron, 160.
Thorp, Amasa, 112.
Thorp, Amos, 112.
Thorp, Andrew, 234.
Thorp, Asher, 201.
Thorp, E., 212.
Thorp, Eliphalet, 181.
Thorp, Esra, 152.
Thorp, James, 117.
Thorp, Jeremiah, 257.
Thorp, John, 138.
Thorp, Joseph, 19, 25.
Thorp, Nehemiah, 16.
Thorp, Peter, 234.
Thorp, Steph, 180.
Thorp, Stephen, 180.
Thrall, John, 209.

Tracy, Gilbart, 186.
Tracy, Giles, 258.
Tracy, Hezekiah, 91.
Tracy, Levi, 174.
Tracy, Moses, 64, 271.
Tracy, Peris, 174.
Tracy, Phineas L., 278.
Tracy, Richmond, 175.
Tracy, S., 213.
Tracy, Solomon, 6.
Tracy, William, 45.
Treadway, David, 4, 163.
Treadway, John, 134.
Treadwell, Benjamin, 109.
Treat, Bethuel, 211, 225.
Treat, Charles, 154, 156.
Treat, Gershom, 74, 228.
Treat, John, 90.
Treat, Joseph, 101.
Treat, Oliver, 153, 155.
Treat, Salmon, 74, 186, 228.
Tredaway, John, 141.
Treet, James, 241.
Treet, Jonathan, 158.
Treet, Mingo, 73.
Trickey, Jered, 61.
Tripp, Isaac, 199.
Trobridg, Seth, 197.
Trobridge, Oliver, 196.
Trowbridg, Eli, 196.
Trowbridge, 22.
Trowbridge, Abel, 196.
Trowbridge, B., 142.
Trowbridge, Caleb, 17, 24.
Trowbridge, Isaac, 37, 266.
Trowbridge, John, 17, 48.
Trowbridge, Stephen, 109.
Trowbridge, William, 67.
Trueman, David, 246.
Truesdel, Ebenezer, 179.
Truesdil, Darius, 131.
Trumble, Jonathan, Jr., 42.
Trumbul, Ezekiel, 201.
Trumbul, Grig, 73.
Trumbull, David, 221.
Trumbull, Ezekiel, 19.
Trumbull, George, 228.
"Trumbull," 237.
Trusdale, Darius, 125.
Trusdell, Darius, 104.
Trusdell, Ebenezer, 9.
Tryon, Edward, 230.
Tryon, Eli, 153, 156.
Tryon, Ezra, 122.
Tryon, Ezry, 61.
Tryon, Josiah, 80.
Tryon, William, 60, 189.
Tubbs, Eleazer, 185.
Tubbs, Elemuel, 137.
Tubbs, Isaac, 158.
Tubbs, Lemuel, 137, 139.
Tubbs, Martin, 111.
Tubbs, Nathan, 39, 124.
Tucker, Daniel, 38, 76.
Tucker, Daniel, Jr., 38.
Tucker, Elisha, 78.
Tucker, Isaac, 212.
Tucker, John, 119, 238, 239.
Tucker, Timothy, 64.
Tucker, Zepheniah, 189.
Tuder, Thomas, 278.
Tudor, Daniel, 278.
Tuels, Samuel, 134.
Tullar, Eli, 125.
Tullar, Israel, 142.
Tuller, Ehud, 164.
Tuller, Eli, 104.
Tuller, Elijah, 164.
Tuller, Joel, 164.
Tuller, John, 184.
Tully, Christopher, 53.
Tupper, Ezra, 95.
Tupper, Mahu, 32.
Tupper, Nathan, 231.
Tupper, William, 111.
Turkens, Tiras, 54.
Turner, 97.
Turner, Charles, 240.
Turner, Enoch, Jr., 271
Turner, Joseph, 184.
Turner, Moses, 39.
Turner, Thomas, 119.
Turner, William, 127.
Turney, Jana, 54.
Turrel, Daniel, 195.
Turrell, Noah, 38.
Turtle Bay, 137.
Tuthill, Daniel, 191.
Tuttle, Aaron, 83, 271.
Tuttle, Beri. 276.
Tuttle, Charles, 24.
Tuttle, Clement, 16, 235.
Tuttle, Edmond, 217.
Tuttle, Eli, 17, 20.
Tuttle, Enos, 72, 104, 109, 130.
Tuttle, Ezekiel, 90.
Tuttle, Hezekiah, 91.
Tuttle, Ichabod, 39.
Tuttle, Jasphat, 19.
Tuttle, Japhat, 24.
Tuttle, Joel, 37.
Tuttle, Jonathan, Jr., 133.
Tuttle, Josiah, 275.
Tuttle, Levi, 271.
Tuttle, Lucius, 223.
Tuttle, Nathaniel, 20, 29, 31.

Washborn, Levy, 159.
Washington, George, 84, 138, 160, 161, 162, 163.
Washington, 52, 80, 82, 88, 89, 91, 110, 268, 279.
Wasson, James, 121.
Waterbury, 24, 267.
Waterbury, David, 17, 18, 19, 21, 22, 23, 24, 25.
Waterbury, John, 201.
Waterbury, William, 104, 131.
Waterbury, 17, 24, 52, 53, 54, 55, 58, 60, 66, 75, 76, 77, 78, 79, 81, 82, 88, 89, 90, 91, 104, 111, 220.
Waterhouse, Isaac, 32.
Waterhouse, John, 35, 211.
Waterhouse, Jonathan, 257.
Waterhouse, Samuel, 37.
Waterman, A., 206.
Waterman, Amasa, 258.
Waterman, Andrew, 5, 134, 159, 160.
Waterman, Chester, 123.
Waterman, Derias, 259.
Waterman, Ezekiel, 185.
Waterman, Gladden, 260.
Waterman, Joseph, 267, 271.
Waterman, N., 207, 209.
Waterman, Nehemiah, 209.
Waterman, Robert, 187.
Waterman, William, 259, 262.
Waters, Benjamin, 55.
Waters, Bigelow, 80.
Waters, Daniel, 159.
Waters, Gideon, 63, 160.
Waters, Joseph, 159.
Waters, Timothy, 163.
Waters, William, 57.
Watertown, 102, 111.
Watkins, John, 244, 247, 248.
Watkins, Nathan, 15.
Watkins, Robart, 97.
Watkins, Thomas, 13, 42, 43.
Watkins, William, 15.
Watrous, Benjamin, 113.
Watrous, Elisha, 160.
Watrous, John R., 47.
Watrous, Richard, 91, 266, 271.
Watrous, Thomas, 61.
Watrous, William, 15.
Watson, Asa, 185.
Watson, Heman, 39.
Watson, John, 20, 22, 23, 227.
Watson, John, Jr., 16, 17, 19, 21.
Watson, Nathaniel, 18, 24.
Watson, Thomas, 95, 117, 127.
Watson, Titus, 39, 48.
Watson, William, 187.
Watterman, Robert, 188.
Watteson, William, 188.
Wattles, Chandlor, 259.
Wattles, Samuel, 260.
Wattles, Samuel, Jr., 5, 160.
Wattles, Thomas, 6.
Wattles, William H., 259.
Watton, Henry, 118.
Waugh, Alexander, 201, 209.
Waugh, Samuel, 69.
Waugh, Thadeus, 69.
Way, 19.
Way, Abner, 193, 276.
Way, Elisha, 132.
Way, Hammon, 91.
Way, John, 273.
Way, Moses, 193.
Way, Seely, 201.
Wayland, James, 271.
Wayland, John, 181, 219.
Wayley, Aaron, 106, 126.
Waymend, Increase, 55.
Wealer, William, 35.
Weathers, Thomas, 135.
Weaver, Francis, 80.
Weaver, Samuel, 63, 87.
Webb, 227, 267.
Webb, Abner, 143.
Webb, Abnor, 185.
Webb, Charles, 16, 17, 20, 21, 22, 23, 28, 29, 30, 265, 267.
Webb, Constant, 266, 271.
Webb, David, 53.
Webb, Isaac, 178.
Webb, John, 262.
Webb, Jonah, 94, 111, 116, 117, 127.
Webb, Jonas, 36.
Webb, Jonathan, 63, 91.
Webb, Jooseph, 240.
Webb, Joseph, 241.
Webb, Nathaniel, 47, 63.
Webb, Samuel B., 80, 100, 104, 129, 265, 267.
Webster, Aaron, 145, 147.
Webster, Abraham, 35.
Webster, Amos, 202.
Webster, Ashbel, 128, 145.
Webster, Ashbil, 137.
Webster, Benjamin, 127, 128, 201.
Webster, David, 6.
Webster, Elijah, 201.
Webster, Elisha, 154, 156.
Webster, George, 6.
Webster, Guida, 6.
Webster, Isaac, 274.
Webster, James, 6, 163.
Webster, Jonathan, Jr., 6.

Wethey, Ephraim, 175.
Wethey, Henry, 175.
Wetmore, Amos, 208.
Wetmore, David, 201.
Wetmore, Jacob, 134.
Wetmore, John, 208.
Wetmore, Josiah, 135.
Whaley, Jonathan, 271.
Whaley, Theophilus, 253.
Whaling, Walter, 35.
Whealer, Caleb, 38.
Whealor, Joseph, 155.
Wheat, Samuel, 209.
Wheaten, Jonathan, 39.
Wheaton, Jeremiah, 99.
Wheaton, Joseph, 242.
Whedon, Roswell, 70. 112.
Whedon, Rufus, 112.
Whedon, Samuel, 9.
Wheedon, Rufus, 72.
Wheeler, A., 84.
Wheeler, Benjamin, 76.
Wheeler, Daniel, 57, 58, 60.
Wheeler, David, 180.
Wheeler, Elizur, 213.
Wheeler, Elnathan, 181, 219.
Wheeler, Ephraim, 68.
Wheeler, Hezekiah, 101.
Wheeler, J., 213.
Wheeler, Jabez, 180.
Wheeler, Jacob, 35.
Wheeler, Job, 237.
Wheeler, John, 56, 124.
Wheeler, Johnson, 213.
Wheeler, Joseph, 154.
Wheeler, Joshua, 53, 122.
Wheeler, M., 190.
Wheeler, N., 177.
Wheeler, Nathaniel, 151.
Wheeler, Samuel, 151.
Wheeler, Stephen, 68.
Wheeler, Thomas, 72, 113, 211.
Wheelock, Thaddeus, 67.
Wheetor, Aaron, 169.
Whelden, Thomas, 252.
Whelding, Jonathan, 246.
Wheler, 150.
Wheler, Abel, 189.
Wheler, Amos, 150.
Wheler, Jeremiah, 150.
Wheler, John, 189.
Wheler, Joseph, 150.
Wheler, Moses, 189.
Wheler, Nathan, 189.
Whelor, Ely, 195.
Whippell, Joseph, 68.
Whipple, Eleazer, 66.
Whipple, Frederick, 102, 124, 130.
Whipple, Jonathan, 82.
Whipple, William, 32.
Whitcomb, John, 94.
Whitcomb, Robert, 37.
Whitcomb, Simon, 34.
White, 56.
White, Aaron, 229.
White, Adonijah, 2, 3, 161.
White, Alexsander, 163.
White, Asa, 162.
White, Charles, 263.
White, Daniel, 115, 161.
White, David, 20.
White, Eli, 56.
White, Fadrick, 163.
White, George, 138.
White, Gideon, 32.
White, John, 27, 120, 138.
White, Jonathan, 100.
White, Joseph, 110.
White, Lemuel, 79.
White, Nathan, 69.
White, Obediah, 162.
White, Oliver, 113.
White, Thomas, 274.
White, William, 95, 111, 117, 127, 135, 163, 184.
White Plains, 139.
Whitehead, Christopher, 141.
Whitehead, Nathaniel, 16.
Whitely, William, 91.
Whitemore, Joseph, 232.
Whiting, 190.
Whiting, Daniel, 58.
Whiting, Frederick J., 143.
Whiting, Henry, 91.
Whiting, Hervy, 105, 202.
Whiting, John, 27, 151, 181, 219, 225.
Whiting, Jonathan, 227.
Whiting, Joseph, 204.
Whiting, Nathan H., 50, 104, 122.
Whiting, Nehemiah, 232.
Whiting, S., 177, 224.
Whiting, Samuel, 18, 22, 23, 24, 143, 151, 152, 177, 180, 212, 222, 225, 226, 227, 265.
Whiting, William, 16, 21, 274.
Whitlock, Justus, 213.
Whitlock, Thaddeus, 85.
Whitman, Jesse, 78.
Whitman, John, 160.
Whitman, Samuel, 21.
Whitmore, Joseph, 211.
Whitnay, John, 138.
Whitney, 111.
Whitney, Cornas, 168.
Whitney, Daniel, 61.

Wolcott, Elizur, 154.
Wolcott, Erastus, 46, 54, 133. 149. 211.
Wolcott, Josiah, 255.
Wolcott, O., 221, 225.
Wolcott, Oliver, 210.
Wolcott, Samuel, 39.
Wolcott, William, 154, 242.
Wolcut, Benajah, 108.
Wolcut, Elijah, 108.
Wolf, Aaron D., 228.
Wolf, Anthony, 240.
Woobrig, Timothy, 146.
Woobury, John, 246, 250.
Wood, Alexander, 255.
Wood, Benjamin, 93, 194.
Wood, Daniel, 198.
Wood, David, 209, 226.
Wood, Eli, 25.
Wood, Elijah, 194.
Wood, Henry, 212.
Wood, Israel, 79.
Wood, Jacob, 61.
Wood, Jacob, Jr., 61.
Wood, James, 56.
Wood, Joel, 135.
Wood, John, 32, 211, 260.
Wood, John, Jr., 175.
Wood, Joseph, 104.
Wood, Lemuel, Jr., 198.
Wood, Samuel, 72, 146, 147.
Wood, Stephen, 218.
Wood, Thomas, 54, 240.
Wood, Timothy, 137.
Woodard, Amos, 14.
Woodard, John, 15.
Woodard, Lee, 172.
Woodard, Samuel, 149.
Woodard, Ward, 167.
Woodbridg, Timothy, 145.
Woodbridge, 146.
Woodbridge, Christopher, 28. 31.
Woodbridge, Hoel, 227.
Woodbridge, Howel, 208.
Woodbridge. Theodore, 12. 41, 42. 43, 48.
Woodbridge, Theophilus, 7. 46, 58. 60.
Woodbridge, Timothy, 146. 147. 148, 261.
Woodburn, Francoes, 233.
Woodbury, 20, 22, 23, 24, 53, 54. 55, 66, 67, 75, 76, 77, 78, 79, 80, 83, 88, 89, 102, 103. 104. 110, 267.
Woodcock, Samuel, 69, 271.
Wooden, Joseph, 202.
Woodfood, Joseph, 79.
Woodford, Joseph, 182, 211.
Woodford, Timothy, 37.
Woodhoop, Lemuel, 153.
Woodhouse, John, 154, 156.
Woodhouse, Lemuel, 155.
Woodhouse, Samuel, 154. 156.
Wooding, Calvin, 187.
Wooding, Jer., 109.
Woodman, Samuel, 173.
Woodmansee, Joseph, 271.
Woodroof, Asa, 52.
Woodrose, David, 179.
Woodruff, 223.
Woodruff, Andrew, 201.
Woodruff, Benjamin, 258.
Woodruff, Enoch, 205, 211.
Woodruff, John, 201, 209, 273.
Woodruff, Judah, 182, 207, 223, 224.
Woodruff, Martin, 21.
Woodruff, Philo, 273.
Woodruff, Samuel, 201.
Woodruff, Solomon, 201, 273.
Woodruff, William, 75. 271.
Woodruff, Zebulon, 59.
Woodstock, 53, 54, 64. 65. 66. 68. 88, 89, 90, 103, 104.
Woodward, Ambrous, 82.
Woodward, Amos, 14, 74, 185. 206, 222.
Woodward, Benjamin, 2.
Woodward, Daniel, 114, 120.
Woodward, Fredrick, 82.
Woodward, John, 15. 140.
Woodward, Lee, 172.
Woodward, Noah, Jr.. 176.
Woodward, Oliver, 91.
Woodwarth, Benjamin, 3.
Woodworth, Abel, 246. 247. 248. 253, 256.
Woodworth, Able, 262.
Woodworth, Azel, 271.
Woodworth, Benjamin, 4
Woodworth, Heman, 116.
Woodworth, James, 163.
Woodworth, Jedediah, 80.
Woodworth, Jonathan. 252.
Woodworth, Joshua, 163.
Woodworth, Josiah, 260, 261.
Woodworth, Recompense, 118.
Woodworth, Reuben, 4.
Woodworth, Ruel, 185.
Woolcot, Erastus, 149.
Woolcott, Elisha, 156.
Woolcott, Elizur, 156.
Woolcott, Simeon, 139.
Woolcott, William. 156.
Woolcut, Bennajor, 70.

Woolcut, Samuel, 82.
Woolf, Anthony, 257.
Woolf, John, 245, 249.
Woolf, Stephen D., 245.
Woolworth, Ebenezer, 68.
Wooster, 190, 221, 265.
Wooster, David, 9, 12, 16, 17, 18, 19, 20, 21, 22, 23, 24, 25, 43.
Wooster, Ephraim, 190.
Wooster, Henman, 78.
Wooster, Thomas, 91.
Worden, Arnold, 95.
Worden, Henry, 31, 51.
Worden, Ichabud, 186.
Worden, Wait, 51.
Wording, Ichabod, 124.
Wordwell, Nathan, 55.
Worner, Eliphaz, 136.
Worthington, 222.
Worthington, E., 210.
Worthington, William, 178, 191, 209, 210, 211, 221, 223, 277.
Worthington, Mass., 103.
Worthylake, George, 246. 247, 253.
Wright, 4, 6, 209.
Wright, Amaziah, 227.
Wright, Asher, 29, 31, 192.
Wright, Beriah, 56.
Wright, Charles, 21, 39, 209.
Wright, Daniel, 59, 65, 116. 185.
Wright, David, 21, 39.
Wright, Ebenezer, 153, 155.
Wright, Ezekiel, 91.
Wright, Frances, 61.
Wright, Isaiah, 91.
Wright, J., 69, 206.
Wright, Jabez, 209, 210, 225.
Wright, James, 68.
Wright, Jeriah, 149.
Wright, Jesse, 163.
Wright, Job, 210.
Wright, John, 58, 61, 97, 230.
Wright, Jonathan, 105.
Wright, Joseph, 154, 156, 192.
Wright, Joseph A., 47.
Wright, Moses, 105.
Wright, Samuel, 25, 34, 64, 211.
Wright, Sim., 18.
Wright, Solomon, 149.
Wright, Timothy, 185.
Write, Abel, 163.
Write, Ezekiel, 163.
Wyard, Lemuel, 138.
Wyett, Benjamin, 259.
Wylder, Moses, 185.
Wylie, John, 171.
Wylie, Robart, 171.
Wyllys, H., 206, 207.
Wyllys, Hezekiah, 84, 207, 222.
Wyllys, J., 206.
Wyllys, John P., 82, 121.
Wyllys, Samuel, 23, 24, 25, 46, 57, 58, 60.
Wyoming, 115.
Wyyaung, Guardin, 264.

Yale, Ameton, 193.
Yale, Asa, 209.
Yale, Asahel, 276.
Yale, Daniel, 193.
Yale, Elihu, 194.
Yale, John, 193.
Yale, Jonathan, 193.
Yale, Nash, 112.
Yale, Nathaniel, 193.
Yale, Noah, 276.
Yarrington, Ezekiel, 175.
Yates, Paul, 223, 225.
Yates, William, 111.
Yatman, James, 32.
Yeates, John, 212.
Yellis, Abram, 77.
Yeomans, Elijah, 193.
Yeomans, Ovorus, 63.
Yerrington, David, 74.
Yeumons, Andrew, 32.
York, Elisha, 175.
York Island, 138, 139.
Yorkshire, Eng., 22.
Young, Alexander, 2, 262.
Young, David, 74, 247, 252.
Young, James, 231, 234.
Young, Levi, 245, 249.
Young, William, 143, 264.
Youngs, Benjamin, 34.
Youngs, Eliphalet, 163.

www.ingramcontent.com/pod-product-compliance
Lightning Source LLC
Chambersburg PA
CBHW070541270326
41926CB00013B/2164